Breaking Ground

STUDIES IN COMPARATIVE ENERGY AND ENVIRONMENTAL POLITICS

Series editors
Todd A. Eisenstadt,
American University, and Joanna I. Lewis, Georgetown University

*The Roots of Engagement: Understanding Opposition and Support
for Resource Extraction*
Moisés Arce, Michael S. Hendricks, and Marc S. Polizzi

*Fueling State Capitalism: How Domestic Politics Shapes Foreign Investments
of National Oil Companies*
Andrew Cheon

*Who Speaks for Nature? Indigenous Movements, Public Opinion, and
the Petro-State in Ecuador*
Todd A. Eisenstadt and Karleen Jones West

A Good Life on a Finite Earth: The Political Economy of Green Growth
Daniel J. Fiorino

*The Politics of Extraction: Territorial Rights, Participatory Institutions, and
Conflict in Latin America*
Maiah Jaskoski

*Democracy in the Woods: Environmental Conservation and Social Justice in India,
Tanzania, and Mexico*
Prakash Kashwan

Breaking Ground: From Extraction Booms to Mining Bans in Latin America
Rose J. Spalding

Breaking Ground

From Extraction Booms to Mining Bans in Latin America

ROSE J. SPALDING

OXFORD
UNIVERSITY PRESS

Oxford University Press is a department of the University of Oxford. It furthers the University's objective of excellence in research, scholarship, and education by publishing worldwide. Oxford is a registered trade mark of Oxford University Press in the UK and certain other countries.

Published in the United States of America by Oxford University Press 198 Madison Avenue, New York, NY 10016, United States of America.

© Oxford University Press 2023

All rights reserved. No part of this publication may be reproduced, stored in a retrieval system, or transmitted, in any form or by any means, without the prior permission in writing of Oxford University Press, or as expressly permitted by law, by license, or under terms agreed with the appropriate reproduction rights organization. Inquiries concerning reproduction outside the scope of the above should be sent to the Rights Department, Oxford University Press, at the address above.

You must not circulate this work in any other form and you must impose this same condition on any acquirer.

Library of Congress Cataloging-in-Publication Data
Names: Spalding, Rose J., author.
Title: Breaking ground : from extraction booms to mining bans in Latin America / Rose J. Spalding.
Description: New York. NY : Oxford University Press, [2023] | Includes bibliographical references and index. |
Contents: Mining conflict and policy alternatives—From community conflicts to policy outcomes : movements, elites and state permeability—Mining friendly : promoting extractivism in Nicaragua—Mining, maybe : intermittent mining in Guatemala—Mining skeptics : environmental resistance in Costa Rica—Mining free : mining prohibition in El Salvador—Mining reform in Latin America : international regimes and the challenges of regulation.
Identifiers: LCCN 2022040735 (print) | LCCN 2022040736 (ebook) | ISBN 9780197643150 (hardback) | ISBN 9780197643181 (ebook) | ISBN 9780197643174 (epub) | ISBN 9780197643167
Subjects: LCSH: Mineral industries—Latin America. | Mineral industries—Government policy—Latin America.
Classification: LCC HD9506.L252 S635 2023 (print) | LCC HD9506.L252 (ebook) | DDC 338.2098—dc23/eng/20221214
LC record available at https://lccn.loc.gov/2022040735
LC ebook record available at https://lccn.loc.gov/2022040736

DOI: 10.1093/oso/9780197643150.001.0001

Printed by Integrated Books International, United States of America

This book is dedicated to my sister Catherine Hamilton Spalding,
who brightened my life

Contents

Acknowledgments	ix
Acronym List	xiii

1. Mining Conflict and Policy Alternatives   1

2. From Community Conflicts to Policy Outcomes: Movements, Elites, and State Permeability   34

3. Mining Friendly: Promoting Extractivism in Nicaragua   64

4. Mining, Maybe: Intermittent Mining in Guatemala   104

5. Mining Skeptics: Environmental Resistance in Costa Rica   142

6. Mining Free: Mining Prohibition in El Salvador   180

7. Mining Reform in Latin America: International Regimes and the Challenges of Regulation   218

References	245
Index	285

Acknowledgments

The push to accelerate "development" fueled a turn to resource extraction during the commodities boom, and returned with a vengeance in the downturn following the appearance of COVID-19. This extractivist era, now deploying new technologies and entering into relatively unexplored regions, brings its own set of problems. In the precious metals sector, the cyanide saturation now needed to extract "invisible" or microscopic particles of gold, and the massive movement of earth required to do so (one metric ton per gram), point to the new environmental challenges associated with modern industrial mining. The location of metallic mining and hydrocarbon reserves in indigenous territories, protected areas, headwaters, watersheds, and offshore locations introduces new risks, with predictable distributional consequences for already marginalized populations living nearby. The urgency of these concerns, during a time of climate crisis and mass migration, calls us to undertake a sustained investigation into extractive sector transition. Under what circumstances might mining be more effectively governed, such that social and environmental harms are effectively mitigated? Under what circumstances might mining be banned entirely, should social and environmental factors so dictate?

Breaking Ground engages those questions with fresh eyes, motivated by a strong commitment to understand both the obstacles to and possibilities for change. Drawing on research conducted in four Latin American countries, and taking over a decade to research and write, this book owes a heavy debt to scores of contributors. Let me begin by thanking the people that I interviewed for sharing their experiences with extractive sector development and the forms of resistance that it inspired. Policymakers, activists, community residents, business leaders, miners, state officials, organizational spokespeople, and development specialists gave generously of their time and expertise to help me identify the patterns I document in this book. Research findings on controversial topics like resource extraction and environmental resistance will never win universal endorsement, but I hope that most of those who contributed to this study will find merit in the results.

X ACKNOWLEDGMENTS

I also want to thank the members of my research group, Research Group MEGA (Mobilization, Extractivism, and Government Action). Led by the inestimable Eduardo Silva of Tulane University, this group has been meeting periodically for almost a decade to produce and discuss cutting-edge work on extractivism and megaprojects in Latin America. Through many years of collaboration, I have benefited from the research and wise counsel of Maria Ackhurin, Moisés Arce, Tony Bebbington, Ludovico Feoli, Julieta Godfrid, Paul Haslam, Kathy Hochstetler, Barbara Hogenboom, Denise Humphreys Bebbington, Arsel Murat, Lorenzo Pellegrini, Roberta Rice, and Katrin Uba. For lively and informed conversation about the issues raised in this book, I also want to thank other specialists in this field, including Robin Broad and Rachel Nadelman, Benedicte Bull, Thomas Chiasson-Lebel, Nick Middeldorp, Ainhoa Montoya, and Manuel Vogt.

This research has taken me to many different communities to consult with participants in the mining debate and to observe their work. In Nicaragua, I carried out field work in Bonanza, La India, Managua, Matagalpa, and Rancho Grande; in Guatemala, I interviewed respondents in Casillas, Guatemala City, San José del Golfo, and Santa Rosa de Lima; in Costa Rica my interview locations and field sites included Alajuela, Heredia, and San José; and in El Salvador, I completed field work in Cinquera, Perquín, San Isidro, San Salvador, Sesuntepeque, and Victoria. For comparative purposes, I consulted with Peruvian participants in the mining debate in Arequipa, Lima, and Puerto Maldonado. For background on mining promotion and investment disputes, I did two rounds of interviews in Washington, DC.

This field work was carried out between 2010 and 2018, and involved a total of 255 interviews. Research involved direct participation in protest marches and *convocatoria*; personal observation of legislative hearings, strategy sessions, roundtable consultations, and corporate reporting events; and informal interactions with miners, both large-scale and small-scale. This work took me to the corporate headquarters of Canadian mining company Infinito Gold's affiliate in San José, Costa Rica, and to Bonanza, Nicaragua, for conversations with informal gold miners as they doused gold-laced sludge with mercury to extract amalgamated nuggets. I met with La Puya protesters organizing against the large-scale gold mine in the El Tambor zone outside of San José del Golfo in Guatemala, and with family members of Marcelo Rivera, an anti-mining activist who was assassinated in Cabañas, El Salvador in 2009. As my project expanded, I carried out interviews with officials, lawyers, and activists in Washington,

DC, to better understand how mining companies use international dispute settlement mechanisms to pressure states for access to mining rights, and how governments fight back, demanding the right to change obsolete practices and invent new rules.

In each of these locations, I benefited from the advice of colleagues and friends too numerous to list. In particular, for their assistance over a long period of time, I want to thank Mauricio Alvarez, Gino Biamonte, Nicolás Boeglin, Arturo Carballo, Carlos Denton, and Ciska Raventós in Costa Rica; Antonio Baños, Rodolfo Calles, Rick Jones, Andrés McKinley, Luis Parada, and Loly de Zúñiga and her family in El Salvador; Mike Dougherty, Becky Kaump, Alba Lucía Morales, Magalí Rey Rosa, Luis Solano, and Simona Yagenova in Guatemala; and Alejandro Bendaña, Judy Butler, David Dye, Laura Enríquez, Lori Hanson, José Alberto Idiáquez, Salvador Martí, and Mario Sánchez in Nicaragua. Additional support was provided by Washington, DC-based colleagues, including David Holiday and Manuel Pérez-Rocha, and, in Peru, by Gerardo Damonte, Carlos Monge, and Cynthia Sanborn. None of these friends and colleagues bears any responsibility for the framework I employ or the conclusions that I draw in this work.

Closer to home, I want to express my gratitude to colleagues at DePaul University. This includes the members of the University Research Council and the Society of Vincent de Paul Professors, who provided financial support for much of the fieldwork; Katy Arnold, Bill Johnson González, Christie Klimas, Susana Martínez, Lourdes Torres, and Guillermo Vásquez de Velasco, for their sustained interest in and support for my work; and Lourdes Contreras, Estelle de Vendegies, Christina Origel, and Linette Sánchez, who provided valuable research assistance. Index preparation was funded by a Late-Stage Research Grant from the College of Liberal Arts and Social Sciences at DePaul University.

On Common Ground Consultants (2010) generously provided access to their report's appendix on legal cases related to the Marlin Mine. Carlos Denton of CID Gallup (2018) produced the comparative public opinion data on attitudes toward mining operations in eight Latin American countries that I present in Chapter 2. An earlier version of Chapter 6 was published as an open access article by the Center for Latin American Research and Documentation (CEDLA) as "From the Streets to the Chamber: Social Movements and the Mining Ban in El Salvador," *European Review of Latin American and Caribbean Studies (ERLACS)* 106 (2018): 49–76, DOI: http://doi.org/10.32992/erlacs.10377.

xii ACKNOWLEDGMENTS

I am grateful for the skilled assistance provided by Angela Chnapko, my editor, and Alexcee Bechthold, senior project editor, at Oxford University Press, and by Todd Eisenstadt, the co-editor of the OUP series Studies in Comparative Energy and Environmental Politics. They offered invaluable support as this project was finalized and provided an excellent home for my work. I also thank the two anonymous readers whose comments and suggestions helped me to clarify and enrich my manuscript.

Finally, with gratitude and deep appreciation, I thank my husband, Will Denton, for his enduring support for my work, even when it takes me far from home; our daughters, Claire and Grace, for their cheerful accompaniment, outstanding logistical support, and unerring inspiration during multiple phases of this work; and my sister Betsy Delmonico for her keen editorial eye and encouragement as this project advanced into its final stages.

I conclude on an autobiographical note. I was born and raised in Kentucky, a place where "King Coal" reigned and mountaintop removal was an entrenched tradition. As a young girl growing up in the nearby Knob Region, I was told that "Kentucky needs coal mining in order to promote development." *Development?* I wondered as I looked around at the gouged topography and slag heaps in those run-down mountain towns. I left that region for graduate school and the world beyond, followed by over three decades of research and teaching about Mexico and Central America, in places that sometimes reminded me of home. My work on *Breaking Ground* allowed me to return to questions that troubled me in my youth, and to explore more fully the possibilities for change in the mining industry. I offer this book to all those searching for better ways to align human needs with environmental constraints, in hope that new political configurations will help to advance that quest.

Acronym List

Costa Rica

AECO	Asociación Ecologista de Costa Rica (Costa Rica Ecologist Association)
APREFLOFAS	Asociación Preservacionista de Flora y Fauna Silvestre (Wildlife Flora and Fauna Preservation Association)
CINDE	Coalición Costarricense de Iniciativas en Desarrollo (Costa Rican Investment Promotion Agency)
COECO-CEIBA	Asociación de Comunidades Ecologistas–La Ceiba (Ecological Communities Association–La Ceiba)
COMEX	Ministerio de Comercio Exterior (Ministry of Foreign Trade)
FA	Frente Amplio (Broad Front)
FECON	Federación Costarricense para la Conservación del Ambiente (Costa Rican Federation for Environmental Conservation)
ICE	Instituto Costarricense de Electricidad (Costa Rican Electrical Institute)
MINAE	Ministerio de Ambiente y Energía (Ministry of Environment and Energy)
ML	Movimiento Libertario (Libertarian Movement)
PAC	Partido de Acción Ciudadana (Citizen Action Party)
PEN	Programa Estado Nación en Desarrollo Humano Sostenible (State of the Nation Program for Sustainable Human Development)
PLN	Partido de Liberación Nacional (National Liberation Party)
PUSC	Partido de Unidad Social Cristiana (Social Christian Unity Party)
SETENA	Secretaría Técnica Nacional Ambiental (National Environmental Technical Secretariat)
SINAC	Sistema Nacional de Áreas de Conservación (National System of Conservation Areas)
SLAPP	Strategic Lawsuit Against Public Participation
TCA	Tribunal Contencioso Administrativo (Administrative Litigation Tribunal)

xiv ACRONYM LIST

UCCAEP	Unión Costarricense de Cámaras y Asociaciones del Sector Empresarial Privado (Costa Rican Union of Private Sector Chambers and Associations)
UCR	Universidad de Costa Rica (University of Costa Rica)
UNOVIDA	Unión Norte Por la Vida (Northern Union for Life)

El Salvador

ADES	Asociación de Desarrollo Económico y Social–Santa Marta (Social and Economic Development Association–Santa Marta)
ANEP	Asociación Nacional de la Empresa Privada (National Association of Private Enterprise)
ARDM	Asociación de Reconstrucción y Desarrollo Municipal (Municipal Association for Reconstruction and Development)
ARENA	Alianza Republicana Nacionalista (Nationalist Republican Alliance)
CAC	Comité Ambiental de Cabañas (Environmental Committee of Cabañas)
CCR	Asociación de Comunidades para el Desarrollo de Chalatenango (Chalatenango Communities Development Association, formerly called the Refugee and Repopulated Communities Coordinator)
CEDES	Conferencia Episcopal de El Salvador (Episcopal Conference of El Salvador)
CEICOM	Centro de Investigación Sobre Inversión y Comercio (Investment and Trade Research Center)
CRIPDES	Asociación de Comunidades Rurales para el Desarrollo de El Salvador (Rural Communities Association for Salvadoran Development)
FESPAD	Fundación de Estudios para la Aplicación del Derecho (Foundation for the Study of the Application of Law)
FMLN	Frente Farabundo Martí de Liberación Nacional (Farabundo Martí National Liberation Front)
FUSADES	Fundación Salvadoreña para el Desarrollo Económico y Social (Salvadoran Social and Economic Development Foundation)
GANA	Gran Alianza por la Unidad Nacional (Grand Alliance for National Unity)
IUDOP	Instituto Universitario de Opinión Pública (University Public Opinion Institute)
JPIC	Justicia, Paz e Integridad de la Creación de los Franciscanos (Franciscan Justice, Peace and Creation Integrity)
MARN	Ministerio de Medio Ambiente y Recursos Naturales (Ministry of the Environment and Natural Resources)
MINEC	Ministerio de Economía (Ministry of the Economy)

UCA	Universidad Centroamericana–José Simeón Cañas (Central American University–José Simeón Cañas)
UNES	Unidad Ecológica Salvadoreña (Salvadoran Ecological Unit)

Guatemala

ASIES	Asociación de Investigación y Estudios Sociales (Research and Social Studies Association)
CACIF	Comité Coordinador de Asociaciones Agrícolas, Comerciales, Industriales y Financieras (Coordinating Committee of Agricultural, Commercial, Industrial, and Financial Associations)
CALAS	Centro de Acción Legal-Ambiental y Social de Guatemala (Environmental and Social Legal Action Center)
CICIG	Comisión Internacional Contra la Impunidad en Guatemala (International Commission Against Impunity in Guatemala)
CIG	Cámara de Industria de Guatemala (Guatemalan Chamber of Industry)
CODIDENA	Comisión Diocesana de la Defensa de la Naturaleza (Diocesan Committee in Defense of Nature)
CPO	Consejo del Pueblo Maya (Maya People's Council, formerly People's Council of the Western Highlands)
EXMINGUA	Exploraciones Mineras de Guatemala (Guatemalan Mining Explorations)
FUNDESA	Fundación para el Desarrollo de Guatemala (Guatemalan Development Foundation)
GHRC	Guatemalan Human Rights Commission
GREMIEXT	Gremial de Industrias Extractivas (Union of Extractive Industries)
ICEFI	Instituto Centroamericano de Estudios Fiscales (Central American Fiscal Studies Institute)
KCA	Kappes, Cassiday & Associates
MARN	Ministerio de Ambiente y Recursos Naturales (Ministry of the Environment and Natural Resources)
MEM	Ministerio de Energía y Minas (Ministry of Energy and Mines)
MSR	Minera San Rafael (San Rafael Mining Company)
NISGUA	Network in Solidarity with the People of Guatemala
ODHAG	Oficina de Derechos Humanos del Arzobispado de Guatemala (Human Rights Office of the Archbishop of Guatemala)
PDH	Procurador de los Derechos Humanos (Human Rights Ombudsman)
UDEFEGUA	Unidad de Protección a Defensoras y Defensores de Derechos Humanos (Unit for the Protection of Guatemalan Human Rights Defenders)

xvi ACRONYM LIST

| URL | Universidad Rafael Landívar (Rafael Landívar University) |
| USAC | Universidad de San Carlos (San Carlos University) |

Nicaragua

ADDAC	Asociación para la Diversificación y el Desarollo Agrícola Comunal (Diversification and Community Agricultural Development Association)
BCN	Banco Central de Nicaragua (Nicaraguan Central Bank)
CAMINIC	Cámara Minera de Nicaragua (Nicaraguan Mining Chamber)
CEN	Conferencia Episcopal de Nicaragua (Episcopal Conference of Nicaragua)
CENIDH	Centro Nicaragüense de Derechos Humanos (Nicaraguan Human Rights Center)
COSEP	Consejo Superior de la Empresa Privada (Superior Council of Private Enterprise)
CPC	Consejos del Poder Ciudadano (Citizen Power Councils)
CST-JBE	Confederación Sindical de Trabajadores-José Benito Escobar (José Benito Escobar Union Federation of Workers, formerly the Sandinista Workers Central)
DGM	Dirección General de Minas (General Directorate for Mining)
ENIMINAS	Empresa Nicaragüense de Minas (Nicaraguan Mining Enterprise)
FSLN	Frente Sandinista de Liberación Nacional (Sandinista National Liberation Front)
FUNIDES	Fundación Nicaragüense para el Desarrollo Económico y Social (Nicaraguan Foundation for Economic and Social Development)
GRUN	Gobierno de Reconciliación y Unidad Nacional (Government of Reconciliation and National Unity)
INMINE	Instituto Nicaragüense de la Minería (Nicaragua Mining Institute)
MARENA	Ministerio del Ambiente y los Recursos Naturales (Ministry of the Environment and Natural Resources)
MEM	Ministerio de Energía y Minas (Ministry of Energy and Mining)
UCA	Universidad Centroamericana (Central American University)

Other

AmCham	American Chamber of Commerce
ASM	artisanal and small-scale mining
BIT	bilateral investment treaty
CAFTA	Central American Free Trade Agreement (or, with the Dominican Republic, DR-CAFTA)
CAO	Compliance Advisor Ombudsman

ACRONYM LIST xvii

CIEL	Center for International Environmental Law
CRS	Catholic Relief Service
CSR	corporate social responsibility
ECLAC	Economic Commission on Latin America and the Caribbean (Comisión Económica para América Latina y el Caribe, CEPAL)
EIA	environmental impact assessment
EJATLAS	Global Environmental Justice Atlas
FDI	foreign direct investment
FLACSO	Facultad Latinoamericana de Ciencias Sociales (Latin American School of Social Sciences)
FPIC	free, prior, and informed consent
GDP	gross domestic product
GTZ	Deutsche Gesellschaft für Internationale Zusammenarbeit
IACHR	Inter-American Commission on Human Rights
IACtHR	Inter-American Court for Human Rights
ICMM	International Council on Mining and Metals
ICSID	International Centre for the Settlement of Investment Disputes (Centro Internacional de Arreglo de Diferencias Relativas a Inversiones, CIADI)
IFC	International Finance Corporation
IGF	Intergovernmental Forum on Mining, Minerals, Metals, and Sustainable Development
IGO	Intergovernmental Organization
ILO 169	International Labour Organization, Convention 169 (Organización Internacional del Trabajo, Convenio 169)
INGO	international nongovernmental organization
ISDS	investor-state dispute settlement
LSM	large-scale mining
NAFTA	North America Free Trade Agreement (subsequently, United States-Mexico-Canada Agreement, USMCA)
NGO	nongovernmental organization
OAS	Organization of American States
OCMAL	Observatorio de Conflictos Mineros de América Latina (Latin American Mining Conflicts Observatory)
OECD	Organisation for Economic Cooperation and Development
SEA	strategic environmental assessment
SLO	social license to operate
UN	United Nations
UNCTAD	United Nations Conference on Trade and Development
USAID	United States Agency for International Development
USGS	United States Geological Survey
WOLA	Washington Office on Latin America

1

Mining Conflict and Policy Alternatives

During the 2010 inauguration ceremony for the newly reopened La Libertad mine, Nicaraguan president Daniel Ortega recalled his father's migration to the town as a young man. Like many others before him, his father had come seeking work in a nearby gold mine. Mine conditions of that era, Ortega observed, were "tragic" (Ortega 2010). Death and disease were rampant; poor living conditions took the lives of Ortega's two older siblings. When his revolutionary government came to power in 1979, it quickly nationalized the mines, claiming that improvements would follow.

State control over mining did not last—mines were soon reprivatized following Ortega's electoral defeat in 1990—but mining itself proved tenacious. When the former revolutionary returned to power for a second time in 2007, he became an avid booster of foreign mining investors. Seeking a new understanding with private capital, he pivoted to discursive support for mining, now depicted as the solution to regional poverty. "What is our grand objective?" he asked rhetorically at the 2010 mine reopening. "Our grand objective is to defeat poverty." As soaring gold prices and favorable tax terms ensured booming investments, mining reemerged as a major source of economic activity in Nicaragua.

As Ortega was returning to his birthplace to inaugurate the reactivated mine, newly elected president Laura Chinchilla was being sworn into office across the border in Costa Rica. Her first act after taking the oath was to decree a ban on new open pit mines (AFP 2010). With 2010 public opinion polls indicating that 75% of the Costa Rican population opposed mining, Chinchilla's decree enjoyed sweeping national approval. Her executive decision was reaffirmed a few months later in a unanimous vote of support by the National Assembly. With that vote, Costa Rica became the first Latin American country to legislate a national mining ban. As Nicaragua moved to ramp up activity in the gold mining sector, Costa Rica was hard at work closing it down.

These two scenarios, found in neighboring Central American countries, underline the sharp divide in mining policies in the region. The present study

Breaking Ground. Rose J. Spalding, Oxford University Press. © Oxford University Press 2023.
DOI: 10.1093/oso/9780197643150.003.0001

offers the first full analysis of this bifurcation. It shows how the prospect of mining investment, and the resulting jobs and revenues that it brings, tends to generate a significant base of support in resource-rich countries, particularly at the elite level. The extent to which public support consolidates and to which pro-mining policies and practices persist, however, varies notably from country to country. Outcomes depend on the kind of resistance movements that emerge, and the obstacles and opportunities they encounter along the way. My task is to map these interconnections and identify those that lead toward divergent paths. Ultimately, this work raises questions about the future of natural resource extraction in the region, and the prospects for a mining U-turn.

Given the visible leadership of anti-mining activists in the push for policy change, I start my story with a discussion of social movements. A large body of research has emerged to interpret social movements, giving particular attention to their origins, alliance structures, and tactics (McAdam, Tarrow, and Tilly 2001; Tarrow 2011; Almeida 2014; Arce and Rice 2019). The connections between movements and their policy consequences (or lack thereof), however, are less well documented and theorized (Bosi, Giugni, and Uba 2016; Silva 2017). Social movement research generally finds that mobilizations have identifiable political goals (Soule and King 2006; King, Bentele, and Soule 2007; Amenta et al. 2010; McAdam and Boudet 2012; Biggs and Andrews 2015; Silva, Akchurin, and Bebbington 2018; Arce and Rice 2019) and that they are often at least partially successful in achieving their objectives. How and why they have an impact remains a matter of dispute. Given the significant role of social movements as an expression of collective demands, and the frequency with which people employ mobilization in search of substantive change, the circumstances under which popular organizing becomes politically consequential should be better understood. To advance this line of inquiry, movement theorists and policy specialists are working to provide a better account of the sequences and interactive effects that animate the movement-policy nexus, and to more accurately map causal processes.

Documenting the connections between movements and policy is intrinsically challenging. The difficulties are in part due to the wide array of processes and timelines involved in both mobilization and policymaking (McAdam and Boudet 2012; Bosi, Giugni, and Uba 2016). As Silva (2017, 6) notes, "the very characteristics that draw us to social movements—their passion, fluidity, malleability, precariousness, creativity, and contingent nature—make it hard to establish their connection to observed changes with high degrees of confidence." Solid research on the movement-policy link requires careful process tracing, a labor-intensive methodology that tends to limit the scope of the analysis to a small number of cases, which can blunt the contribution to theory building and rigorous testing.

This kind of research also requires a commitment to studying movement dynamics and policy processes over an extended period of time, so that interactions can be monitored across various phases and any longer-term consequences can be identified. This method—what I call "slow movement studies"—permits multidimensional analysis of the ways in which movements affect and are affected by social and political processes across various phases of conflict. Slow movement studies also make it possible to weigh evidence about outcomes, including both policy changes and institutional adaptations that unfold over time.

Social movement analysts and public policy specialists have begun to develop these long-term, connective frameworks. In an ambitious study of ecology, anti-nuclear, and peace movements in the United States, Switzerland, and Italy over the twenty-four-year period between 1975 and 1999, Marco Giugni (2004) found that protest by itself had "at best a marginal to moderate effect" on policy, at least as defined in terms of adoption of legislation and increases or decreases in spending (p. 70). Instead, policy change was more likely to depend on a "joint effects" process in which several factors were impacted simultaneously. In his formulation, which followed shifts in three kinds of policy, joint effects referred to the combined impact of movement mobilization (typically in the form of increased protest), alliances with strategic political elites in the institutional arena, and shifts in public opinion that demonstrate increased support for movement goals.[1]

Amenta et al. (2010) also call attention to this interactive effect. Reviewing the literature on the political consequences of movements, these authors found that movements achieved desired policy impacts in 70% of the case studies published in leading sociology journals between 2001 and 2009 (having a "strong" influence in 33% and a "modest" influence in 37%) (p. 292). In their research databank, movement success was associated with

---

[1] The extent and direction of policy change varied by thematic area, with policies relating to domestic and low-intensity issues being more responsive, and policies relating to high-intensity and international issues being less so (Giugni 2004, 215–222). Amenta et al. (2010, 295) also found social movements to have weaker impacts on issues related to "the national cleavage structure," in cases when political and material stakes were high, in military affairs, and when public opinion was unfavorable.

organizational size, multisectoralism, and diverse and complex leadership structures; with the construction of "resonant prognostic and diagnostic frames" that identified problems clearly and presented viable solutions; and with the successful use of political and electoral strategies to gain penetration and leverage, including the insertion of activists into formal institutional roles (pp. 296–297).

To trace the connection between movement activities and policy results, Amenta et al. employed a "political mediation model," which highlighted the importance of "engaging in collective action that changes the calculations of institutional political actors, such as elected officials and state bureaucrats, and adopting organizational forms and strategic action that fit political circumstances" (p. 298). Arce and Rice (2019) also focus on political causation, employing political process theory to construct a model of interconnections between movements and policy change. In their analysis of the recent global protest cycle, which witnessed regional movements for democracy in the Middle East and against neoliberal globalization in the United States, Europe, and Latin America, they posit three conditions that connect mobilization and change. Impact is more likely to occur, they argue, when protest is part of a global cycle of mobilizations, reflects grievances that resonate broadly in the society, and occurs in a "responsive" political system.

My book turns our attention to movements that focus on environmental and community rights in a region undergoing an extractive sector boom. Mining policy in Latin America sits at the crossroads between a continuation of mine-promoting advances and an increase in regulatory restriction. While some countries continue to sell themselves as mining-friendly oases, others are establishing more ambitious constraints. In my analysis, three factors are found to shape the emerging policy divergence: (1) the degree of elite unity in support of mining, (2) the breadth and cohesion of the mining opposition, and (3) the institutional "docking" points available to citizens who engage the political process. Pressures to open up national territory to mining interests are powerful and multidimensional, but national anti-mining coalitions can and do impose restrictions under particular conditions. The goal of this book is to lay out these contrasting paths and identify the political logistics that lead toward different ends. In the process, I trace the routes followed by movement actors who have pursued an environmental and community rights agenda, calling attention to the circumstances under which different opportunities opened and closed and the combination of effects that tended to make movements consequential.

What follows is a five-part introduction. I begin with a brief discussion of the "new Latin American extractive complex" (Bebbington and Bury 2013) and describe the crescendo of opposition and protest that followed in its wake. The gold mining sector provides the grist for this book's mill. Gold, which is mined in around ninety countries worldwide, gives us a particularly lucrative and bloody arena for our exploration. It stands at the intersection of jewelry and fashion, financial security and risk management, and, as a highly efficient conductor of tiny electronic currents, a number of other new manufacturing processes that pave the way for future technologies.[2]

The second section summarizes the dominant frameworks under which mining advanced in the 1990s and early 2000s. It highlights the development of the "commodities consensus" in Latin America (Svampa 2019) and examines the strategies used by mining companies to gain access to extraction sites, including de rigueur corporate social responsibility (CSR) initiatives. The third section provides an overview of a six-part policy reform spectrum that frames the contemporary call for change in the mining sector. This section sketches the main proposals advanced by mining opposition networks and identifies two reform clusters: one that emphasizes regulatory change and a second that calls for outright prohibition. The fourth section details the research methodology employed in this book. The fifth presents an overview of the chapters to come.

The "New Latin American Extractive Complex" and Its Discontents

In *Subterranean Struggles: New Dynamics of Mining, Oil, and Gas in Latin America*, Anthony Bebbington and Jeffrey Bury (2013) describe the rapid expansion of mining investment that gave rise to a "new Latin American extractive complex." This mining boom was visible in much of the region, emerging first in traditional mining centers and expanding quickly into territory where significant mine development had not previously occurred. Between 2003 and 2017, foreign direct investment (FDI) in mining topped $171 billion in Latin America, with over 40% of that from Canadian

---

[2] According to 2010 World Gold Council estimates, 50% of total aboveground stocks are found in jewelry, 36% in private investments and official holdings, and 12% in "other fabrication," with 2% unaccounted for (see Bloomfield 2017, 7–8).

6 BREAKING GROUND

corporations (Bárcena 2018). "Junior" firms aggressively scoured the countryside, searching for commercially viable finds to be developed, and global mining giants acquired control over the largest complexes.[3] Although artisanal and small gold miners produced around 17% of gold output and involved an estimated workforce of 1.4 million people in Latin America in 2014 (Bury and Bebbington 2013, 55; IGF 2017, 1), mining technology, financing, and scale generally required large capital investments, and transnational firms dominated the industry.

The rapid expansion of the mining sector in Latin America resulted from the confluence of several factors. New technologies allowed extraction of small traces of dispersed ores using open pit mining and chemical processing, and increased the profitability of mining investments in what had previously been unpromising territory.[4] Deregulation and the creation of specialized agencies to promote foreign investment during the heyday of neoliberal reform in Latin America coincided with regulatory tightening in the mining sector in the United States, Canada, and European countries (Dashwood 2012, 180–181), shifting investment to the global South. Commodity prices increased in the early 2000s due in part to rapid growth in China and India. Economic volatility in the United States and Europe after the 2008 financial crisis and during the 2020 COVID-19 pandemic pumped up profit margins for gold, sparking new investment in precious metals extraction.

Extractivism may be defined as the large-scale removal of economically valuable natural resources and their export to other markets, where they are processed and incorporated into higher-value goods (Acosta 2013, 62).[5] In the mining sector, this process requires the movement of large amounts of earth, with the ratio of earth to extracted metal rising sharply over time.

[3] "Juniors" are small mining companies that focus on exploration activities and are typically financed with risk capital. When they are successful, their assets are usually acquired by larger and better-resourced "senior" mining corporations, which bring the mine into production.

[4] New methods for dissolving and extracting thinly dispersed, microscopic gold deposits were developed in the United States in the late 1970s and introduced in Latin America in 1994 by the Newmont Mining Corporation at its Yanacocha cyanide heap leach gold mine in Northern Peru (Bury and Bebbington 2013, 45–46). The process involves large-scale open pit mining in which extracted materials are crushed, placed onto plastic liners, and exposed to a solution of cyanide, which flows through the ore, dissolving the gold particles and carrying them to a processing facility in which the gold is concentrated.

[5] This definition of extractivism focuses on production processes involved in the commercialization of natural resources. The term "neo-extractivism," which has come into wide academic use, is understood here to highlight state roles in the extraction process and the use of the resulting resource rents to finance social programs (Gudynas 2018; Svampa 2019). These terms are sometimes conflated.

MINING CONFLICT AND POLICY ALTERNATIVES 7

A geological economics rule called Lasky's law observes that as the mineral grade declines arithmetically, the tonnage of ore extracted increases geometrically (Studnicki-Gizbert 2017, 34). Trillions of tons of earth are processed as concentrated deposits are depleted and ore grade declines, leaving behind vast quantities of waste rock and tailings.[6] The collapse of tailings dams, as with the Brumadinho disaster in Brazil in January 2019, which released 9.7 million cubic meters of tailings and killed over 250 people, illustrates the vulnerabilities of nearby communities.[7] Even without catastrophic failures, ecological systems are permanently disrupted as mining spreads across a region.

As mining exploration and extraction grew in Latin America, an array of social groups mobilized to challenge this advance. Supportive international observers and allies developed databases to document the most visible conflicts. Although constrained by data limitations due to their unofficial nature and to the herding and clustering tendencies in NGO organizing and media reporting, these collections provide an initial take on the patterns of conflict.[8] As of December 2021, the Observatorio de Conflictos Mineros de América Latina (OCMAL) registered 284 mining conflicts involving 301 mines in twenty Latin American and Caribbean countries.[9] While the highest number of conflicts in that database occurred in Mexico (58), Chile (49), and Peru (46), repeated and enduring mining protests were also registered in Argentina (28), Brazil (26), and Colombia (19).[10] Thirty-five conflicts occurred in Central America, including Panama, with the largest concentration in Guatemala (10). Environmental threats served as a major catalyst for protest activism across the region. In Central America, as Paul Almeida (2015) concluded, "environmental harms appear to be creating conditions for dozens of mass struggles throughout the region" (p. 106).

---

[6] Tailings are what remains after the target mineral is extracted from rock compound, and include ground-up rock, process water, and chemicals used in extraction.

[7] Owen et al. (2019) report sixty-three major tailings dam failures globally since 1969, with the trend rising since 1990, and at least 2,375 people killed as a result between 1961 and 2019.

[8] The EJATLAS database (https://ejatlas.org/) included 2,836 environmental justice conflicts around the world as of July 2019, 454 of them in the mineral ore extraction sector. This database follows the "most significant" cases as determined by investment size, media attention, and activist opinion (Temper et al. 2018, 580).

[9] See https://mapa.conflictosmineros.net/ocmal_db-v2/, accessed December 7, 2021.

[10] International databases tend to undercount conflicts. Peru's Defensoría del Pueblo registered 117 socio-environmental conflicts in June 2019, 62% of them in the mining sector. See https://www.defensoria.gob.pe/wp-content/uploads/2019/07/Conflictos-Sociales-N%C2%B0-184-Junio-2019.pdf.

8   BREAKING GROUND

The effort to trace and explain the growth of these conflicts has given rise to a large and expanding body of literature.[11] Although much of this work focuses on experiences in countries where mining and hydrocarbon extraction have been traditional economic mainstays, analysis is expanding to cover the conflicts erupting in newer mining territories, including in Central America.

Natural Resource Dependence and Mining Promotion Frameworks

Research on extractive sector development and "reprimarization" of Latin American economies tends to homogenize the region by painting with a broad brush.[12] Dependency on natural resource rents actually varies significantly by country. According to the World Development Indicators measuring the economic impact of natural resource rents, which includes returns to oil, gas, coal, mineral mining, and forestry, the average of natural resource rents as a percentage of GDP was 5.6% in Latin America in 2014 (see Figure 1.1). Three levels of resource rent dependence can be identified: high (above 7% of GDP), medium (2–7% of GDP), and low (less than 2%). Chile has long been the most dependent on these rents, which accounted for 14.7% of GDP in 2014. Bolivia (11.3%), Ecuador (11.7%), Venezuela (11.8%), and Peru (7.4%) were also in the high cluster. Several South American countries, including Argentina (3.0%), Brazil (4.1%), and Colombia (6.6%), were located in the more typical middle cluster, as were three Central American countries, Guatemala (3.2%), Honduras (2.7%), and Nicaragua (4.4%). In still others, including Costa Rica and El Salvador, where mining was suspended, and Panama, natural resource rents contributed little to the national economy.

Variation in extractive sector dependence is in part related to the concentration of mineral and fossil fuel deposits in different geological zones. That

---

[11] See, for example, Delgado-Ramos 2010; Bebbington and Bury 2013; Saade Hazin 2013; Arce 2014; Ponce and McClintock 2014; Dupuy 2014; Broad 2014; Dawson 2014; Veltmeyer and Petras 2014; Li 2015; de Castro, Hogenboom, and Baud 2016; Haslam and Heidrich 2016; Deonandan and Dougherty 2016; McNeill and Vrtis 2017; Bebbington et al. 2018; Gustafsson 2018; Svampa 2019; Eisenstadt and West 2019; Kröger 2020; Broad and Cavanagh 2021; Shapiro and McNeish 2021; Jaskoski 2022; and Arce, Hendricks, and Polizzi 2022.

[12] Reprimarization is the return to economic dependence on primary sector activities, including mining, oil and gas, and resource-intensive forms of forest use and agricultural production.

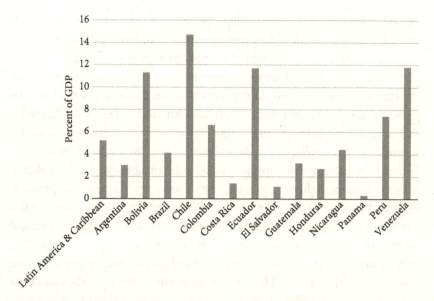

Figure 1.1 Natural resource rents as % of GDP (2014). Data from World Development Indicators.

feature, however, captures only part of the mining story. Exploration activities and the identification of deposit locations respond to a wide range of additional factors, some of them related to variation in public policies. Using a ranking of the top twenty criteria for investment decisions reported by representatives of forty junior and senior mining companies, Otto et al. (2006, 215–216) identified the key policy conditions favored by the industry. Their ranking demonstrates investors' strong commitment to profitability, asset control, and policy stability, including security of tenure and stability of tax liabilities and environmental rules.

The Fraser Institute, a libertarian think tank based in Vancouver, Canada, conducts an annual survey of mining company officials to assess their views about desirable locations for mining investment. The Fraser metric combines a Best Practices Mineral Potential Index, based on a country's geologic attractiveness, with a Policy Perception Index, which registers the reaction of mining managers to government policies. These scores feed into an overall Investment Attractiveness Index, with totals calculated for each country or province assessed. According to an in-house report on the 2018 survey results, policy factors like the taxation regime, regulatory burdens

10 BREAKING GROUND

and uncertainties, and quality of legal protections determine approximately 40% of mining investment decisions (Stedman and Green 2019, 1).

In Latin America, public and private policies related to mining have varied across time, with three patterns commanding attention. First, investment in the industry was promoted during the 1980s and 1990s era of *neoliberal reform*, encouraged by processes of privatization and deregulation. Conflicts that emerged between mining companies and communities encouraged a second pattern, in which corporations introduced *corporate social responsibility initiatives* and accepted new forms of stakeholder engagement. Finally, a shift to *resource nationalism* in the 2000s sparked a third round of mining promotion, now justified in terms of funding for social development projects. In spite of this newfound rationale for mine promotion, the local impacts and environmental costs intrinsic to the industry meant that protest often continued, especially in agricultural communities and those territories where vulnerability to harm was most acute (Arce 2014; Haslam and Tanimoune 2016; Eisenstadt and West 2019). Except in "sacrifice zones" (Klinger 2017), where extensive prior degradation had undermined alternative aspirations, mining proved to be a sustained source of tension and conflict.

Mining and Neoliberal Reform

During the heyday of the developmental state in the 1930s–1970s, state ownership of subsoil rights, mining nationalizations, and restrictions on foreign ownership in the sector restrained private mining development. Privatization and deregulation in the wake of the 1980s debt crisis sparked the return of business interest. Many countries rewrote their mining laws in keeping with recommendations from the World Bank (Sánchez Albavera, Ortiz, and Moussa 2001; Otto et al. 2006). Tax inducements and infrastructural supports helped to increase the return on investment, and labor "flexibilization" permitted easier layoffs and reassignments. Royalties in the mining sector were reduced and remained low in spite of the spike in commodity profits during the boom years (Haslam and Heidrich 2016, 6–11; Altomonte and Sánchez 2016, 186–194).

Even countries with a long history of mining restriction began opening up the sector. In the 1990s, for example, Mexico approved a new mining law (1992) that privatized state-owned mining companies, adopted a new Foreign Investment Law (1993), and entered into the North American Free Trade Agreement (NAFTA) (1994), as neoliberal reforms interlaced and accumulated (Moreno-Brid and Puyana 2016, 141–157).[13] Whereas foreign ownership had previously been restricted, it was now permitted "with the simple establishment of a mailing address in Mexico" (Holland 2018, 126). The state extended the period for mining concessions to fifty years, up from twenty-five, and taxes were lowered. Public hearings were eliminated in 1999 and red tape was reduced. In the event of environmental damage, Mexican mining regulations permitted only fines and precluded permit cancellation. Subsoil concessions came with privileged access to surface rights, superseding restrictions on transfers of protected areas, *ejido* land, and other forms of private property (Studnicki-Gizbert 2017, 33). NAFTA ratification gave U.S. and Canadian investors additional protections, including the right to present demands against the Mexican state at the World Bank's International Centre for the Settlement of Investment Disputes (ICSID), rather than depending on domestic courts to hear their claims.

Soft Law Adaptations: Corporate Social Responsibility and Social License to Operate

As mining conflicts heated up, international norm-setting by extractive sector promoters encouraged corporate attention to community relations. The World Bank not only promoted mining policy reforms as a general strategy for accelerating growth but also became an investor itself through its International Finance Corporation (IFC). As a stakeholder in mine development, the IFC used its investor status to encourage improved standards in the industry (IFC 2014b). It called for early strategic stakeholder engagement and recommended the inclusion of citizen participation in project discussions and environmental impact assessment (EIA) review. Over time, these steps became accepted as "best practice" guidelines.

As the boom continued, the IFC developed a more extensive set of recommendations and tailored them for junior mining companies, which, as short-term and risk-prone actors, often had a troubled history (Dougherty 2011; IFC 2014b). These IFC guidelines encouraged mining juniors to seek local "partnership" with communities and to promote the "psychological identification" of local actors with the mining project. The goal, at the

---

[13] Studnicki-Gizbert (2017, 33) described this reform as "essentially a repeat of the Porfiriato's 1892 code," albeit with modifications tailored to accommodate open pit chemical mining.

12 BREAKING GROUND

end of a series of trust-building and dialogue exercises, was for community members to become mining "advocates and defenders," serving in a "united front against critics" (IFC 2014b, 17).

During the initial wave of mining expansion, community members had little opportunity to weigh in on proposed projects (Jaskoski 2022). The conditions under which local residents had been authorized to participate were often very limited. During the small window (ten working days) open for public comment on Pacific Rim's El Dorado mine project in El Salvador in 2005, for example, the EIA was available only in the central office of the Ministry of the Environment in the capital city, with no photocopying permitted (Moran 2005b). In Guatemala, residents in overwhelmingly indigenous communities near the Marlin mine complained that announcements about the public comment period were not disseminated widely or made available in local languages (IACHR 2014). Without document access, translation into indigenous languages, and explanations using nontechnical forms of expression, the mandated public comment period routinely failed to facilitate informed participation.

When excluded, communities could challenge the company's EIA submission and pressure the government to withhold approval. With the assistance of transnational partners, they could also draw the attention of the media, including international news sources, and alert current or potential company stockholders to project deficiencies and community disapproval. If the project was funded in part by the World Bank, they could use the Bank's Compliance Advisor Ombudsman (CAO) complaint system and call for an independent investigation.

To avoid these conflicts, more responsive mining companies commonly sought a "social license to operate" (SLO).[14] Although not generally a legal requirement, evidence of community approval of the project reduces conflict and investment risks, and international mining associations urge corporations to pursue it as a best practice. Stock market reporting requirements generally mandate public disclosure of investment risks, including strikes and protests, making it cost-effective to strive for social acceptance.[15]

---

[14] The IFC (2014b, 15) notes that there is no one approach to the concept but identifies two definitions: "ongoing acceptance by the people who live and work in the area of impact and influence of any given project," and "improved risk management, as failure to gain and maintain SLO can lead to conflict, delays, and additional costs associated with a project."

[15] Ernst and Young ranked problems with securing a social license as the fourth-largest business risk faced by the mining industry (as cited in IFC 2014b, 15).

To secure a social license, companies regularly provide community services beyond those mandated by law, including periodic garbage pickup drives, funding for school projects, health worker visits, and housing and reforestation initiatives. The resulting corporate social responsibility initiatives may also include voluntary corporate improvements in environmental performance, corporate funding for community development initiatives, and resource access for artisanal and small miners who populate the zone (Costanza 2016; Haslam 2018; Gustafsson 2018, 59–60). Some of these behaviors are further incentivized by the state through tax reductions and exonerations, as with Nicaragua's tax write-offs for reforestation projects. These initiatives enter the realm of "soft law" as nonbinding normative instruments that may be adopted and diffused quickly, even in the absence of enforcement mechanisms (Walker-Said and Kelly 2015). Gustafsson (2018) uses the phrase "private politics" to refer to the arrangements that emerge via exchanges between corporate representatives and community actors.

The development of CSR commitments in the mining sector has been the subject of a growing body of academic research, and analysts point to wide variation in their forms and impacts (Horton 2007; Slack 2009; Moran 2011; Dashwood 2012; Haslam 2018; Hertel 2019). Pressures to secure community approval frequently lead corporate spokespeople and public relations professionals to manipulate information and pursue acquiescence through discursive trickery and deception (Goodland 2011, 22; Kirsch 2014; Broad 2014; Walker-Said and Kelly 2015; Torres Wong 2019). In some cases, corporate responses begin with artifice and improve over time. Dashwood (2012, 146) traces a shift in corporate attitudes toward environmental sustainability from the early "redneck" stage, characterized by the absence of any corporate environmental policy and an environmentally disengaged workforce; through the "lip service" stage, in which verbal expressions of concern emerged, unaccompanied by substantive action; into a "clean and green" phase in which environmental commitments permeate management training and workforce values, and reward systems embrace norms of environmental sustainability.

Resource Nationalism

Opposition to mining can be softened through greater state absorption of mining rents and application of these funds to social programming for a

14   BREAKING GROUND

previously underserved part of society. The political shift to the left in several extraction-dependent countries in Latin America during the first decades of the twenty-first century encouraged this revenue transfer and produced a new line of defense for extractivism (Veltmeyer and Petras 2014; Haslam and Heidrich 2016; Lewis 2016; Riofrancos 2020). With the ascendance of "resource nationalism," progressive governments in Argentina, Bolivia, Ecuador, and Venezuela adopted new legislation that laid greater state claim to subsoil resources. Common practices involved full or partial nationalization of extractive resources, creation or expansion of state-owned enterprises, the enactment of new taxes and fiscal obligations, and the establishment of institutions and regulatory agencies to manage the increased resource inflows.

Bolivia's Hydrocarbons Law #3058 (2005), Supreme Decree #28701 (2006), and Mining Law #3787 (2007) reestablished state ownership of hydrocarbons resources and substantially increased revenues from the natural gas and mining industries. The resulting increase in rents allowed the government to fund new social programs and develop an array of conditional cash transfers. Under Evo Morales, Bolivia established universal cash transfer programs to support schoolchildren and their families (Bono Juancito Pinto), new mothers and pregnant women (Bono Juana Azurduy), and the elderly (Renta Dignidad), reaching around 30% of the population in 2014 (Vargas and Garriga 2015, 25). This alignment of extractive revenues and social programs brought this wave of Latin America's progressive governments firmly into the pro-mining camp. Tax incentives designed to promote mining investment continued or even increased under some "pink tide" governments, as did openings to and partnerships with transnational mining corporations (IGF 2019, 5–6).

Looking at this double thrust of neoliberal support for extractive sector development and the enthusiasm for extraction found in post-neoliberal regimes, Svampa (2019) describes a "commodities consensus," which aligned the traditional neoliberal governments in the region with those claiming to embrace redistributive social change. In spite of political differences between the two, both endorsed an economic model based on the appropriation of natural resources (mining, oil and gas, timber, fishing, and plantation agriculture) using a top-down development approach. And both pursued alliances with transnational capital and global markets in order to accelerate economic growth.

As resource extraction accelerated, so too did community and environmental critiques, even in neo-extractivist regimes. Martinez-Alier, Baud, and Sejenovich (2016) identify a broad array of environmentalisms that surfaced in Latin America. These range from traditional conservationist approaches and government-supported sustainable development initiatives to the more redistributive visions expressed in the "environmentalism of the poor" and in projects rooted in indigenous principles of *buen vivir*. Lewis (2016), tracing the development of environmental movements in Ecuador, identifies four clusters: "ecoimperialists," who impose norms from the global North; "ecodependents," who bend their proposals into line with funder preferences; "ecoentrepreneurs," who establish sustainable-development-oriented business projects; and "ecoresisters," who reject the developmentalist vision held by neo-extractivist promoters and search for alternatives.

Whether due to active support for megaprojects or because of inertia and their own organizational limitations, some communities did not mobilize in opposition. In their study of 302 electricity projects financed by the Brazilian development bank BNDES, Hochstetler and Tarjan (2016) found that only 29% generated conflicts. Haslam and Tanimoune (2016) found in their study of 640 geolocated mining properties in Latin America that conflicts had been recorded in only 21%.[16] Some in Latin America's impacted communities endorsed megaprojects, seeing potential for gains that outweighed the harm. Others, however, moved to challenge the commodity "consensus," breaking new ground in the resource struggle.

Reform Alternatives and Proposals for Change

For the large and growing number of communities that develop mining resistance movements, reform proposals tend to cluster around two broad policy nodes. The first favors *restrictive regulation*, while the second calls for outright *prohibition*. These approaches are not absolutely divergent or necessarily radically opposed, although they may become so in particular conflicts. For many mining critics, these positions may be best understood as mutually conditioning and sequenced, with one approach perceived as a stopgap measure on the way to the other. Mining critics may call for

---

[16] Their results may reflect the undercount of conflicts in the OCMAL database, on which they draw.

16 BREAKING GROUND

prohibition but only if restrictive regulation cannot be achieved or only until well-enforced restrictive regulation becomes possible. Alternatively, restrictive regulation may be endorsed, but in a bid to limit the range and number of mining projects as a step in the journey toward eventual elimination of the industry.

Still, these proposals are distinct enough to permit the construction of a reform policy spectrum (see Table 1.1). Proposals on this spectrum range from modest forms of regulatory tightening that adjust the distribution of returns to transformative interventions that eliminate the industry altogether. Both of these policy nodes include significant variations, as summarized in Table 1.1.

Restrictive Regulation

For many mining protesters, the goal is not to halt mining but to negotiate for better terms. Such conflicts strive for the tightening of regulations, better implementation of laws and guidelines, larger royalties and tax revenues, increased wages and payments to the localities, improved cleanup or closedown processes, fuller and more consequential consultation with the community, and more regulatory transparency. These "adverse governmental actions" may also increase national participation requirements or in-country "beneficiation" rules regarding exports or domestic processing (Burnett and Bret 2017, 47–58). Restrictive regulatory changes are designed to reduce the risks associated with mining operations and increase the local benefits, including evidence of company respect for residents and recognition of their basic rights (Bebbington et al. 2013, 263–264).

Discussing the 2011 mobilizations in Puno, Peru, for example, Bebbington et al. (2013) conclude: "This was not necessarily a generalized call for a Puno without mining. It was, though, a call to start over and to find different modes and criteria for planning and making decisions about how extractive industry should unfold in a region" (pp. 262–263). This call for revision in the mode of interaction may, of course, become a call for termination if the possibility of reform is eliminated or if confidence in the good faith of bargaining partners is missing. Many protesters, however, may be willing to accept development of a mining industry if the terms and conditions of operation are altered.

Table 1.1 Restrictive Policy Demands: Mining Sector Reforms Sought by Opposition Networks

RESTRICTIVE REGULATION			PROHIBITION		
Greater Local Compensation	**Stricter Environmental Control**	**Consultation with Affected Community**	**Provisional (Temporary) Bans**	**Partial (Geo-specific) Bans**	**Full National Bans**
• Increased wages, labor protections for miners • Increased tax payments (royalties, income and land use taxes) • Shifts in the way tax and royalty payments are distributed or monitored • Reduced tax incentives (exonerations) for investors • Strengthened legal commitments to job creation, local buying, and social program funding	• Detailed and externally validated environmental impact assessment (EIA) prior to each stage • Improved environmental monitoring and intervention, with stronger penalties for violations • Higher bond and insurance requirements • Stronger "life-cycle" and land reclamation standards	• Local access to project information and planning documents • "Free, prior and informed consent" by indigenous communities • Binding "prior consultation" by affected populations (including both indigenous and non-indigenous residents) • Ongoing and renewed consultation as the project expands and winds down	• Mining suspension, moratorium, shelving, or delay • Project postponement pending citizen review, independent technical analysis, new legislation, or strengthened regulations • Moratorium pending completion of processes to build institutional management capacity	• Ban on mining in populated or protected areas • Ban on mining in indigenous territories • Ban on mining in disaster-prone areas • Ban on mining in headwaters or in proximity to vulnerable water resources • Ban on mining by zone (tropical, agricultural, offshore, deep sea) • Ban on mining in areas that register broad community opposition (lack social license to operate)	• Legal prohibition on all metallic mining • Legal prohibition on all open pit mining • Legal prohibition on large-scale mining • Legal prohibition on use of cyanide and mercury in mining

18   BREAKING GROUND

Three issues that commonly drive such conflicts are compensation contests, calls for improved environmental control, and a push for community recognition and voice (see Table 1.1).

Compensation Contests

To begin with a common demand, mining protests frequently raise distributional claims related to the allocation of mining revenues. The resulting "distributive conflicts," discussed in more detail in Chapter 3, involve mobilizations designed to shift the way mining rents are divvied up and increase the portion received by local actors. As Raymond Vernon (1971) noted in his seminal study of state-corporation bargaining, petroleum and mining investment is typified by the "obsolescing bargain," in which state-investor agreements in phase one front-load favorable treatment in order to attract high-risk investment into exploration and start-up, only to be replaced in phase two, once investment risks dissipate and sunk costs allow recalibration by states seeking to gain better terms.

Mining companies are often enticed to invest with offers of tax exonerations, leaving little fiscal reward for the countries in which they operate (IGF 2019). This dynamic puts pressure on the stability of the fiscal regime and opens another arena of contestation over time. Charges of corruption and bribery associated with concession access and generous fiscal incentives, all too common in the extractive sector, exacerbate these political tensions (Moran 2011: 12, 18–20; Vieyra and Masson 2014). Forceful voices now question preferential treatment for mining investors and call for a crackdown on any corruption that eased the way for megaproject development.[17] These shifts in investor-state bargaining point to a regular rhythm of escalating tension as the investment moves from stage one to stage two.

Conflict also emerges over the division of resources between national and subnational levels of government (Dupuy 2014). Traditionally, royalties tended to accumulate at the central government level, leaving few gains for the localities in which the mines are located. In addition, jobs created by the capital-intensive modern mine are few in number beyond the construction phase, and the quick depletion of extractable ores may make mine work quite short-term. The enclave characteristics of the industry result in low spillover benefits and may widen the local class divide, setting persistent

---

[17] An OECD (2014, 21–22) study of 427 foreign bribery cases concluded between 1999 and 2013 found that 19% involved companies in the extractive sector, which led all other economic activities.

social tensions into motion. In addition, funds set aside to cover mine closing and land reclamation post-mining are often inadequate, leaving localities to struggle with the long-term costs.[18] These issues fuel collateral demands, ones that are designed to ensure a better distribution of the financial costs and rewards associated with industry operations.

Environmental Controls

Second, mining critics have been in the forefront of calls for improved environmental regulation. Mining is widely recognized as an environmentally challenging industry because of its potential to release harmful substances into the air, soil, and water (Bell and Donnelly 2006). Chemicals and heavy metals that are deposited into waterways as a result of mining have been implicated in human health problems in communities surrounding the mines (Rosario and Ault 1997; Picado et al. 2010; Sequeira-León, Luna-Avilés, and Huete-Pérez 2011; McNeill and Vrtis 2017). Even inactive mines may continue to produce acid mine drainage and leave behind toxic pools that threaten local water sources long after mine closure (Studnicki-Gizbert 2017; Pacheco Cueva 2017). These concerns lead environmental activists to play a forceful role in mobilizing mining protests and to call for rigorous regulation and abatement, if not outright mine closure.

Reducing the risks associated with mining requires the deployment of strong incentives, rigorous regulation, attentive monitoring, and vigorous enforcement to ensure compliance. Even with careful controls, unplanned events such as chemical spills and leaks, landslides, and mismanagement lead to major damages, in both the formal and informal mining sectors (IGF 2017; ICMM, UNEP, and PRI 2020). Mining protesters have played a leading role in advancing the agenda for rigorous and independent environmental impact assessments at every stage in the permitting process. The most significant demand concerns controlling the impact of mining on water access and quality, given the large quantities of water required in open pit chemical leach mining.

The local response to environmental concerns has been found to vary depending on the extent to which mining competes with or complements local needs. In barren regions, with relatively limited productive prospects,

---

[18] Dawson (2014, 4) reports that the amount of the original bond to cover closure costs for the Marlin mine in Guatemala was only US$1 million, an amount that even shareholders recognized as inadequate. They called for a US$49 million increase to cover expected real costs.

20   BREAKING GROUND

mining conflicts tend to focus on access to jobs and the distribution of gains—that is, compensation issues, which are generally less difficult to resolve. In productive agricultural zones, where competition for land and water pits mining promoters directly against agricultural producers, mining conflict tends to be more visible and intense (Arce 2014; Haslam and Tanimoune 2016). Those whose livelihoods and survival needs make them particularly vulnerable to environmental harm tend to prioritize this set of concerns (Eisenstadt and West 2019).

Mining critics note the need to improve state capacity in order to implement regulations that address perceived needs.[19] In the absence of a professional and well-equipped state bureaucracy, efforts to enforce restrictions will almost certainly fall prey to clientelism and corruption. If past is prologue, the results are in. Without a strong and effective state apparatus, protected areas will not be protected, water quality will not be monitored, toxic spills will not be reported, and corrective interventions will not be undertaken. "Green criminology," or investigative practices used by state officials to detect violations of environmental rules and to better penalize infractions and enforce compliance, will fail to produce results if underfunded and inadequately staffed (Ungar 2017). The environmental protection process is further undermined when state resources are mobilized principally on behalf of corporations, as when protest is criminalized and mining critics are subject to judicial persecution.

To achieve regulatory control, governments also need to negotiate and enforce agreements with artisanal and small-scale miners. This step requires moving beyond periodic clampdowns and camp invasions, which the authorities tend to favor, to providing access to territory, training, fair compensation, and safety. Environmental protection in this sector involves support for the introduction of appropriate technologies, such as shaking tables using gravitational separation (an alternative to mercury amalgamation) and retort equipment (which prevents the vaporized mercury from escaping into the air and waterways).

Recognition and Voice

Finally, mining critics commonly seek to carve out a meaningful role for local populations in decision-making about project contours and authorization.

---

[19] See Altomonte and Sánchez (2016) on the widespread failure in institutional capacity for water management and the implementation of mine closing regulations.

Activists have called for the introduction of "free, prior, and informed consent" (FPIC) processes that would recognize and give voice to those local populations most immediately affected (Voss and Greenspan 2012; Fontana and Grugel 2016; Leifsen et al. 2017; Falleti and Riofrancos 2018; Torres Wong 2019; Riofrancos 2020; Le Billon and Middeldorp 2021; Jaskoski 2022).

The right to consultation has been promoted using a variety of legal protocols. In Latin America the obligation has been most actively defended as a requirement under ILO 169, the Indigenous and Tribal Peoples Convention, an international convention introduced in 1989 that is designed to protect indigenous rights. Article 6 of this agreement requires signatory states to ensure consultation with indigenous communities regarding development projects that affect their territory.[20] Consultation rights for non-indigenous communities have also been promoted with laws permitting national referenda and municipal codes that institutionalize community participation in development policy implementation.

The enforcement of consultation rights remains infrequent, however, even in countries under a legal obligation to carry them out. Mining critics express frustration over the "information sessions" and public relations campaigns that mining companies attempt to pass off as consultations, as well as the use of state-led processes in strategically selected communities that invariably register project support (Flemmer and Schilling-Vacaflor 2016; Zaremberg and Torres 2018; Eisenstadt and West 2019; Le Billon and Middeldorp 2021). In response to this manipulation, critics sometimes organize consultations of their own (Walter and Urkidi 2016; Leifsen et al. 2017; Copeland 2019a), orchestrating performances that likewise respond to political calculations with largely predetermined results, but in the opposite direction. Divergence in these outcomes reinvigorates debate about whether community consultation can contribute to indigenous rights and the enhancement of democratic quality, and the conditions under which those outcomes occur (Falleti and Riofrancos 2018).

The push for prior consultation puts to the side the question of whether this ritual offers meaningful space for addressing the enormous structural power imbalances that characterize community-company relations in the extractive sector. Debate continues about how best to lift the barriers to implementation

---

[20] As of December 2021, twenty-four countries had signed the convention, including fifteen in Latin America and the Caribbean (Argentina, Bolivia, Brazil, Chile, Colombia, Costa Rica, Dominica, Ecuador, Guatemala, Honduras, Mexico, Nicaragua, Paraguay, Peru, and Venezuela).

22 BREAKING GROUND

of consultation rights and improve the quality of the results. In the absence of inclusive, informative, and iterative consultations that are well institutionalized, enjoy a strong sense of legitimacy, and whose results are accepted as binding, this issue will continue to spark conflict and calls for further reform.

Mining Prohibition

Given the impediments to effective regulation and the desire of many community residents to prevent cultural and economic losses, resisters may shift to the other end of the spectrum and call for outright prohibition. Mining bans have been declared in a number of countries, most commonly at the state or provincial level, as in Argentina, the United States, and the Philippines, but sometimes at the national level, as in Costa Rica, El Salvador, the Czech Republic, and Germany (Laitos 2012; Dawson 2014; Janíková et al. 2015; Walter and Urkidi 2016; Ali 2021). Bans may focus on particular commodities, such as uranium, or specific production practices, such as deep sea mining. The remaining three categories presented in Table 1.1 involve actions that would halt mining activities, whether informally or formally, partially or fully, or on a temporary or permanent basis.

Seven provinces in Argentina introduced mining bans between 2003 and 2011, generally by prohibiting the use of chemicals that were central to the extraction process. The state of Virginia approved a moratorium on uranium mining in 1982, a decision that was challenged by the mining industry but upheld by the U.S. Supreme Court in 2019. Montana banned cyanide use in mining in 1998 through referendum, a decision that was upheld by the Montana Supreme Court. New Mexico (1993), Michigan (2004), and Maine (2017) prohibited mines when cleanup plans would require perpetual water treatment post-closedown due to acid mine drainage (Laitos 2012; Wright 2018). In the Philippines, several provinces declared a moratorium on mining following a major tailings spill at the Marcopper mine in March 1996, and Executive Order 79 introduced a national moratorium on new mining permits in 2012 (Chaloping-March 2014; Dawson 2014).

A national mining ban, such as the one adopted in El Salvador in 2017, may be defended as sound policy, especially in a country characterized by small geographic size, high population density, heavy dependence on a single waterway, and underdeveloped regulatory capacity (Tau Consultora Ambiental 2011; Bebbington, Fash, and Rogan 2019). In settings where mine disasters would quickly have national impacts, prohibitions can be explained in technocratic terms as well as social and political ones.

But mining bans and moratoria affecting even a partly advanced exploration concession can lead to costly legal challenges, increasingly lodged at the international level and based on provisions and guarantees in bilateral investment treaties and free trade agreements (Schneiderman 2008; Tienhaara 2011; Moore and Pérez-Rocha 2019; Remmer 2019). Faced with the prospect of punishing costs, and often dealing with an unfavorable legal or political hand, some mining critics advocate for or acquiesce to a limited type of ban that falls short of comprehensiveness. Community ambivalence and division over the gains and losses associated with mine development may also result in provisional or partial measures. Gradations of variation in the prohibition cluster can help us identify the way that different combinations of resources affect strategic choices and serve as catalysts for different policy demands.

Provisional Bans: De Facto and Temporary Prohibitions
Some anti-mining movements culminate in de facto restrictions, rather than legislated ones. De facto bans, which do not take the form of formal legal measures, may emerge as extended delays, permit suspensions, or informal moratoria. Mining projects may be stalled by sustained protests, roadblocks, and occupations.[21] If the delay or postponement endures and tensions continue to escalate, the project may be halted by additional bureaucratic interventions (belatedly noting a defect in the application or incomplete paperwork, for example) or by a company's decision to withdraw given its inability to cover costs (Franks et al. 2014). Informal restrictions may signal a softening of state support or an internal division within the state apparatus. They may also be adopted by officials in lieu of formal action, in hope of avoiding a ruling of "indirect expropriation" or findings that go against the state in international investor-state investment disputes. In this regard, all four of the Central American case studies will be instructive.

The push for restriction could also wind up producing a *temporary ban*, rather than a permanent one, as state officials attempt to buy time or negotiate a new political agreement. These short-term bans may provide a pause during which conflict cools, damage is assessed, and further investigation is

---

[21] Latin American mining resistance movements claimed $30 billion in "paralyzed" mining investments in 2013. https://www.ocmal.org/la-resistencia-a-la-mineria-en-america-latina-tiene-paralizados-us-30-mil-millones/, accessed July 21, 2019.

conducted. Although temporary bans may deescalate tension or remove a dispute from the path of a high-stakes electoral campaign, they fail to resolve core issues and may themselves become the source of political agonism.

Temporary bans on new concessions may be declared in response to environmental disaster and court actions, as in Honduras in 2004 following exposure of environmental damages at the San Martín mine, and in 2006, when the Honduran Supreme Court ruled that sixteen articles in the 1998 mining law violated the constitution. These temporary measures may be reversed following shifts in the dominant political alliance structure and the passage of new legislation. After Honduran president Manuel "Mel" Zelaya, who endorsed a mining ban, was overthrown in a 2009 coup, the new governing coalition promoted a revised mining law, which was approved in 2013. This new law, while tightening protections in the articles that the Supreme Court had identified as problematic, encouraged the renewal of mining investment and left various gaps unattended (Dawson 2014; ICEFI 2014a). This policy was again contested when Zelaya's wife, Xiomara Castro, became president in January 2022 and announced a ban on new open pit mining.

In Ecuador as well, the initial suspension of large-scale mining introduced by the Constituent Assembly in the 2008 Mining Mandate, which revoked mineral concessions for almost half of the territory under exploration (Moore and Velásquez 2013, 122, 141; see also Warmaars 2013), was subsequently reversed. Ecuadorian president Rafael Correa's aggressive push for mine development and his palpable irritation with "infantile environmentalists" (Becker 2014, 280) illustrate the ways in which "rentier populism" (Mazzuca 2013) may undo temporary measures and restart mining ventures.

Partial Bans: Territorial Prohibitions

The second category of prohibitions involves partial bans that designate particular territories as off-limits. Environmental regulations often specify closed or prohibited areas, as mining regulators engage in triage that reflects their perceptions of the greatest threats. Partial bans, for example, may restrict mining in territories occupied by particularly vulnerable populations. They may also single out zones rich in biodiversity and ecotourism potential, or sites where mining advances have generated intense social conflict (Goodland 2011).[22] Prohibitions may respond to the political contours of

---

[22] In a policy paper prepared for the Colombian government, former World Bank extractive sector adviser Robert Goodland (2011) recommended that the following five areas be classified as "no-go"

particular mining struggles and mirror variation in movement organizational strength, succeeding in the territorial home of the best-organized forces of resistance.

Territorial bans could also be enacted through the use of binding community consultations that allow residents of affected communities to determine whether to grant a mining license. This is a frequent demand within the mining resistance camp, and would seem to be consistent with both the legal affirmation of indigenous territorial rights and the idea of a social license. Debate continues about the extent to which indigenous people, under the guarantees provided in ILO 169, and local communities, under a wide array of legal instruments that emerged during decentralization processes, should be able to veto mining projects. A June 12, 2013, community referendum in Piedras, Colombia, saw community residents vote overwhelmingly against a proposed mining project. This process was initially accepted as consistent with constitutional guarantees by the Colombia Constitutional Court, in spite of strong opposition by the presidency and attorney general (McNeish 2017). But as more communities followed suit, attempting to place their neighborhoods off-limits to extraction, the Colombian court reversed itself in October 2018, leaving mining decisions under the purview of the national government.

Full Bans: Legal and Permanent Prohibitions of National Scope

The gold standard for the prohibitionist camp is a permanent, legal ban on metallic mining. A full ban may target a form of extraction, as with the Costa Rican ban on all open pit mining, or it may prohibit all forms of metallic mining, including even that by artisanal and small miners, as in El Salvador. This outcome reduces the risk and uncertainty associated with moratoria and partial measures, and directs development initiatives toward other activities, ideally those with fewer social and environmental costs. Chapters 5 and 6, which describe the adoption of prohibitions in Costa Rica and El Salvador, respectively, provide a detailed analysis of the key features and dynamics that governed those outcomes.

---

zones for mining projects: indigenous peoples' territories; conflict zones (including those where the conflict was not about mining); fragile watersheds, including *paramos* and areas of active seismicity; conservation units (national parks, protected forests, and their buffer zones) and areas of high biodiversity and endemism; and areas of "cultural property," such as religious and archaeological sites and places of historical significance.

26 BREAKING GROUND

This end of the policy reform spectrum is less frequently employed than threatened. But outright prohibition becomes a meaningful option under certain sets of circumstances, as we will see in the coming chapters. Even when national prohibition is not implemented, the call for "[X country] without mining" prompts mining advocates to take notice of the resistance, and becomes a powerful tool in the conflict arsenal.

Argument and Methods

This book focuses on the political logistics of mine development during the most recent commodity boom. It draws attention to the ways in which policies governing mining vary with political dynamics and patterns of contention. Alternative approaches, some of which follow the simple logic of path dependence (production trends mirror the historical trajectory) or economic variables (global commodity price fluctuations dictate production increases and decreases), fall short as explanations of the complex processes that tease mines down into the earth and propel extraction policies in divergent directions.

This study employs a political process approach to identify the factors that contribute to extraction policy variation. It argues that social mobilization is a necessary but not sufficient condition for mining policy reform. Mining restrictions are unlikely to occur in the absence of a movement pushing for significant change. Powerful actors with a vested interest in keeping investment easy and regulations light impede adjustments, even when technocrats endorse reform and international codes call for new standards. A robust multisectoral and multiscalar reform movement is needed, one that negotiates frame alignment among movement sectors, raises recognition of these issues to the national level, and successfully highlights the costs of inaction.

But even well-networked mining resistance movements are not, by themselves, able to achieve changes in the rules and regulations that govern sectoral activities, much less to determine which kinds of policies will be implemented and enforced. Explanations of policy change that emphasize the "will" (Kröger 2020) or "smarts" (Broad and Cavanagh 2021) of resisters capture only a piece of the puzzle. As Giugni (2007) and Amenta et al. (2010) observe, movements normally impact policy change as components of larger processes, in which several factors combine to animate the policymaking process and reshape visions, protocols, and procedures. In addition to social mobilization, this study identifies two other factors that influence policy change: the extent of elite cohesion in support of mining, and the availability of portals through which the movement can penetrate the state apparatus. The interplay of these three factors shapes the fate of mining ambitions.

If elites form a pact for continuity, substantive reform is unlikely to advance. To achieve policy change, movement activists need to find or create fissures in the "political settlement" (Bebbington et al. 2018) and recruit elite allies to serve as sponsors and protectors. As they cross into the realm of formal institutional politics, activists need to engage actors within penetration points of the state apparatus, finding or creating institutional docks where they can insert their demands into the policymaking process. If elite fragmentation and state penetration can be achieved, then nationally networked coalitions may be able to achieve policy reform. If elite pro-mining cohesion is maintained and the state apparatus is unresponsive, then mining resistance movements will be unlikely to achieve their goals, particularly if they are themselves riven by internal division.

To identify the conditions under which mining reform advances or stalls, I used the methods of comparative historical analysis (Mahoney and Thelen 2015). This approach, which involves careful process tracing of a theoretically informed set of dynamics in a small number of closely observed cases, permits us to build a robust argument about the connections between social mobilization and policy. To trace these dynamics, I use a "controlled comparison" technique (Slater and Ziblatt 2013). Controlled comparison involves the selection of a small number of cases that narrow the range of variation and focus attention on a subset of recurring patterns. My use of this method entails process tracing of mining promotion and resistance in four countries, two of which opened up to and promoted metallic mining investment (Nicaragua and Guatemala) and two of which adopted policies that closed it down (Costa Rica and El Salvador).

This approach allows us to use John Stuart Mill's (1843) "method of agreement" and "method of difference" comparison to eliminate features that might seem to explain variation but do not, and to extract evidence of commonalities that initially escape attention because of the apparent significance of overwhelming difference. In spite of apparent similarities, Nicaragua and El Salvador, both economically stressed countries located in the Central American "Gold Belt," where former revolutionaries gained power in the wake of civil war, took sharply divergent paths on metallic mining policy. Meanwhile, violence-torn and remittance-dependent El Salvador and peaceful and prosperous Costa Rica both hacked their way toward similar outcomes by adopting innovative prohibitions in spite of their apparent political and economic differences. Analyzing the circumstances under which similar countries diverged and dissimilar countries converged helps to clarify those factors that led to counterintuitive outcomes.

My use of a four-case comparison instead of a more conventional two-case approach allows me to avoid confusing case particularities with category rules. Comparing multiple cases with similar outcomes forces conceptual work that goes beyond the narrow recounting of unique details. It propels discussion toward a higher level of generalization, where theoretically informed hypotheses are better birthed. Our question becomes not just what happened in Nicaragua that led to mine-promoting regulation but what happened in both Nicaragua and Guatemala that contributed to that outcome.

The small-n comparison, even one that builds in multiplicity, does not permit the kind of quantitative testing that characterizes large-n analysis. But it does allow nuanced analysis of the interplay of multiple factors and improves the quality of generalizations that emerge. Using a small number of cases also allows scholars to prioritize depth of familiarity and length of observation, both of which become possible only when limiting the scope of the data.

To reduce variation, all four of the cases analyzed in this book were drawn from Central America, a region in which I have worked for several decades. To eliminate differences that might be commodity- or time-dependent, I focus on gold and silver extraction and look closely at the 2002–2020 period. Precious metals have historically been produced in all four of these Central American countries, and all four were found to have the potential for commercial production of these metals during the recent commodity boom. Although narrowing the case material to a particular commodity and subregion is a good research strategy, one commonly followed by those who work in Andean countries, it could limit my ability to speak to mining policy debates elsewhere. To address that limitation, I include references to similar developments with other natural resource commodities and in other Latin American and Caribbean countries, and I note when the Central American examples are unique.

This analysis draws on four kinds of source materials: interviews, direct observation, official documents, and public opinion data. Between 2010 and 2018, I carried out 255 semistructured interviews with 216 individual respondents in Costa Rica, El Salvador, Guatemala, Nicaragua, and the United States (Chicago, Colorado, and Washington, DC). Central American interviews were conducted with community activists and mineworkers; local and national political leaders; church officials; government officials (including former presidents and vice presidents, ministry officials, legislators, judges, mayors, and other municipal officials); mining company representatives and their business allies; and legal representatives and spokespeople from national and international governmental and nongovernmental organizations. To my repository of Central American interviews, I added a small number of respondents in Washington, DC, including individuals from the World Bank's International Centre for the Settlement of Investment Disputes (ICSID) and International Finance Corporation (IFC), the Inter-American Development Bank (IADB), and international NGOs connected to Central American mining struggles as funders and allies.

With the exception of public officials who are mentioned by name, I reference individual interviews using a country code, an arbitrarily assigned individual interview number, and the last two digits of the interview year (e.g., 18 = 2018).[23] To follow up on responses and capture shifting perspectives over time, I conducted repeat interviews with a subset of thirty-nine respondents.[24] Appendices following each of the four empirical chapters include a list of interviews cited in that chapter.

Second, I undertook direct observation of mining processes and protest activities. In Nicaragua, I observed large-scale mining operations, small-scale extraction, and mercury-based gold processing in the informal sector. I participated in a public comment process that was part of the mining permit requirement for a proposed new mine in Chontales and in a strategy session for mining resisters in Rancho Grande. In Guatemala, I accompanied protesters who were attempting to close down mining operations by staging roadblocks and occupations in and around San José del Golfo, San Rafael Las

[23] CR = Costa Rica; ES = El Salvador; GT = Guatemala; and NI = Nicaragua. Except for respondents from the United States and Canada, interviews were conducted in Spanish. Translations are by the author.

[24] Nicaragua interviews were conducted in and around Bonanza, La India, Managua, Matagalpa, and Rancho Grande in 2012, 2015, 2016, 2017, and 2018. Guatemala interviews were conducted in Guatemala City, Santa Rosa de Lima, Casillas, and San José del Golfo in 2015, 2016, 2017, and 2018. For the Costa Rican case, interviews took place in and around San José, Heredia, and Alajuela in 2010, 2014, and 2017. Interviews in El Salvador were conducted in and around San Salvador, Cinquera, Sesuntepeque, San Isidro, Victoria, and Perquín in 2010, 2012, 2017, and 2018. Additional interviews were conducted in Chicago during Salvadoran and Guatemalan delegation visits in 2015 and 2017, and with respondents in Washington, DC, in 2012, 2013, and 2017. Follow-up electronic exchanges with key participants in 2020 and 2021 are not included in the interview tally.

30 BREAKING GROUND

Flores, and Guatemala City. In Costa Rica, I attended community strategy sessions, academic seminars, and press conferences related to the Crucitas case. In El Salvador, I attended legislative committee sessions in San Salvador and memorial services for anti-mining activists who had been assassinated in Cabañas. I both joined and presented at academic forums where extractive industry impacts were analyzed and debated in Nicaragua, Guatemala, and El Salvador.

Third, in addition to an extensive review of conventional and gray literature, this study incorporates information from a trove of official documents, including court testimony and legal rulings, campaign platforms and electoral results, draft bills and legislative commission reports, and official findings resulting from national and international investigations. Finally, it draws on public opinion data, including the results of both local and national polls, some of which were repeated in different years. To place Central American public opinion within a larger regional context, I commissioned an international poll about attitudes toward industrial mining in eight Latin American countries in 2018. These polls allowed me to trace shifts in attitudes over time and to compare perspectives in a variety of Latin American countries, including the four highlighted in this book.

Chapter Overviews

Chapter 2, "From Community Conflicts to Policy Outcomes: Movements, Elites, and State Permeability," provides a fuller introduction to the central argument of the book. It describes the three processes—elite alignment, movement organization, and state penetration—that shape the trajectory of mining policy development. The chapter draws on theories and concepts from the interdisciplinary subfields of political economy, social movement theory, and comparative politics to develop the arguments on which this analysis is built. Literature from political economy supplies the criteria by which to define an elite, interpret the relationship between political and business elites, and assess the extent of internal elite agreement. Social movement theory provides the tools to analyze networking strategies and to trace the bridging, bonding, and brokerage processes of frame construction and alignment that foster multisectoral and multiscalar collaboration. The insights of comparative politics permit exploration of institutional "docking

MINING CONFLICT AND POLICY ALTERNATIVES   31

points"—that is, spaces in the political apparatus where popular movements can insert resonant demands into policy deliberation processes and influence the outcome. Together these elements offer a comprehensive model to explain variation in mining policy.

Chapters 3 to 6 explore mining policy variations using empirical cases and illustrations. These chapters move systematically across the spectrum from pro-mining settings where state interventions encouraged rapid growth in the industry to contexts where mining opposition disrupted elite alliances and secured a comprehensive legislative ban on metallic mining. Along the way, we analyze the policy ambiguities that emerge under mixed configurations, and the production disruptions and project delays that tended to follow.

Chapter 3, "Mining Friendly: Promoting Extractivism in Nicaragua," uses the Nicaraguan case to trace the processes supporting the advancement of gold mining. It shows how elite unity, resistance movement fragmentation, and low levels of state penetrability combined to encourage the adoption of policies favored by the industry. This chapter follows mine advancement from the Sandinista revolution in the 1980s to the post-revolutionary neoliberal reforms of the 1990s, and concludes with the legal and discursive mine promotion activities that followed Daniel Ortega's return to power in 2007. Although community-level resistance emerged, mining conflicts fractured into three types (distributive, definitional, and scale), each with their own distinct goals. The opposition's political capacity was further undermined by the consolidation of hegemonic rule under Ortega and the withering of participatory practices in the 2010s. This chapter introduces the central argument about how elite cohesion, resistance disarray, and state insularity combine to sustain the mine-friendly policy outcomes into the post-neoliberal era.

Chapter 4, "Mining, Maybe: Intermittent Mining in Guatemala," examines the mixed conditions that favor stop-and-go mining, in which favorable policies are followed by moratoria and suspensions before the cycle begins again. This chapter focuses on the Guatemalan case, where gold mining advanced more episodically. Developed by a cohesive pro-mining elite, the Guatemalan gold and silver mining industry triggered decentralized forms of mobilization, where grassroots community referenda and creative legal strategies intermittently stalled but did not derail industry expansion. While tracing the way environmental and

32 BREAKING GROUND

indigenous rights movements employed strategic litigation to promote institutional change, this chapter also demonstrates the tenacious hold of pro-mining elite networks in the context of movement fragmentation and state opacity.

Chapter 5, "Mining Skeptics: Environmental Resistance in Costa Rica," tracks what happens when elites are divided, protestors develop organizational breadth, and state institutions include participatory pathways. Although mining enjoyed elite backing at the outset in Costa Rica, few government officials or business leaders rallied to defend the industry as it fell under attack by grassroots activists. This chapter traces the dynamics involved in successful mining regulation by observing how environmental protesters achieved organizational cohesion and successfully opened up docking points to carry the resistance message forward. Mining permits that failed to adhere to regulatory standards were successfully challenged in the courts. As public opinion moved strongly against mining, the Costa Rican mining debate concluded in 2010 with a unanimous legislative vote to ban new open pit metal mining, making that country a global pioneer in mining curtailment.

Chapter 6, "Mining Free: Mining Prohibition in El Salvador," shows how elite division and opposition mobilization led to a mining moratorium and eventual ban. Unlike "green" Costa Rica, with its relatively responsive and penetrable state institutions, El Salvador suffered from multiple political deficits, and resistance movements there faced a range of obstacles, including activist assassinations. Fissures in elite support, which widened over time, created opportunities for mobilization, and mining opponents drew on bridging, bonding, and brokerage processes to build a broad resistance network. Introducing the concepts of "tipping points" and legislative "social cascades," this chapter shows how cohesive opposition, in the absence of elite unity, and in the context of an opening institutional setting, can use docking opportunities in the bureaucracy and the legislature to secure policy outcomes that bring mining to a halt.

Chapter 7, "Mining Reform in Latin America: International Regimes and the Challenges of Regulation," restates the argument, showing how variation in levels of elite consensus, anti-mining organization, and state penetrability aligns with four kinds of mining policies: those that favor *sustained promotion*, that lead to *intermittent approval*, that support *resistant authorization and prohibition*, and that result in an *extended moratorium and ban*. I conclude by discussing the challenges introduced by investor-state dispute settlement (ISDS) claims, and I briefly analyze the three ICSID cases filed against Central American countries involved in mining suspensions. While recognizing the pressures imposed by the globalization of investment rules and the push for neoliberal policy homogenization, this study concludes by noting that space for national-level mining policy variation remains, informed by identifiable differences in domestic political conjunctures.

2

From Community Conflicts to Policy Outcomes

Movements, Elites, and State Permeability

The goal of this book is to introduce a second generation of mining studies—one that goes beyond descriptive discussion of community conflicts to examine the circumstances under which conflict and mobilization give rise to policy and institutional change. This chapter introduces my analytical framework and provides an overview of the argument, which combines an analysis of elite alliances, movement characteristics, and institutional dynamics to create a multidimensional model of mining policy stasis and change.

Research on extractive sector conflict traditionally focuses on struggles at the community level (Bebbington and Bury 2013; Arce 2014; Kirsch 2014; Li 2015; McNeill and Vrtis 2017; Gustafsson 2018; Shapiro and McNeish 2021; Jaskoski 2022). As noted in this extensive literature, these local conflicts assume different forms and vary widely in their outcomes. Anti-mining mobilizations are commonly checked by corporate and government interventions and by their own organizational limitations. Some defy the odds, however, and demonstrate a capacity to deepen and grow. A few become emblematic, and come to serve as a cause célèbre in the activist world.

In a study of 346 mining conflicts reported in the Environmental Justice Organizations, Liabilities and Trade (EJOLT) database, an online resource compiled by environmental activists, Özkaynak, Rodríguez-Labajos, and Aydin (2015) found that 46% of these mobilizations were classified as failures.[1] A third (33%) were found to have mixed results, with achievements noted along with significant costs. A relatively modest 21% were deemed successful, typically because the mining project was suspended. Project

---

[1] Outcomes were scored from 0 (complete failure, no positive outcomes) to 5 (complete success, exclusively favorable observations). Scores of 0 (35%) and 1 (11%) were classified as failures; 2 (28%) and 3 (5%) were classified as mixed; and 4 (8%) and 5 (13%) were considered to be successful (Özkaynak, Rodríguez-Labajos, and Aydin 2015, 53).

Breaking Ground. Rose J. Spalding, Oxford University Press. © Oxford University Press 2023.
DOI: 10.1093/oso/9780197643150.003.0002

suspension is a significant outcome for those who, often at great personal risk, dedicate their scarce resources to the effort. It tells us little, however, about the broader consequences of the mobilization, and even less about whether the struggle has a policy consequence. Since national policy change is the central issue in this book, our task is to search for the processes with that kind of impact.

One factor associated with policy difference is variation in public opinion. Given the regularity and intensity of mining conflict in Latin America, it is not surprising that public opinion on this topic has been divided. Attitudes vary by country and issue salience, and are affected by the usual media campaigns designed to soften or intensify public views. To get a snapshot of this variation, at least at one moment in time, I commissioned a cross-national poll of attitudes toward industrial mining in eight Latin American and Caribbean countries in January 2018. Respondents were asked whether they believed that mining company operations should be permitted or pro-hibited. Table 2.1 reports the results.

In this set of surveys, only the Peruvian respondents clearly favored mining company operations, with 57% stating that these should be permitted while only 36% called for their prohibition. Given Peru's rela-tively high level of economic dependence on mining exports and strong role in the global supply chain, majority support for mining activities in

Table 2.1 Public Opinion on Mining Company Operation in Eight Latin American Countries

Country	Permit	Prohibit	DK/NR
Peru*	57%	36%	7%
Dominican Republic	48	43	9
Honduras	41	49	10
Nicaragua	40	45	15
Panama*	37	51	12
Guatemala*	33	52	15
Costa Rica*	26	59	15
El Salvador*	24	58	18

Question: Do you think the operation of mining companies should be permitted, or do you think they should be prohibited? ("¿Cree usted que debería permitir la operación de empresas mineras o más bien cree que se deberían prohibir?"). CID Gallup, January 2018.

* Difference exceeds margin of error.

36 BREAKING GROUND

that country is not surprising. But even in Peru, more than one-third of the respondents indicated a preference for mining prohibition, and mining protests were both common and consequential (Arce 2014; Li 2015; Gustafsson 2018).

The attitudinal outlook in the Dominican Republic, Honduras, and Nicaragua was mixed, with no statistically significant preference emerging in this dataset, although national policy remained mining friendly. In the other four countries, public opinion tilted toward the opposition. The outcomes in Panama and Guatemala showed a modest majority in support of prohibition, while approximately one-third of the respondents stated a position in favor of mining. Respondents in Costa Rica and El Salvador, the two countries in which either open pit (Costa Rica) or all forms of metallic mining (El Salvador) have been banned, provided the clearest signal of opposition, with the percentage in favor of prohibition more than double that in favor of mining authorization.

These survey results align loosely with several mining policy outcomes, and public opinion has clearly played a role in policy enactment. But public opinion may vary across the policymaking cycle and be as much an outcome of policy change as a cause.[2] By itself, it does not tell us much about how policy packages emerge or what factors are most consequential in shaping the results. As policy analysts have noted, public opinion plays a role in policymaking, particularly in putatively democratic regimes, but when and how much needs clarification (Giugni 2004; Amenta et al. 2010; Bosi, Giugni, and Uba 2016). Nor does a model that starts and stops with public opinion tell us much about the origins of these attitudes and how they shift over time. Fuller explanation of these linkages comes with the development of more complex models, followed by rigorous process tracing to assess their accuracy. To address these larger questions, we turn to the framework that is employed throughout this book. This broader model allows us to trace the shifts and adjustments that took place as mining policy packages were put

---

[2] The timing of the survey, conducted more than seven years after the Costa Rican legislature approved a ban on open pit mining and ten months after the Salvadoran legislature banned metallic mining, leaves in question how well these results capture the attitudes that prevailed at the time of the legislative votes. But other polls conducted in these countries around the time of ban adoption suggest that opposition was pervasive, and perhaps even stronger at that time. CID Gallup's 2010 poll in Costa Rica found that 85% of respondents expressed some level of opposition to open pit mining, and only 10% were in favor when the mining moratorium was declared (CID Gallup 2010a). A 2015 poll in El Salvador, which tallied attitudes in *municipios* where mining licenses had been issued, found that four out of five respondents thought that mining was not appropriate for El Salvador (IUDOP 2015).

together, and to capture the changes that unfolded as mining policy underwent change.

This book proposes an approach to theory building that highlights three elements: the extent of elite cohesion in support of mine development, the characteristics of mining resistance networks and the frames they employ, and the degree to which state institutions are open and penetrable versus restricted and insular. Each serves as a necessary but not, in isolation, sufficient condition to explain policy variation. In conjunction, I argue, these factors chart the course of extraction policy development and lead to divergent outcomes.

The role of social movements in determining the shape of mining policy has drawn analytical and activist attention (Kröger 2020; Broad and Cavanagh 2021), so let's begin with this element. Much does depend on the kind of social movement that emerges to challenge extractive sector expansion, including the possibility that no significant mobilization occurs or that mobilization remains scattered in disconnected pieces. To achieve a broad-based regulatory shift, movement actors need not only to mobilize across social sectors but also to scale up community activities to the national level and engage in the laborious work of coordinating their claims and sharing resources. Resistance movements may be assessed in terms of their *spatial reach* (ability to connect across local and national scales), *sectoral breadth* (ability to link across multiple sectors), and *frame alignment* (ability to define overlapping objectives)—all features that are necessary to build a comprehensive network.

But mining policy is not just an artifact of movement mobilization. Theories of policymaking that depend exclusively on the work of movements place too much analytical burden on that component of the process. Linkages to policy impact are often elusive, and require the addition of two more factors. One concerns the degree of cohesion found within the political and economic elite in support of mining-based development. An elite-driven "political settlement" (Bebbington et al. 2018) in favor of extraction-based development raises the challenge level faced by activists, and stands as a serious obstacle to internally induced reform. Fissures within the elite, on the other hand, create opportunities for activists to find allies and champions, and to mobilize resources needed for broader change.

The final element added to this model concerns the ability of activists and their allies to enter into the inner chambers of the state apparatus itself. This third condition requires an assessment of the political permeability of the

38 BREAKING GROUND

regime, or the extent to which movement actors can either locate or construct new points of entry into policy formulation and implementation dynamics. This component probes the mechanisms that channel public preferences into public policy, assessing the availability of "docking points"—that is, institutional locations within the state where engaged citizens can introduce initiatives and maneuver public officials to advance toward their preferred policy response.

The next three sections take up each of these features in turn. They each begin with discussion of the general linkages that connect the given feature to the policy process, and then narrow the focus to mining policy. The last section provides an overview of the full model and summarizes the alignment of features that result in divergent outcomes.

Social Movement Organization: From Localized Threats to National Networking

Social movements are made up of diverse actors who mobilize collectively based on shared concerns, often in response to perceived grievances or threats (McAdam, Tarrow, and Tilly 2001; Tarrow 2011). They vary widely in terms of their catalysts, resonance, durability, and reach. Market reform and economic globalization have historically triggered waves of multisectoral mobilization as people sought protection against the associated dislocation and loss (Polanyi 2001). Late twentieth-century neoliberal reform in Latin America, accompanied by austerity and precarity, proved a catalyst to widespread protest and collective action, in some cases contributing to regime change and new forms of political incorporation (Silva 2009; Almeida 2014; Rossi 2017).

Analyzing threat-induced mobilization, Almeida (2015) identifies environmental destruction as a major motivation for increased resistance activism in Latin America. Simmons (2016) argues that "meaningful grievances," such as those arising from subsistence threats that bring cultural identity and survival into question, serve as catalysts to broad-based mobilizations, as in the Bolivian water wars and Mexican mobilizations over maize and tortilla production. Eisenstadt and West (2019) employ *vulnerability theory* to explore public reactions to environmental threats, hypothesizing that people who are most at risk from a proximate harm are more likely to register awareness and respond. Analyzing the intersection of vulnerability, extraction, and public opinion in Ecuador, they use survey results and geocoding of respondent location to show that those who face objective vulnerability to harm from environmental deterioration (who experience water scarcity or work in ecotourism, for example) are more likely to prioritize environmental concerns in their rankings of current problems (p. 61). They found environmental concern to be elevated among those residing in areas targeted for oil sector expansion, although such commitments fell sharply among those in areas that had already experienced extensive environmental degradation (pp. 127–145).

In addition to catalysts and motivations, movements also vary in terms of the character and quality of the linkages they forge. As della Porta and Diani (2006, 159) note, "Social movement action on a large scale has always been organized in network form." The underlying structure of movement networks includes building blocks that connect through relational mechanisms to facilitate the dissemination of information, distribution of resources, framing of grievances, recruitment of affiliates, burden sharing and collaboration on tasks, and identification of leaders, both formal and informal. Analysis of social movement networks generally involves either quantitative analysis of large-n data sets using data visualization techniques or small-n studies of archival and interview materials using process tracing to map affiliations and relationships (Diani 2015; Spalding 2023). The present study draws on this latter approach to identify and assess the networks involved in mining resistance.

Movements may begin locally by connecting those most directly affected by perceived threats, and then expand outward by constructing nodes and links through "bonding" and "bridging" techniques (Putnam 2000) that mobilize both "close" and "weak" ties (Granovetter 1982; Marsden and Campbell 2012; Biggs and Andrews 2015). Together, these processes expand the reach of social actors and build relational resources that increase capacity. Bonding-based networks build on close ties where participants have frequent, routine, and often organic (based on family, friendship, and neighborhood) connections. These links are imbued with familiarity and permit a ready flow of interaction and communication. This kind of mechanism produces closed-circuit patterns of information diffusion that tend to reinforce message content through repetition and trust-based validation. Bridging networks, in contrast, build on weak ties that link actors beyond their primary groups. They provide more distinctive and less predictable flows of information.

40 BREAKING GROUND

As the literature on the strength of weak ties indicates, bridging connections allow networks to extend beyond the clusters of redundant communication that characterize close-tie alliances, and kindle new linkages that can both broaden and accelerate the diffusion of mobilizing information. The cultivation of weak ties can also facilitate multisectoralism, as people in different social groups connect, and permit greater functional specialization in keeping with the variation in resources that broadened networks can mobilize. These differences in capacity encourage repertoire diversification by connecting those, for example, who have different kinds of expertise with regard to lobbying, fundraising, media access, legal strategies, and political party ties.

In terms of social movement impacts on public policy, close ties built on bonding techniques can stoke attitudinal uniformity and inspire recurring mobilization, including passion-driven protest and electoral engagement, by providing emotional support and validation. Weak ties built on bridging principles, in contrast, can extend the network beyond its historical boundaries and encourage broader awareness of issues, promoting fuller shifts in public opinion. Although bridging ties increase the risk of internal tensions, mistrust, and network fragmentation, they may also provide the leverage needed to affect a broader swath of popular views. This strategy, however, requires brokers who can link previously disconnected movement segments and build bridges that span the gaps (McAdam, Tarrow, and Tilly 2001; Gurza Lavalle and von Bülow 2015).

Mining Resistance Movements: Alliance Variations and Organizational Challenges

The twenty-first-century expansion of extractive industries in Latin America triggered a groundswell of protest regarding environmental threats and social injuries. The dramatically increased ratio in modern mining between the amount of earth moved relative to the quantity of minerals and metals extracted meant that the historically unprecedented levels of mining output lay waste to growing territories in the extraction zone (Studnicki-Gizbert 2017). The toxicity of chemical extraction processes employed in contemporary mining heightened concern, even in some regions where traditional forms of mining previously existed. The interconnection between large-scale mining and other megaprojects required to meet modern mining needs (water management, electricity generation, transportation and communication infrastructure) multiplied the tensions around mine development. Expansion into new territory included remote regions inhabited by indigenous and Afro-descendent populations, and fresh wounds layered on top of the old (Shapiro and McNeish 2021).

Although sharing a common catalyst, mining mobilizations vary significantly in terms of their goals and cohesion. Analyzing this variation in the Peruvian case, De Echave (2017, 137) differentiates between *conflictos de convivencia* (coexistence conflicts) and *conflictos de resistencia* (resistance conflicts). In coexistence conflicts, De Echave observes, community residents tell the mining companies:

> If you want to remain here for another 20, 30, 40 years, recognize that this is my territory. Respect my rights—economic, social, cultural, and environmental. I want to know how you are going to control the environmental impact. I want to know how you are going to manage the social environment. I want to know if I'm going to have any type of benefit.

These conflicts involve struggles over the rules governing relationships in the mining sector and entail competition over the way resources are parceled out among the parties involved.

Resistance conflicts, in contrast, involve opposition to mining itself. In these conflicts, De Echave continues, people say:

> I see this project as a menace. It's going to affect me. It's going to affect my economic, cultural, and environmental rights, my way of life [*forma de vivir*]. It's going to dispossess me, and so I resist. I reject it.

Protests in this second scenario are designed to prevent mining projects from operating—either from being established, expanding beyond their original parameters, or continuing to operate at the site after costs begin to accumulate.

Arce's (2014, 50–54) analysis of mining protests in Peru follows De Echave's logic and distinguishes between those focused on improving *services* and those organized around *rights*. Service-oriented movements involve distributional struggles that focus on the division of royalties and tax revenues or other economic benefits associated with mining. These movements do not oppose mining activity per se, nor do they seek mine closure as an

42   BREAKING GROUND

ultimate goal. Usually local, shorter-term, and more narrowly pitched, these movements aim for financial improvement, job growth, or funds to support cleanup or reclamation projects. Rights-oriented movements, in contrast, focus on the tensions between mining and the exercise of basic guarantees, including the right to water, health, or cultural survival. These movements tend to be more comprehensive and to more readily scale up to the national and international levels. The discourse surrounding the latter mobilizations often calls for closing the mines or denying the permits that would allow them to operate.

My own analysis builds on these distinctions and expands into a third variation. My framework identifies *distributive conflicts*, which are similar to De Echave's coexistence conflicts and Arce's service-based ones and focus on the allocation of mining rents. These struggles highlight concerns about the labor rights of mineworkers, including attention to occupational hazards, job security and compensation, and the community impacts of mining royalties and financial flows. My second category, which resembles De Echave's resistance conflicts and Arce's rights-based ones, focuses on *definitional conflicts*. Those conflicts raise fundamental questions about how the community is going to be understood in terms of its economic and cultural place in the world. Such conflicts invoke deeper struggles about the significance of place-derived meaning and post-mining trajectories; they involve the complex task of imagining current versus future possibilities. These struggles highlight the long-term costs to local communities of mine-centered development and foster outright rejection of mining intrusion.

To these familiar categories I add a third, which I describe as *scale conflicts*. Scale conflicts focus on the competition between small- and large-scale mining. Contrary to the dominant trend in mining studies, which focuses on large-scale mining (LSM), my work offers a needed corrective by broadening the discussion to include artisanal and small-scale mining (ASM). Internationally, an estimated 10 to 15 million artisanal and small-scale miners work in gold production, producing 15–20% of annual world gold output (Seccatore et al. 2014; Veiga and Morais 2015). According to a global assessment of the sector by ICMM and IFC (Wall 2015, 4), the number of artisanal and small miners surpasses 500,000 in Brazil, 150,000 in Colombia, and 50,000 in Bolivia and Ecuador, and ranges between 5,000 and 50,000 in Nicaragua, Mexico, and Peru. Yet this sector, and its conflicts with both the state and its large-scale counterpart, has received limited attention in the Latin American mining literature.[3] The size, output, and vulnerability of this sector, and its role in the diffusion of mercury, call for increased analytical effort.[4]

Globally, the ASM sector is responsible for the release of 1,000 tons of mercury annually, according to the UN Industrial Development Organization (UNIDO), with a third released as atmospheric emissions (Wall 2015, 9). The 2013 Minamata Convention, which commits signatory states to formalize the sector and reduce the use of mercury-based processing, should have beneficial consequences over the long run, but progress has been slow and the environmental impact of ASM remains problematic. Environmental harms associated with large-scale mining, including water sedimentation, acid mine drainage, and deforestation, are present in the ASM sector as well. Occupational health problems, including silicosis, hearing loss, and muscular strains, are common, and marginalized miners often receive inadequate medical attention (Wall 2015). Working conditions are frequently hazardous, with predictable consequences in terms of injuries and fatalities. ASM thus becomes a focus of concern for analysts and policymakers attempting to address social and environmental problems in the mining sector.

State responses to ASM expansion vary widely. Unregulated ASM growth attests to the failures of national development policy, whether the structural adjustments related to neoliberal reform in much of the region or the collapse of rentier socialism in Venezuela. The connection between ASM development and regional economic duress adds to the complexity of the problem, since this sector often serves as an escape valve for the economically displaced. Some states declare unregistered mining to be illegal and periodically send in the military and police, as in environmentally fragile Madre de Díos, Peru (Damonte 2018). Harsh enforcement, however, often alternates with regulatory inaction, whether due to lack of capacity, intentional forbearance, or elite complicity and enrichment (Rosales 2019; Baraybar Hidalgo and Dargent 2020). Informality and corruption may push the unregulated sector

---

[3] Notable exceptions include work by Hinton (2005); Veiga et al. (2014); Veiga and Morais (2015); Hilson et al. (2018); Damonte (2018); Rosales (2019); and Baraybar Hidalgo and Dargent (2020).

[4] Mercury is a neurotoxin that builds up along the food chain and can lead to brain damage, tremors, loss of hearing and sight, and death in humans (IGF 2017). Vaporizing mercury to separate out the gold from milled ore slurry has especially dangerous consequences for those in the vicinity. This process repeatedly exposes artisanal miners, others nearby, and those living downstream to a toxic chemical with known harmful health consequences, particularly for pregnant women and children, due to the bioaccumulation of methylmercury in aquatic food chains.

44 BREAKING GROUND

underground, to align with criminal actors who source workers and precursor materials, provide protection, and engage in illegal export (Rosales 2019; Ebus and Martinelli 2021). These relationships involve complex connections between small- and medium-scale miners, large-scale mining corporations, and state actors, including security forces.

New exploration for ore deposits by foreign mining corporations often concentrates in areas where mining took place previously. Not only are cultural barriers to mining often less pronounced in these zones, where prior experience sometimes fades into nostalgic yearning, but investment in brownfield sites tends to reduce risks of failure for the exploration companies charged with finding new deposits. Geological conditions may be propitious for new discoveries in once-productive regions, and mining waste discarded by antecedent companies may be reprocessed using newer technologies, permitting another round of profitable extraction.

Complications soon arise, however, when artisanal and small miners, some trained during prior boom eras, continue to extract material in these zones, using low-tech practices and operating in legally precarious ways. The return of large-scale mining ventures to these areas creates a distinctive kind of conflict between artisan and small miners, who may operate informally in family-based or cooperative forms, and large-scale investors, who generally plan capital-intensive operations that will drill to exhaustion. Scale conflicts, which entail literal "accumulation by dispossession" (Harvey 2004), pit small miners against large ones, calling for checks on the latter to bolster the territorial and resource claims of the former. Like distributional conflicts, scale conflicts are not designed to eliminate all forms of mining; like definitional conflicts, scale struggles see large-scale mines as inimical to the small-scale way of life. Artisanal and small miners support mining as an activity but may fight existential battles to prevent LSM ensconcement.

This overview of distributional, definitional, and scale conflicts underscores the challenges involved in building a broad national network of activists who will push in the same direction toward an agreed-upon policy change. Frame alignment may become impossible; activists in different camps may even be pitted against each other, as when mineworkers mobilizing for better wages shift into battle against peasants and farmers who seek to prevent concession extension or the opening of new extraction zones. This diversity of activist goals and assumptions may undermine movement bricolage, in which "familiar themes are arrayed to entice citizens to become supporters; and new themes are soldered onto them to activate them in new and creative directions"

FROM COMMUNITY CONFLICTS TO POLICY OUTCOMES   45

(Tarrow 2011, 146). Even as public concern about sustainability deepens and formal commitments to decentralization advance, environmental and community organizers often fail to achieve the kind of sustained cross-regional collaboration required for effective mobilization and policy impact.

In spite of these tendencies, which will be discussed in more detail in Chapter 3, on Nicaragua, movement fragmentation is not predestined. When frame differences are successfully brokered and diverse organizations protesting mining development identify overlapping objectives, the resulting alliance may be able to achieve network cohesion. Building on both strong and weak ties, an alliance may grow into a diverse but well-connected network that mobilizes across difference and scale. Sources of agglutination include what Federico Rossi (2017) calls a "stock of legacies" and Paul Almeida (2014) describes as "strategic capital." These concepts, derived from research projects that trace movement organizing over a long period of time, reference the relationships and learning that accumulate through recurring practices of collaboration and adaptation among a subset of organizers and activists. Anti-mining movements that use these forms of collective learning to develop both sectoral breadth and spatial reach, as in the Costa Rica and Salvadoran cases, are more likely to advance toward mining policy reform, including even mining prohibition. The conditions that produce sustained collaboration in extraction struggles call for close observation and analysis.

From Fused to Fragmented Elites

The ability of activists to impact mining policy depends not just on their own organizational capacity but also on the intensity of elite cohesion and resistance. Extraction studies often portray the pro-mining elite as a unified whole, looming as a monolith and shorn of variation. But grounded analysis of an empirical bent often points to crevices in the sector, revealing internal differentiation and rivalries (Spalding 1994; Schneider 2013; Ondetti 2021). This sense that elite networks differ in terms of their levels of coordination and homogeneity invites discussion about variation in their configurations and in the mechanisms that unite and divide them.

Higley and Gunther (1992, 8) define elites as "persons who are able, by virtue of their strategic positions in powerful organizations, to affect national political outcomes regularly and substantially." Elites are the "principal decision makers in the largest or most resource-rich political, governmental,

46 BREAKING GROUND

economic, military, professional, communications, and cultural organizations and movements in a society." Necessarily small in number, those defined as elites have "acknowledged authority" (p. 9), which gives them outsized influence over the lives of everyone else.

For our purposes, two categories of elites are significant: those involved in the political sphere and those in the business sector. Political elites dominate official rulemaking and regulatory enforcement, and negotiate agreements among themselves about formal and informal priorities and policies. This segment includes key government officials, such as presidents, but also legislative leaders, heads of bureaucratic agencies, and leaders of the main political parties. Economic elites define and dominate the business sector. As Ben Ross Schneider's (2013) research on business elites in Latin America demonstrates, leading businesses tend to create formal or informal groups that oversee complex multisectoral holdings, with diversification serving as a risk management strategy. "Family capitalism," characterized by direct family control over business groups, is "endemic" in Latin America (Schneider 2013, 47), and leadership sometimes spans generations. This description applies not just to business giants like Mexico's Carlos Slim and Grupo Carso but also to business groups across the region, including in Central America (Segovia 2005; Bull, Castellacci, and Kasahara 2014; Bull and Aguilar-Støen 2015).

The distinctions between political and economic elites sometimes blur in practice. Business elites have a wide repertoire of strategies they deploy—individual and collective, formal and informal, associational and electoral—to pursue their political goals (Fairfield 2015).[5] In addition to obvious instruments such as campaign contributions and media ownership, these elites may establish their own political parties and finance think tanks that prioritize their interests, as with the Nationalist Republican Alliance (ARENA) and the Salvadoran Social and Economic Development Foundation (FUSADES) in El Salvador. They may cut out intermediaries and run for office directly, as did Sebastián Piñera in Chile and Mauricio Macri in Argentina, or Tony Saca in El Salvador and Enrique Bolaños in Nicaragua. Business leaders may promote their interests through the strategic placement of representatives in the cabinet as ministers of the economy or of finance, or through their veto power over such appointments. Business elites

---

[5] Fairfield (2015) differentiates between the structural power of economic elites, which derives from the aggregate economic consequences of investment decisions, and their instrumental power, which is associated with deliberate political actions.

also participate in government commissions and assume seats on boards that relate to business interests, such as the central bank, wage tribunals, and committees involved in negotiations regarding subsidies, exonerations, taxes, and trade. Since government officials need private sector investment and growth in order to achieve state consolidation and stability (i.e., "the structural dependence of the state on capital"), business elites wield systemic power that political elites ignore at their peril (Przeworski and Wallerstein 1988).

At the same time, the ability of business elites to exercise this influence depends on the extent to which they attenuate the differences among themselves through negotiation, persuasion, intimidation, or exclusion of weaker segments. Although historically state-dependent and fragmented in many countries, Latin America's business organizations often gained organizational capacity during and after market transitions (Durand and Silva 1998). Complex multisectoral peak associations, such as the Mexican Council of Businessmen or Guatemala's Coordinating Committee of Agricultural, Commercial, Industrial, and Financial Associations (CACIF), worked to unify the business voice and amplify its impact on both domestic policy and international agreements.[6]

Coordination across the business elite often presents challenges and requires persistent ideological and relationship work. Domestic business groups tend to operate separately from transnational corporations, many of which arrived more recently and organize independently through the numerous AmChams (American Chambers of Commerce) found across Latin America (Schneider 2013, 86). However, domestic and transnational business groups generally have an overlapping interest in low taxes and thin regulation, and in keeping the state responsive to their demands. A perception of shared needs often inspires collaboration, in spite of organizational variations (p. 151).

Business elites pursue organizational alignment for multiple reasons, including corporatist representational incentives proffered by the state, "self-help" initiatives that align with traditional pluralist views of interest group behavior, and defensive responses to perceived threats from social movements and political rivals (Schneider 2004; Bull 2014). Gabriel Ondetti

---

[6] Business peak associations, also called encompassing associations, are umbrella organizations that integrate sectoral associations and provide representation to business as a whole (see Durand and Silva 1998; Schneider 2004).

48 BREAKING GROUND

(2021) argues that variations in collective threat levels faced by business elites in different Latin American countries triggered divergence in levels of organizational cohesion that was then sustained by path dependence and institutional stickiness. Business organizations that were mobilized by high threat levels, as in Chile, Mexico, and Guatemala, tended to produce cohesive associations, whereas those in Brazil and Uruguay, where such historical threats had not registered as fully, retained a tendency toward fragmentation.

Negotiation and consultation between the economic and political elites may produce durable agreement and lead to a "political settlement." As defined by Bebbington et al. (2018, 8), political settlements are bargains struck by political and economic elites that hold "different relationships of power together in stable form." Settlements occur when contending elites negotiate a mutually compatible and relatively long-lived agreement about the distribution of power, and design policies and institutions to sustain that balance. They forge understandings about how potentially contentious issues will be resolved, thereby lending predictability to elite interactions and reducing uncertainty. As these understandings are embedded in law and regulation, settlement durability may be enhanced.

Although political settlements tend to reduce intra-elite conflict, they are neither comprehensive nor permanent. Market reform deals both winning and losing hands to business elites, commonly producing fissures that may lead to fragmentation and organizational reconfiguration. Hierarchies among business groups with differential access to policymakers foster policy reforms that favor some interests over others. The particular coalitional formation that emerges between state and economic elites may direct economic policy toward different benchmarks. Business elites who are neglected or harmed by the prevailing rules of the game may prefer to abscond.

In addition to unresolved tensions within the business sector, conflicts may erupt between business and political leaders. State leaders need to cultivate an independent sense of legitimacy, especially in putatively democratic regimes. This may mean separating themselves from the business class in order to attend to other collective needs, or at least pursuing that appearance. Electoral competition among contending political elites may also disrupt previous understandings with business, particularly during critical junctures when established parties and officials face a real prospect of defeat. Elite cohesion, both within the economic and political spheres and between political and economic elites, may deepen, but it may also falter.

FROM COMMUNITY CONFLICTS TO POLICY OUTCOMES   49

Elite fragmentation both reflects and facilitates mobilization by subordinate groups. In his overview of the impact of political opportunities and constraints on social mobilization, Tarrow (2011, 166) observes, "Divisions among elites not only provide incentives to resource-poor groups to take the risks of collective action; they encourage portions of the elite that are out of power to seize the role of 'tribunes of the people.'" He continues, "History provides numerous examples of divided elites bringing resources to emerging movements" (p. 166). Elite fragmentation is a potential source of what Tarrow calls "influential allies," those domestic or international sectors that can provide movements with resources (funds, recognition, media access) that are in scarce supply. Fissures within the state apparatus or among segments of the elite create opportunities for reformers to introduce change and to alter an established policy trajectory.

Elites and Mining

In much of Latin America, business elites supported extractive sector development, and political elites mobilized to promote its advance. Although large-scale metallic mining companies were largely foreign-owned and provided few direct economic opportunities for domestic producers, national business elites envisioned roles as junior partners, suppliers, and service providers. Local elites sought contracts for construction and security services, and business leaders secured positions as local managers, lobbyists, legal representatives, environmental consultants, and public relations specialists (Bull and Aguilar-Støen 2015; Dougherty 2019a). Even for those in unrelated sectors, mining taxes and royalties were sometimes perceived as offsetting tax increases on their own activities, and served as an indirect boon.

Looking for alliances and protection, mining companies often sought out connections with local business associations. The Nicaraguan Mining Chamber (CAMINIC), for example, provided an organizational home for both foreign investors and local vendors of mining services. Established soon after mining privatization, and ensconced inside Nicaragua's business peak association, the Superior Council of Private Enterprise (COSEP), CAMINIC affiliates enjoyed opportunities for networking and the insider benefits of representation on government boards and commissions. The Guatemalan mining chamber (Union of Extractive Industries, GREMIEXT) likewise affiliated with CACIF, Guatemala's powerful business peak association, through

50 BREAKING GROUND

its politically muscular Chamber of Industry (CIG). When resisters challenged mining operations in the Guatemalan courts, CACIF and CIG provided a full-throated defense, buying full-page newspaper ads emblazoned with chamber logos. Nestled within these powerful business associations as an active member and funder, mining chambers positioned their activities to stoke state support.

Government officials regularly defended mining in terms of its expected contribution to economic growth, job creation, and poverty reduction, as we saw in Chapter 1 with Daniel Ortega's comments at the 2010 reopening ceremony for the mine at La Libertad. The prospect of increased tax revenues proved a powerful lure, as did the optics of national success associated with rising exports and FDI. Revenue flows were particularly compelling for post-neoliberal elites pursuing resource nationalism, where increased state appropriation of extractive sector rents provided funding for social programs and poverty alleviation.

Public support for mining, which sometimes rose in the wake of corporate public relations campaigns, further encouraged government officials to align with mining interests. Corporations worked hard to win hearts and minds. Infinito Gold's PR campaign in Costa Rica, for example, included trailers about "green mining" that aired before popular films in local cinemas. B2Gold offered repeated CSR initiatives in Rancho Grande during the run-up to the 2015 environmental permit decision in Nicaragua. Although the environmental risks associated with the industry raised alarm in some quarters, mining supporters in the government consoled followers with industry-generated claims about clean mining techniques.[7]

From Alan García in Peru to Rafael Correa in Ecuador, Latin American presidents provided public endorsement of extractive sector expansion and dismissed mining opponents for their "irresponsibility" and for subverting national interests.[8] In Central America, Guatemalan president Óscar Berger (2004–2008) issued Governmental Accord 499-2007, which declared a

[7] Political sponsors also played the degradation card, arguing that the environment was already so degraded that there was nothing left to protect, or that the degradation that would result from mining was no worse than that produced by industries that already exist. The latter position was taken by the former minister of finance in El Salvador in his consultant's report on Pacific Rim's proposed El Dorado mine (Hinds 2007).

[8] In 2007 and 2008, García criticized opponents of his executive degrees that opened the Peruvian Amazon to extraction, and claimed that indigenous resisters exhibited the "dog in the manger syndrome" by displaying irrational resentment that prevented others from accessing gains (see Arce 2014, 103–107). Correa angrily denounced anti-mining protesters as "nobodies," and "allies of the right" (see Lewis 2016, 184–190).

FROM COMMUNITY CONFLICTS TO POLICY OUTCOMES   51

national interest in energy and mining (Yagenova 2012, 219; Aguilar-Støen 2015, 135). Costa Rican president Óscar Arias did likewise in 2008 when he authorized a suspension of forest regulations by declaring Infinito Gold's mining permit to be in the public interest. Top-level support for mining investments persisted through the decades and across presidential periods in Nicaragua, where mining featured prominently in government invest-ment promotion brochures and national development plans. This affinity for mining was also apparent in the routine criminalization of mining protesters (Moore et al. 2015). Deploying the police and the military in service of mining interests, political elites forcibly cleared out objectors, and favorable investment conditions were assured.

But elite support, as this book will demonstrate, was not universal. Business elites may become divided when mining poses threats to other activities, such as agriculture, ranching, and ecotourism, or where competition for water, land, and landscape can set off alarm. Local elites may develop a sense that losses associated with mining will not be offset by gains, or that the long-term costs of cleanup and remediation will not be absorbed by the industry but will instead fall on the communities or the society at large. Tensions can emerge over issues as varied as who pays the costs of environmental cleanup or the privileged access that foreign investors have to diplomatic interven-tion and international arbitration. Crevices may appear in the business front. Foreign mining companies may wind up facing the gauntlet alone.

Political elites may also reject the mining lobby if extraction clashes with their party's or their personal stance on environmental and indige-nous rights. Fissures may widen due to pressures from other influential elite institutions, such as the Catholic Church hierarchy, as in El Salvador, or the university community, as in Costa Rica. Public opinion, as we will see in the coming chapters, may shift as anti-mining campaigns advance and issue salience rises. When public attitudes tilt against mining, electoral risks in-crease for parties and candidates perceived to be mining allies. Under these circumstances, elites may divide, and the prospects for restrictive regulation improve.

Docking Points and Policy Deliberation

The final factor that allows some movements to reshape policy boundaries while others founder concerns the availability of *docking points*. Docking points are institutional spaces into which civil society and social movement networks introduce demands and through which they activate policy review and deliberation. This section shifts our attention from the role of threats as a trigger to mobilization to the role of opportunities as a gateway to impact.

Early formulations in the social movement literature suggested that mobilization depended on the presence of opportunity structures that offered certain guarantees and reduced risks. This approach was criticized as overly static and inadequately attentive to the role of perception and agency in eliciting action (Goodwin and Jasper 1999). Subsequent analysis tended to conceptualize opportunity in more fluid and innovative terms. Arce and Rice (2019) argue that an open political opportunity structure may be less significant as a precondition for social mobilization, which often emerges even when political systems are closed, than as a factor that conditions its success. To explain when movements have a greater propensity for impact, they call attention to the significance of state "permeability" (p. 3), along with the readiness and willingness of protesters to participate in the process.

My analysis of social mobilization builds on those observations. I trace the activities of mining resistance coalitions as they search for institutional spaces where relations with state actors might be cultivated in order to attract recognition and elicit a sympathetic or concordant response. I use the concept of docking to convey the idea that activists pursuing policy and institutional reform need to locate or create sites where demands, complaints, proposals, and ideas can be inserted, formally or informally, into the policymaking process. This linking activity allows activists to enter the flow of negotiation and decision-making that ultimately determines which rules advance and what is actually implemented. This process may involve locating preexisting openings, where demands have previously been introduced and engaged, or creating new opportunities by prying open an institutional space that was previously unavailable.

My work highlights opportunities for docking in three domains. The first is located in political parties and electoral campaigns. The second moves beyond elections and focuses on participatory space within existing political institutions such as the courts, bureaucracies, legislative committees, and local governments. The third examines direct forms of citizen participation, including a wide array of grassroots initiatives, community consultations, plebiscites, and referenda, some of which are under development.

Docking and Political Parties

Electoral democratization opens institutional doors through which activists can move beyond the protest phase of oppositional politics. Social movements seeking to inform policy change can connect with or build political parties and lend their organizational capacity to electoral campaigns. As Mische (2015, 46–47) observes in her work on youth activism and partisan politics in Brazil during the 1990s, "Many leaders in labor and popular movements went to the party; in the case of the PT [Workers' Party] in particular, they were building the party at the grassroots level." This strategy involves channeling movement resources into party politics in order to influence the political identity and electoral rhetoric of the party and its candidates.

Connections between movements and parties are often complex. Hoping to create new subjectivities from below and to avoid simply replicating the hierarchies that define the established order, some activists reject "insider" strategies that seek to influence the composition of the state (Holloway 2002; Stahler-Sholk, Vanden, and Becker 2014). Long histories of betrayal and disappointment over party promises that were never fulfilled often inspire skepticism about party alliances among movement activists. But efforts to influence policy guidelines and change the contents of the law generally compel activists to engage the state, and collaboration with reform-oriented political parties can offer unique possibilities for innovation. A growing body of literature analyzes movement-based political parties in Latin America, finding that the Movement toward Socialism (MAS) in Bolivia, the Alianza País in Ecuador, and the Farabundo Martí National Liberation Front (FMLN) in El Salvador served as conduits for promoting movement demands, at least at certain junctures (Van Cott 2005; Almeida 2006; Anria 2013).

Movement-party links emerge when movement actors support a political party's electoral work (i.e., encourage identification with a party, share its messages, and get out the vote in favor of the party's candidates); when a political party assumes the discourse, frames, and mobilization strategies deployed by social movements; and when, if victorious, party leaders name social movement actors to positions in government and champion their causes. Although this bond raises the risk that the movement will be co-opted by party leaders and lose its independent identity, this connection can also allow movement actors to raise the profile of the issues that concern them and secure commitments for desired actions in the event of electoral success.

54 BREAKING GROUND

Through party connections, activists can affect what issues get placed on the legislative agenda and advance through the lawmaking process. Close alliance with an electorally significant political party opens a potentially propitious docking point.

Docking and Institutional Engagement

In addition to their role in electoral processes, movement actors may seek access to non-elected officials, including those who staff institutions and agencies that affect how legislation is interpreted and implemented. These institutions influence the pace, rigor, and consistency of policy application, and can ultimately determine the priorities that emerge in practice. Key institutional actors include the courts and bureaucracies that oversee formal policy implementation. Research seeking to map the diverse ways in which movements have impacts calls for greater attention to these potentially powerful and often neglected institutional actors (Rich, Mayka, and Montero 2019).

Although courts frequently serve the interests of the powerful, they can be retooled as a weapon of the weak (Sarat and Scheingold 1998; Rhode 2013). As domestic courts developed increasing capacity in Latin America, they have become active players in political contention (Santos and Rodríguez-Garavito 2005; Couso, Huneeus, and Sieder 2010; Helmke and Rios-Figueroa 2011; Kapiszewski, Silvestein, and Kagan 2013; Rodríguez-Garavito and Rodríguez-Franco 2015; Langford, Rodríguez-Garavito, and Rossi 2017; Brinks and Blass 2018). Justice-oriented activists often look to judicial institutions for validation or relief, using references to constitutional guarantees, officially declared rights, and legal traditions. Constitutional courts now hear and rule on a wide range of cases, including those involving disputes on community and environmental rights (McNeish 2017; Dietz 2019).

The extent to which movements initiate judicial involvement obviously varies, depending in part on the "legal opportunity structure" (Wilson and Rodríguez-Cordero 2006). Legal opportunity structures differ based on factors such as the court system's geographical and financial accessibility, willingness to adjudicate, capacity to elicit enforcement, and local perceptions of its legitimacy. When legal opportunities are available, strategic litigation becomes a useful tool for advancing social and economic rights. Activists in Costa Rica, where the courts enjoy a relatively high level of accessibility and public trust, regularly add legal filings to their arsenal of strategic resources. Courts have also become a powerful source of rights promotion in Colombia (Rodríguez-Garavito and Rodríguez-Franco 2015; McNeish 2017; Dietz 2019; Wilson and Gianella-Malca 2019). International assistance, as in the case of the UN-sponsored International Commission Against Impunity in Guatemala (CICIG), can encourage use of the courts by promoting judicial independence and professionalism (Hudson and Taylor 2010). Training programs designed to expand the pool of indigenous lawyers and knowledge of indigenous law can add new players to the legal game.

On the other hand, persistent problems of impunity, corruption, and nonenforcement discourage legal activism. In Nicaragua, where rule of law is weak, activists rarely pursue legal recourse. When they do, this step is generally taken only to fulfill the requirement to exhaust domestic remedies before bringing a case to the Inter-American Commission on Human Rights (IACHR). The IACHR and its companion, the Inter-American Court for Human Rights (IACtHR), serve as alternative legal options for the activist community, in spite of their limited enforcement powers, due to their perceived ability to exercise judicial independence (Wilson and Gianella-Malca 2019, 142).

In addition to the courts, activists may attempt to affect policy through engagement with the bureaucracy. Bureaucracies in modern states are sometimes referred to as a "fourth branch of government" (Potter 2019). In terms of their role in regulation and rulemaking, they generally outpace the productivity of elected officials, whose legislative work involves sketching the general outlines for a relatively modest number of policy initiatives.[9] Put in terms of the conventional policymaking cycle, bureaucrats exercise significant power as crafters and proposers at the policy formulation stage, and as interpreters and managers in the policy implementation phase. Their regulatory work is guided by their own need for political support and desire for influence, along with the dictates of institutional mission and resource constraints. Securing compliance with regulations generally requires a high degree of voluntary cooperation, making regulators attentive to the preferences of those they purportedly

---

[9] In the United States, for example, Congress and the president approved 224 laws in 2014, while the federal agencies collectively produced around 3,500 new regulations (Potter 2019, 2).

56 BREAKING GROUND

regulate, even without the extra inducements associated with the revolving door and corruption.[10]

An emerging body of literature addresses the intersection between social movements and bureaucratic decision-making. One point of convergence is found in the literature on "institutional activism." As defined by Abers and Tatagiba (2015, 73), institutional activism is "what people are doing when they take jobs in government bureaucracies with the purpose of advancing the political agenda or projects proposed by social movements." These processes embed activists within an agency, including at the ministerial level, following the election of party leaders aligned with movement mission. This occurred in Brazil under PT president Lula da Silva, for example, with the appointment of noted environmental activist Marina Silva as minister of the environment (Hochstetler and Keck 2007). Bureaucrats may adopt practices and problem-solving preferences supported by social movements due to their own sense of professionalism or perceived institutional mission, even without personal membership in a movement organization or direction from superiors who hold such ties (Abers 2019).

Activists may also attempt to exercise influence by joining advisory boards or consultation committees that monitor and review agency work. They can burrow into government agencies by engaging with project funders, who may be eager to promote an image of transparency or mission-driven proposals, or by working with or as consultants, who provide independent reporting based on prior experience or technical expertise. Policy experts elevated to blue ribbon commissions or bureaucratic roles because of specialized knowledge may facilitate contact between movement actors, state agencies, universities, and NGOs, as in the case of environmental specialists in Costa Rica (discussed in Chapter 5) and El Salvador (discussed in Chapter 6).

Alternatively, bureaucracies may be characterized by mission vacuity or drift, mechanical and unresponsive rule enforcement, or corruption. They may be governed by clientelistic norms, requiring bureaucrats to take direction from political patrons who demand loyalty and subservience in exchange for employment. They may be split, with different ministries and agencies working at cross-purposes. Agencies characterized by isolation and insularity provide few opportunities for activist engagement. Faced with impenetrable bureaucracies, social movement interactions may come in the

---

[10] The revolving door refers to hiring practices that allow government officials (legislators, regulators) to take positions in an industry for which they previously had regulatory responsibility, and representatives of or consultants working for an industry to assume positions in the government.

FROM COMMUNITY CONFLICTS TO POLICY OUTCOMES 57

form of protests that target these institutions, sometimes through long-term occupations staged outside the offending agency's front door.

Docking and Community Consultation

Democratization gave rise to new forms of participation in Latin America, including direct citizen involvement in the identification of policy priorities and decision-making (Fung and Wright 2003; Selee and Peruzzotti 2009; Fung 2011; Rich, Mayka, and Montero 2019). Post-neoliberal regimes often declared a participatory vocation and added plebiscitary mechanisms, some of them embedded in new constitutions (Goldfrank 2011). Breuer (2007, 562, 565) found that fifteen of Latin America's eighteen presidential democracies introduced a referendum option, and twenty-four popular consultations were carried out between 1978 and 2004. These innovations were frequently designed to address deficiencies in or dissatisfaction with the conventions of liberal democracy.

Perhaps the best studied participatory practice in Latin America is participatory budgeting, which was pioneered by the PT in Brazil and quickly diffused to other parts of the region (Wampler and Avritzer 2005; Fung 2011). Participatory budgeting allowed residents to determine budgetary priorities through direct vote at the community level. Other citizen initiatives allowed voters to propose their own bills for legislative debate and approval, as with Mexico's 3X3 anti-corruption law and Costa Rica's wildlife protection legislation (Carballo Madrigal 2013). Laws authorizing the use of referenda allowed citizens to resolve debates directly on matters of public concern, as with the 2006 referendum through which Costa Rican voters ratified their entry into the Central American Free Trade Agreement (CAFTA) (Willis and Seiz 2012; Spalding 2014, 141–151).

Decentralization initiatives, intended to make government more accessible and to improve accountability, enjoyed support from international organizations, including the World Bank (World Bank 2008). These processes have been accompanied by a medley of community participation innovations, including the establishment of local citizen councils and adoption of grassroots petition mechanisms authorizing municipal-level consultations (Selee and Peruzzotti 2009). Although subject to considerable debate and litigation, some municipal codes contained provisions for binding decisions, providing for the devolution of decision-making authority to the local level.

58 BREAKING GROUND

One contentious arena for local-level docking concerned the rights of indigenous communities to be consulted about development projects that impact their territories. The mandate for free, prior, and informed consultation (FPIC), as defined in ILO Convention 169, raises complex issues, including how indigeneity is defined, whether consultation takes place in a single instance or as an iterative process, and whether the results are regarded as binding. Debate rages in the extraction zone over who should call and oversee this process; at what point(s) in the project development process; with what kind of information provided; and whether this right should be extended to all residents in impacted communities, not just those defined as indigenous (Fontana and Grugel 2016; McNeish 2017; Zaremberg and Torres 2018; Falleti and Riofrancos 2018; Torres Wong 2019; Eisenstadt and West 2019; Riofrancos 2020; Le Billon and Middeldorp 2021; Jaskoski 2022).

In the absence of agreement about what constitutes community consultation, wide variation has emerged in practice. Analyzing the sharp divergence in consultation dynamics and outcomes, Dietz (2019) differentiates between what she calls top-down and bottom-up operations. *Top-down* consultations are typically managed by the state, which determines where they will be staged and oversees the voting process. *Bottom-up* processes, in contrast, are organized by community activists, and they generally take place in areas where opposition to mining has fired up community interest. Bottom-up or grassroots consultation frequently involves mobilization outside of a formal legal framework (Rasch 2012; Copeland 2019a).

Walter and Urkidi (2016) describe sixty-eight bottom-up consultations concerning metal mining carried out in Argentina, Colombia, Ecuador, Guatemala, and Peru between 2002 and 2012. They interpret this process as an effort to construct "hybrid governance," an approach to decision-making that rejects state-centric rulemaking and top-down control. Instead, activists orchestrating these processes design complex, multiscalar environmental justice campaigns that follow "travel paths" (p. 292) across regions and national boundaries. Using videos and presentations that highlight mining damage elsewhere, they mount counterhegemonic educational campaigns to challenge the positive messaging disseminated by mining companies and their allies. Subsequent turnout in these grassroots consultations has generally been high and the vote tally in opposition to mining overwhelming.[11]

---

[11] The highest pro-mining vote reported in their study was 17% in the 2003 Esquel case in Argentina (Walter and Urkidi 2016, 295).

These early consultations proceeded in a legislative void, as legislation to codify consultation unfolded in "a process of stop and go, advances and retreats" (Sanborn, Hurtado, and Ramírez 2016, 4). Legal guidelines setting up top-down consultations were subsequently adopted in Peru, Bolivia, and Mexico, but these government-run processes restricted consultation to certain narrowly defined sectors and limited the range of people allowed to participate (Torres Wong 2019).[12] Critics of these official consultations note that they occurred only when the national government so dictated and that these maneuvers routinely concluded with project acceptance (Sanborn, Hurtado, and Ramírez 2016; Eisenstadt and West 2019; Le Billon and Middeldorp 2021). In a study of more than 170 state-authorized consultations held between 2007 and 2017 in Bolivia, Peru, and Mexico, Zaremberg and Torres Wong (2018) found that none of the top-down consultations led to rejection of the project, although they did serve, in some cases, as a space in which the community could negotiate for greater compensation.[13] The pattern of careful selection of communities, which were chosen for consultation by state actors with a strong pro-extraction agenda, has been found elsewhere, sometimes accompanied by coercion. Mayer (2019, 99) found in Nicaragua that the Ortega government used "heavy-handed government tactics that fostered division and stifled dissent" to secure community acceptance of its signature Gran Canal project, to be built through Rama-Kriol territory. Le Billon and Middeldorp (2021) note the frequent imposition of projects in spite of the lack of local consent.

In Eisenstadt and West's (2019, 96) analysis, prior consultation in practice served more as a "bargaining table" than a "veto point." Based on their observation of top-down indigenous consultations in the Andes, they call for the elimination of this practice, at least as it is currently constituted. They challenge the distorted forms of reified ("frozen in time") ethnic boundary-making that characterize indigenous rights regimes, and they call instead

---

[12] Consultation was prioritized in the oil and gas sector, and few mining zone projects were opened up for this level of community review. Indigenous consultation in Peru was placed under the Vice Ministry of Intercultural Affairs within the Ministry of Culture, one of the weakest ministries in the cabinet. According to Sanborn, Hurtado, and Ramírez (2016, 10), this ministry received "less than one half of one percent of the national budget, and has had relatively high turnover in staffing." Indigenous consultation in Mexico was legislated under the 2014 hydrocarbon law, and not formalized in the mining sector, leaving mining consultation undeveloped in spite of ILO 169 commitments.

[13] Consultation was associated with the reduced use of state repression against protesters in these communities, although this outcome may be due to the absence of large-scale resistance in these carefully selected areas (Zaremberg and Torres Wong 2018).

60 BREAKING GROUND

for "polycentric pluralism," or joint deliberation by indigenous and non-indigenous populations involved in "solving issues via many different fronts" (p. 3). Their approach would "universalize the prior consultation mechanism among their entire population, thereby recognizing the rights of all citizens to use legal mechanisms to guarantee their rights" (p. 216). This call for rethinking the protocol for community consultation raises new possibilities for stakeholders in the mining resistance movement.

In sum, movement actors found numerous institutional docking points that opened pathways into the policymaking process. They got their own leaders elected to high office or appointed to leading administrative and judicial positions. They engaged the courts and bureaucracies through litigation and complaints mechanisms, and served as consultants and community representatives on advisory or decision-making boards. Although the impediments to grassroots influence are notorious, and insular networks of political power stood in the way of direct consequences, growing pressure for community consultation created incipient docking spaces for local-level mining resisters to register their demands and, under some circumstances, influence the direction of policy change, albeit in the face of multiple challenges.

Summary and Conclusions

This chapter argues that mining protest movements can play a role in policy development but that movements, by themselves, are unlikely to have significant impact on mining beyond, perhaps, the occasional suspension or closing down of particularly objectionable projects. Project cancellation, while important, may mean simply moving the operations down the road or trimming out the piece located in a particularly hostile community. To determine the circumstances under which more substantive change takes place, we need to begin with a broader framework and ask a different set of questions. What combinations of political and economic features can propel mining policy parameters and national practices toward cleaner and greener outcomes? How might we explain the cancellation of mining operations in a whole region, or even a whole country? Why have so many countries failed to implement regulatory reform or enforce environmental laws, even after the adoption of protocols that were painstakingly approved? What are the main processes that stand in the way of change?

FROM COMMUNITY CONFLICTS TO POLICY OUTCOMES   61

Table 2.2 Factors Leading to Divergent Outcomes: Framework Summary

Factors	Mine-Promoting Policies	Mine-Restricting Policies
Mining resistance movement	Mining opposition • Is weak or episodic • Displays internal rivalries and sectoral rupture • Attains only local presence or subregional reach • Generates frame competition	Mining opposition • Is resilient and well networked • Displays multisectoral membership and organizational breadth • Is grounded in communities but scales up to the national level • Generates frame alignment
Elite position on mining	• Major political leaders and parties endorse mining. • Pro-mining perspectives persist even when the party in power shifts. • The business sector is characterized by cohesion and unanimity. • Mining company representatives develop cooperative ties with other business interests.	• Major parties take opposing positions on mining. • Electoral victory rotates, periodically improving prospects for mining critics. • The business sector is characterized by division and fissure. • Competition erupts between mining and other business interests.
Institutional docking points	• Political parties and candidates are inaccessible and unresponsive. • State institutions are weak or insulated. • Local governments lack autonomy and responsiveness. • Prior consultation mechanisms are missing or are applied selectively and lack transparency.	• Political parties and candidates are receptive to movement demands. • State institutions are open to civil society input. • Relatively autonomous local governments are responsive to community preferences. • Prior consultation mechanisms permit broad participation and informed deliberation.

This book argues that larger dynamics explaining mining development result from the interplay of three distinct factors. This framework is summarized in Table 2.2.

First, to achieve policy impact, mining resistance movements need to move beyond disconnected mobilizations operating at the community level and build integrated networks that operate at both the local and national levels. This process requires bridging and bonding efforts to connect disparate pieces, including linkage mechanisms that tie together indigenous communities, peasant associations, environmental activists, women, labor, and religious organizations. Alliances that extend beyond in-group

62   BREAKING GROUND

trust networks need to be built and to travel to the national scale. This networking involves laborious processes of frame alignment as groups work to define a common agenda based on widely shared values, like the need for water (El Salvador) or the preservation of the national environmental brand (Costa Rica).

If the issues that mobilize activists at the community level cannot be linked and scaled up, then the prospects for policy reform are limited. Reform proposals may still emerge under the guidance of technocrats or due to international pressure, as with anti-corruption initiatives of the Organisation for Economic Co-operation and Development (OECD), but they are unlikely to advance toward multidimensional regulatory improvement or the construction of alternative development strategies without broad-based movement support.

Second, when elite-based political settlements favor extraction-based development, the prospects for institutional reform and policy change become remote. Oppositional forces face a heavier lift as they attempt to advance reform proposals, and they have fewer potential allies and champions within the system to lend a hand. If all of the major parties align around mining promotion, as in Nicaragua and Guatemala, then space for review and reconsideration of extractive policy will be slim. If the party system is noncompetitive and the hegemonic party does not need to expand its base or broaden its appeal in order to win, then policy innovation becomes less likely. Cohesive support for mining interests within the business elite and the embedding of mining chambers inside the national business association, as occurred in both Nicaragua and Guatemala, serve to ensure reinforcement and continuation of the status quo.

Elite rupture and internal tension, in contrast, provide an opening that improves the prospects for reform. Elite fracture and recombination, as occurred in Costa Rica and El Salvador during the mining debate, opened up possibilities for significant realignments and policy shifts. Competing economic interests in agriculture and ecotourism can fracture the common front forged by pro-mining interests. Activists can encourage division in the political elite by turning public opinion toward greater environmental care and engaging the electoral process in search of supportive parties and candidates.

Finally, democratic systems offer an array of mechanisms through which activists can press for an institutional response. In addition to liaison work with leading candidates and parties, institutional openings permit the filing

FROM COMMUNITY CONFLICTS TO POLICY OUTCOMES   63

of legal demands, participation on policy advisory boards, networking within bureaucratic agencies that carry out regulation and implementation, and mobilizing for consultations from below. If these institutional crevices are accessible to civic actors, then movements have opportunities to penetrate the state apparatus and locate spaces where they can exercise influence. These processes offer an organizational terrain that is propitious for deliberation about policy reform.

Without these docking spaces, institutions remain off-limits to activist networks, and dominant actors can use their privileged position to dictate their preferred policy direction and priorities. Under these circumstances, neither the cluster of reforms that promote regulatory restriction nor the spaces of deliberation needed to define alternative directions are likely to emerge.

This discussion provides a road map for the chapters that follow. We begin with the Nicaraguan case, where the combination of movement fragmentation, durable elite alliances, and limited docking options tilted the outcome toward mining promotion.

3

Mining Friendly

Promoting Extractivism in Nicaragua

The *municipio* of Bonanza nestles deep in Nicaragua's northeastern Atlantic Coast region, connected to the capital city, Managua, by one daily twelve-passenger plane or a hard fourteen-hour bus trip. The town sprawls thinly alongside the main paved road. Wending along a serpentine topography, a steady stream of trucks moves mounds of rock to processing centers owned by HEMCO, where chemical treatment extracts microscopic particles of gold. Outside of the town, construction follows the Caribbean style. Wood-slat homes built on stilts keep residents safe from the floodwaters that surge during tropical storms.

Founded in the 1880s, Bonanza did not achieve municipal status until a century later, at the tail end of the Sandinista Revolution (1979–1990). The town struggles still with its origins as a migrant camp. A local hydroelectric plant has long provided electricity, on which the mine depends, but safe drinking water is limited and a third of the town's residents lack access to sewage facilities (FUNIDES 2016, 29–30). With HEMCO's funding, the town completed construction of its first municipal park and opened a public library in 2015 (HEMCO and Mineros 2016, 15–17), but public transportation remains unreliable, as is internet service.

Bonanza is a company town. Life revolves around activities at HEMCO, one of three large-scale gold mines operating in Nicaragua during my field work in 2018. The recent gold boom fueled migration to the area and filled the town with young men looking for work. Employment outside of mining is scarce, intensifying household dependence on the extractive sector. HEMCO, which opened in the 1940s as Neptune Gold Mining and was nationalized by the Sandinista government in 1979, was reprivatized in the 1990s, as the country underwent post-revolutionary market reform. In 2013, it was acquired by Mineros S.A., a family-owned Colombian firm.

Encouraged by the success of current mines, a half-dozen other gold mining companies have started exploration projects in Nicaragua, none

Breaking Ground. Rose J. Spalding, Oxford University Press. © Oxford University Press 2023.
DOI: 10.1093/oso/9780197643150.003.0003

more audaciously than Calibre Mining Corp., a Canadian junior that acquired the other two large mines, El Limón and La Libertad, in 2019. These extraction and exploration projects signal the country's growing commitment to gold mining. Even as operations were halted in neighboring Costa Rica and El Salvador, where metallic mining has been banned by law, and suspended in Honduras and Guatemala, where court decisions mandated legal review, gold mining advanced without interruption in Nicaragua. In 2020, gold was once again Nicaragua's number one export (BCN 2021, 94).

This chapter focuses on the political logistics of mine development during the most recent commodity boom. It uses the Nicaraguan case to map the ways that state actors and investors collaborate on the construction of a pro-mining policy framework. Process tracing allows us to identify the sequences, disconnections, and combinations that shaped particular outcomes in the Nicaragua case. Our task is to explain not only how and why Nicaraguan elites linked arms around the promotion of mining but also how and why mining opposition movements proved unable to influence the policy trajectory. The argument, described conceptually in Chapter 2, is briefly summarized below for the Nicaraguan case.

Elite consensus: Unlike political elites in Costa Rica and El Salvador, who proved deeply divided on the mining question, Nicaragua's political leaders united across partisan and ideological lines to endorse the recrudescence of mineral extraction in the 1990s. Both the outgoing revolutionary government and the incoming neoliberal one concurred on the development potential of the industry. During the difficult postwar transition period following economic collapse, mine officials presented extractive sector investment as a catalyst that could absorb underemployed labor and trigger expansion in related services. Government support for mining persisted across the post-revolutionary administrations of Violeta Chamorro (1990–1996), Arnoldo Alemán (1996–2002), and Enrique Bolaños (2002–2007), and continued after FSLN leader Daniel Ortega (1984–1990, 2007–) was reelected and returned to power during the mining boom. Mining advocacy penetrated deeply into the state apparatus, precluding the development of opposition enclaves within executive agencies, legislative commissions, municipal governments, or the courts. Unlike other Central American countries, where state actors in opposition enclaves disrupted the mining advance, Nicaraguan legislators, bureaucrats, mayors, and judges maintained a common pro-mining front.

The durability of elite mining support through the decades and across presidential periods in Nicaragua demonstrates how this arrangement became part of the post-revolutionary "political settlement" (Bebbington et al. 2018). Political settlements occur when government officials and business elites come to agreement about development priorities and design policies that reflect and sustain that agreement. The pro-mining consensus among political elites in Nicaragua echoed the mining endorsement by economic elites, as mining investors and their local suppliers networked inside the country's main business chamber and secured the backing of powerful internal and external leaders.

Mining Opposition: Although voices emerged in opposition to mining, Nicaraguan opponents lacked the internal consensus and organizational resources needed to confront a cohesive pro-mining elite. For much of this period, opponents were geographically scattered and disarticulated, and were unable to forge a durable coalition. Mobilized critics divided into three kinds of groups, each employing a different frame. Those that engaged in *distributive conflicts* struggled over the allocation of mining rents and highlighted concerns about labor rights, compensation, and the allocation and use of mining royalties. Those that engaged in *definitional conflicts* raised more fundamental questions about the costs to local communities of mine-centered development and advocated the outright rejection of mining operations. A third group, involved in *scale conflicts*, highlighted the competition between large-scale and small-scale mining, calling for checks on the former to secure the advance of the latter.

With the resistance movement segmented into different kinds of struggles, frame alignment proved difficult, as did movement bricolage. Public concern about environmental impacts grew, but anti-mining activists failed to achieve the multisectoral and multiscalar collaboration required for effective mobilization and policy impact.

Docking Points: Standard democratic theory envisions multiple points of entry for citizen demands and presumes the activation of both *vertical* (citizen participation) and *horizontal* (institutional cross-checks) accountability mechanisms (O'Donnell 2003). Citizen demand-making is expected to operate through a competitive electoral process, in which voters select candidates and political parties that reflect their preferences and dismiss those who fail to do so. In addition to vertical pressures exercised through electoral competition, democratic systems include an array of mechanisms through which organized civil society can press for fuller inclusion (Kapiszewski, Levitsky, and Yashar 2021). These openings provide opportunities for ordinary people to participate in diverse citizenship-building activities, such as voting in a referendum, filing legal demands in court, taking seats on policy advisory boards, and networking within bureaucratic agencies that carry out regulation and implementation. These institutional spaces for public participation are what I describe as "docking points."

Elsewhere in Central America, these forms of participation played a significant role in shaping the mining policy debate. In Nicaragua, however, docking points remained largely inaccessible. Nicaragua's "hybrid regime" (Close 2016, 9), which gradually became more insular, limited the opportunities for the assertion of demands and restricted access to the policymaking process. Pact-making between formally competing political elites created a closed circle at the top, in which power-sharing arrangements produced predetermined deals unmoored from popular preferences (Close 2016; Martí 2018; Sánchez and Osorio Mercado 2020). Constraints on access in the post-revolutionary era intensified following the shift to one-party dominance in the 2010s.

The FSLN, which governed the country for a decade before losing power electorally in 1990, recovered control of the presidency in 2007 and began building a new electoral monopoly under its perennial leader, Daniel Ortega. By the 2010s, major policy initiatives were ratified with little discussion or simply appeared in the form of presidential decrees. Laws, particularly those related to the economy, were crafted in closed negotiations with business elites rather than through a public process of legislative debate (COSEP 2012; Spalding 2017). Under these circumstances, political space for policy deliberation tightened, and mining policymaking became increasingly centralized.

The following four sections trace the development of this process.[1] The first offers an overview of Nicaragua's recent mine development history, and analyzes the evolution of elite consensus in favor of friendly rules and mining investment. The second describes the diverse forms of movement organizing that emerged in opposition to mining in Nicaragua and traces their fragmentation into distributive, definitional, scale-based conflicts. The third focuses on the problem of institutional access and maps the contraction

---

[1] This chapter draws on seventy-six semi-structured interviews carried out in Nicaragua between 2012 and 2018. See Appendix 3.1 for a list of the interviews cited in this chapter. This chapter also incorporates information from Nicaraguan environmental and human rights NGOs; official government documents and reports; corporate reports and press releases of Nicaraguan mining companies; briefs submitted to domestic court and the IACHR; and public opinion data provided by CID-Gallup. For additional information about the research methodology, see the "Argument and Methods" section of Chapter 1.

68 BREAKING GROUND

of docking points, those locations within the state apparatus where mining resisters elsewhere were embedding their claims and agitating for a greater policymaking role. The final section concludes by retracing the political logistics that permitted the continuation of mine development, even as nodes of opposition began to appear. Facing a high level of elite consensus in support of mine reactivation, their own internal divisions, and a policymaking process that restricted public participation, geographically scattered resistance movements gained little traction in Nicaragua.

The Logistics of Extractivist Ascendance: Constructing Elite Cohesion

As we saw in the model presented in Chapter 2, a sustained pro-mining policy landscape is promoted by a high degree of elite consensus in favor of extraction-based development. To assess the extent of elite consensus regarding mining in Nicaragua, this section traces mining policy development across recent decades. I look for evidence of elite convergence and divergence at three key junctures: first, among political elites in competing political parties, as they rotate in and out of office; second, among officials located in different segments of the state apparatus, where positions that are distinct from those adopted by national leaders might signal internal disconnection; and third, between political and economic elites.

Mining Transitions in the Revolutionary Period

All four of the Central American countries analyzed in this book had a gold mining legacy inherited from the colonial period. In the early twentieth century, precious metals represented the second- or third-most-important export in countries across the region.[2] Although earnings in this sector remained far below those for the dominant agro-export crops (coffee and bananas), gold and silver export value in 1913 passed US$1 million in Costa Rica, El Salvador, and Nicaragua (Bulmer-Thomas 1987, 8). Nicaragua was distinctive only in the degree to which gold mining activities persisted well

---

[2] The percentage of total export value represented by precious metals in 1913 was as follows: Costa Rica, 10%; El Salvador, 16%; Honduras, 26%; Nicaragua, 14% (Bulmer-Thomas 1987, 8).

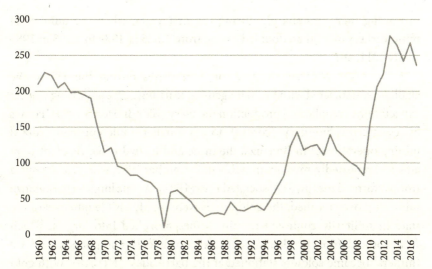

Figure 3.1 Nicaraguan gold exports, 1960–2017 (thousands of troy ounces). Data from BCN 2011, BCN 2018.

into the twentieth century, albeit in an attenuated form even there (Bulmer-Thomas 1987, 8, and table A.7, 320–321).[3]

Although mining outposts demonstrated considerable staying power in Nicaragua, midcentury production was never simply a matter of sectoral inertia. Nor did production rise and fall in keeping with international gold prices, which soared in the 1970s even as Nicaraguan production crashed.[4] Production levels during this era reflected the country's turbulent political events, suggesting the relevance of including political context in any explanatory framework of production patterns. The FSLN insurrection against the Somoza dynasty triggered capital flight and decapitalization, and mining production collapsed in 1979 (see Figure 3.1). The incoming revolutionary government nationalized the gold mines and attempted to bring them back into production, defending state ownership as necessary for sectoral reactivation. The newly created state mining company, Instituto Nicaragüense de la Minería (INMINE), reorganized the mining sector, which became part of the "mixed economy" model under which the state managed key economic activities (MIPLAN 1980; Martínez Cuenca 1992). Formal employment

---

[3] Annual gold production topped 200,000 troy ounces in 1941 and did not drop below that level until the mid-1960s (FUNIDES 2014). See also Parsons 1955, 49–51.

[4] "Gold Prices—100 Year Historical Chart," accessed April 15, 2019, https://www.macrotrends.net/1333/historical-gold-prices-100-year-chart.

70 BREAKING GROUND

in mining increased sharply during the first years, when the number of mineworkers more than doubled, rising from 1,625 in 1979 to 3,353 in 1980 (BCN 2011, 46).

As in other Nicaraguan state-run enterprises during the 1980s, the challenges associated with the management learning curve and rising worker expectations complicated production recovery (Biondi-Morra 1993). Forays by counterrevolutionary (contra) forces further undercut nationalized mining operations.[5] In Bonanza, the mine and its hydroelectric plant were attacked repeatedly, most memorably in December 1987, when 7,000 contra troops stormed the town (Associated Press 1987). As one long-term Bonanza mine employee recalled, the gold mines were highly visible outposts of the state in militarily contested terrain. Mines morphed into targets, which "transformed from production centers into defense compounds, and we [miners] became soldiers stationed at the barricades" (NI1818). With gold mines located in the interior region where contra attacks were concentrated, and with machinery dependent on replacement parts that were inaccessible following the 1985 Reagan administration export ban, production levels soon tumbled. National gold output reached only 25,000 troy ounces in 1985, less than one-tenth of its 1953 peak (FUNIDES 2014).

Ironically, the FSLN government never embraced the full-scale socialist vision it was often accused of following, and the regime's commitment to state-led development had faded by the end of the 1980s (Spalding 1987; Martínez Cuenca 1992, 69–84). Economic setbacks and monetary collapse made Sandinista leaders increasingly cautious about the viability of revolutionary change and more inclined to negotiate with domestic economic elites. Postwar transformation, including leadership embourgeoisement, fostered a growing willingness among top Sandinista leaders to accept a market-oriented transition, which soon followed.

Post-Revolutionary Mining Growth and Development

After Ortega's loss in the 1990 presidential election, the post-revolutionary government of Violeta Chamorro (1990–1996) convoked the Concertación

---

[5] Presenting the Sandinista government as an extension of the "Soviet-Cuban-Nicaraguan axis," the Reagan administration (1980–1988) funded and trained a paramilitary force of counter-revolutionaries that pursued the goal of regime change. In 1985, the administration declared a freeze on trade and credit for Nicaragua in an effort to further destabilize the Sandinista government.

Económica y Social, a multiphase dialogue process (CIPRES 1992; Spalding 1994, 171–177; de Franco 1996; Close 1999, 130–135). Sidestepping the fractious legislature, the government brought together thirty-five representatives, evenly split between the business chambers and worker federations, to hammer out agreements about new economic rules. Intense negotiations in 1990 and again in 1991 produced agreement to privatize 351 state enterprises, using a combination of property returns to former owners, sales to new private investors, and transfers to workers or to demobilized troops from both sides of the conflict. Workers in these enterprises secured a commitment for 25% of these assets, but without agreement about specific allocations or terms.

Between 1991 and 1994, Corporaciones Nacionales del Sector Público (CORNAP), the government holding company, negotiated 1,237 separate privatization transactions (de Franco 1996, 24) and released 98% of the state companies then prioritized for transfer. These agreements reprivatized the mining sector, along with banking, export trade, and a broad swath of agricultural production.[6] Privatization was accompanied by the layoff of over 40% of mineworkers (BCN 2011, 46).[7]

In 1994, Greenstone Resources, a Canadian mining junior, acquired 75% of the mine in La Libertad, Chontales (Rabchevsky 1994, 593). In the same year, Texas oil tycoon Bunker Hunt got a ten-year concession in the Mining Triangle for his Hunt Exploration and Mining Company (HEMCO), which included the mine in Bonanza (Rabchevsky 1994, 594). In 1996, Triton Mining Corporation of Canada acquired 95% of the El Limón mine, then the country's largest gold producer (Doan 1996, 1). Unionized workers secured 5% of El Limón (and, from 1994 to 1996, 25% of La Libertad), and local capital wound up with 10% of the Bonanza mine, offering a patina of domestic business participation. Ownership came with financial obligations that were often unmet, and concessions were handed off quickly to other investors and partners (Tolvanen 2001), in the familiar shell game that characterizes the junior mining sector.

[6] In the initial agreement, mining workers received the right to acquire 100% of four mines (La Libertad gold mine and three non-metallic mines in the quarrying subsector) for US$4 million, with Swedish foreign aid used to support this purchase (CIPRES 1992, 109–111). Over the next two years, ownership arrangements were renegotiated as debts and production problems mounted.

[7] The *concertación* processes that designed the template for post-revolutionary privatization allowed severance packages for laid-off workers and the partial transfer of assets to workers and demobilized troops (Spalding 1994). Mineworkers acquired a modest ownership percentage in the company, which was managed by the holding company Inversiones Mineras, S.A. (INMISA), or received compensation in bonds that were sold off quickly at bargain basement prices (NI1818).

72   BREAKING GROUND

Gold production began to recover, with exports reaching 143,000 troy ounces in 1999. Demobilized military and contra troops moved into artisanal mining, which grew rapidly during this transition phase. Between the renewal of industrial mining and the expansion of informal mining, environmental contamination worsened, triggering public inquiry and investigation by international donors, including Germany's Gesellschaft für Internationale Zusammenarbeit (GTZ) and the US Agency for International Development (USAID).[8] Large-scale mines had traditionally dumped mining wastes directly into nearby rivers, and artisanal miners used mercury to amalgamate gold, inhaling the vapor as they burned it off and dumping contaminated wastewater at widely scattered work sites (Tolvanen 2001; Rosario and Ault 1997). Hurricane Mitch, which hit the region hard in 1998, left large-scale flooding and mudslides that further complicated environmental remediation and mine rebuilding efforts.

Bent on reactivating and growing the industry, the post-revolutionary government approved a series of laws and regulations to create a favorable investment climate for mining. To woo foreign investment, for which countries across the region were competing, the Alemán administration approved the Foreign Investment Promotion Law #344 in 2000 and the Special Mining Exploration and Extraction Law #387 in 2001 (see Table 3.1). The new mining law permitted concessions up to a maximum of 50,000 hectares for a twenty-five-year period, a generous spatial allocation and time frame that were extendable for an additional twenty-five years. Annual royalties were fixed at 3% of the value of the extracted material. This rate was higher than that approved in new mining laws in Guatemala (1%) and El Salvador (2%), but was a deductible expense for income tax purposes, substantially easing the financial burden.[9] The combination of deductions and exemptions allowed the industry to develop while contributing little to state revenues (Centro Humboldt and IEEPP 2017). To reduce uncertainties for potential investors, the law granted exploration and extraction rights simultaneously, pending approval of an environmental impact assessment (EIA). EIAs were to be reviewed by

[8] Rosario and Ault (1997), USAID consultants, found that 8% of examined residents in a targeted area near the Bonanza mine had mercury levels that exceeded 10 ppm in hair samples, a benchmark for exposure normally regarded as hazardous to health.

[9] In 2006, royalty rates in Latin America varied by country, product, and price, with top rates of 7% and 5% for gold in Bolivia and the Dominican Republic, respectively, and a bottom rate of zero percent in Mexico. See Otto et al. 2006.

MINING FRIENDLY: NICARAGUA   73

Table 3.1 Nicaraguan Mining Policy Timeline

Mining Policies and Related Actions (Year)	Presidential Administration and Political Party/Coalition	Term
Concertación Económica y Social agreements (1990, 1991) Mine privatization in Bonanza, La Libertad, and El Limón (1991–1994) CAMINIC established (1995), joined COSEP	Chamorro, UNO	1990–1996
Foreign Investment Promotion Law approved (2000) Special Mining Exploration and Extraction Law approved (2001)	Alemán, Liberal Alliance	1996–2002
PRONicaragua created (2002) Mining "cluster" prioritized in National Development Plan (2003)	Bolaños, PLC, APRE	2002–2007
MEM created (2007) La Libertad and El Limón mines acquired by B2Gold (2007) PODU established in Bonanza (2008) Ortega inaugurated La Libertad reopening (2010)	Ortega, FSLN	2007–2012
Mineros acquired HEMCO (2013) International Mining Congresses jointly sponsored by CAMINIC, MEM, and PRONicaragua (2014, 2016) Environmental permit denied for El Pavón project (2015)	Ortega, FSLN	2012–2017
ENIMINAS created (2017) Environmental Law "streamlined" (2017) Environmental permit granted for La India (2018) B2Gold's Nicaragua properties acquired by Calibre (2019) Environmental permit granted for El Pavón Norte (2020)	Ortega, FSLN	2017–2022

the Ministerio del Ambiente y los Recursos Naturales (MARENA), an underfunded environmental agency with limited administrative capacity (McGinley and Cubbage 2012).

Pro-mining policies continued into the Bolaños administration, which, with World Bank (2007) assistance, oversaw the creation of PRONicaragua, a public-private agency designed to attract foreign investment. Gold mining was identified as one of the nine "clusters" targeted for development in the 2003 National Development Plan (Bolaños 2003, 138–140).

"Nicaragua," the plan concluded, "possesses enviable mining potential, which places it in a privileged position with respect to the rest of Central America" (Bolaños 2003, 138). Over the next decade, mining became a featured sector that was actively promoted in PRONicaragua publications and presentations.

Elite consensus entails not just cohesion within the political elite but also the development of shared assumptions that unite political and economic elites. Although normally the political dependence of the state on capital implies a high degree of business-state connection in market economies, in practice variation emerges, creating subtle shades of alliance and distance. This variation is in part due to the rotation of political elites among various political parties, which differ in terms of their histories and constituencies, affecting their affinity for positions held by the business sector. Distinctions also occur due to internal fissures within the business elite, which may be characterized by diverse histories, resources, and needs.

Several processes affect the ability of the business sector to attenuate internal divisions, and one of these processes is organization (Schneider 2004). As Fairfield and Garay note (2017, 1879):

> Organization is a fundamental source of business power. Strong encompassing associations, as opposed to fragmented, overlapping, or rival associations, help business advance their interests through two main mechanisms. First, encompassing associations facilitate unity and collective action, which legitimates business demands. When business is uncoordinated, their demands can more easily be dismissed as narrow, particularistic, and against the public good. Second, strong organization strengthens business's bargaining position by making it harder for policymakers to divide and conquer.

In the Nicaraguan case, the convergence of pro-mining preferences across the political elite was reinforced by unity within the business elite, represented by the Consejo Superior de la Empresa Privada (COSEP), Nicaragua's business peak association (Spalding 1994). As a mechanism to promote business cohesion and improve its bargaining position, COSEP came to enjoy a privileged relationship with post-revolutionary governments (Spalding 2017). Two of Nicaragua's presidents (Alemán and Bolaños) had served as leaders in the business sector prior to entering the partisan political fray, with Bolaños presiding over COSEP during the long years of conflict with the revolutionary government. This relationship allowed economic elites to gain special access to negotiations about wages, taxes, and economic development policy, as the government undertook economic stabilization and structural adjustment in the 1990s.

Within a year of mine privatization, investors founded the Nicaraguan Mining Chamber (CAMINIC). COSEP quickly absorbed and accommodated the new mining chamber, adding it to a growing list of sectoral affiliates. CAMINIC representatives became active members in the business alliance, serving as association officers and donors, and using their relationship with this prominent lobby to gain access to policymaking circles. Like other business representatives, CAMINIC officers collaborated with the government to secure roles for their appointees on key boards and commissions, including the National Energy and Mines Commission, National Commission on Minimum Wages, National Labor Council, and National Health and Safety Board (Ríos 2012). PRONicaragua became a natural ally, with CAMINIC officials attending and co-hosting international trade fairs and congresses, where government officials lauded the sector's achievements and prospects.

By 2013, CAMINIC membership had grown to include eleven metallic mining companies at different stages of exploration, plus a small mill designated for artisanal miners (Plantel Los Ángeles) and a host of local mining service providers. Combining both metallic and nonmetallic sectors, mining producers and related services, and corporate and cooperative affiliates, CAMINIC had extended membership to thirty companies in 2013 (PRONicaragua 2013, 15).

Gold Mining During the Boom

When you talk to people in Nicaragua about the country's history of gold mining, and particularly about mining policy development under Ortega, they sometimes jokingly say, "Daniel was born in a mine." While not literally true, that statement makes a broader point. As we saw in the opening to Chapter 1, Ortega was born in the mining town of La Libertad, Chontales, and his father worked in the business, at one point holding a low-level administrative position in La Esmeralda gold mine (Kinzer 1999, 186). Ortega's up-close familiarity with the industry is widely assumed to have predisposed him to view mining as a development opportunity, and to have reinforced

76 BREAKING GROUND

his active promotion of mine expansion.[10] Investors and observers alike described him as a reliable recruiter for new mine investment and an eager performer in mining-symbolic celebrations.[11]

The returning Ortega administration created a Ministry of Energy and Mining (MEM) in 2007 and put Carlos Zarruk, the former head of state mining company INMINE, in charge of the MEM's Dirección General de Minas (DGM). To attract mining investment, PRONicaragua drew attention to the country's tax exemptions on inputs and mining machinery and the absence of import and export taxes on the activity, as well as the growing availability of clean energy sources (PRONicaragua 2013, 2014). Investment promotion featured the country's low labor costs, bilateral investment treaties and free trade agreements, and guaranteed access to international tribunals in the event of investment disputes. PRONicaragua staff worked to overcome investor reservations by highlighting Nicaragua's relatively strong Doing Business rankings for contract completion, bankruptcy provisions, and investment protection, as well as the country's reputation for safety. Like other state leaders in Latin America, Ortega was eager to cultivate natural resource investment that would allow the country to ride the commodity boom.

Ortega's return to power raised concerns in some business quarters, given the expropriations and regulatory controls adopted by the Sandinista government during the revolution and its prior record of hostile relations with the United States. Ortega, however, had embraced a form of "populist capitalism" (Veltmeyer and Petras 2014, 225), blending anti-imperialist discourse and modest social spending with market-friendly policies negotiated with business elites. His return ushered in an era of economic co-governance wherein COSEP leaders had access to monthly meetings with high-level economic officials. According to COSEP's internal assessment, the business association

---

[10] In a 2015 speech that addressed mining, Ortega bemoaned the way mining investors had taken wealth (a "montonón de plata") out of the country, and he expressed a wish that the industry were still under national control ("We would have liked for Nicaragua to have enough resources to make these investments, and to not depend on foreign investors"). But he concluded that the Nicaraguan government would not have the ability to develop the mines, and that the loss to Nicaragua of the wealth associated with mining is the price to be paid for the mining sector jobs and their multiplier effect ("The benefit that it leaves is that it provides work, provides direct employment for the [mine] workers, and also commercial activity for all the people who live nearby, for people who live in the town, for those who sell food, for those who wash clothes, for those who iron clothes, for those who sell beer") ("Comandante Daniel Ortega" 2015).

[11] Interviewed in 2012 (Reuters Staff 2012), B2Gold CEO Clive Johnson reported that his first act in pursuing expansion in Nicaragua after his arrival in 2007 was to meet with Ortega, a twenty-minute appointment that turned into a two-hour conversation.

collaborated in the drafting of 105 laws and 42 regulations approved by the legislature between 2008 and 2015 (COSEP 2016, 9).[12]

As elsewhere in the region, mining investment and production in Nicaragua increased during the boom cycle. The volume of Nicaraguan gold exports tripled between 2006 and 2013. Rising prices allowed gold export value to increase even more rapidly.[13] The number of metallic mining concessions doubled from 85 in 2007 to 172 in 2014 (MEM-DGM 2014b, 18; MEM-DGM 2015). Overall mining investment increased as well, rising from US$25 million in 2010, when it represented a modest 5% of total foreign investment, to US$274 million in 2013, when it represented 20% of the total (PRONicaragua 2014). By 2014, 11.8% of national territory had been concessioned for metallic mining, and concessions had been solicited for an additional 4.1% (MEM-DGM 2014b, 19). Eager to attract more investment, the government's mining bureau advertised that an additional 45% of national territory remained available (p. 19). Nicaragua, as the director general of mining, Carlos Zarruk, observed in the *Mining Weekly Online* in 2014, was "open for business" (as quoted in Lazenby 2014).

When I asked Zarruk early in 2018 if he considered Nicaragua to be a *país minero* (mining country), a label sometimes used by Nicaraguan mining advocates, he told me no. Following up the next day on WhatsApp, he sent me a screenshot of a publication by Peru's Ministry of Energy and Mining with the headline "Perú, País Minero." This colorful table showed national rankings for regional and global production of seven metals, with Peru ranked either first (gold, zinc, and lead) or second (copper, silver, tin, and molybdenum) in Latin America and between second and sixth in the world. Peru, he had told me, was a *país minero*, not Nicaragua. The best way to describe Nicaragua, he said, was "mining friendly."

Warmly supported in elite circles, gold mining continued to expand in the years that followed. The regime even developed a small stake in the sector, creating a state-owned mining company in 2017. The Empresa Nicaragüense de Minas (ENIMINAS) allowed the government to establish joint venture

---

[12] In 2012, COSEP reported having representation on eleven supervisory boards for public-private institutions, ten councils, and four ministries and government agencies, including the Central Bank, national social security institute, and institutions in charge of technical education, tourism, and competition (COSEP 2012, 2–3). Its representatives served on the tripartite commission that negotiated annual increases in the minimum wage and participated in consultation processes that designed changes in the tax code.

[13] As gold production levels doubled and then tripled, mining reached 9% of export value in 2013, up from 3.3% in 2009, and became Nicaragua's highest-value export, surpassing even the top agribusiness mainstays in 2013 (BCN 2014, 133).

78   BREAKING GROUND

partnerships with private investors in a newly designated area called the Mining Reserve (GRUN 2018). Inching toward this thin version of resource nationalism,[14] administration officials focused their efforts on building small mills for the artisanal mining sector, refraining from direct competition with large-scale mines, and ultimately secured business approval (NI1118; NI2318).[15] By the end of 2020, a total of 227 metallic mining concessions had been either granted (146) or solicited (81), affecting 22% of national territory (MEM-DGM 2021). Gold was again the country's main export, generating over one-third of export earnings (BCN 2021, 94). Both the governing FSLN and its main rivals endorsed mine development, and both political and economic elites offered positive assessments of Nicaragua's mining potential.

Mining Opposition in Extractivist-Oriented Nicaragua

As the framework presented in Chapter 2 indicates, mining prospects do not depend on elite preferences alone. The second element in my argument focuses on the organizational characteristics of the mining resistance movement. Mining expansion sparked opposition in Nicaragua, and two organizations served as network nodes. The Humboldt Center provided coordination for Nicaragua's nascent environmental movement, and the Catholic Church leadership came to galvanize and accompany community-led struggles. In a pattern repeated in different proportions across Latin America, environmental and religious leaders served as significant sources of information and moral suasion in the mining opposition movements that unfolded.

Founded in 1990 in the wake of the Sandinista revolution, the Humboldt Center quickly became Nicaragua's lead organization engaging the environmental policy debate. Seeking to "open a conversation" (NI1418) about mining policy as the sector expanded, Humboldt Center staff members prepared a series of reports that identified significant problems in the industry,

---

[14] Unlike more radical versions of resource nationalism developed in Bolivia, Ecuador, and Venezuela, which claimed to break neocolonial patterns of foreign exploitation and to deliver the benefits of extraction to the citizenry at large (Haslam and Heidrich 2016), the Nicaraguan version simply sought status as a minority partner in new mines to be developed in a delimited area.

[15] The MEM was authorized to define the boundaries of the Mining Reserve using strategic targeting and concession forfeiture. For any new mining project developed in the reserve, the state would be a required minority partner, with a mandatory, non-dilutable 15% ownership stake. The government presented ENIMINAS as a mechanism that would promote small mill development and help Nicaragua fulfill its obligations under the Minamata Convention, an international agreement to reduce mercury contamination, which Nicaragua had signed in 2014 (GRUN 2018; NI1118).

most importantly the issues of water contamination and inadequate administrative and regulatory control (Centro Humboldt 2008, 2014; Centro Humboldt and IEEPP 2017). Their research provided documentation of the environmental damages associated with mine development and helped to build a nascent epistemic community of environmental researchers and activists.[16] Humboldt Center reports also challenged the government's policy of concessioning territory in buffer zones (*zonas de amortiguamiento*) surrounding the officially declared Protected Areas, and of actively promoting mine approval in indigenous communities in the Atlantic Coast. In addition, they questioned the policy of allowing concessioners to acquire multiple holdings, which let key investors control far more than the legal maximum of 50,000 hectares and helped spur ownership concentration (Centro Humboldt 2008, 43–45; 2014, 21, 73).

Unlike most NGOs in Nicaragua, which tended to focus their work in Managua, the Humboldt Center established a sprinkling of local offices outside the capital, including two in the Atlantic Coast region (Bonanza and Siuna). In 2008 its staff collaborated with local teams in fifty-six municipalities, playing a role in advancing land use planning and municipal-level disaster management. Staff members networked with leaders in several communities, and provided informational workshops on environmental protection and mining laws as part of their environmental advocacy work. Local-level work brought Humboldt Center representatives into contact with an emerging array of regional and departmental NGOs, including those embracing the principles of agroecology and sustainability.

While research dissemination and local networking advanced in the environmental community, attention to these issues deepened in sectors of the Catholic Church. Bishops in nearby Honduras and Guatemala took leadership roles in the protest movements as mining investments entered those countries in the early 2000s (Holden and Jacobson 2011; Arellano-Yanguas

---

[16] This research documented cyanide contamination by Greenstone Mining, heavy metal contamination of Río Mico by DESMINIC at La Libertad, and water and soil contamination by Tritón Minera at El Limón, among others (Centro Humboldt 2008, 45–47; 2014). Centro Humboldt (2014) provided the results of water sample testing near mining sites by technicians at the Centro para la Investigación en Recursos Acuáticos de Nicaragua, a hydrology research center affiliated with the Universidad Nacional Autónoma de Nicaragua. Comparing those results against the standards established by Nicaragua's regulatory framework and the benchmarks recommended by the World Health Organization, Humboldt Center researchers identified health hazards associated with the release of toxic levels of several metals into local waters and pinpointed environmental hot spots. For additional documentation of toxic discharges in waterways related to mining in Nicaragua, see Picado et al. 2010; Sequeira-León, Luna-Avilés, and Huete-Pérez 2011; Corrales-Pérez and Romero 2013; and Veiga et al. 2014.

80 BREAKING GROUND

2014; see also Chapter 4). As natural resource extraction expanded across Latin America, other religious leaders joined the chorus. Meeting in Aparecida, Brazil, in 2007, the region's Catholic bishops declared, "Today the natural wealth of Latin America and the Caribbean is being subjected to an irrational exploitation that is leaving ruin and death in its wake" (CELAM 2007, para. 473). Pope Francis's 2015 encyclical "Laudato Si'" echoed environmental teachings long rumbling within the Latin American Catholic Church.

The Nicaraguan church hierarchy was slower than others to develop an environmental voice. Nicaragua's long-term Catholic leader, Cardinal Miguel Obando y Bravo, developed a belated affinity for the Ortega regime, his earlier hostility diluted by FSLN legislative support for an absolute ban on abortion in 2006 and the regime's self-proclaimed description of Nicaragua as "Christian, Socialist and Caring (*Solidaria*)." Obando and Ortega became political allies, collaborating on a range of initiatives, including mine promotion.[17] Individual parish priests and local bishops, however, began to register environmental criticism, in tones that became more emphatic as the mining industry grew.

Following the February 2014 elevation of Bishop Leopoldo Brenes to the position of cardinal, church officials struck a more critical tone, as seen in their 2014 pronouncement "En búsqueda de nuevos horizontes para una Nicaragua mejor" (CEN 2014). Presented to Ortega in a four-hour exchange, this document referenced an array of environmental issues, including the destruction of forests by a "timber mafia" that operated in violation of national laws and "without restrictions of any type." The officials called on the government to improve environmental practices in currently existing mines and to "expressly deny permission for such projects in virgin mining territories, as in the case of the *municipio* of Rancho Grande in Matagalpa, respecting the decision of its population." As elsewhere in Latin America, Nicaraguan church leaders entered into environmental struggles through both their reading of church social doctrine and the pastoral practice of community accompaniment.

In spite of these sources of support, the mining opposition movement in Nicaragua failed to develop traction, at least at the national level. One stumbling block was the absence of alignment across local-level movements. The

---

[17] Cardinal Obando, who was also born in La Libertad, joined Ortega on the stage to celebrate the 2010 reopening of La Libertad mine.

literature on mining protest points to the need for careful analysis of the networks that are constructed within the resistance camp (Bebbington and Bury 2013; Kirsch 2014; Arce 2014; Li 2015; De Echave 2017; Kröger 2020; Broad and Cavanagh 2021). To better understand the circumstances under which protest becomes consequential, forensic investigation of the linkages between and among opposition groups is required.

Close analysis of the Nicaraguan case points to three major variations in mining struggles. *Distributive* conflicts focus on competition over how large-scale mining rents are divided up. *Definitional* contests center on struggles over incompatible development trajectories and the negative impact of mining on community livelihoods and cultural practices. Finally, *scale* struggles pit small-scale against large-scale mining, with corollary disputes about ownership claims and the environmental impacts of mining technologies. The literature on mining conflict in Latin America has focused on the first two types of contests (Arce 2014; De Echave 2017), overlooking or misinterpreting the third. Underexamination of scale struggles is a by-product of the general neglect of artisanal and small-scale mining in academic analysis and, consequently, inadequate conceptualizations of the conflicts in which this sector engages. Neglect persists even though most of the economically active population involved in gold mining is located in the ASM sector and this sector plays a critical role in global gold production.

The following descriptions of three mining conflicts in Nicaragua demonstrate this variation, with each capturing a different type of struggle. Labor conflicts at El Limón mine illustrate distributive struggles; community resistance in Rancho Grande demonstrates definitional conflicts; and scale conflicts erupted in La India, where artisanal miners attempted to thwart the return of large-scale mining a half century after its departure.

Distributive Conflicts: Competition over Economic Resources in El Limón

As in other countries where mining became a mainstay of economic life, Nicaragua had communities that built up around the extraction site. Mining expansion created jobs, as its proponents had advertised, including much sought-after positions in the formal sector. Although exonerations and deductions trimmed the tax transfers substantially (Centro Humboldt and IEEPP 2017), gold mining generated modest royalty payments, with a portion

82 BREAKING GROUND

disseminated at the local level.[18] Comparing data on social, economic, and demographic indicators in five mining and five nonmining towns that had been selected with an eye to comparability, the Fundación Nicaragüense para el Desarrollo Económico y Social (FUNIDES) found that household income in mining towns was double that in nonmining communities; mining towns also had lower multidimensional poverty rates and better access to electricity (FUNIDES 2016, 43, 30).[19]

On the other hand, fewer households in Bonanza (HEMCO) and Larreynaga (Mina El Limón) had access to safe drinking water and sanitation than their counterparts in nonmining communities. These mining town residents also reported higher levels of unemployment and lower levels of home enterprise business development (FUNIDES 2016, 34–35, 43).[20] Although several living standard indicators pointed to relatively positive outcomes, at least during the active extraction period before ore exhaustion and mine closure, others showed mixed results. New and persistent deficits in mining sector performance triggered recurring episodes of mobilization.

Tensions between mine operators and community activists in established mining towns typically revolved around economic issues of employment access, collective bargaining, and wages and working conditions, as in classic labor disputes, or around the distribution of tax revenues, royalty payments, and voluntary contributions, which accounted for a significant portion of municipal budgets and determined the availability of local services. These diverse forms of competition, which Arce (2014) describes as "service" conflicts, appeared repeatedly in Nicaragua's mining zones, periodically flaring into roadblocks and strikes that temporarily closed down operations.

---

[18] In Nicaragua, the tax formula allocated 35% of mining royalties to municipal governments. For projects located in the Atlantic Coast autonomous regions, an additional 20% of royalties was transferred to the regional council. Municipalities with the largest mines were the main beneficiaries of these resource flows. La Libertad received 26% of the total municipal transfers in 2013 and Bonanza received 22%.

[19] The study, which was commissioned by CAMINIC, included three metallic mining and two non-metallic mining *municipios*, each of which was matched with a nonmining town based on similar demographic, social, and economic characteristics using 2005 census data (FUNIDES 2016). The survey involved a random sample of 394 households in mining towns, 350 in nonmining towns, and an additional 50 in Bonanza's artisanal mining sector. In metallic mining towns, the percentage of households without electricity was 10% (Larreynaga), 7% (Bonanza), and 2% (La Libertad), whereas in their matched nonmining towns, it was 46% (Telica), 20% (Río Blanco), and 10% (Camoapa), respectively (FUNIDES 2016, 30).

[20] Twenty-six percent of households in Bonanza and 20% in Larreynaga lacked potable water, whereas no households in their respective nonmining counterparts, Río Blanco and Telica, reported this deficit (FUNIDES 2016, 29). Thirty-four percent of households in Bonanza and 75% in Larreynaga lacked sanitation services, whereas 25% of households in Río Blanco and 31% in Telica reported this problem (p. 30).

Labor conflict at El Limón mine, where lengthy strikes were a recurring feature of community life, illustrates the point. Six strikes and protests involving salaries and collective contracts took place at El Limón between 2002 and 2015. After acquiring the Limón mine in 2009, B2Gold faced regular community complaints about sinkholes related to excavation and interruptions in water and electricity services. When the free electricity supplied to residents by the mine was cut back following a management change in 2015, and three members of the Pedro Roque Blandón union were dismissed following the resulting protests, activists blocked access to the mine for three weeks and brought production to a halt. The roadblock was broken and the mine reopened only after a second police deployment, marked by injuries and death, and the direct intervention of the president (García Peralta 2015; "Comandante Daniel Ortega" 2015).

Unions are generally weak in Nicaragua (Bickham Mendez 2005) and are absent altogether in some large enterprises, including the Bonanza mine. Tensions were typically contained by the mobilization of Sandinista loyalties in those unions that were historically aligned with the FSLN and by voluntary corporate contributions to social projects and operations focusing on community relations. Both B2Gold and HEMCO managers set up offices dedicated to softer operations, working to strengthen community ties and ensure a "social license." "Not your grandfather's mining company," proclaimed B2Gold (2017a) as it showcased its projects for reforestation, water treatment, mosquito fumigation, and local business development.

HEMCO attenuated local distributive conflicts by melding its efforts with a fledgling city planning initiative. Faced with a well-documented and decades-long complaint about how wealth washed out of the town without leaving infrastructure or social development behind, the company launched a municipal planning process in 2008. The goal was to identify a visible set of investments that the town could undertake using both royalty transfers and CSR donations, and to set a timeline for their initiation. The resulting Plan de Ordenamiento y Desarrollo Urbano (PODU) introduced an urban infrastructural development process that included the construction of roads, parks, and water lines, and the distribution of a wide array of cultural and social services (HEMCO and Mineros 2016; HEMCO 2018). As the principal funder of most of Bonanza's municipal development projects, HEMCO enjoyed close collaboration with the FSLN-dominated municipal government (NI1818). Social tensions, which flared periodically, were generally tamped down through these interactions.

Definitional Conflicts: Struggle over Community Identity and Agroecology in Rancho Grande (El Pavón)

As gold prices rose and the government's encouragement of mine investment bore fruit, prospectors moved beyond brownfield sites and spread into previously untapped parts of Nicaraguan territory, searching for commercially viable deposits and the requisite water resources. In areas identified as propitious, such as Rancho Grande, an agricultural community in the department of Matagalpa, exploratory work turned up a promising combination. Two years after the 2001 mining law was approved, the Bolaños administration granted concessions in this zone, and exploration advanced.

The Canadian mining company B2Gold, quickly becoming Nicaragua's lead corporate investor, acquired the Rancho Grande concession in 2009 and approved the financing and project design for El Pavón, a new open pit mine, in 2012. To cultivate support and assuage the concerns of local residents, the company launched a social outreach campaign, installed a microfinance program, and repainted the local school. To counter this advance, local activists reached out to allies in departmental- and national-level nongovernmental organizations that had established a growing presence in the region during the postwar era. The Asociación para la Diversificación y Desarrollo Agrícola Comunal (ADDAC), whose founders in the late 1980s included demobilized Sandinista troops, had spent over a decade promoting local organic and sustainable agricultural practices in the Matagalpa area (ADDAC 2010; NI0415). ADDAC leaders encouraged residents of Rancho Grande and the nearby communities to embrace development that centered on the area's rich soil and abundant rainfall. By emphasizing survival strategies for peasant economies and skill development for local cooperatives, ADDAC promoted improvements in the quality of cacao and coffee production in the zone. ADDAC affiliates became significant actors in the emerging antimining movement.

As Arce (2014) observed in Peru, and Haslam and Tanimoune (2016) found more broadly in Latin America, mining conflict tends to increase when mine development competes with agricultural production, particularly when available cropland is relatively scarce. In Rancho Grande, 90% of the residents lived in rural hamlets (*comarcas*), and economic activity was eminently agricultural (Sosa 2015). Interviews with Rancho Grande antimining activists (NI0615; López and Dávila 2014; Gutiérrez Elizondo 2015; Sánchez 2017) call attention to the interaction between the local sensitivity to cropland loss, agroecology principles, and mining resistance. Describing these escalating environmental concerns, one anti-mining peasant leader offered these thoughts: "Rancho Grande is a paradise that some people want to destroy. . . . If we let this company operate here we'd end up living in a desert. The fertile topsoil would be blown away who knows where and they'd leave us with land that produces nothing, where not even one tree could grow" (López and Dávila 2014).

Religious leaders reinforced the message, providing moral framing and expanding the resistance base. Movement origin stories highlight the catalytic role played by Father Teodoro Custer, a Maryknoll priest who became pastor of Rancho Grande's Catholic parish in 1999. In our Facebook exchanges regarding his work, Father Custer described being influenced by Maryknoll sisters who were organizing against the Marlin mine in Guatemala in the early 2000s. Calling his anti-mining work in Rancho Grande "probably the greatest achievement of my life," Custer recounted his experience:

> I had heard one day that that Canadian mining company was not only trying to get in, but was actually "in," and working. I found out they were sneaking in under the radar, so to speak, in violation of the government's regulations. No public hearing had ever been held. When nothing was done, I started by posting some banners over the main road . . . with some pithy messages about how gold mining was done and what happens to the underground water. R[ancho] G[rande] sits on top of one of the most plenteous pure underground water supplies in all Nicaragua. (NI0116)[21]

Bolstered by support from development specialists long active in the area, and armed with information from trusted sources about the harmful impact of mining on water access and quality, Rancho Grande activists began organizing against mining in 2004 (López and Dávila 2014; Pérez González 2015; Gutiérrez Elizondo 2015; Sánchez 2017; Arce, Hendricks, and Polizzi 2022, chap. 4). Anti-mining activists in Rancho Grande and nearby communities merged their efforts, naming themselves Defenders of the Yaoska River (Guardianes de Yaoska), which flowed through the region, and setting up a five-member directorate to network supporters across thirty-eight communities. Contending that mining would compete directly with

---

[21] See also "Empresa Minera" 2006 for comments by Rancho Grande community leaders and organizational spokespeople as opposition to mining began to develop.

86 BREAKING GROUND

the agricultural production for which the region was known, and would offer only short-term return at the expense of long-term development, resisters called for space for citizen participation in the process.

By 2013, a multisectoral anti-mining coalition had been constructed in this region. At the municipal level, leadership was provided by the local Catholic parish, the Guardianes de Yaoska, Evangelical activists, and individual political party leaders from both the FSLN and the PLI, its principal local competitor at the time. A network of allies developed in Matagalpa, the departmental capital, calling themselves the Strategic Group Against Mining (Grupo Estratégico contra la Minería).[22] The bishop responsible for the Diocese of Matagalpa, Monsignor Rolando José Álvarez Lagos, and Father Pablo Espinoza, then pastor of Nuestra Señora de Fátima church in Rancho Grande, organized protest marches with a growing number of participants (Silva and Martínez 2013). At the national level, Centro Humboldt and the national human rights organization Centro Nicaragüense de los Derechos Humanos (CENIDH) offered information and accompaniment, and documented the movement's efforts (CENIDH 2013a; Centro Humboldt 2014, 41–51; López and Dávila 2014; Sánchez 2017).

During my interviews in Rancho Grande in July 2015, community members offered a variety of explanations for their involvement in the movement. One man who had spent time in the Mining Triangle, where Bonanza is located, focused on mining town vices, deploring the way mineworkers drank their earnings away. Another, originally from a water-stressed community in a neighboring department, marveled at the abundant water and lush vegetation in Rancho Grande, which he feared would be lost should mining advance. A third, inspired by religious views, replied to my question with a question of his own. "How," he asked, "would God feel if he gave me something beautiful and pure when I was born, and I returned it to him as a dirty and degraded thing upon my death?" (NI0815). For this activist, religious strictures required an active commitment to environmental protection.[23]

---

[22] This network included ADDAC, Asociación para el Desarrollo Integral Comunitario (ADIC), Radio Comunal Católica, the Movimiento de Mujeres de Matagalpa, the local Movimiento Comunal Nicaragüense (MCN), and the Ríos de Agua Viva Cooperative, among others.

[23] In a 2018 survey in which 408 Rancho Grande respondents were asked if they would "permit a mining company to extract resources in benefit of the country," 86% said no; only 14% expressed approval (Sánchez 2018). Anti-mining views were particularly strong among respondents who identified as Catholic and those who earned all or a great part of their income from agricultural activities. In their study of individual attitudes toward mining in four widely dispersed communities that were confronting mining projects (Tía María in Peru, Rancho Grande and Santo Domingo in Nicaragua, and Fuleni in South Africa), Arce, Hendricks, and Polizzi (2022) found that people who

Local FSLN municipal officials initially stood with the townspeople in opposition to the mine. In both 2010 and 2012, the Municipal Council approved resolutions registering their opposition, and Rancho Grande's FSLN mayor aligned publicly with resisters (Sánchez 2017, 34). As the conflict tightened, however, FSLN national party leaders pressured local officials to support the mine, and the mayor stepped away from her earlier anti-mining stance. On August 15, 2014, Ortega administration officials, including the ministers of education and environment and the vice minister of energy and mining, joined the FSLN mayors of Rancho Grande and Matagalpa at a packed public meeting in Rancho Grande in an unsuccessful attempt to quell opposition. Alluding to the prospect of an investment freeze should the government deny mine authorization, the MEM vice minister, Lorena Lanzas, declared,

> No company will come to a country to invest a great deal of money, more than 10 or 15 million dollars on a mining exploration project, and suddenly not have the right to bring it to production. So, in a certain sense, we have to guarantee that, if they find gold, they can extract it and recover the investment they have made in the country.[24]

The government, in this framing, had no choice once gold was found but to approve the environmental license.

The tenacity of Rancho Grande's resistance movement, its religious leadership, and evidence of rising strength raised the costs of authorizing approval and led to a temporary pause in project advancement. Nine days after Bishop Álvarez (2015) staged a well-attended anti-mining "pilgrimage" in Rancho Grande on October 3, 2015, presidential spokesperson and First Lady Rosario Murillo (2015) announced that the Pavón application had failed its environmental review. This victory for anti-mining forces turned out to be short-lived, however, as elite cohesion, movement fragmentation, and state impenetrability took their toll. With the 2019 arrival of Calibre Mining Corp., which bought out B2Gold and acquired the Pavón concession, a subsequent round of applications brought MARENA approval. Arguing that inadequate ore delivery would threaten the survival of the

---

were embedded in robust networks of social ties were more likely to reject mining advances and participate in anti-mining mobilizations than those who were more socially isolated.

[24] As quoted in Sosa 2015, 14.

88 BREAKING GROUND

"hungry mine"[25] at La Libertad, and developing an aggressive concession application protocol wherein they solicited over 10% of national territory in 2020 alone, Calibre Mining Corp. advanced a bold growth strategy that secured strong state support. In the context of national movement disarticulation and increased state repression, Calibre's stepped-up strategy of new concession applications and robust investment commitments tightened elite support and put the Pavón project back on track.

Scale Conflicts: The Large-Scale and Small-Scale Face-Off in La India

The third type of opposition organizing emerges at the intersection between the formal and informal sectors of the mining complex. These scale conflicts reflect tensions between industrial and small-scale miners and frequently involve rivalries over territory.

Nicaragua's 2001 mining law required companies to permit continued territorial access for small miners who traditionally operated in concessioned areas, and to allocate up to 1% of concessioned land to artisanal miners. Concession owners and artisanal miners sometimes clashed in negotiations over the demarcation of established worksites and the identification of spots where access would be granted. Because artisanal miners typically used extraction processes that involve mercury, and operated without adequate protective equipment or modern chemical recovery systems, they contributed to contamination of the zone and complicated the task of improving environmental performance in the mining sector. These issues fueled a complex relationship between industrial and artisanal/small-scale mining (World Bank 2009).

Forty percent of the economically active population in La Libertad and the neighboring town of Santo Domingo reportedly worked in artisanal or small-scale mining (B2Gold 2017b, 2). In Bonanza, that figure was 52% (Hemco and Mineros 2016, 6). Official government sources estimated in early 2018 that 20,000 people were employed in this sector (NI1118), and some external

---

[25] Mines are often composed of both extraction and processing facilities. A mine is called "hungry" when its ore processing facility does not have a sufficient supply of ore to process. Ore supplies near La Libertad were approaching exhaustion and the company was eager to find new supply sources that would keep the processing facility operating at capacity.

estimates ran even higher (Veiga et al. 2014). HEMCO reported 6,000 artisanal miners in Bonanza alone (HEMCO and Mineros 2016, 6).

Known locally as *guiriseros*, artisanal miners in Nicaragua generally work in small groups, often without licenses or oversight, and on land and riverbanks to which they had little or no legal claim. Descending into narrow shafts on hand-hewn ladders or riding down on roped-up planks, most *guiriseros* work directly in extraction, picking out and carting off buckets of rock, either for themselves or as helpers (*mozos*) assisting small miners who control a site. A subset of small mine leaders and cooperatives run rudimentary gold processing centers called *rastras* or *tómbolas*. There, extracted rock is bathed in water and ground into a slurry that is doused with mercury as an amalgamating element. As illustrated in Figure 3.2, gold is commonly extracted by hand in small balls from which the mercury is subsequently vaporized by burning. Wastewater is dumped without treatment, leading to further contamination as mercury enters waterways, where it bioaccumulates in the aquatic food chain. According to the Nicaragua government's 2018 internal studies, 4,000 *rastras* were scattered around the country (GRUN 2018).

Figure 3.2 An artisanal miner in Bonanza, Nicaragua, holding gold extracted from ore slurry using mercury as an amalgamating element. Photo by author.

90 BREAKING GROUND

As more Nicaraguan territory was concessioned to industrial mining companies, some small miners were pushed off "their" plots or threatened with expulsion. This resulted in recurring conflicts at the contact point between small miners and large-scale mines. To reduce the friction, control the use of mercury, and derive increased gain from the labor power provided by artisanal miners, large-scale mine managers in Nicaragua developed a system that formalized collaboration with artisanal miners. In return for exclusive, albeit temporary, access to designated plots on company concessions, small miner collaborators were required to organize into cooperatives; participate in health, safety, and environmental training; and bring all of their product to the company's processing facilities or to small mills specifically designed to accommodate their deposits (B2Gold 2017b; NI1918; HEMCO 2018). Use of this system expanded rapidly during the gold boom.[26]

The small miner sector generated 27% of Nicaraguan gold output in 2015, according to CAMINIC president, Sergio Ríos.[27] This sector was both vital to the expansion of the industry and, Ríos argued, a significant source of economic benefit to the community, where it promoted rural economic diversification, channeled a portion of the returns from mining into the local economy, and helped to stabilize the population more generally. At the same time, ASM activity has been associated with a host of social, economic, and environmental ills (Veiga et al. 2014; Wall 2015; Veiga and Morais 2015; IGF 2017). Earnings for ASM run far below those for formal sector mine work, and living conditions are generally much worse. According to the previously mentioned FUNIDES (2016) study, while the general incidence of multidimensional poverty in Bonanza was 34%, this figure rose to 78% for artisanal mining families—more than double the average rate for the community as a whole (p. 25).

Additional problems include the difficulty of eliminating child labor in artisanal mining sector and the heightened dangers inherent in this work, in spite of industry efforts to reduce mercury use and improve worker safety.[28] Newspapers in Nicaragua report a steady drumbeat of cave-ins and deaths at unlicensed gold mining sites. Even with efforts to promote formalization and safety training, occupational hazards remain pronounced. The Comisión

---

[26] HEMCO (2018, 7) reported 1,690 artisanal miner collaborators legally operating within its Bonanza concession in 2016, up from 295 in 2008. B2Gold (2017b, 3) reported 847 artisanal and small miners working secondary veins on its concession in La Libertad and Santo Domingo in 2017.

[27] As quoted in B2Gold 2017b, 1.

[28] Hinton (2007) reported that fatality rates in ASM were up to ninety times higher than in large-scale industrial mining.

MINING FRIENDLY: NICARAGUA   91

Municipal de Minería Artesanal Bonanza (2018, 16) reported 126 ASM accidents during 2013–2017, with 32 resulting in fatalities.

Scale conflicts between large and small miners erupted repeatedly in Nicaragua, as seen when the British mining junior Condor Gold accelerated its exploratory work in the village of La Cruz de la India in 2015. This village sprang up in an old mining zone that had been abandoned to *guiriseros* following massive flooding in 1956. By the time of the recent gold boom, a population of around 1,000 had settled there, most in some way linked to ASM.[29]

Condor Gold, frozen out of mine development in El Salvador when anti-mining mobilization halted extraction licensing there, turned its sights to Nicaragua beginning in 2006. Mining juniors in Nicaragua relied heavily on a brownfield exploration strategy, focusing their search in old mining districts to reduce costs and improve the odds of success. Condor's exploration in La India's beehive of ASM activity indicated strong commercial possibilities. In its December 2014 pre-feasibility study, Condor projected the extraction of 675,000 ounces of gold over a seven-year period, with the construction of an open pit mine that would take out the residential center of the town. The board of the World Bank's International Finance Corporation (IFC) approved a $10 million investment in the project in 2014, taking a 9% stake in the company (IFC 2014a). The company completed a 700-page environmental and social impact assessment and submitted an environmental permit application to MARENA in December 2015. PRONicaragua pledged legal assistance with clearing land titles so the company could advance quickly toward extraction (Condor Gold 2018).

As company representatives launched resettlement negotiations, local residents "woke up" to the prospect of imminent displacement (NI1618) and moved to resist. Handmade mine shafts dotted the landscape around the town and offered community members ready access to gold-laced rock. An estimated eighty artisanal mills were scattered around La India, employing on average between ten and fifteen workers (NI1618; NI0818). The prospect of industrial mining returning sixty years after its exit meant the livelihood of community residents would now be in jeopardy. As one resident explained, "Even if the new town [that the company proposed to build for them] could provide water and health services, what would we live on?" (NI1618). With

---

[29] IFC 2014a; Cuffe 2017; NI0117; NI0217; NI2818; NI1618; NI0818; community site visit on February 24, 2018; field notes from presentations by community leaders at the Conversatorio at the UCA, Managua, February 27, 2018.

92 BREAKING GROUND

heightened corporate control over access to territory and state monitoring of the use of mercury, livelihood practices woven into the fiber of community economic life were now being called into question.

In April 2016, La India activists launched their campaign against industrial mining, going house to house to survey respondents and make their case. With support from Central American allies, they shared videos produced abroad depicting the dangers of large-scale operations. When the company began to install equipment at the edge of town in early 2017, local residents ruptured the platform base and challenged the legality of the company's permit to bring it in. Tensions mounted as seven leaders were charged with "aggravated damage" to mining company property, and hundreds of community members rallied to accompany them to court. Contention resurfaced in August when the company introduced drilling equipment, now accompanied by a phalanx of police officers. In response to the 24/7 roadblock that followed, 150 riot police flooded the town on August 8, maintaining a "military-style" occupation for over three months (NI1618).

In the midst of this brewing conflict, and still waiting for approval of its environmental permit, Condor Gold announced the relocation of the open pit: full community resettlement would no longer be required (Condor Gold 2018). This revision addressed some community concerns but did little to respond to the "lack of community consultation" (NI0818) and the cultural and environmental risks associated with having a large-scale mine next door.[30] Perhaps most importantly, the new version of the project would still allow the company to deplete the area's gold resources in a seven-year production burst, diminishing access to what had been communally available ore and economic opportunities that had allowed the community to persist for decades.

Extractive struggles that pit small miners against industrial mines are a distinct subtype of conflict. Closely aligned with David Harvey's (2004) concept of *accumulation by dispossession*, these conflicts involve zero-sum struggles over the division of a finite set of resources, in which the gains of one entail losses for the other. Scale conflicts raise livelihood issues resulting from restricted access to previously established resources and the forfeiture

---

[30] Artisanal miners in La India recognized that their mercury use contaminated the environment, but they contended that those harmful consequences were small ("we contaminate, but only a little" [NI1618]) and could be addressed with retort equipment donations they hope to secure. By contrast, LSM use of cyanide-based processing was described as a highly dangerous activity ("peligrosísima") that placed the whole community at risk.

of economic independence. This interface also triggers community identity issues that are difficult to resolve. Threats include corporate appropriation of extraction sites, some of which were discovered due to ASM exploration skills, and challenges to established social status hierarchies in the ASM community, where small mill owners, local gold buyers, and informal moneylenders can be formidable opponents. At the same time, corporate alliances with the state, including access to police controls and the court system, serve to undermine local organizing and deepen political resentment and fear.

To the difficulties associated with organizing any one of these conflict variants, we must add the challenges associated with organizing across the three types. In Nicaragua, sharp variations in the circumstances that drove mining community mobilizations played a significant role in disarticulating the mining opposition network and undermining its contribution to a policy dialogue. Strikes and standoffs over union rights in mining towns did not cohere with community protests designed to prevent the encroachment of mining altogether. And neither form of opposition connected easily with movements to protect and promote artisanal mining. Without solid national alliances to promote frame alignment and movement bricolage, the prospects were limited for finding common ground and coordinating mobilization across distributive, definitional, and scale conflicts.[31] The opportunities to advance proposals and secure a policy response were further undermined by the absence of robust docking points, the topic to which we now turn.

Docking Points: Institutional Spaces for Inserting Demands

As described in Chapter 2, the final piece of my three-part argument focuses on the availability of docking points. Policy impact requires more than the activation of protest movements or the construction of a cohesive resistance network. The ability of citizens to influence policy ultimately requires

---

[31] With support from the Humboldt Center and Catholic Church activists, leaders from the Guardianes de Yaoska (Matagalpa), Salvemos Santo Domingo (Chontales), Movimiento Comunal Santa Cruz de La India (León), Movimiento San Antonio (Nuevo Segovia), and Llegó la Hora de Acción del Pueblo (Nueva Segovia) came together to announce formation of the National Movement Against Industrial Mining (MONAFMI) in 2017. Movement formalization did not produce a sustained mechanism for strategic collaboration, however, and left a tangle of unanswered questions about social and environmental goals and policy objectives.

94   BREAKING GROUND

access to institutional actors—those candidates and elected officials, committee chairs and record keepers, bureaucrats and budget authorities, legal representatives and judges who serve as the final gatekeepers in the policy process (Giugni 2004; Amenta 2006; Biggs and Andrews 2015; Bosi, Giugni, and Uba 2016). The space to engage state actors in the institutional locations where policy gets made is the third and final element of my analytical framework.

Formally, post-revolutionary Nicaragua constructed an open political system characterized by multiparty competition and leadership rotation, with state policies and decisions that were susceptible to citizen influence. Political participation ran strong, with average turnout of registered voters topping 74% in the seven presidential elections held between 1984 and 2016.[32] In the decades following the reestablishment of municipal elections at the end of the 1980s, local governments became directly responsible to their communities and acquired a degree of financial and administrative autonomy (Prado and Mejía 2009; Prado 2020). Some towns were able to develop independent initiatives and secure their own financial flows, including funding from international sources (Anderson and Park 2018). In the heyday of decentralization during the Bolaños administration, the 2003 Citizen Participation Law (#475) added community participation mechanisms to encourage local-level involvement in municipal policy discussions.

Although national-level politics undercut democratic contestation through the construction of elite pacts (Close 2016), as with the Olivos Pact in 2000 between outgoing president Arnoldo Alemán and soon-to-return president Daniel Ortega, local-level political leaders displayed a measure of independence, even when hailing from the same political party as national leaders. Even after Ortega returned to the presidency in 2007, Leslie E. Anderson (2010, 7) concluded that Ortega was "held in check" by three "countercurrents": the legislature, which the FSLN did not initially control; Sandinista defectors, who served as forceful critics; and the independence of the mayors operating at the local level, initially including those from within the FSLN.

Increasingly centralized control over the state apparatus in the 2010s, however, soon led these democratic openings to narrow. Citizen

---

[32] Voting is not compulsory in Nicaragua. Turnout data are from the International Institute for Democracy and Electoral Assistance (IDEA, www.idea.int). Turnout estimates by the Instituto para el Desarrollo y la Democracia (IPADE 2012, 12), which excludes null ballots, offer a similar finding (72.1%) for the five presidential races held in the 1990–2011 period.

MINING FRIENDLY: NICARAGUA   95

participation mechanisms created in the early 2000s proved difficult to activate (Babinia and Sirias 2010) and were replaced under Ortega with local Citizens Power Councils (CPCs; later, Family Cabinets), a top-down mechanism that had a distinctly partisan flavor (Prado and Mejía 2009; Stuart Almendárez 2010; Close 2016).[33] Unlike other countries in Latin America, where legal opportunities for grassroots referenda and indigenous rights commitments under ILO 169 created spaces for direct participation in consultation processes (and court challenges in their absence), Nicaragua provided few institutional opportunities for organized citizens to exercise leverage over local development, even in formally autonomous regions and indigenous communities (Baracco 2019). By the 2010s, mayors and city council members, increasingly aligned with the FSLN, were pressured to follow the lead of the national authorities, further closing up spaces for independent action within the dominant party (Prado 2020; Sánchez and Osorio Mercado 2020).[34]

Laws and constitutional provisions limiting the concentration of power went unenforced. The judicial and electoral authorities became closely aligned with the president's party and offered no check on presidential power. The Sala Constitucional de la Corte Suprema de Justicia (CSJ), claiming that term limits violated constitutional rights, permitted Ortega to run for the presidency again in 2011 in spite of the constitutional prohibitions on consecutive and third terms. The FSLN moved to purge dissidents in a series of party congresses, and the party fell increasingly under the control of Ortega and close allies (Martí 2010). Strong party discipline meant that those who did not follow party directives lost political rights and were removed from office (Sánchez and Osorio Mercado 2020). After the FSLN's electoral sweep in 2016, when the party took seventy-one of the ninety-two national assembly seats, the legislature became a rubber stamp.

The opportunities for grassroots activists to organize in defiance of national FSLN preferences were strikingly limited, especially in comparison with those available to citizens elsewhere in Central America. In Costa Rica, Guatemala, and El Salvador, anti-mining activists were turning to the courts, holding local referenda, and scaling up into national networks

---

[33] Drawing on results from a M&R public opinion poll, Stuart Almendárez (2010, 37) noted that eight out of every ten respondents who participated in CPCs indicated that they sympathized with or had voted for the FSLN.

[34] Eighty-eight percent (135 out of 153) of the *municipios* in Nicaragua were governed by FSLN mayors in 2017 (Prado 2020, 153).

96 BREAKING GROUND

to gain access and policy influence. Although well-networked community movements in Nicaragua could momentarily impact government decisions, as in Rancho Grande, their impact was local and temporary. In the end, civil society activism played little role in national mining policy deliberation or regulatory decisions. Intermediate state actors (courts, agencies, municipal governments) lacked the legal space and political autonomy required to promote transparency or intervene.

This limited impact was not due to the lack of familiarity with mining protest dynamics in neighboring countries. To the contrary, the leaders of mining opposition movements in Nicaragua reported following the work of their counterparts in the region with great interest. Asked, in 2015, about how Rancho Grande's anti-mining movement designed its mobilization strategy, a Guardianes de Yaoska leader described their efforts to learn from and replicate the opposition techniques deployed in neighboring countries (NI0615). Like their counterparts elsewhere in Central America, Rancho Grande activists attempted to use national courts to advance their claims. With legal assistance from the national human rights organization CENIDH, they filed for an injunction to prevent mine authorization in January 2015, calling on the district court to halt the issuance of the El Pavón permit due to health and environmental concerns and the absence of community consultation. Unlike the case with resisters in Guatemala and Costa Rica, however, where legal strategies led to the suspension of mining operations, the injunction request in Nicaragua failed to advance (NI0615; Centro Humboldt 2015; Recurso de Amparo 2015).

Nicaraguan organizers also traveled to El Salvador to observe preparations for a community mining referendum (NI0615), but local-level consultation options were more constrained at home. In both El Salvador and Guatemala, mining opponents took advantage of municipal codes that included provisions for local-level plebiscites. No such legal mechanisms existed in Nicaragua. Efforts to scale up local networks to the national level, as occurred in El Salvador, also came to naught, in part because of the effectiveness of the Nicaraguan state in containing protest activities. When CAMINIC, MEM, and PRONicaragua hosted their first International Mining Congress in Managua in August 2014, mining opponents attempted to coordinate a national protest. Caravans of mining opponents headed to Managua from Matagalpa and Chontales, with banners proclaiming "Protejamos Nuestra Madre Tierra" (Let's Protect Our Mother Earth). The national government moved fast to avoid dilution of affirmative messaging to prospective investors. Would-be protesters were detained on the road, with driver's licenses and vehicle registrations confiscated, long before they approached the entrances to the capital city (NI0215; NI0415; NI0615; Pérez González 2015, 79).

Democratic Deterioration and Deepening Conflict

In April 2018, the political situation worsened. A forest fire raging in the Indio Maíz Biological Reserve sparked a student movement demanding government action to protect the area. Students mobilized again a week later when the government unilaterally decreed a reform decreasing benefits and raising costs in the social security system following pressure by international financial institutions to address a projected funding shortfall. The student protest was met with attacks by shock forces and the police, which sparked further mobilization. Huge throngs began to attend the protest marches, with many participants calling for Ortega and Rosario Murillo, his wife and now vice president, to resign.

The death toll climbed as Hilux trucks filled with heavily armed and masked men patrolled the streets and snipers intermixed with police picked off protesters and bystanders. Moral indignation and the need to protect their communities led the *autoconvocados* (self-convened) to build barricades in the roadways and defend them with mostly homemade weapons. As police and paramilitary forces bore down on the protesters, human rights violations increased and were widely documented. A six-month investigation carried out in the aftermath by an expert group appointed by the Inter-American Commission on Human Rights, the OAS, and the Nicaraguan government (GIEI 2018) found that the clash had led to at least 109 deaths, 1,400 wounded, and 690 imprisoned just in the first six weeks. By 2020, the death toll had reportedly tripled, and over 100,000 had gone into exile (IACHR 2020, 17).

As repeated rounds of negotiation failed, the regime deepened the divide by prohibiting public protest and canceling the legal registration of many of the country's best-established civil society and human rights organizations. Additional restrictions were approved as Nicaragua's 2021 presidential election came into view, including laws that required NGO leaders who received foreign funding to register as foreign agents and legislation barring anyone who had endorsed economic sanctions or called for Ortega's

98   BREAKING GROUND

removal from running for public office.[35] The 2021 detention of all major opposition candidates, along with the arrest of prominent business and civic leaders, demonstrated how far the regime had departed from the formal requirements of electoral democracy. As officials tightened their control over the political system, independent NGOs (including the Humboldt Center) lost their legal status, and docking points for civil society all but vanished.

Meanwhile, mining investment continued with only a brief interruption imposed by the social distancing requirements of COVID-19. Without the docking points that allowed mining critics elsewhere to press demands for legally stipulated carve-out zones in environmentally vulnerable or residential areas, and absent meaningful public deliberation and consultation, Nicaraguan extraction projects grew apace.

Interpreting Mining Conflict in Nicaragua

As elsewhere in Latin America, the mining boom in Nicaragua gave rise to new investments and community conflicts. Company managers, hoping to reduce local wariness, hired public relations professionals to improve communications and deploy affirmative messaging. Over time, they became increasingly attentive to management "soft issues," replacing foreign managers with experienced nationals and adding new administrative units to focus on community relations and social service delivery. Companies donated millions for paving roads, building houses, collecting garbage, opening landfills, and reforesting damaged territory in order to secure an elusive social license. The mining business chamber, CAMINIC, coordinated sectoral efforts, negotiating policy planning with the government and commissioning studies to quantify the economic benefits associated with the industry (see, for example, FUNIDES 2016; Avendaño 2017).

Through it all, the government played a critical role in bolstering mine development. In addition to the fiscal and regulatory exemptions, labor

---

[35] Nicaragua's political crisis contributed to an escalation of US pressures and sanctions, including adoption of the Nicaragua Human Rights and Anticorruption Act of 2018, which prohibited US support for multilateral loans to Nicaragua, and the designation of targeted financial restrictions under the Global Magnitsky Human Rights Accountability Act. Sanctions were imposed on high-level government officials, including Vice President Murillo, several of the Ortega Murillo children, and the Nicaraguan National Police, among others (Taft-Morales 2021). Officials and investments in the gold sector were explicitly targeted by the Trump and Biden administrations under US Executive Order 13851 and its revisions.

stability guarantees, and quick response times that drew investment to the country, state actors provided multiple forms of discursive support. They highlighted mining achievements in national planning documents, displayed visible presidential approval at the inauguration of new processing plants, co-sponsored international mining congresses, and incorporated mine representatives in celebratory public events. To ensure that the mine-friendly perspective of state leaders reached down into the mining communities, the national government exerted top-down executive pressure on local FSLN officials, as in Rancho Grande, requiring them to detach from community preferences and adhere to the pro-mining position adopted by the national leadership. When resistance levels grew, state capacity to defer or recalibrate conflict, as seen with the temporary denial of environmental authorization for the Pavón mine, gave way to behind-the-scenes negotiations and coercive practices that forced dissenters to desist. This political landscape was strikingly unfavorable for mining resisters, who confronted three major obstacles.

First, Nicaraguan elites displayed high levels of support for mining, both within and across administrations and between the political and the economic elite. Throughout these decades of political change, the FSLN remained supportive of metallic mining, an activity it had controlled directly during the period of the revolution and that it advocated for after returning to power. Although formally anchoring divergent positions on the ideological spectrum, the FSLN and opposing parties joined forces in support of market reforms during the post-revolutionary transition and concurred on the development potential of the mining industry. They presented mining investment as a mechanism that could absorb underemployed labor associated with military demobilization following the contra war and the economic dislocation associated with neoliberal transition. All four post-revolutionary presidents endorsed incentives and protections that encouraged the entry of mining investment. They all provided the sector with organizational space and official recognition on boards and commissions where mining-related policy was negotiated. And they all celebrated the progress of the industry as growing swaths of national territory were concessioned and moved into production.

A rupture in the government's official alliance with the business class following the 2018 political crisis points to disruption in the established dynamics of elite cohesion. But the elite consensus about extractive sector development, with its mine-friendly mentality and commitment to limited regulatory intervention, remained unbroken across the post-revolutionary period. The breakdown of elite consensus over the management of political conflict did not imply a rupture in the elite agreement about the economic model. Nicaragua's underlying political settlement in favor of mining continued to hold, thwarting movement toward improved regulation and inclusionary participation.

Second, mining resistance forces, while cropping up repeatedly in different regions of the country, were locally focused and organizationally fragmented. Mining opposition in Nicaragua possessed limited territorial reach and remained largely community-based. Movement composition and goals differed by town, with three distinct variations taking root. Distributive conflicts, which focused on disputes over wages, the cost of services, and revenue transfers, erupted in communities with well-established mines, where the desirability of mining was not in question but rent distribution sometimes was. Definitional conflicts emerged in agricultural communities with no mining tradition and where extractivism was perceived as harmful to local livelihoods and values. Finally, scale conflicts developed in established mining areas where artisanal and small mining actors butted up against large mining investors, sparking new tensions over access to mineral resources and control over social hierarchies. These differences in frames and objectives made it difficult for protesters to fashion a shared agenda, with predictable consequences in terms of policy impact.

Third, the scarcity of institutional "docking points," into which organized citizens could insert their claims, made the prospects for regulatory restriction yet more remote. Unlike other Central American countries where mining protesters could use party ties and electoral processes to embed proposals in official deliberations, or where institutional openings required officials to deliver information or issue a formal response, Nicaragua was marked by institutional opacity and regime insularity. Institutionally, Nicaragua lacked legislation permitting the holding of local referenda or allowing citizen groups to initiate the introduction of bills for legislative deliberation. Its courts were largely inaccessible to public interest claimants and failed to serve as a check on the powerful. In spite of well-known abuses and reports of corruption, no ombudsman or UN-sponsored monitor provided independent oversight or review. Electorally, mining opponents had few options as the country's political parties proved unable to absorb grassroots demands and as party competition withered.

Over the course of the post-revolutionary period, Nicaragua shifted from a system of low-intensity democracy toward a system of electoral authoritarianism. As defined by Andreas Schedler (2006, 3), electoral authoritarian regimes "play the game of multiparty elections by holding regular elections for the chief executive and a national legislative assembly. Yet they violate the liberal-democratic principles of freedom and fairness so profoundly and systematically as to render elections instruments of authoritarian rule." The Nicaraguan political system, never fully inclusive nor transparent, became increasingly authoritarian following Ortega's return to the presidency in 2007 (Pérez-Baltodano 2012; Close 2016; Martí 2018; Sánchez and Osorio Mercado 2020).

Unlike other Central American cases, in which mining opponents could find common cause with a political party ally and secure representation in elected bodies, or embed testimony about environmental damage in court or commission proceedings and secure regulatory intervention to ensure community consultation, Nicaragua offered few opportunities for such issue docking. Facing the sunk costs of its mining history, elite consensus in support of continued mine promotion, fragmentation of resistance, and limited access to lawmakers, the courts, and regulatory agencies, Nicaraguan mining critics were unable to launch a significant movement in favor of tightened environmental regulation, a slowdown on new projects, or consultation with affected communities. Protest episodes did not precipitate a policy shift, or even meaningful policy debate.

Production in Nicaragua's gold sector continued to attract attention and outpace that in neighboring countries. International investors migrated over to Nicaragua after mining was banned in Costa Rica (2010) and El Salvador (2017). New players were drawn to the area by supportive government agencies and prospects of high return. Sustained exploration work pointed toward future growth, as mining projects, in territories both inside and outside the traditional mining zones, continue to advance.

102 BREAKING GROUND

Appendix 3.1 Nicaragua: List of Cited Interviews

Code	Affiliation	Sector	Interview date	Location
NI0118	Former president	Government—executive	February 12, 2018	Masaya
NI0318	Humboldt Center	Civil society—environmental	February 7, 2018	Managua
NI0418	Independent researcher	Academic	February 6, 2018	Managua
NI0818	Movimiento Comunal Santa Cruz de la India	Civil society—anti-mining	February 9, 2018	Managua
NI0918	IEEPP	Civil society—policy research	February 9, 2018	Managua
NI1018	COPADES	Economic analysis	February 9, 2018	Managua
NI1118	Presidency	Government—executive	February 8, 2018	Managua
NI1218	B2Gold	Business—mining company	February 20, 2018	Managua
NI1418	Humboldt Center	Civil society—environmental	February 27, 2018	Managua
NI1518	MEM	Government—executive	February 23, 2018	Managua
NI1618	Movimiento Comunal Santa Cruz de la India	Civil society—anti-mining	February 24, 2018	La India
NI1818	HEMCO	Business—mining company	March 1–2, 2018	Bonanza
NI1918	HEMCO	Business—mining company	March 1, 2018	Bonanza
NI2118	Rastra owner	Business—small mill	March 1, 2018	Bonanza (Los Cocos)
NI2218	HEMCO—"spot" holder	Business—small miner	March 1, 2018	Bonanza
NI2318	CAMINIC	Business—mining association	February 15, 2018	Managua
NI2418	Former minister	Government—executive	February 16, 2018	Managua
NI2818	Condor Gold	Business—mining company	February 21, 2018	Managua
NI3018	CST-JBE	Labor union	March 2, 2018	Managua
NI0117	World Bank Group	IGO	September 11, 2017	Washington, DC
NI0217	World Bank Group	IGO	September 11, 2017	Washington, DC

MINING FRIENDLY: NICARAGUA   103

Appendix 3.1 Continued

Code	Affiliation	Sector	Interview date	Location
NI0317	Rancho Grande church official	Civil society—religious	August 9, 2017	Guatemala (via Facebook)
NI0116	Rancho Grande church official	Civil society—religious	February 5, 2016	Guatemala (via Facebook)
NI0215	Grupo Venancia	Civil society—women's movement	June 23, 2015	Matagalpa
NI0415	ADDAC	Civil society—development	June 23, 2015	Matagalpa
NI0615	Guardianes de Yaoska	Civil society—environmental	June 24, 2015	Rancho Grande
NI0715	Mayor's office	Government—municipal	June 24, 2015	Rancho Grande
NI0815	Rancho Grande church official	Civil society—religious	June 24, 2015	Rancho Grande
NI0312	CAMINIC	Business—mining association	December 12, 2012	Managua
NI0812	PRONicaragua	Government—investment promotion	December 13, 2012	Managua

4

Mining, Maybe

Intermittent Mining in Guatemala

This chapter focuses on the political logistics of mining development in settings where the industry has advanced in a discontinuous fashion. It draws on the Guatemalan case to trace the developments that promoted the growth of mining activities in the opening phase but that shifted to impede mining advancement as the sector developed. Here, initially robust mining activities slowed and faced a temporary suspension but were not permanently halted or banned by law. This variation, characterized by its stop-and-go patterns, illustrates the operation of a second model of mining development, the *intermittent approval framework*.

Guatemala pursued pro-mining development in the wake of its 1996 peace process, and extractive sector investments increased substantially during the commodity boom. This dynamic followed the now-familiar formula described in detail in Chapter 2. As in Nicaragua, *strong elite consensus* bolstered mining development, while *resistance forces remained fragmented,* and mining critics had *limited access to docking points.* The outcome was eager exploration and a rapid initial takeoff of mine development.

Elite support for the industry was affirmed in Guatemala's 1985 constitution and expressed in mine-friendly legislation and investment promotion activities. Strong backing came from Guatemala's powerful business association, which opened space internally for mining company membership. The business chamber proved a forceful advocate in negotiations with the government, and president after president defended extraction-oriented policies. Resistance grew as mining projects secured state authorization, but organizing was reactive, not proactive, and largely confined to the local level. Opposition networks lacked national-level brokers who could link up disconnected nodes and negotiate frame alignment. Public access to policymakers through political parties and state institutions was limited by the exclusionary nature of Guatemalan politics and the thin and underfunded character of the state apparatus, which routinely defaulted to

Breaking Ground. Rose J. Spalding, Oxford University Press. © Oxford University Press 2023.
DOI: 10.1093/oso/9780197643150.003.0004

business preferences. This combination of elite support and ineffective opposition allowed Guatemala to become a Central American leader in gold production during the 2006–2011 period.

But unlike in the Nicaraguan case discussed in Chapter 3, mining opponents in Guatemala proved capable of adapting their resistance strategies, and they gained momentum as they did. Never achieving the national-level organizational capacity that emerged in Costa Rica (discussed in Chapter 5) and El Salvador (discussed in Chapter 6), Guatemalan mining resisters did succeed in building multisectoral coalitions. Anti-mining clusters brought together indigenous rights activists, Catholic Church officials, local community leaders, and national organizers promoting environmental and human rights. Postwar Guatemala also received international governmental and nongovernmental support for ongoing institutional development, which promoted new spaces for public participation.

With local and international support, docking points associated with strategic litigation and activist courts expanded. Although mining resistance networks were not cohesive enough and state penetrability was not high enough to instigate a formal national debate over extractivist policy, repeated bouts of conflict produced both licensing moratoriums and mine suspensions, and stymied the growth of the sector. By 2018, the production of precious metals had ground to a halt in Guatemala, and mining development was placed on pause.

This confluence of processes led to a disrupted and intermittent pattern of metallic mining advancement. In this model, mining is initially endorsed by a curated coalition of political and economic elites, but support for mining is countered over time through the construction of multiple centers of opposition. The subordinate status and sparse presence of opponents in official circles leave them unable to reshape the national policy direction. But institutional adaptations open up spaces during policy implementation that serve to disrupt the consolidation of a pro-mining framework, at least temporarily.

What follows is a description of mining policy and mining activities in Guatemala that highlights the three features addressed in my argument. The first section focuses on the character of pro-mining elite networks that persisted during this period. The second section analyzes the shape of the dispersed resistance networks that emerged alongside mining advances. Next, the chapter explores the docking strategies that led to mining interruption. The last section reviews and summarizes the findings. Through rigorous process tracing, this chapter points to a second model of mining policy

106 BREAKING GROUND

advancement, in which elite pro-mining consensus, resistance fragmentation, and docking through the judicial process led to mining development combined with periodic reversals.[1]

Elite Support and Extractivist Ascendance in Guatemala

As elsewhere in the region, Guatemalan gold and silver extraction during pre-Columbian times continued in the colonial era, when extractivist accumulation activated a region-wide search for deposits. Exploration took place across the Central American isthmus, with resources in Honduras attracting particular attention in the centuries that followed (Soto 2011, 92; Bulmer-Thomas 1987, 320–321). Although colonial-era mining took place in Guatemala and continued into the twentieth century, production there lagged behind that in Honduras and Nicaragua. Gold export in Guatemala was relatively modest, with production "mainly used in the country for minting, jewelry and sacred goods" (Soto 2011, 93). In the 1934–1954 period, even El Salvador produced higher value added in the mining and quarrying sector. Guatemala's extended period of military conflict and genocidal war (1961–1996) sped the exit of foreign mining interests and further depressed extractive sector activities. The military assault on indigenous communities during the war, inspired by a combination of anti-communism, brutal racism, and territorial acquisitiveness, led to destruction of over 440 Mayan villages and over 200,000 killings and disappearances, 93% reportedly at the hands of state agents (CEH 1999).

As the process of ending the civil war advanced, political and economic elites moved to open the country up for mining, embedding language in support of the activity in the emerging legal framework (see Table 4.1). The 1985 constitution, written under the military government by a Constituent Assembly composed largely of right-wing, pro-market forces (Brinks and Blass 2018, 127), affirmed a commitment to mining development. Article 125

---

[1] This chapter draws on fifty-four semistructured interviews conducted in Guatemala and the United States between 2015 and 2018. See Appendix 4.1 for a list of the interviews cited in this chapter. This chapter also draws on information posted to Guatemalan NGO websites; reports by government agencies and international human rights monitors; newspaper archives; corporate reports and mining company press releases; legal filings in domestic and international venues, including *Kappes/KCA v. Guatemala*; and public opinion data compiled by multiple sources. For additional information about the research methodology, see the "Argument and Methods" section in Chapter 1.

Table 4.1 Guatemalan Mining Policy Timeline

Mining Policies and Related Actions (Year)	Presidential Administration and Political Party/Coalition	Term
Constitution (1985)	Mejía Víctores, Brigadier General, chief of state	1983–1986
Environmental protection law approved (1986)	Cerezo, Christian Democrat	1986–1991
ILO 169 ratified in Guatemala (1996) Mining Law approved (1997)	Arzú, PAN	1996–2000
MARN established (2000) Decentralization laws approved (2002) MEM granted Marlin Mine extraction license (2003)	Portillo, FRG	2000–2004
Grassroots mining *consultas* began (2004) Presidential declaration that mining is in national interest (2007) MEM granted Cerro Blanco Mine extraction license (2007) Constitutional Court ruled that consultation is legal but not binding (2007) CICIG established (2007)	Berger, GANA	2004–2008
Constitutional Court ruled seven articles in Mining Law unconstitutional (2008) Inter-American Commission on Human Rights called on government to suspend Marlin Mine (2008) MEM granted Progreso VII Mine extraction license (2011)	Colom, UNE	2008–2012
Voluntary royalties negotiated (2012) MEM granted Escobal Mine extraction license (2013) President declared two-year moratorium on new mining licenses to prepare new mining law (2013)	Pérez Molina, PP	2012–2015
Progreso VII license suspended by Supreme Court (2016) Suspension of Progreso VII sustained by Constitutional Court (2017) Marlin Mine closed (2017) Escobal license suspended by Supreme Court (2017) Suspension of Escobal sustained by Constitutional Court (2018) Kappes, Cassiday & Associates filed ICSID case against Guatemala (2018) CICIG closed (2019)	Morales, FCN	2016–2020
MEM began pre-consultation with Xinka Parliament regarding Escobal Mine (2021)	Giammattei, VAMOS	2020–2024

108 BREAKING GROUND

stated, "The technical and rational exploitation of hydrocarbons, minerals, and other non-renewable natural resources is declared to be of public utility and necessity. The State will establish and propitiate the conditions for their exploration, exploitation, and commercialization" (República de Guatemala 1985).

The peace accord, signed in 1996 under President Álvaro Arzú, led to military demobilization and a push for economic recovery. Arzú, a former mayor of Guatemala City who hailed from Guatemala's traditional oligarchy, led the move for privatization in electricity, telecommunication, airlines, and railroads as the Guatemalan government embraced neoliberal reform. This new juncture permitted negotiation of legislation to encourage mining investment.

Guatemala's 1997 Mining Law included an array of features that were commonly sought by mining companies. This mining-friendly legislation reduced royalties from 6% to 1%, to be split evenly between the national and municipal governments, and permitted fully foreign-owned mine development. It established a short window for the MEM to respond to license applications (thirty days) and permitted administrative silence (inaction) to be interpreted as approval of pending applications. It allowed mine concessions to be granted in protected areas and on land held by indigenous communities. Companies were not required to notify landowners of their activities during the reconnaissance or exploration stages. The law and its regulatory stipulations required a full environmental impact assessment (EIA) only in the final stage of the process, when extraction permits were solicited. Monitoring and remediation depended on corporate self-assessment and did not require independent or third-party review (Aldana and Abate 2016; ICEFI 2016).

International best practices in mine development (social impact assessment, plan for health and safety, plan for employment and skills development, plan for community and local business development, and plan for reclamation and rehabilitation) were all missing, as was legislation regarding water pricing and regulation (UNCTAD 2011, 104–109). Although Guatemala had ratified ILO 169 in 1996 and was obliged to ensure prior consultation when development projects affected indigenous communities, the mining law failed to include discussion of a consultation process, leaving the public participation requirement unaddressed (Yagenova 2014, 20; Aldana and Abate 2016).

This new law attracted a swarm of exploration companies, leading quickly to the location of commercially viable gold deposits in several parts of the country. Montana Exploradora de Guatemala became the production pioneer, introducing gold extraction at the Marlin Mine in the Western Highlands in 2004. As the local affiliate of Canadian mining company Glamis Gold, Montana acquired concessions and land titles in the *municipios* of San Miguel Ixtahuacán and Sipacapa in the department of San Marcos, and secured an extraction permit from the MEM on November 29, 2003.[2] This licensing agreement placed the opening of Guatemala's new gold mining industry into the middle of indigenous territory.

To support mine development, Montana secured a $45 million investment from the World Bank's International Finance Corporation in 2004. World Bank policy encouraged the introduction of extractive sector activities in new territories, and IFC investments helped industries overcome uncertainties through financing and partnership. IFC protocols were designed to introduce international standards and benchmarks in new extractive sites and help emerging mines attract international investment attention. Proving success of concept, Montana was acquired by the Canadian mining company Goldcorp, the number two gold mining company in North America, in 2006. As the Marlin Mine entered into full production, Guatemala jumped out of the gate as the region's largest gold producer, quickly surpassing Nicaragua, as seen in Figure 4.1.

Precious metal mining investments quickly spread to other parts of the country. The Goldcorp portfolio soon included the Cerro Blanco project in southeastern Guatemala near the border with El Salvador, which received an extraction permit in 2007. On behalf of Radius Gold, the Guatemalan subsidiary Exploraciones Mineras de Guatemala (EXMINGUA) acquired an extraction permit in 2011 for Progreso VII Derivada, its proposed open pit gold mine in the El Tambor zone, located in the department of Guatemala, just north of Guatemala City. Meanwhile, Minera San Rafael S.A. (MSR), the local affiliate of Canadian mining company (and Goldcorp offshoot) Tahoe Resources, secured an extraction permit in 2013 for an underground silver mine, El Escobal, which was located in the *municipio* of San Rafael Las Flores in the department of Santa Rosa. All of these mines soon registered

---

[2] Sipacapa is the official spelling of the name of the *municipio*. Indigenous leaders of the community and activists use an alternative spelling, Sipakapa, which is adopted in the rest of this chapter.

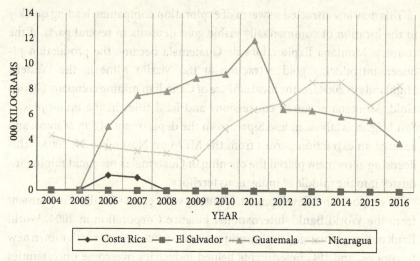

Figure 4.1 Central American gold output by country and year (2004–2016). Data from USGS, *Minerals Yearbook Volume III: Area Reports—International—Latin America and Canada,* various years.

political, legal, and/or technical difficulties. None was in active production as of mid-2022.

Business Elite Organization and Advocacy

As I argued in Chapter 2, mine development does not occur just because of rising prices or growing demand; it responds to a complex interplay of political processes, beginning with the endorsement by national elites. Mine development received strong backing from Guatemalan business elites, who played a forceful role in defending mining interests.

The literature on economic elites in Guatemala divides the sector into a traditional cluster, composed of families that were prominent in the nineteenth and early twentieth centuries and historically anchored in agroexport production, and a cluster that emerged subsequently in the industrial, service, and financial sectors, associated with new forms of internationalization (Dosal 1995; Paige 1998; Segovia 2005; Casaús Arzú 2006; Bull, Castellacci, and Kasahara 2014; Valdez 2015; Díaz 2016). These segments were interlinked through business dealings and political interests, and both were represented in Guatemala's powerful business peak association, the

Comité Coordinador de Asociaciones Agrícolas, Comerciales, Industriales y Financieras (CACIF), which served as the sector's public voice.

Formed in 1957, CACIF brought together business associations from agribusiness, commerce, industry, and finance to create a united business front in the wake of the Guatemalan Revolution of 1944–1954. The organization's self-description emphasizes the role of threat in the founders' decision to combine forces.[3] Organizational catalysts included the 1957 assassination of General Carlos Castillo Armas, the military leader whose 1954 invasion triggered the resignation of the Arbenz government and the end of the Guatemalan Revolution.[4] Ongoing threats, including murders and kidnappings of business elites during the subsequent waves of civil war, reinforced CACIF's militant anti-communism and hyperpoliticization.

As documented elsewhere in Latin America, business associations forged in response to perceived class-based threats tend to develop relatively high levels of unity and cohesion (Schneider 2004; Ondetti 2021). Competing priorities created periodic tensions, but Guatemala's business sector successfully used CACIF to promote the projection of consensus. Academic and policy analysts regularly call attention to CACIF's outsized political role and influence (McCleary 1999; Schneider 2012; ICEFI 2015b; Bull and Aguilar-Støen 2015).[5] As Alexander Segovia (2019) notes, "There is an academic consensus that the most powerful elites in Central America, with the most influence, the most hegemonic, and the ones least disposed to social change, were the Guatemalans." A 2006 cable from the US Embassy in Guatemala concluded similarly, noting that CACIF "has been the dominant business voice for the last four decades," and "has had extraordinary power over Guatemala's political and economic destiny, whether it gets directly involved or through its proxies in the government and Congress."[6]

CACIF played a direct role in defining public policy, particularly in the fiscal arena, where the association's enduring success in preventing tax

---

[3] See CACIF, "Nuestra Historia," https://www.cacif.org.gt/nuestra-historia, accessed September 14, 2021.

[4] The Guatemalan Revolution of 1944–1954 was a democratic experience that introduced labor and land reforms under the presidencies of Juan José Arévalo and Jacobo Arbenz. This short-lived transition was overthrown by a combination of US cold war interventionism and Guatemalan military action, and was followed by three decades of military rule.

[5] The decision by CACIF leaders to reject the auto-coup by President Jorge Antonio Serrano in 1993 played a significant role in his ouster (McCleary 1999). CACIF's call for Otto Pérez Molina's resignation in 2015, following a tidal wave of corruption allegations, also made the tarnished president's political isolation clear, hastening his departure from office and arrest.

[6] Cable 06GUATEMALA431, March 1, 2006, WikiLeaks, http://wikileaks.wikimee.net/cable/2006/03/06GUATEMALA431.html, accessed June 24, 2021.

112 BREAKING GROUND

increases has drawn close analytical attention. Guatemalan tax revenues totaled only 10.3% of GDP in 2009, one of the lowest levels in Latin America, and were no higher than they had been in 1998, in spite of commitments in the peace accord to increased services and revenue generation (ICEFI 2015b, 78). The opposition of CACIF leaders to fiscal reform, made evident in the chamber's strategy of repeatedly filing for injunctions against legislated increases, played a major role in preserving the country's long history of low tax collection.[7] Due to these persistent legal challenges, the Guatemalan tax system remained stunted and regressive (Schneider 2012). Revenues depended heavily on the general value-added tax, whose burden fell most heavily on the poor. Low corporate and income tax rates and high tax evasion levels kept Guatemalan social services chronically underfunded while facilitating wealth accumulation at the top.

CACIF's power was, in part, a reflection of the weakness of other actors, including political parties. As noted in Stein et al. (2006, 98):

> The business sector plays a role in policymaking throughout Latin America, but nowhere more than in Guatemala. . . . The ability of Guatemalan business to influence the policymaking process rests on the fact that it is the best-organized sector in the country, and has been since colonial times, when power resided in the hands of large farmers and traders. The effectiveness of the Guatemalan business sector contrasts with the limitations of other organized sectors of society and of the State itself. Unions, peasant and indigenous movements, public servants, academics, and much of the rest of civil society have had limited influence throughout much of Guatemala's modern history.

Although the business sector failed to develop its "own" political party to advance its preferred candidates, the absence of any strong party on the left made business partisan organizing less necessary for the preservation of elite power. Business interests exerted ideological influence through alternative mechanisms, including mainstream media ownership and a network of avatars in think tanks and universities.[8] The Universidad Francisco

---

[7] According to an ICEFI (2015b) study of fiscal policy in Guatemala, of the seventy legal claims for an injunction against a tax increase for violating the constitution in the 2000–2003 period, forty-three (61%) were brought by CACIF, a business chamber, or a company.

[8] Prominent think tanks on the right include the Centro de Estudios Económicos y Sociales (CEES), the Centro de Investigaciones Económicas Nacionales (CIEN), and the Fundación para el Desarrollo (FUNDESA), among others.

Marroquín, founded by libertarian business leader Manuel Ayau in 1971 with financial support from a network of prominent business allies, played a notable role in elite ideological formation. The university provided an alternative to public and religious universities and actively promoted a promarket agenda; all of its students, regardless of their area of study, had required classes on the virtues of a free market system, with an emphasis on the anti-statist ideas of Mises and Hayek (Marroquín and Thomas 2015, 464). Network analysis of the leadership of Guatemala's major right-wing think tanks has found strong connections with a sector of local CEOs and corporate board members, who serve as funders, directors, and allies (Fischer and Waxenecker 2020).

Guatemalan business leaders also connected to government officials by running for office themselves (as in the case of Arzú and Berger), making strategic campaign contributions, and paying salary supplements to top state officials. CACIF officials served as key advisers and cabinet members, as seen in President Alejandro Giammattei's 2020 appointment of former CACIF president Roberto Antonio Malouf Morales as his first minister of the economy and coordinator of the cabinet. Businesses released their executives to take stints in the technical ministries, and permitted their smooth return after this period of service was rendered (GT1318). These financial flows and informal links gave business leaders what Segovia (2005, 90) called a perceived "derecho de picaporte" (right to knock and be received).

CACIF included nine sectoral chambers, the presidents of which met regularly to determine strategies and policy positions. By one account, business chambers held designated seats on more than fifty-eight *juntas directivas,* commissions, and committees involved in the governance of state institutions, with many slots allocated directly in the constitution or specified by law (Rodríguez Quiroa 2018). CACIF, which reportedly represented over 200,000 affiliates (Bull, Castellacci, and Kasahara 2014), contained dozens of *gremios,* or smaller clusters of businesses organized by interest. Extractive sector companies participated directly in CACIF as members of the Guatemalan Chamber of Industry (CIG), which provided forceful support for their activities. CIG, in turn, included the Gremial de Industrias Extractivas (GREMIEXT), which brought together twenty-seven corporations involved in metallic (gold, silver, nickel) and nonmetallic (stone, sand, rock) extraction, along with foreign and locally owned shipping, machinery, energy, and construction businesses (CIG 2015, 137–138).

114   BREAKING GROUND

Unlike some countries, where foreign mining interests did not participate actively in local business chambers and affiliated only with local AmChams, if at all, mining companies in Guatemala were members of major national business associations, taking membership through their local subsidiaries, which formally oversaw their domestic operations. Like COSEP in Nicaragua, CACIF absorbed local branches of transnational corporations and represented their interests. Describing this relationship, one CIG spokesperson explained that the chamber provides "accompaniment," so that foreign investors do not have to navigate the political maze alone: "In countries where the *gremio* does not assume the role of defending them, foreign investors are left all on their own" (GT1518). Without close ties to the national business association, the thick blanket of local support and avenues to access were not available. In a country like Guatemala, where rules and regulations are often vague and contested, and much depends on insider information and personal contacts, having a local support system was critical to business success.

Few Guatemalan elites were directly involved in gold mining, an activity that normally requires specialized expertise and heavy up-front investments with a high degree of risk.[9] As elsewhere in Latin America, industrial gold mining was dominated by foreign, especially Canadian, corporations (Imai, Gardner, and Weinberger 2017). Nonetheless, several bridges linked local and foreign capital in Guatemala's mining sector. Members of elite families took management positions in the emerging mining companies, serving as corporate representatives and spokespeople.[10] Guatemalan business elites became invested in precious metals as minority partners. Guatemalan companies provided real estate and land acquisition services, and lined up to offer heavy equipment, environmental consulting (preparation of EIAs), construction services, and energy supplies. Well-placed Guatemalan lawyers served as legal representatives, handling registration requirements and defending the mining corporations in court (Solano 2013, 2015; Yagenova 2014, 18; Aguilar-Støen and Bull 2016, 23–28).

The business chamber's discourse served to conflate all mining interests, implicitly connecting foreign firms with local quarrying and construction

---

[9] El Sastre, a small gold mine acquired by the local partners after Canadian junior Argonaut Gold withdrew in 2010, was an exception.

[10] For example, Rodrigo Carlos Maegli Novella, vice president of the Grupo Tecún and member of the family that owned Cementos Progreso, served as corporate manager of Exmingua, the company that managed the El Tambor project (Yagenova 2014, 33).

operations. Metal mining was buffered by powerful local companies, including Cementos Progreso, owned by the Novella family, one of the country's wealthiest. The nonmetallic mining industry repeatedly self-defined as a partner to gold miners, defending the sector as a similarly situated ally and providing a strong local voice (see, for example, Cementos Progreso 2014).

Listed in investment consultant reports as a sector ripe for development, mining was promoted as a priority activity by business chambers and their think tank allies (see, for example, Lée L. and Bonilla de Anzueto 2009). CACIF and its policy arm, FUNDESA, identified mining and petroleum as one of twenty-five "clusters" highlighted in their 2012 development proposal, *Revista Mejoremos Guate* (FUNDESA and CACIF 2016). In 2014, Invest in Guatemala (2014), the country's leading investment promotion agency, placed mining as number seven on their list of highlighted opportunities for foreign investors. Among other attractive features, they called attention to Guatemala's "stable legal framework," and identified eleven minerals and metals that were available for extractive sector investment.

Seeking to stimulate foreign investments, the Guatemalan government requested that the UN Conference on Trade and Development (UNCTAD) prepare a case report outlining investment promotion strategies for three priority sectors—energy, roads, and mining. Despite what it identified as Guatemala's "high potential" for mining and oil extraction, the report (UNCTAD 2011, 15) included a long list of obstacles to mining development—features that led to the Guatemalan mining sector's "underperformance." One area identified as deficient was environmental regulation. Although Guatemala was described as "a pioneer in adopting modern environmental legislation," having approved its first environmental protection law in 1986, the report noted long delays in actually opening the Ministerio de Medio Ambiente y Recursos Naturales (MARN, Ministry of the Environment and Natural Resources, which did not begin functioning until 2000) and in drafting its regulatory provisions (not approved until 2003).

UNCTAD interviews and field research in Guatemala pointed to six areas of MARN weakness (UNCTAD 2011, 62–63): lack of institutional capacity resulting from the small number of personnel (twenty people) in the office in charge of environmental evaluations; substandard environmental assessments, where important environmental security standards (seismic criteria, for example) were not routinely considered; inadequate capacity to monitor compliance (only five inspectors for the whole country); inability to close down activities that "present eminent risks to the environment"; lack

116 BREAKING GROUND

of capacity to implement strategic environmental evaluations; and the propensity for these institutional weaknesses to trigger local community opposition. MARN's practice of depending on company-hired consultants to produce the EIAs and giving a swift nod to 90% of their reports, along with its reliance on companies to self-monitor and self-report their compliance, produced assessments of uneven quality that often fell below international standards. These deficiencies, some of which were flagged by international consultants, fueled recurring complaints about harmful impacts of mine operations on residents and local water supplies (Moran 2005a; Aguilar-Støen 2015; Aguilar-Støen and Hirsch 2017; CECON-USAC and CODIDENA 2019). As mining expanded, so did resistance.

Mining and Resistance in Guatemala

Mining, along with other megaprojects (hydroelectricity, petroleum extraction, monocrop agriculture, and transportation infrastructure), generated a high level of conflict in communities across Guatemala. A study of conflict at the *municipio* level conducted by the Guatemalan research center ASIES (2010, 27) in 2009–2010 found that protests and demonstrations had erupted in almost 80% of the *municipios* that had a mining license, whereas only 20% of communities without mining projects registered such conflicts. Yagenova (2016, 102–103) documented conflict in two-thirds (thirteen) of the twenty departments where megaprojects were approved or in process in 2012.

As is common in resource conflicts, mining resistance movements in Guatemala erupted first at the local level. Unlike Nicaragua, where conflicts included three variations—distributive protests over wages and royalties, definitional struggles over the community's social and economic meaning, and scale conflicts between artisanal gold miners and large industrial mines—Guatemalan resistance was largely definitional (see discussion of conflict subtypes in Chapter 3). Anti-mining struggles in Guatemala focused on the competition between mining and other forms of livelihood, like food crop production, which were understood to be mutually antagonistic, and resisters aimed at project derailment. At the policy level, mining critics commonly called for a mining moratorium, often an indefinite one.

In spite of their basic narrative affinity, mining resistance movements in Guatemala failed to develop into a cohesive network or to channel activist energies into a national movement. Unlike the anti-mining movement in

Costa Rica, which built up around a preexisting national environmental network and drew on abeyance structures related to prior social mobilizations against privatization and trade liberalization, the Guatemalan movement had little organizational infrastructure on which to grow. And unlike the movement in El Salvador, which drew on wartime alliances at the grassroots level and aligned its agenda with that of political party leaders in the FMLN, the movement in Guatemala found little uptake among the political parties. The absence of any strong party on the left created an organizational void, dimming the prospects for programmatic liaisons with state officials or access to potential bureaucratic allies.

At the same time, mining resisters did have access to some tools in Guatemala, particularly regarding indigenous community rights. Mining exploration in Guatemala often targeted territories where the indigenous population was concentrated, pitting indigenous communities against the encroachment of mining projects. Indigenous leaders who were drawn into the struggle attempted to build on both preexisting and new organizational structures to acquire information and coordinate a response. Formally representing 44% of the total population, and overwhelmingly Mayan (96%) in terms of self-identification, Guatemala's indigenous population had the demographic potential to develop into a significant political force.[11] But the absence of a politically empowered national movement, where mining issues could be collectively processed and responses configured, meant that community actions tended to be piecemeal and disarticulated, and often had limited impact.

Although detailed discussion of the mechanisms that disrupted national organizing among Guatemala's indigenous peoples extends beyond the boundaries of the present study, the country's long history of racism and genocidal violence, combined with the sustained practice of criminalization of protest, took a heavy toll on collective action.[12] Organizational capacity was further weakened by bouts of disanimating clientelism and tightly circumscribed forms of indigenous self-expression, where postwar affirmation of multiculturalism prioritized consumerist visions consistent with the dominant neoliberal model (Hale 2002; McAllister and Nelson 2013; Copeland 2019b). The resulting individuation and social disarticulation

---

[11] "Resultados del Censo 2018," https://www.censopoblacion.gt/mapas.

[12] For fuller discussion of the Guatemalan case in comparison with more successful national indigenous mobilizations elsewhere in Latin America, see Van Cott 2005; Vogt 2019.

118   BREAKING GROUND

tended to undermine successful organizing and constrain the political reach of indigenous activists. As one Guatemalan academic analyst observed during our interview, "There is no national indigenous agenda in Guatemala. What indigenous people want is local autonomy. What they want is to be left alone" (GT2418). This quest for local-level separation and decisional control complicated the effort to redefine national metallic mining policy and ensure protections for territorially dispersed indigenous peoples. But concerns about cultural, spiritual, and environmental dislocations did energize local-level opposition, producing resistance clusters that soon dotted the terrain.

Guatemalan Mining Resistance: Strategies and Tactics

Anti-mining activists, attempting to protect their local communities, demonstrated notable strategic dexterity in Guatemala. They deployed an array of actions designed to halt mine development, some of which they borrowed from each other. Their main strategies involved a four-part medley of roadblocks, "scientific activism," demands for local-level consultation, and a call for judicial intervention.

Roadblocks are a common form of protest activity in Latin America. As intentionally disruptive actions in areas where roads are few and alternative routes are not readily accessible, roadblocks provide highly visible flashpoints that quickly draw attention. Once the MEM granted an extraction license for the first of the new mines, protesters repeatedly moved to deploy this maneuver. When a large mill ball used for industrial grinding was trucked slowly down the highway toward the Marlin mine site in December 2004, protesters mobilized in Los Encuentros, a transportation crossroads in the indigenous municipality of Sololá. Residents had been attempting for months to figure out what mines were being planned for their region and to determine what the impact would be. Local leaders feared that the mill ball would be going into an unannounced mine in their own community, and the indigenous mayor of Sololá, Dominga Vásquez, had gone to the national Congress to seek information (Sibrián and van der Bough 2014, 75–76). To halt advancement toward mine production, protesters placed their bodies on the line.

Resisters detained this equipment for over five weeks before the Berger government moved to break up the blockade. Over 1,000 members of a special police force and 300 soldiers were reportedly sent to rupture the human

MINING, MAYBE: GUATEMALA   119

barrier and accompany the equipment to its final destination (Sibrián and van der Bough 2014). Blaming the mayor for these events, the minister of the interior, Carlos Veilman, issued a warrant for her arrest for the crimes of "terrorism, sabotage, threats, injuries, and damages to private property" (p. 76). Another fifteen people were classified as "principal instigators" and also charged with punishable offenses.[13]

Charges brought against mining protesters attempting to advance environmental and community rights included crimes such as "terrorism" and vague categories such as "illegal detention," an accusation sometimes leveled for merely impeding the flow of traffic. At times these charges were raised against people who were not present during the event or who were present in their capacity as community leaders seeking mediation and conflict resolution (Sibrián and van der Bough 2014; Yagenova 2014; Consejo del Pueblo Maya-CPO 2016a). Arrest could mean prolonged detention prior to trial, often under poor conditions. Court delays could extend the process, adding to costs and psychological pressures on detainees frequently far from home. When finally delivered, sentences could be lengthy.[14]

As the anti-mining movement grew and began to draw on the resources of national NGOs, resistance networks added the tactic of *scientific activism*. Scientific activism, as defined by Marta Conde (2014, 68), involves activists "engaging with professional scientists to learn from them the tools and the scientific language they need to produce a new and alternative knowledge with which they can challenge dominant discourses and engage in practical activism." Put simply, it involves the mobilization of scientific knowledge and expertise to advance social claims. In debates about development projects, this approach commonly entails calls for rigorous economic or environmental assessment of the impacts by independent experts. This form of activism carries fewer risks of criminalization and can help to delegitimize the mine licensing process, even in elite circles.

Expert scrutiny often involves critical review of the environmental impact assessments that have been approved by the government, with close attention

---

[13] See Equipo Nizkor, "La orden de captura contra la alcaldesa indígena de Sololá, 'es injuriosa,'" January 12, 2005, http://www.derechos.org/nizkor/guatemala/doc/solola4.html.

[14] Under Guatemalan law, paying fines could provide a reprieve from prison time for some convictions, but the fines were often unaffordable in these communities. The fine reported for one La Puya resister, sentenced to nine years for "illegal detention" of mineworkers who claimed their path was blocked by aggressive protesters, was Q10 a day for the nine-year period of their sentence (Yagenova 2014, 86). This amount, if paid in full, would total US$4,338 based on the 2014 exchange rate.

120 BREAKING GROUND

to gaps or mistakes and the risks or harms that result. In Guatemala, this approach involved hiring foreign experts like Robert Moran, a US geochemist and hydrologist with extensive international mining experience, who was contracted to reexamine the approved EIAs for both the Marlin and Progreso VII mines.[15] The deficiencies Moran identified added fuel to the arguments that environmental risks had not been properly assessed in Guatemala, and that the licenses that had been granted based on faulty assessments should be withdrawn (see also CECON-USAC and CODIDENA 2019).

The third resistance strategy involved calling for *community consultation*. As discussed in Chapter 2, mining projects triggered calls for local consultations across Latin America, generating both top-down (official) processes and bottom-up (grassroots) campaigns (Walter and Urkidi 2016; Dietz 2019; Torres Wong 2019; Riofrancos 2020; Jaskoski 2022). Mining companies generally provided pro forma information sessions for town authorities and community leaders, and claimed that these sessions indicated community consent. Mining critics persistently rejected that diagnosis, and in regions where many people self-identified as indigenous they called attention to the provisions in ILO 169 that required a consultation process that was free, prior, and informed. Although Guatemala had ratified ILO 169 as part of the peace accord process, it failed to legislate a consultation process, even as development projects spread through indigenous territories in the Western Highlands. This gap put the government out of compliance with its obligations under the convention—obligations recognized in the Guatemalan constitution as having coequal weight to the constitution itself.

In response to this participatory failure, some indigenous communities introduced "good faith community consultations" (*consultas comunitarias de buena fe*), adapting and resignifying processes that resonated with local traditions and preferences. Practices of community dialogue and collective assessment persisted in some indigenous communities and governed routine decision-making about such things as the timing of seasonal planting, allocation of communal work, approval of marriages, and entry of traveling salespeople into their territory (Tzul Tzul 2018; Mayén and Ochoa 2018; GT0418; GT3918). Many of these processes involved gathering residents

---

[15] Moran spent six years working for the US Geological Survey followed by twenty years as a hydrologist for private clients, including mining companies. He then began working for community groups, offering critical appraisals of mining EIAs in eight Latin American countries. See Moran 2005a; ES3710. Other external technical consultants contracted by local groups in Guatemala included Robert Robinson and Steve Laudeman (GT3018) and water quality analysts at Virginia Tech University (CECON-USAC and CODIDENA 2019).

for an assembly and public voting by raising hands. Some communities adopted broadly inclusive participatory criteria and allowed unregistered voters and children to engage as participants.[16] Such features were at odds with the rules governing conventional electoral processes, which required secret-ballot voting and restricted participation to registered voters over the age of eighteen. Defenders noted, however, that ILO 169 provisions called for participation to proceed according to the customs and traditions of indigenous communities, which were not tethered to conventional voting rules. As Rasch (2012) observed, this less restrictive approach served to increase the participation of women, who were less likely to be registered voters in some Highland communities.

In addition to demanding the rights embedded in the ILO 169 text, mining opponents also drew on consultation opportunities made available in recently approved decentralization laws. In line with World Bank recommendations, Guatemala had adopted three decentralization measures in 2002: the Ley de los Consejos de Desarrollo Urbano y Rural, the Código Municipal de Guatemala (Municipal Code), and the Ley General de Decentralización. These reforms permitted community consultation as a component of decentralized decision-making (Aldana and Abate 2016, 639). The Municipal Code allowed residents to convoke consultations on issues affecting their communities and bring the matter to a vote if a referendum was requested by more than 10% of registered voters. The results were to be binding if at least 20% of registered voters participated (Código Municipal, title IV, chap. 1, art. 64). This legal framework provided a mechanism through which mining resisters could register their views and challenge those projects that lacked community support, whether in indigenous or non-indigenous communities, and however those concepts were defined.

Consultation opportunities inspired considerable excitement and controversy in Guatemala. Beginning in 2004, *consultas* spread through indigenous communities in the Western Highlands and then beyond. Communities employed a variety of participatory practices, ranging from traditional community gatherings to formal voting under the Municipal Code. Assemblies were generally organized by coalitions of Mayan activist leaders who formalized under the name of the People's Council of the Western Highlands (Consejo

---

[16] As one indigenous defender of the practice of child voting explained to me, children "would bear the consequences of the decision, which would shape their future," and therefore had views that deserved full incorporation. In addition, they were only invited to join the voting if they "had demonstrated an ability to make choices based on their preferences" (GT0218).

122 BREAKING GROUND

de Pueblos de Occidente, CPO) in 2008 (van de Sandt 2009; Mash-Mash and Gómez 2014).[17] The CPO reported that more than sixty-five consultations took place between 2004 and 2014, most of them in the Western Highlands.[18] Mining opponents won overwhelmingly in every case, reflecting the intensely mobilized character of these processes.[19] Of the 851,037 *consulta* votes registered in the CPO database between 2004 and 2014, only 3,514 (0.4%) of the participants took a position in favor of the project.

Driven by concern about the social and environmental consequences of mining and hydroelectric projects in the region, even communities that were not threatened by active projects moved to hold referendums. Most of these votes were described as "anticipatory" and "preventative," and were designed to discourage interest by demonstrating the high potential for conflict and associated reputational costs (GT0317). As mining projects expanded into other regions of the country, including those traditionally regarded as *ladino* or non-indigenous, a second wave of consultations began in 2011, shifting to the southeastern department of Santa Rosa. These results paralleled those in the Highlands, with mining projects also soundly rejected.

Mining Resistance Clusters: Marlin, Progreso VII, and Escobal

The actors, frames, and tactics of mining resistance movements showed significant parallels in different regions of Guatemala, although each had distinctive features and organized separately. The Marlin resistance network that emerged in the Highlands drew on indigenous cultural claims about the

---

[17] The CPO, subsequently called the Consejo del Pueblo Maya-CPO (Maya People's Council-CPO), included representatives of the Mam, Sipakapense, K'ichè, Kaqchiquel, Q'anjob'al, Chuj, Akateko, and Poptí peoples. See Mash-Mash and Gómez 2014.

[18] Based on CPO database, www.cpo.org.gt/mapa/prueba13.php, accessed September 12, 2015. Since CPO-registered *consultas* were decentralized grassroots processes, not centrally administered state procedures, details on the vote results were not always standardized. Fifty-eight of the sixty-five cases in the CPO database included vote tallies; fifty-nine cases specified the issue (mining, hydroelectric, or both), with 90% related to mining. Reviewing additional databases of "good faith" consultations (also called *autoconsultas*) between 2004 and 2014, Xiloj Cuin (2016, 24) found their numbers ranged from 84 to 114, revealing substantial variation in the way these tallies were reported.

[19] Dougherty (2019b, 166) reports that about 25% of respondents in indigenous communities across Latin America express positive views of mining, although support levels vary by region and context. His values and attitudes survey in four Guatemalan communities found that 79% of respondents disagreed with the statement "Mining is more beneficial than damaging," but that individual attitudes varied by level of community exposure to mining and personal concepts of development.

primacy of nature and the sacredness of the land (Mash-Mash and Gómez 2014; GT1418; GT3918). Inspired by word of a mining consultation that had taken place three years previously in Tambogrande, Peru, where participants had registered strong opposition to the mine, indigenous community leaders of Sipakapa organized a consultation process on June 18, 2005, citing Guatemala's obligation to consult under ILO 169. The community rejected the Marlin project by a large margin, with eleven of the thirteen villages in the *municipio* and 95.5% of all voters expressing opposition to mining (Walter and Urkidi 2016, 296; Yagenova 2012; van de Sandt 2009). The message of community empowerment embedded in the Sipakapa plebiscite proved resonant, inspiring media attention and emulation. A widely distributed documentary, *Sipakapa No Se Vende*, fueled an emerging national and international opposition network (Walter and Urkidi 2016; Costanza 2016). As the practice of holding community referenda spread across the Western Highlands in the years that followed, indigenous communities claimed the right to self-determination and the legal authority to reject the national government's monopoly control over mining decisions.[20]

Marlin resisters raised alarm about the impact of industrial mining on access to and the quality of water. Residents worried about springs drying up and water "hiding" as water resources were redirected to meet the needs of the mine (GT0216). Supported by Bishop (subsequently Cardinal) Álvaro Ramazzini, one of three Guatemalan bishops who adopted a forceful position against mining, this network established the Pastoral Commission for Peace and Ecology (COPAE) in the department of San Marcos.[21] MadreSelva, the country's main environmental activist association, provided assistance, beginning a process of community accompaniment that it continued as megaprojects proliferated.

Evidence gathered subsequently from water, soil, and blood testing pointed to harmful concentrations of arsenic near the mine, although the absence of baseline studies conducted prior to mine opening made it difficult to lay responsibility at the feet of the company. Resisters drew on the IFC's complaint process to demand intervention by the Compliance Advisor

---

[20] A local civil court's ruling that the Sipakapa consultation was not legally valid led activists to challenge this finding in the Guatemalan Constitutional Court. Although the Constitutional Court upheld the community's legal right to conduct a referendum, it concluded that the results were not legally binding because the constitution gave control over natural resources to the central, not local, government.

[21] Along with Ramazzini, Bishops Bernabé Sagastume in Santa Rosa de Lima and Julio Edgar Cabrera Ovalle in Jalapa took forceful positions against the mining projects (GT1818).

124   BREAKING GROUND

Ombudsman (CAO 2005), triggering a round of external review. An independent assessment of the project that was commissioned by Goldcorp called for increased corporate control over the activities of the Guatemalan management team, whose heavy-handed dealings and legal aggressiveness with local populations were found to contribute to conflict escalation (On Common Ground 2010).

Forewarned about potential mining risks, community residents near Guatemala's second gold mine, Progreso VII Derivada, began organizing soon after mine licensing began. They were likewise not consulted prior to the issuance of the mining permit, and were also misled about the nature and status of the project. As one movement participant put it, "The company came in like a thief," without informing residents of its interests or its plans (GT0218). This mine was located in a zone called El Tambor, between the *ladino* town of San José del Golfo and the ethnically diverse San Pedro Ayampuc, not far from Guatemala City and the access to media attention that proximity provided. In March 2012, as heavy equipment began to appear en route to the mine, residents launched La Puya, with a well-organized, permanently installed occupation designed to halt mine construction. La Puya's goals and actions, which also centered on concerns about water rights, were often framed in religious terms, with protesters kneeling and praying as they stated their petitions and withstood assault. Local religious leaders provided visible support and assisted with coordination.[22]

La Puya activists maintained an around-the-clock presence at the site for over two years, organizing shift changes, sleeping quarters, meal preparation, and religious services. Protesters impeded the installation of mining equipment on repeated occasions, holding out in spite of countermobilizations orchestrated by the mining company personnel. After several unsuccessful efforts to clear protesters from the site, the government forcibly dislodged the activists on May 23, 2014. Thirty-five police vehicles and around 500 agents from the Policía Nacional Civil (PNC) reportedly arrived with shields, batons, and tear gas (Yagenova 2014, 73, 90). Having captured national and international attention and won public sympathy with a nonviolent stance and strategic profiling of elderly women, activists soon returned, now with a twenty-four-hour-a-day police detachment settled within sight of their

---

[22] National allies included the Conferencia de Religiosos de Guatemala (CONFREGUA), MadreSelva, Comité de Unidad Campesina (CUC), Waqib' Kej, UDEFEGUA, and alternative media outlets, including Prensa Comunitaria Kilómetro 169 and Plaza Pública (Yagenova 2014; Yagenova et al. 2015; Pedersen 2014).

camp. Although the local power structure (business, teachers, officials) in San José del Golfo showed signs of support for the mine, other surrounding communities registered sustained opposition (Yagenova et al. 2015, 105).

Meanwhile, community leaders at the third site, located in the southeastern department of Santa Rosa, signaled concern about the impact of the proposed Escobal mine, which was projected to become the third-largest silver mine in the world. Developed by MSR for the Canadian company Tahoe Resources, the project soon sparked a third wave of conflict. Local residents in San Rafael Las Flores invited MadreSelva to provide information about the social and environmental impacts, leading to the formation of the anti-mining Committee in Defense of Life and Peace in 2010 (GT1918). Information about anti-mining organizing spread through nearby populations, including indigenous residents affiliated with the Xinka Parliament, one of the two key organizations for Guatemala's main non-Maya indigenous group (Rogers 2017). When Santa Rosa activists called for the creation of pastoral committees that would organize around the mining debate in nearby communities, Bishop Bernabé Sagastume of Santa Rosa de Lima established a regional religious-environmental network under the Diocesan Committee in Defense of Nature (CODIDENA).

Continued organizational work culminated in a series of local plebiscites convened under decentralization laws in 2011 and 2012. Four were held in the departments of Santa Rosa and Jalapa, with each one demonstrating overwhelming opposition (98–99%) to the silver mining project (Solano 2015, 9). Between 2013 and 2015, ten additional plebiscites took place in communities near the Escobal mine, with all but one, in Sabana Redonda, where the sleeping quarters of mineworkers were located, producing a strong negative vote.[23]

As with Marlin and Progreso VII, the Escobal mine had been granted a license without community consultation and in the face of growing tensions. Charges of kidnapping, terrorism, and burglary were brought repeatedly against those organizing in opposition (Solano 2015, 12–13). News that the Escobal extraction license had been granted, in spite of local opposition, provoked another surge of anti-mine mobilization in April 2013. On April 11, police arrested twenty-six people for allegedly blocking freedom of movement and preventing mineworkers from getting to work, charges that were later dropped for lack of evidence (CALAS 2016, 18–32). Mine employees

[23] The "yes" option won in Sabana Redonda with 53% of the vote in January 2014 (Solano 2015, 10).

126 BREAKING GROUND

escalated the conflict the following week, when the company's security personnel pursued and shot fleeing protesters with rubber bullets, leading to the injury of seven people.

As tensions heightened, President Otto Pérez Molina declared a thirty-day "state of siege" in the zone. On May 2, 2013, he deployed a reported contingent of several thousand police officers into nearby communities, in a now-routine effort to repress dissent (Justice and Accountability Project 2016, 12). Having negotiated a "voluntary" increase in mining royalties only a year before, and having made a commitment to update the Mining Law and address its legal deficiencies, Pérez Molina was firmly committed to mine promotion.[24] He visited the zone on July 12, 2013, descending by helicopter to offer full-throated support for the Escobal project and to celebrate the job growth and opportunities that the mine would bring (Tahoe Resources 2013).

Supported by powerful state actors, Escobal quickly went into production. Operations were soon disrupted, however, when resisters launched a 24/7 roadblock in June 2017 in the nearby town of Casillas. This roadblock, which prevented the shipment of any extracted ore, effectively brought mine production to a halt.

These capsule summaries of events at Guatemala's three large-scale gold and silver mines capture both the mobilization of mining opponents and the push to develop the industry by mining managers, accompanied by state officials who provided the legal framing and repressive capacity. The repeated movement of protesters, followed by massive deployment of security forces, soon made Guatemala a Latin American leader in the tally of mining's human costs. According to a Justice and Corporate Responsibility Project report on violence and Canadian mining companies in fourteen Latin American countries, between 2000 and 2015 Guatemala ranked first in terms of the recorded number of deaths (12 out of the 44) and injuries (89 out of 403), and third (after Argentina and Honduras) in terms of the number of arrests, detentions, and charges (71 out of 537) (Imai, Gardner, and Weinberger 2017, 12).[25]

---

[24] Marlin Mine owner Montana agreed to contribute an additional 4% to the legally mandated 1% when the gold price per ounce topped US$975, and other precious metals miners also upped their contributions. With this more lucrative arrangement in place, the MEM granted twenty-one new mining licenses in 2012, sixteen of them for extraction (MEM 2020, 18).

[25] The Guatemalan data in this report included violence at the Fénix nickel mine, where there was one reported death, twelve injuries, and eleven cases of sexual violence (Imai, Gardner, and Weinberger 2017, 64–65). This fourth mining conflict site is not examined in the present study, which focuses on precious metals.

Although Guatemalan resistance movements developed multisectoral linkages that brought together indigenous, religious, environmental, and human rights actors, their networks remained essentially local operations, and failed to develop into a national resistance front. Expressions of solidarity provided connections across the grid, and local networks shared some national-level allies. But the movements operated separately, a strategic limitation that allowed police actions and countermovements by pro-mining elites to thwart them, one by one.

The remaining tool in the resisters' arsenal, however, brought mining operations to a durable pause. Strategic litigation had come into growing use in postwar Guatemala. The clash between legal obligations (those embedded in the mining law, the constitution, and international conventions) and on-the-ground developments as mines became operational—the "parchment versus practice" gap aptly described by Kapiszewski, Levitsky, and Yashar (2021)—generated growing tensions over performance failures. Engagement with the courts, in turn, provided a mechanism for institutional docking, and effectively slowed the mining advance.

Mining and Docking in Guatemala

The Guatemalan political system is characterized by weak institutions and political insularity. Although formally an electoral democracy, public access to elite decision-making is restricted, both by the large gaps between legislated rules and actual practice and by the "predatory informal rules" (Schwartz 2021) and "clandestine control" (Bowen 2017) that coexist alongside democratic reforms. Whether understood in terms of structural historical conditions, including the hierarchical legacies of colonial rule, large indigenous populations, and persistence of labor-repressive agriculture (Cameron 2021), or in terms of the more recent penetration by ex-military networks and criminal organizations (Yashar 2018; Schwartz 2021), the Guatemalan state is commonly regarded as insular, exclusionary, and unresponsive. In his depiction of Latin American cases along an inclusionary-exclusionary spectrum, Cameron (2021 416, 413) locates Guatemala at the far end of the exclusionary side, describing it as a "counterinsurgent state" characterized by an "uneven citizenship regime." Copeland's (2019b) anthropological analysis emphasizes the consolidation of "authoritarian populism" in the Mayan Highlands, spun up by the onslaught of neoliberal reform and

128 BREAKING GROUND

"radical pessimism" (pp. 109–136) in the wake of the war. None of this work suggests a regime that is responsive to civil society or receptive to popular participation.

Even those mechanisms that mobilize voters for electoral participation were inadequate to the task. Guatemalan political parties serve primarily as electoral instruments under the control of individual aspirants to political power (Sánchez-Sibony 2016). They lack established programs, membership, or voting bases, and operate only briefly during election season. Each of the successful presidential candidates during the postwar period has hailed from a different party—all of recent vintage, and almost all of which fizzled in the aftermath.[26] As Sánchez-Sibony (pp. 128–129) notes, "all political formations that were at some juncture electorally important (evincing a large parliamentary presence) became marginal (or extinguished) within two or three electoral cycles," making Guatemala notorious as "the cemetery of political parties." Studies of electoral volatility and party system institutionalization find that Guatemala has one of Latin America's most "weakly institutionalized" (Jones 2011) and "inchoate" (Espana-Nájera 2018, 308) party systems (see also Schneider 2012, 180–183).

Not all elements of the political system were equally ineffective, however. Participatory spaces did periodically open in some parts of the state apparatus, most notably in the judicial arena. Mining resistance in Guatemala involved intense engagement in legal disputes, much of it due to the criminalization of protest. But resisters also engaged the judicial system voluntarily, gaining skill in accessing legal tools and initiating strategic litigation. This side of the judicialization process provided opportunities for docking, or inserting demands into the state apparatus in order to secure resources or relief. Judicialization was used to increasing effect by activist organizers over time. It also introduced a caveat to the depiction of the Guatemala state as closed and inaccessible.

The concept of "judicialization of social movements" describes the juncture between contentious mass-based movements for social change and legal institutions and processes related to the administration of justice (Sarat and Scheingold 1998; Santos and Rodríguez-Garavito 2005; Rodríguez-Garavito and Rodríguez-Franco 2015). A growing willingness to turn to the courts

---

[26] Schneider (2012, 182) reported that 42% of Guatemalan legislators changed parties in the 1986–1991 period. An OAS (2015) report on the 2015 election found that "within a day of taking office, virtually one of every three deputies changed parties or joined a new organization, and the number increased later on."

MINING, MAYBE: GUATEMALA 129

to seek a mandate for formally declared but functionally absent rights has allowed social movements to expand their repertoires and devise complex strategies by which to advance their cause. Legal action can provide activists with remedy to duress even when group voting power is weak and organizational resources offer little hope of positive action. As such, it can shield vulnerable populations and constrain unilateral decision-making by dominant actors. Although legal intervention frequently serves the interests of the powerful, it can also become a significant tool for resisters. That judicial strategies may fail, or that they may be used with greater prowess and insider advantage by movement adversaries, does not obviate the potential that this mechanism holds for grassroots activists.

Judicial Institutions and Processes in Guatemala

Legal institutions have been notoriously weak in Guatemala (Camus, Bastos, and López García 2015; OHCHR-Guatemala 2016). Characterized by corruption and impunity, the Guatemalan judicial system has proven incapable of protecting even the most basic rights (see Brett 2011; Yashar 2018). The combination of high crime levels and ineffective prosecution has led some communities to circumvent the courts; mob killings and lynching became a local practice in some areas (Sieder 2010, 172). Even considered alongside other Central American countries, Guatemala generally scores at or near the bottom on judicial power metrics.[27]

Of the four countries analyzed in the present study, Guatemala placed last in terms of rule of law on the World DataBank's 2015 Worldwide Governance Indicators, a relative ranking that persisted across the 2005–2015 period (see Table 4.2).[28] Already at the regional bottom in 2005, Guatemala's rule of law percentile ranking fell yet lower in 2010, and declined still further across the decade. Guatemala's 2019 score was well below those received by Costa Rica and El Salvador, topping only that received by Nicaragua, which

---

[27] There is no internationally agreed upon measure of judicial power or rule of law, concepts that are notoriously difficult to quantify (Bowen 2017, 5; Yashar 2018; Brinks and Blass 2019, 20; Esquirol 2020).

[28] World Bank DataBank's scores for rule of law are based on perceptions of the extent to which people confide in and adhere to the rules on contract enforcement, property rights, court and police performance, and the likelihood of crime and violence. "Percentile rank" reflects the country's overall score relative to that of other countries in the database, with a score of 0 given to the country with the lowest rank and 100 to that with the highest.

130 BREAKING GROUND

Table 4.2 Rule of Law, Worldwide Percentile Rank of Four Central American Countries

	2005	2010	2015	2019
Costa Rica	64.1	64.5	69.2	70.2
El Salvador	39.2	22.3	31.7	23.6
Guatemala	*22.5*	*16.6*	*15.4*	*13.9*
Nicaragua	32.5	24.2	27.9	9.6

Source: World Bank DataBank, Worldwide Governance Indicators, accessed May 1, 2020.

dropped precipitously following the Ortega regime's escalation of repression in 2018.

Recognition of the failings in the Guatemalan judicial system led to a two-prong push for change. First, Guatemalan activists worked to develop an organizational infrastructure that would build legal capacity and promote a rights-oriented agenda within civil society. Second, international and state actors collaborated to strengthen the autonomy of the Guatemalan court system and improve its performance.

Building a Legal Rights Infrastructure

Formal rights commitments expanded with Guatemala's 1996 peace accord agreements, and a network of legal rights organizations emerged in the wake (Sieder 2010; Hessbruegge and Ochoa García 2011). Often operating with international financial assistance, these organizations took on a range of issues, including the promotion of indigenous cultural rights, decentralization, and community empowerment. This legal support structure provided critical assistance to the mining resistance movements.

Early support for activists who mobilized in opposition to mining licenses was provided by MadreSelva, an environmental organization founded as the war officially concluded in 1996. MadreSelva provided accompaniment and resistance training to the communities located near the Marlin mine and the legal defense of La Puya protesters who had been charged in 2012 with threatening and illegally detaining mineworkers at the El Tambor project site (Colectivo MadreSelva 2006; Yagenova 2014, 86–87; Yagenova et al. 2015). A second organization, the Environmental and Social Legal Action Center (Centro de Acción Legal-Ambiental y Social, CALAS), was established in

MINING, MAYBE: GUATEMALA 131

2000 with a focus on providing legal assistance to environmental activists. The CALAS legal team repeatedly took up the defense of resistance activists accused of protest-related crimes, contributing to the legal defense of anti-mining protesters in both the La Puya movement and at the Escobal mine (CALAS 2016).

Over time, Guatemala's legal support infrastructure added organizations staffed by a growing network of Maya lawyers and legal professionals.[29] The Nim Ajpu Association of Maya Lawyers and Notaries, established in 2004 by a group of Maya lawyers and legal rights experts, offered free legal services to Maya communities, drawing on donations from European funders, including the Association of Lawyers of Norway (Picq 2016a, 2016b; GT0118). The People's Council of the Western Highlands, formed officially in 2008, also expanded the Maya community's organizational and legal capacity (CPO 2012). In addition to its work promoting grassroots consultations and the legal defense of indigenous leaders facing criminal charges, the organization's legal commission represented indigenous leaders in their successful 2016 demand for the suspension of six mining licenses that had been granted without community consultation (Consejo del Pueblo Maya-CPO 2016b).

Xinka organizations added an additional indigenous voice to the medley. Xinka identity, while recognized in the peace process and national-languages laws, had been "all but extinguished by the extreme discrimination and civil war throughout Guatemala's history" (Rogers 2017). Efforts to recover this identity led to the formation of two grassroots cultural organizations in the southeastern departments of Santa Rosa, Jalapa, and Jutiapa: the Council of the Xinka People of Guatemala, formed in 1996, and the Xinka Parliament, founded in 2002 (Dary 2017).[30] The legal representative of the Xinka Parliament used the courts to challenge the way state administrative practices diluted and diminished Xinka identity, and brought a case against the MEM for its failures to adhere to its own consultation and complaints procedures prior to the issuance of the Escobal license.

---

[29] The Maya Programme, initiated in 2009 with funding from the government of Norway, financed technical training in strategic litigation for critical sectors, offering rights-defense training for indigenous communities; training in international indigenous rights standards for legal professionals; and instruction in public interest law, indigenous rights, and indigenous customary law for university and law students (OHCHR-Guatemala 2014).

[30] As the penalties for indigenous identity became less acute, recuperative spaces led 264,167 Guatemalans (1.8% of the total population) to self-identify as Xinka in the 2018 census, up from 16,214 in 2002 (Instituto Nacional de Estadística Guatemala 2019, 25).

132 BREAKING GROUND

In addition to these and other domestic organizations, international NGOs contributed critical resources and outreach to support legal activism around mining in Guatemala. International allies included human rights and solidarity organizations whose work in the country dated back to the civil war era, such as the Network in Solidarity with the People of Guatemala (NISGUA), the Guatemalan Human Rights Commission (GHRC), and the Canadian solidarity organization Maritimes–Breaking the Silence (BTS). Canadian mining-focused organizations like MiningWatch Canada also became significant supporters, hosting delegations, providing community accompaniment, and producing on-the-ground reports about local conflicts. An array of allies, including the Washington-based Center for International Environmental Law (CIEL), the Justice and Corporate Accountability Project at York University, and the Canadian Centre for International Justice, among others, provided support for legal action in international venues.

This thickening and multiscalar judicial rights network permitted notable breakthroughs. At a time when the anti-mining movement had no major patrons in political leadership and few bases of support in the country's feckless political parties, and where the fragmented Congress proved uniquely ill-prepared to address the problems raised by the mining resistance movement, the courts opened a door.[31]

Legal action required not just the development of a legal rights infrastructure but also the promotion of a functioning court system. Evidence of corruption and impunity, and a crime rate that alarmed even elites, fueled the Berger administration's decision to support creation of the International Commission Against Impunity in Guatemala (CICIG) in December 2006. This innovative collaboration allowed the Guatemalan state to draw on the resources of the United Nations and key donors to tackle some of the failings of the judicial system.

CICIG introduced a hybrid mechanism designed to strengthen criminal investigations and improve the prosecutorial capacity of the Guatemalan court system through the collaborative work of an UN-appointed commissioner and the Guatemalan Public Prosecutor's office (Ministerio Público).

---

[31] The Guatemalan court system is complex, with two high courts (the Supreme Court of Justice and the Constitutional Court), a legal process that facilitates injunctions and appeals, and a rulings process that includes both provisional and final decisions. Terms for magistrates on the Constitutional Court are relatively short (five years) and replacement is highly politicized. Magistrate selection is disbursed among five institutions: the president, congress, the Supreme Court, the bar association, and the Universidad de San Carlos (USAC), the main public university, with each one naming a justice and a substitute (Bowen 2017; Brinks and Blass 2018; Call and Hallock 2020).

During its twelve-year mission (2007–2019), CICIG promoted piecemeal improvements in judicial autonomy. In conjunction with its Guatemalan partners, it prosecuted over 120 cases, with more than 1,540 indictments and over 400 convictions, with outcomes that impacted more than 70 criminal networks (WOLA 2019; Call and Hallock 2020, 11).[32] The growing capacity of CICIG, under its third commissioner, Iván Velásquez, and the Guatemalan public prosecutor, Thelma Aldana, to conduct rigorous investigations and prosecute high-level corruption affected the balance of power and lent critical support to the court system's work (Hudson and Taylor 2010; Open Society Justice Initiative 2016; Carrera 2017; WOLA 2019; Call and Hallock 2020). With Guatemala's legal rights infrastructure expanding, and a new alliance of international and domestic actors working to strengthen the autonomy and transparency of the courts, new docking possibilities began to emerge.

Court Cases and Mining Conflicts

As noted previously, Guatemala's 1997 mining law failed to include provisions for indigenous community consultation, as required by ILO 169, and mining critics quickly contested the law's constitutionality (Fulmer, Godoy, and Neff 2008; ICEFI 2014b, 21; On Common Ground 2010; van de Sandt 2009). With CALAS support, Mam, Mayan, and Sipakapense community leaders in San Marcos presented a legal challenge to the law and called into question the validity of permits secured under its terms. In 2008, the Guatemalan Constitutional Court declared that seven articles of the 1997 Mining Law were unconstitutional, leaving the status of the law in question (EITI 2014; van de Sandt 2009) and temporarily slowing the pace of mine licensing.

Sipakapa leaders also filed a 2007 petition with the Inter-American Commission on Human Rights (IACHR), claiming that they had been denied the right to meaningful consultation prior to the granting of the Marlin license. They further claimed that the MEM had published the notice

---

[32] The weakness of the Guatemalan court system encouraged activists to pursue relief abroad, in settings where the judicial system was better institutionalized and court decisions would carry more weight (Davis and Warner 2007). By 2010, complaints about the Marlin Mine had been brought to four international bodies, including the ILO Committee of Experts, the Inter-American Human Rights Commission, the Compliance Advisor and Ombudsman of the International Finance Corporation, and Canada's National Contact Point for the OECD Guidelines for Multinational Enterprise (On Common Ground Consultants 2010, 182). Abuse by the security subcontractor hired by the Tahoe Resources at the Escobal mine in 2013 led injured Guatemalans to seek justice in the courts in British Columbia, Canada, where the company had its headquarters. The case was settled by the new owner, Pan American Silver, in 2019, for an apology and undisclosed compensation.

134 BREAKING GROUND

of the mining license application only in Spanish and in newspapers that were not distributed in their communities. In addition, they contended that the company's EIA did not cover all of the affected territory, was written in technical terms, and was not translated into local languages. Informing themselves about the content of the project required community leaders to assume financial responsibility for traveling to Guatemala City to view the EIA and hire attorneys to interpret it, activities that were beyond their means. They further alleged that a study of water quality downstream from the mine found contamination affecting the health of local residents (IACHR 2014, 2–5).

IACHR responded with a precautionary measure in 2010, calling on the Guatemalan government to suspend mining operations affecting eighteen Mayan indigenous communities in San Marcos and instructing the government to ensure these communities had access to water supplies that were safe for human consumption and irrigation purposes (IACHR 2014, 2). The Colom administration initially indicated that it would comply with the ruling and suspend the mine (IACHR 2014, 7), but it soon reversed course and pressured IACHR to lift the suspension order while the investigation progressed (Sibrián and van der Borgh 2014).

Legal contestation continued in both domestic and international courts as mining entered its second postwar decade in Guatemala. In 2014, CALAS lawyer Pedro Rafael Maldonado launched a set of new legal challenges in Guatemalan courts, claiming that mining licenses that had been granted without indigenous community consultation were invalid. As court scrutiny of government transactions intensified, the Guatemalan Supreme Court approved a provisional injunction that called for the suspension of Progreso VII's license in November 2015 (Corte Supremo de Justicia 2015; Pitán and Sánchez 2016).

By this time, the country had entered into a major political crisis, triggered by corruption charges against President Pérez Molina and Vice President Roxana Baldetti. These charges resulted from a CICIG investigation into state complicity in La Línea, a large-scale tax evasion scheme. Evidence of corruption in the La Línea case pointed directly to illegal enrichment by the president and vice president, among others. CICIG's exposé triggered the largest and most sustained anti-corruption protests in Guatemalan history. Unprecedented demonstrations swelled in central plazas in Guatemala City and other major urban centers, connecting activists in local communities with the mobilizing urban youth (Solís Miranda 2016; Gutiérrez 2017; Sáenz de Tejada 2017). This "Guatemala Spring" culminated in the resignation and arrest of Pérez Molina in September 2015.

With state officials who had authorized mining licenses now badly discredited by corruption scandals, and the high courts increasingly attentive to issues of administrative malfeasance, mining companies became vulnerable to adverse rulings. Following a second Supreme Court ruling against the MEM over the Progreso VII license, the public prosecutor finally directed the takeover of the mine by the national civil police in May 2016. That same month, the Constitutional Court upheld the Progreso VII license suspension, based on the MEM's failure to conduct the required indigenous community consultation.

Meanwhile, conflicts over Escobal were also making their way into the courts. In July 2017, the Supreme Court granted CALAS's request for an injunction suspending the Escobal mine on behalf of the Xinka people living in the vicinity, again due to the failure of the MEM to carry out a consultation. In September 2018, the Constitutional Court produced a 554-page ruling that confirmed the suspension and laid out a process through which free, prior, and informed consent could be pursued (Corte de Constitucionalidad 2018). This ruling, which meticulously reviewed the case and the arguments advanced in a host of pro and con amicus filings, concluded with a definitive suspension of mining operations, pending the completion of a consultation process. With the Marlin Mine decommissioned and the Progreso VII and Escobal mines legally suspended, gold and silver mining in Guatemala now drew to a temporary close.

Mining Outcomes in Guatemala

The present chapter demonstrates how the interplay of elite consensus, resistance fragmentation, and state impenetrability for non-elite actors—conditions that favor mining promotion—prevailed in Guatemala at the beginning of the mining cycle. Elite support for mining was most visible in CACIF's embrace of the sector and the declarations of pro-business presidents in the postwar era. Resistance movements emerged and became well entrenched wherever industrial mines sprang up, but they remained primarily decentralized operations. Signaling localism and organizational fragmentation, these networks did not scale up to the national level. With limited docking options, opponents found it difficult to gain access to state institutions where fuller national discussion of mining regulation might advance. This political void persisted in spite of strong evidence that the Guatemalan Mining Law was legally flawed and that the environmental ministry was too weak to provide reliable protection.

Roadblocks and grassroots consultations at the municipal level raised awareness of the conflict, and public opinion supported the opposition, at least in the mining zone.[33] But critical views and protests failed to prevent the approval of mine licenses and the growth of the industry. The Marlin mine opened on schedule in 2005 and was mined to exhaustion in 2017. The La Puya mobilization did not prevent the opening of the Progreso VII in 2014. The negative votes on mining in municipalities and communities surrounding the Escobal mine did not prevent the construction and commercial launch of that project in early 2014. The question for resisters became whether it is possible to turn community opposition into a legal outcome and use the instruments of the state to restrain mining investment. That magic act required effective judicial docking.

In spite of the entrenched challenges, mining resisters repeatedly looked to the judicial branch for leverage against the mining advance. The onslaught of legal challenges contributed to a dramatic slowdown in the issuance of new mining permits (van de Sandt 2009; EITI 2014, 10). The number of new exploration and extraction permits issued by the MEM peaked at fifty in 2007 and then declined sharply, falling to seven in 2009 (MEM [Guatemala] 2020, 18). Licensing numbers increased briefly in 2012 and 2013, bolstered by Pérez Molina's mining enthusiasm, before they plateaued and then tumbled to zero at the end of the Jimmy Morales administration. Without access to new licenses, mining investments fizzled and production soon followed.

Between 2015 and 2020, the Constitutional Court issued a series of rulings that pressed state institutions to adhere to their own legal requirements, particularly regarding indigenous rights. Initially ruling that the MEM should deny license applications when indigenous communities had not been consulted, the court then escalated pressure by halting production in mines

---

[33] A 2010 ASIES survey of the forty-eight *municipios* that had at least one active metallic mining license (either exploration or extraction) found that 58% of the 720 survey respondents either "completely disapproved" or "disapproved" of mining in Guatemala (64% held that position with regard to mining in their *municipio*) (ASIES 2010, 57). Asked whether they thought metallic mining would impact a list of items, half of the respondents stated that it would have some ("algo") or much ("mucho") impact on jobs increases (50%). But higher percentages thought it would produce water pollution (88%), soil contamination (77%), illness (75%), forest loss (74%), water loss (74%), drought (71%), and the violation of indigenous rights (56%) (pp. 55–57). When asked whether they thought the Guatemalan government had the capacity to monitor and regulate mining, 72% of the respondents said no (p. 49).

MINING, MAYBE: GUATEMALA   137

where defective licenses had already been issued. One by one, Constitutional Court rulings detained the operations of the large-scale metallic mines, first at Progreso VII (2016), and then Escobal (2018), in each case requiring production suspension until official consultation was complete. With no legislation in place to govern indigenous consultation, and considerable debate about how this process should be carried out, these rulings put metallic mining operations on extended standby.[34]

As mining fell on hard times, CACIF followed a course of active resistance. Chamber support for the mining industry popped up in news articles and full-page ads highlighting the mining sector's contribution to the economy. CACIF ads bemoaned the costs of "legal uncertainty" to investment promotion efforts and the country's credit ratings, and business chambers became outspoken critics of the courts. The Constitutional Court's September 2018 decision to suspend Escobal operations added animus to a festering campaign against the magistrates. This new pattern of judicial activism, interpreted locally as an artifact of CICIG's interventionism, drew swelling elite criticism. "For over three years," a CACIF press release proclaimed in 2019, "certain magistrates of the [Constitutional] Court have systematically ruled in an irresponsible and ideological manner. In addition, we have seen how these magistrates have changed the jurisprudence of the Court, destroying legal certainty in the country" (CACIF 2019).

Already troubled by the early morning arrest and subsequent conviction of a prominent business leader in CICIG anti-corruption operations (CACIF 2018), business elites joined the Morales administration's push to oust CICIG's crusading commissioner, Iván Velázquez, lobbying in both Guatemala City and Washington, DC, to weaken the operation and bring CICIG to a rapid end (García 2018; WOLA 2019; Call and Hallock 2020). Velázquez was declared persona non grata by President Morales in 2017 and prevented from returning to Guatemala in 2018. In spite of widespread public support for CICIG, the commission rolled up operations in September 2019. Reform-oriented magistrates soldiered on, attempting to prosecute the ongoing cases and use the court system to advance indigenous political rights. But the tide had begun to turn.[35]

---

[34] After a three-year delay, the MEM initiated a pre-consultation process in 2021 with representatives of the Xinka Parliament and Escobal's new owner, Pan American Silver (Spalding 2022). This process was ongoing in mid-2022.

[35] See Beltrán 2020, Porras 2021, and WOLA 2021 for discussion of abuses and anomalies surrounding Guatemalan Supreme Court and Constitutional Court appointments in 2021.

138 BREAKING GROUND

The Guatemalan case illustrates how a pro-mining regime can face obstacles as features that initially favored mining being to shift. As with Nicaragua, Guatemalan political and economic elites provided strong support for mining, presenting this sector as a source of economic growth and job creation. Following protocols suggested by the World Bank and mining company representatives, these elites produced favorable legislation and investment guarantees, and succeeded in attracting exploration companies that located promising deposits.

Resistance mobilization in Guatemala was not as deeply fractured as that found in Nicaragua, where conflicts included highly divergent types of struggle. Gold and silver mining conflicts in Guatemala all involved introducing mines into new terrain, and the struggles were all definitional. In spite of their basic conceptual affinity, the variation in regional settings, ethnolinguistic identity, and localist traditions led each of these mobilizations to emerge as a distinct cluster in Guatemala, rising and falling in keeping with local dynamics. In the absence of a scale shift to the national level, antimining activists were unable to engage a broader policy debate. This absence favored the expansion of mining, as we saw in the Nicaraguan case.

But unlike Nicaragua, the Guatemalan resistance movement secured political leverage by gaining access to the courts. As the Guatemalan high courts developed a capacity to scrutinize state practices and expanded the state's institutional commitment to indigenous rights, their rulings began to favor the mining resisters. The metallic mining industry was then put on pause.

This disruption did not, however, mean that mining had come to an end. The mining suspensions dictated by the Constitutional Court were designed to be temporary, pending the completion of required consultations with nearby indigenous communities. Procedures to operationalize a multiphase consultation process triggered renewed debate in Guatemala about indigenous identity, what it means to be informed and decide freely, and the meaning and legal significance of consent. The Constitutional Court's requirement of free, prior, and informed consultation as a prerequisite to mining authorization, and its prescriptions regarding the sequence of steps to be followed, could improve official recognition and access for Guatemala's indigenous communities and support state institution-building.

The experience of other Latin American countries that have legislated prior consultation, however, suggests that this maneuver may reactivate established power hierarchies and produce limited benefits for the impacted communities (Eisenstadt and West 2019; Torres Wong 2019; Le Billon and

Middeldorp 2021). Although previous bottom-up *consultas* and municipal-level plebiscites in Guatemala called attention to risks and regulatory gaps in the mining industry and provided strong evidence of local rejection, the current round of indigenous *consultas* taking place under state auspices introduces new constraints. Whether Guatemalan consultations will conform to the disappointing Latin American pattern or will set a new standard remains to be seen.

Meanwhile, Guatemalan mining companies and their supporters prepare for the next surge in mine development. President Alejandro Giammattei (2020–2024) campaigned in support of investment promotion and appointed former mining officials to high-level administrative positions. The MEM launched a multiphase consultation process for the Xinka people in the vicinity of Escobal in 2021 but made no commitment to adhere to local preferences. New owners took over some of the languishing mines, making plans for their reactivation. With gold prices up during the COVID-19 pandemic, mining investors were eager to get Guatemalan projects back on track.

These cross-pressures situate the Guatemalan case inside the *intermittent approval framework*. This model is characterized by phases of expansion, when mining advocates align to push authorization and construction, even in the face of local resistance, and phases of suspension, when resistance movements halt operations for indefinite, albeit temporary, periods, and investor enthusiasm recalibrates. Along this uneven path, the prognosis for Guatemala's mining industry is primed to be discontinuous.

140 BREAKING GROUND

Appendix 4.1 Guatemala: List of Cited Interviews

Code	Affiliation	Sector	Date	Location
GT0118	Nim Ajpu ANMAG	Civil society—legal and Indigenous	March 22, 2018	Guatemala City
GT0218	La Puya	Civil society—anti-mining	March 20, 2018	Guatemala City
GT0418	PDH	Government—ombudsman	March 21, 2018	Guatemala City
GT1318	FUNDESA	Business, policy	March 23, 2018	Guatemala City
GT1418	Legislator, Convergencia	Government—legislature	March 21, 2018	Guatemala City
GT1518	CIG	Business association	March 15, 2018	Guatemala City
GT1618	Mayor's office	Government—municipal	March 16, 2018	Santa Rosa de Lima
GT1818	ODHAG	Civil society—religious	March 21, 2018	Guatemala City
GT1918	MadreSelva	Civil society—environmental	March 9, 2018	Guatemala City
GT2318	CALAS	Civil society—legal and environmental	March 19, 2018	Guatemala City
GT2418	USAC	Academic	March 16, 2018	Guatemala City
GT2618	JOVID	Civil society—anti-mining	March 14, 2018	Mataquescuintla
GT2918	ICEFI	INGO—transparency	March 20, 2018	Guatemala City
GT3018	URL	Academic	March 26, 2018	Guatemala City
GT3618	Ministry of Labor	Government—executive	March 14, 2018	Guatemala City
GT3718	Legislator, Partido Patriota/ Independent	Government—legislature	March 14, 2018	Guatemala City
GT3918	Legal consultant	Civil society—legal and indigenous	March 14, 2018	Guatemala City
GT0117	GHRC	INGO—human rights	September 8, 2017	Washington, DC
GT0317	NISGUA	INGO—human rights	October 9, 2017	Chicago
GT0116	FLACSO	Academic	June 21, 2016	Guatemala City
GT0216	MadreSelva	Civil society—environmental	June 28, 2016	Guatemala City

Appendix 4.1 Continued

Code	Affiliation	Sector	Date	Location
GT0316	Plataforma Internacional Contra Impunidad	Civil society— human rights	June 22, 2016	Guatemala City
GT0516	Former vice president	Government— executive	June 28, 2016	Guatemala City
GT1116	La Puya	Civil society— anti-mining	June 20, 2016	La Puya
GT0115	CODIDENA	Civil society— anti-mining	October 14, 2015	Chicago
ES3710	EIA consultant	International technical expert	September 3, 2010	Colorado

5

Mining Skeptics

Environmental Resistance in Costa Rica

Much like Nicaragua and Guatemala, Costa Rica and El Salvador adopted pro-mining legislation and actively encouraged mine development during the market transition era. But unlike the first two cases, Costa Rica and El Salvador reversed course and ultimately legislated national mining bans. Following years of mine advancement and waves of protest against it, open pit mining was legally eliminated in Costa Rica in 2010, and all forms of metal mining were prohibited in El Salvador in 2017. Whereas prominent Costa Rican and Salvadoran political leaders had lobbied hard for mining-friendly policies in the 1980s and 1990s, much like political leaders in Nicaragua and Guatemala, by the 2010s, enthusiasm for mine development had waned and new priorities had consolidated. How, then, did these two countries come to reject policies that had secured strong support only a few years before? Drawing on concepts and theories from the study of elites, social movements, and political institutions, Chapters 5 and 6 trace the processes that culminated in mining prohibition.

As we saw in Chapter 2, understanding the push for mining restriction requires us to pay close attention to three interactive processes: *shifts in the level of elite consensus, the organizational characteristics of the anti-mining networks,* and *the availability of docking points in the state apparatus where civil society actors can insert demands.* Policies that restrict mining activity are more likely to be found where pro-mining elite consensus has ruptured and elites have become sharply divided over the sector. Although some business and governmental elites will still tend to support mining investment, in keeping with the general advocacy of resource-based development promoted by international funders, mining companies, and corporate home governments, others may come to see mining in negative terms. To the extent that significant sectors of the elite call attention to long-term costs, unacceptable risk levels, and economic distortions related to mining dependence,

Breaking Ground. Rose J. Spalding, Oxford University Press. © Oxford University Press 2023.
DOI: 10.1093/oso/9780197643150.003.0005

these divisions within the elite create opportunities for renegotiation of mining policy.

Second, policy change is more likely when mining resistance networks gain multisectoral breadth, spatial reach, and frame alignment, thereby overcoming their tendency toward local-level fragmentation and frame dispersal. In both Costa Rica and El Salvador, as we will see, the anti-mining movements achieved a high degree of agreement about ultimate goals and were able to effectively link actors across the local-national divide. Third, mining restrictions are more likely to be adopted if the political system includes at least some entry points through which engaged citizens can gain access to state institutions and influence the behaviors of public officials. These docking points, whether providing access to the presidency, legislature, courts, bureaucracies, or municipal offices, allow mining critics to place policy reform on the national agenda and to advance discussion of policy remedies.

Parallels between the two cases are readily apparent. A new burst of gold mine exploration in Costa Rica and El Salvador began in the 1990s, when the governments in both countries actively promoted the development of the industry.[1] Mine-friendly legislation attracted prospectors, concessions were sought and granted, and exploratory investments were made in the early 2000s, when investors located commercially viable deposits. In both cases, the administrative gear-up for permit approval triggered intense rounds of debate, and anti-mining mobilization cycled through several phases over the following decade. In the end, elite support broke, resistance movements coalesced, and the national legislatures in both Costa Rica and El Salvador voted, unanimously, to prohibit industrial mining.

In spite of these parallels, these two cases also contain striking variations. The ways in which activists mobilized, political parties operated, state institutions functioned, and policy decisions unfolded reflected the significant differences in the way political life operated in these two settings. Our controlled comparison allows us to explore how a particular kind of policy outcome can emerge in two seemingly divergent contexts. Tracing the dynamics leading to a specific policy outcome, while also integrating the

---

[1] Although their gold exports tended to be smaller than those from Nicaragua and Honduras, Costa Rica and El Salvador shared the regional history of gold mining (Bulmer-Thomas 1987, 77). United Fruit Company founder Minor Cooper Keith, who controlled Central American regional railroads and banana exports, invested in Costa Rican gold mining in the 1890s, and ultimately acquired eight industrial gold mines that employed over 500 workers (Niesenbaum and Elliott 2019, 35–40).

144 BREAKING GROUND

significant variation that emerges across different cases, permits a richer and more robust interpretation of social movement dynamics and their impacts on the policymaking process. This analysis argues for the incorporation of complexity and texture in our explanatory frameworks, and demonstrates the usefulness of a comparative framework as a tool for avoiding simplistic generalizations based on single cases. The goal of this approach is to reach beyond mere description and push toward more robust forms of analysis and explanation.

This chapter is designed to address mining policy change by examining developments in Costa Rica, the first of these two cases. A parallel analysis of the Salvadoran case is presented in Chapter 6. As noted in Chapter 2, this book draws on "political process theory" (McAdam, Tarrow, and Tilly 2001), which embeds contentious action within the broader political arena. It employs a "political mediation" model (Amenta et al. 2010), which examines ways in which social movement activists interact with state actors and institutions as they pursue policy objectives. In keeping with the broader framework of the book, this study pays close attention to the interconnections among elites, the character and resilience of movement networks, and the availability of *docking points*, or institutional spaces in which activist coalitions can lodge demands, elicit recognition, and register objections that oblige state actors to respond.

This chapter is divided into five parts. The first section explores the background on Costa Rica's heterodox market reform and the early development of its environmental movement. The second part focuses on the advancement of the mining industry and growing evidence of elite division. The next section traces the construction of Costa Rica's decentralized anti-mining coalition. The fourth section maps the two-track docking strategy through which activists engaged both the courts and the legislature, ultimately leading to mining prohibition. As in Guatemala, Costa Rican activists used litigation to insert legal claims into judicial decision-making and to elicit court rulings that challenged extractivist practices. This action brought mining critics into an array of legal and quasi-legal spaces where the mining advance could be challenged and disrupted. Unlike in Guatemala, anti-mining activists in Costa Rica also developed an electoral strategy, impacting the composition of the legislature and reshaping legislative deliberations. This section shows how anti-mining organizations channeled a combination of curated information and political pressure toward key state positions and opened new institutional spaces. The final part

MINING SKEPTICS: COSTA RICA   145

reviews the mining policy outcomes and the post-extractivism challenges that remain.[2]

Market Reform and Environmental Initiatives

Modern conflicts over metal mining emerged in Costa Rica in the 1970s and 1980s, fueled by a clash between neoliberal reform and an emerging popular commitment to conservation and environmental sustainability (van den Holmbergh 2004; Araya 2010, 309; Graef 2013; Almeida 2014, 36–37). State leaders adopted a suite of market reforms in the wake of the debt crisis, which hit Costa Rica hard in the early 1980s (Spalding 2014, 34–43). With substantial early assistance from the US government through USAID, followed by sustained support from international financial institutions, Costa Rica became an early Latin American leader in structural adjustment. Tariffs and regulations were slashed, agro-exports were promoted, and new forms of economic development were pursued. The new model prioritized foreign investment and export growth achieved through market liberalization and global integration.

External financial flows supported the creation of pro-market institutions and think tanks that lent organizational and ideological support to the transition. A new generation of globalizing elites rose to prominence in Costa Rica and aligned with external advisers to oversee increased opening to foreign investment and trade. USAID funding supported the creation of the Costa Rican Investment Promotion Agency (CINDE) in 1983 and the establishment of the Ministry of Foreign Trade (COMEX) three years later. Between 1985 and 1987, the IMF provided six loans for Costa Rica, which contained thirty-four performance criteria and fifty-six total conditions that promoted deregulation (Copelovitch 2010, 321).

Pro-market guru Eduardo Lizano was named central bank president, a post he held across four administrations. Lizano lent personal conviction

---

[2] This chapter draws on forty interviews conducted in Costa Rica and Washington, DC, between 2010 and 2017 and subsequent email exchanges with leading participants in 2020 and 2021. See Appendix 5.2 for a list of the interviews cited in this chapter. The chapter also incorporates information from environmental and anti-mining networks; reports from government ministries and regulatory bodies; mining company documents; legal filings from domestic court and the *Infinito v. Costa Rica* international investment dispute; the database of Asamblea Legislativa proceedings; and CID-Gallup public opinion data. For additional information about the research methodology, see the "Argument and Methods" section in Chapter 1.

146 BREAKING GROUND

and local knowledge to the transition process, and inspired a generation of Costa Rican economists to embrace neoliberal change. The Academia de Centroamérica, a self-described "thought center" under Lizano's leadership, provided a gathering place for market-promoting economists and policy specialists where they could coordinate research and advance policy prescriptions (Spalding 2014, 39–40). Institution-building included the creation of new business chambers to coordinate the efforts of emerging exporters. Among other changes that opened up the Costa Rican economy was the creation of a new Ministry of Industry, Energy, and Mines. A new mining law was adopted in 1982. (See the policy transition timeline in Table 5.1.)

Ultimately Costa Rica moved toward a heterodox version of neoliberal reform that emphasized market opening but preserved social programs (Seligson and Martínez Franzoni 2010; Huber and Stephens 2010). Costa Rica's traditional support for state economic participation, which included state control of the banking system, electricity, and telecommunications, was tested at this juncture but not broken. Commitment to the "solidarity state" model, with guarantees of universal health and education services, was also sustained. Another area where we continue to find active state engagement was in environmental protection.

Costa Rica has a long history of creating public environmental institutions, which predated the 1949 founding of its modern state and persisted across periods of economic adjustment. In the 1980s and 1990s, as the country underwent market reform, environmental institution building persisted and grew.[3] Preexisting environmental services were elevated to ministerial rank in 1988, with the creation of the Ministry of Natural Resources, Energy and Mines (MIRENEM, later Ministry of Environment and Energy, MINAE). This ministry oversaw a network of protected areas and national parks, many initially established by foreign scientists and organizations but soon embraced by Costa Rican scientists as a source of national distinction (Evans 1999; Campbell 2002). New international ideas about sustainability emerged at the 1992 Rio Earth Summit and encouraged the adoption of additional legislation to protect forests and biodiversity. Costa Rica ratified the

---

[3] According to PEN-Región (2016, 236), the number of public environmental institutions established in Costa Rica between 1908 and 2010 exceeded that for any other Central American country. This pattern of institutional development dates back to the 1908–1950 era and continued across the next sixty years. Of the 186 public environmental institutions identified in Central America in 2010, over a third (64) were located in Costa Rica.

MINING SKEPTICS: COSTA RICA 147

Table 5.1 Costa Rican Mining Policy Timeline

Mining Policies and Related Actions (Years)	Presidential Administration and Political Party/Coalition	Term
Ministry of Industry, Energy, and Mines created (1982) Mining Code adopted (1982)	Monge, PLN	1982–1986
Ministry of Natural Resources, Energy, and Mines created (1988) FECON established (1989)	Arias, PLN	1986–1990
Law mandated instruction on environmental awareness in primary and secondary education (1991) Crucitas Project received exploration permit (1993)	Calderón, PUSC	1990–1994
New Forestry Law adopted (1996) Canada and Costa Rica signed BIT (1998)	Figueres Olsen, PLN	1994–1998
Biodiversity Law adopted (1998) Rodríguez proclaimed mining resolution granting Crucitas concession (2001)	Rodríguez, PUSC	1998–2002
Pacheco declared open pit mining moratorium (2002) SETENA rejected Crucitas EIA (March 2003) Infinito filed for an injunction with Constitutional Court and presented an ISDS notice to Ministry of Foreign Trade (April 2003) MINAE ordered SETENA to conduct a new EIA evaluation (October 2003) Infinito filed first request for arbitration (June 2005) SETENA approved Crucitas EIA (December 2005) Bellavista Mine extraction permit approved (December 2005)	Pacheco, PUSC	2002–2006
Bellavista Mine leach pad liner cracked, mudslide destroyed mine infrastructure (2007) Arias declared Crucitas in the "national interest," authorized extraction permit; forest removal began (October 2008) Activists secured injunction; logging and mine preparation halted at Crucitas (October 2008)	Arias, PLN	2006–2010
Chinchilla declared open pit mining moratorium (May 2010) Legislature approved ban on new open pit mines (November 2010) TCA declared Crucitas license invalid due to administrative violations (December 2010) ICSID registered Infinito Gold's arbitration request (2014)	Chinchilla, PLN	2010–2014

(continued)

148 BREAKING GROUND

Table 5.1 Continued

Mining Policies and Related Actions (Years)	Presidential Administration and Political Party/Coalition	Term
ICSID accepted jurisdiction for *Infinito Gold Ltd. v. Republic of Costa Rica* (2017)	Solís, PAC	2014–2018
New legislative proposals to legalize small- and medium-scale gold mining (2020) ICSID tribunal ruled against Infinito Gold (2021)	Alvarado, PAC	2018–2022

Convention on Biodiversity in 1992 and adopted its own Biodiversity Law in 1998 (Miller 2006).

The emerging epistemic community of environmental scientists documented the impact of expanded agricultural and beef production on deforestation, as Costa Rica's forest cover fell from 53% of national territory in 1961 to 21% in 1987 (LeCoq et al. 2015, 256). Recognition of the associated losses moved the government to advance a series of forest laws in the 1980s and 1990s. Attention culminated in the 1996 Forest Law, which expanded forest protection on privately held land, using an innovative payment system that compensated private owners for forest maintenance.[4]

By 2010, forests had begun to recover, once again covering over half of Costa Rica's national territory, a feat unparalleled in the rest of the region (see Table 5.2). Much of Costa Rica's conservation legislation was advanced through technocratic initiatives, often with financial support from international organizations and allies (Evans 1999; Campbell 2002; Zimmerer 2011; Le Coq et al. 2015). The payment structure circumvented the prohibitions on trade subsidies that the IMF and WTO had mandated, and compensatory payments secured the acquiescence of the forest industry (Le Coq et al. 2015). Government support for forest stabilization became a matter of cross-party consensus and consolidated as part of Costa Rica's national brand as an environmentally sustainable haven (Silva 2003; Le Coq et al. 2015; Isla 2015).

---

[4] The 1996 Forestry Law built on the forestry law of 1969, which had established a Department of National Parks within the Ministry of Agriculture and Livestock. Funding for the National Park Service increased substantially during the Oduber administration (1974–1978) (Hopkins 1995, 42–50), and expanded park services "gave impetus to environmental education in Costa Rica" (p. 70).

MINING SKEPTICS: COSTA RICA   149

Table 5.2 Forest Cover as a Percentage of National Territory in Central America, 2000–2015

Country	2000	2005	2010	2015
Costa Rica	47.0%	48.8%	51.5%	54.0%
El Salvador	15.8	14.9	13.6	12.8
Guatemala	38.8	36.7	33.6	33.0
Honduras	56.1	51.8	45.3	41.0
Nicaragua	31.1	28.8	25.3	25.9

Sources: CEPALSTAT databases; PEN-Región (2014, 78); PEN-Región (2016, 212).

Social Movement Organizing and Environmental Activism

Although Costa Rica's early environmental protection policies were largely top-down projects, environmental organizations also emerged within civil society, adopting goals that ranged from radical ecologism to market-friendly sustainability (Evans 1999, 198–214; van den Hombergh 2004). The Asociación Preservacionista de Flora y Fauna Silvestre (APREFLOFAS), founded in 1985, focused on wildlife preservation and skewed toward a conservationist discourse (see Figure 5.1). In contrast, the activist-oriented Asociación Ecologista de Costa Rica (AECO), founded in 1988, developed a critical discourse using a "social ecology" frame that focused on an intrinsic antagonism between ecology and capitalism.[5] Still others focused on advancing environmental sustainability within a market framework and worked to develop Costa Rica's ecotourism brand (see discussion in van den Hombergh 2004; Campbell 2002).

These organizations and activists became loosely linked in a national alliance under the Federación Costarricense para la Conservación del Ambiente (FECON). Established in October 1989, FECON attempted to strengthen the impact of environmental activism through improved collaboration. FECON reported thirty-six institutional members in 2008, many of them operating at the subnational level.[6] Although the dominant issues in

---

[5] AECO dissolved due to internal divisions in 1999, and COECE-CIEBA, the Costa Rica affiliate of Friends of the Earth, assumed leadership of the social ecology wing (van den Hombergh 2004).

[6] See FECON's website, https://feconcr.org.

Figure 5.1 APREFLOFAS anti-mining graphic that references local wildlife and painted ox cart (*carreta*), a traditional national symbol of Costa Rica. Reproduced with permission.

the environmentalist movement shifted across the decades, mobilizations advanced by these activists were recognizably interconnected and often targeted similar adversaries, even as their discourse and frames responded differentially and dynamically to international resource flows and the development of public awareness and sensitivities (Graef 2013).

Mining controversies generated debate in Costa Rica's incipient environmental movement as early as the 1970s, when environmental activists moved to derail a bauxite mine the Aluminum Company of America (ALCOA) had proposed in the Valle de El General. The two months of protest in 1970, involving over 50,000 participants from a reported eighty-three organizations, has been called the birth of the ecology movement in Costa Rica (Quesada 2010). At the end of the 1980s, protest also erupted over a proposed sulfur mine project in what later became the Parque del Agua Juan Castro Blanco. Organizing against industrial gold mining began in the early 1990s in the communities of Cutris and Santa Rosa de Pocosol in Alajuela province. Local residents connected around the theme of mining resistance, citing concerns about property security, agricultural production losses, and fears of social decay that would result from mining incursions. Community leaders soon connected with national-level actors to share information and frame a response.

In the 1970s and 1980s, Costa Rica's anti-mining activists often incorporated a pro-sovereignty frame, registering opposition to foreign ownership of the country's natural resources and pushing for more state-centric control. In a complex process of frame transformation, the dominant discourse shifted over time and "transmogrified" into concern about environmental damage as the concept of ecological sustainability took root in the public imagination (Graef 2013, 304). Over time the environmentalist frame itself became internally variegated, with traditional conservation narratives contested by and coexisting with emerging counternarratives focusing on social ecology (Campbell 2002; van den Hombergh 2004; CR1314).

Mining Sector Debate: From Mining Promotion to Elite Division

As this environmentalist framework unfolded, the rush to commercialize Costa Rica's abundant natural resources advanced in tandem, setting up a collision course. The investment-friendly mining code that was adopted in 1982 encouraged gold mining prospectors to launch exploratory work in the 1990s, as they sought to develop a foothold in a country where no significant large-scale gold industry was then in operation. According to Ana Isla (2015, 149), by August 1996, sixty-six mining permits had been issued by MINAE, many of which expedited exploration inside protected areas, wildlife refuges, and forestry reserves. Two large-scale gold mine projects, Crucitas and Bellavista, advanced most quickly, and these provide the focus for our Costa Rica account.

In 1991, Canadian geologist Maurice Eugene Coates filed for an exploration permit in north-central Costa Rica to search for gold deposits near the Rio San Juan border with Nicaragua (Soto 2013, 22). Over the next ten years, a mine project designated as Las Crucitas was repeatedly bought and sold. Assets of the Costa Rican mine development company Industrias Infinito S.A. were transferred in quick succession to Placer Dome, Lyon Lake

152 BREAKING GROUND

Mines, and finally Vannessa Ventures, the Canadian junior that developed the project. After locating commercially viable quantities of gold, Industrias Infinito (henceforth Infinito) applied for an extraction permit in 1999 to build Crucitas, envisioned as a large open pit mine to extract gold, silver, copper, and other minerals.

Mining critics stepped up their preventative work, compiling information about the environmental risks associated with chemical mining and the negative impacts on water resources. With support from the diocesan Pastoral Social committees and Bishop Ángel San Casimiro of the Ciudad Quesada diocese (1995–2007), local opposition expanded into neighboring communities (Cartagena Cruz 2000; Soto 2013; CR0514). Movement entrepreneurs began to gather information and raise complaints with local media and authorities, and soon networked into regional and national clusters. In April 1996, mining opponents created the National Front for the Opposition to Open Pit Mining, linking seventeen groups and organizations (Cartagena Cruz 2000, 76) in a campaign against open pit mining. Their September 26, 1996, march For Peace, Life, and Justice in Ciudad Quesada reportedly mobilized a crowd of 5,000–8,000 anti-mining protesters, and drew coverage by two national and one local TV news programs (p. 7).

Facing a political and regulatory logjam, Infinito pressed for official intervention. Following almost two decades of structural adjustment and market opening, a powerful segment of the Costa Rican political elite had aligned with foreign investors, and they rallied in support. On December 17, 2001, outgoing president Miguel Angel Rodríguez and his minister of the environment, Elizabeth Odio, granted the rights to establish an open pit gold mine to Vannessa, issuing a proclamation that became official following its publication only three days before the 2002 presidential election. With this pronouncement, Costa Rica cleared the way for construction of a new gold mine industry.

The boldness of Rodríguez's declaration disguised the reality of political and legal division. Not all business sectors were enthusiastic about the advent of mining, and a growing interest in ecotourism, which was rapidly becoming a major industry, prompted questions about the impact of large-scale extraction projects on the country's tourism brand. Whereas in Nicaragua and Guatemala the dominant business association absorbed a newly established mining chamber and became a powerful defender of its interests, in Costa Rica the industry secured only isolated statements of support and did not integrate into the Union of Private Sector Chambers and Associations (UCCAEP), the country's business peak association (CR0110).[7] Divisions were even clearer among Costa Rican political elites, where the split was palpable, with competing party leaders endorsing widely divergent views.

As evidence of elite division accumulated, the advance toward and resistance against gold mining in Costa Rica then moved through three phases: official disenchantment and vacillation during the administration of Abel Pacheco (2002–2006); a government-backed mining advance that brought the country to the brink of mine development during the second administration of Óscar Arias (2006–2010); and finally a successful, multilayered mobilization that ended with cancellation of the Crucitas permit and a mining moratorium declared during the administration of Laura Chinchilla (2010–2014). In the space of a year, Costa Rica went from a presidential declaration in favor of mining (2001) to a presidential declaration announcing a mining moratorium (2002); 2008 brought another presidential declaration that mining was in the national interest, a position revoked two years later with another moratorium declaration. These policy switchbacks demonstrated the absence of elite consensus and the growing political capacity of environmental actors, who called for policy reversal.

Corporate Pressure and Government Vacillation

The 1983–1998 period was characterized by a two-party system in Costa Rica, wherein political leaders were generally drawn from one of two main political coalitions. The historically dominant National Liberation Party (PLN), which represented most of the winners from the 1948 civil war, was traditionally viewed as a center-left, social democratic party; the Social Christian Unity Party (PUSC), which consolidated more slowly and unevenly, generally anchored the center right (Rosenblatt 2018, 126–140). Although the PLN had historically been associated with Costa Rica's developmentalism, elites from both of these parties converged around the 1980s market transition, forming an alignment that their critics sometimes labeled as "PLUSC"

---

[7] UCCAEP was founded in 1973. Its membership had expanded to forty-six chambers in 2011 (UCCAEP 2011).

154   BREAKING GROUND

to indicate their overlap.[8] But this labeling concealed crevices, even within the same party, that became visible at key junctures.

During the 2002 presidential campaign, candidates for both the PLN and PUSC publicly proclaimed their opposition to gold mining (Soto 2013, 91), highlighting the clash between the pro-mining sentiments of the outgoing Rodríguez administration and the extraction policy preferences of in-coming political leaders. This early hesitancy about the industry by a cross-party sector of political elites demonstrated the significance that the anti-mining coalition had already acquired in important corners of the country.

PUSC candidate Abel Pacheco emerged victorious in 2002, and immediately issued Decreto #30477-MINAE (2002), an executive decree banning open pit gold mining in Costa Rican territory.[9] Speaking in opposition to mining during his inaugural address on May 8, 2002, Pacheco (2002) declared, "The true gold of the future will be water and oxygen." To consolidate this perspective, he called for new constitutional provisions that would further affirm environmental protection and create an absolute prohibition on cutting down primary forests.

As Costa Rican environmental and political forces began to coalesce in support of a mining ban, mining company representatives responded. The mining projects with the most advanced status in Costa Rica were Canadian owned. Under the terms of Costa Rica's 1998 bilateral investment treaty (BIT) with Canada, mining company lawyers argued, the government had an obligation to protect Canadian investors, and previously acquired rights could not be retroactively denied under a new decree.[10] In this framing, Pacheco's mining moratorium could only be applied to new investors, not those like Infinito that had already acquired an exploration permit. Any effort to thwart their claim now would be met with legal action in an international investment tribunal, where the case would be adjudicated by international arbitrators and hefty penalties could be imposed. Facing these financial threats, Pacheco then stepped back, agreeing that, under the ban's transition

[8] See also Robles-Rivera 2019, 31–52, on the Costa Rican elite's ideological convergence in support of the market transition.

[9] This initiative, Pacheco said, came at the suggestion of, among others, his youngest son, Fabián Pacheco, a noted environmentalist who went on to head FECON and lead various environmental initiatives. https://www.oceanforest.org/guariadeosa.com/cr_president.htm, accessed August 17, 2021.

[10] This position was affirmed by Sala IV, the Constitutional Chamber of Costa Rica's Supreme Court, in a case brought by the owners of a second gold mining project at the Bellavista mine.

MINING SKEPTICS: COSTA RICA   155

features, investors who already had secured "acquired rights" could not have them annulled.[11]

Institutional reticence about imposing retroactive restraints also allowed the Toronto-based Wheaton River Minerals Limited's project near the Gulf of Nicoya to obtain mining permits and to advance toward production at the Bellavista open pit gold mine. Receiving free zone status and exemption from import and export taxes (Isla 2015, 152), Bellavista began construction in 2003, and "first bar" production was announced in July 2005 (Viales Hurtado and Marín Hernández 2012). This project sparked conflict with local communities over access to freshwater springs and logging in the zone. Anti-mining activists in the area formed the Miramar Front in Opposition to Mining to build community-level resistance (Isla 2015).

In spite of Costa Rica's much-vaunted status as a democratic model, Costa Rican mining opponents lacked legal mechanisms for initiating community consultation, and they struggled to confront corporations that entered their localities having secured national-level authorization. Mining corporations also proved adept at using Costa Rican courts to secure protections and intimidate opponents. Bellavista managers brought repeated legal charges of defamation against their local critics (Isla 2015, 153–155), and they soon secured the conviction and fining of an anti-mining municipal council member from the nearby town of Miramar de Montes de Oro. Although this conviction was overturned on appeal, defamation charges leveled against activists raised the costs of opposition. Geographically disconnected and outgunned, the Miramar Front was unable to prevent the launch of Costa Rica's gold mining industry.

Conflict over the legal framework governing mining continued for the next decade and spread from the regional to the national level. The National Environmental Technical Secretariat (Secretaría Técnica Nacional Ambiental, SETENA), the government agency in charge of certifying the environmental viability of construction projects, rejected Infinito's environmental impact study in 2003. This step halted the advance of Crucitas, Costa Rica's second gold mine project, slowing the momentum for extractive sector development.

---

[11] One legal question was whether Infinito, which had been given an exploitation permit but had not completed the environmental impact review, had fully established its "acquired rights."

156 BREAKING GROUND

Mining companies deployed both carrots and sticks to force their way into resistant terrain. Using domestic courts, Infinito challenged SETENA's review process and, in April 2003, again raised the international investment dispute threat, now notifying the Costa Rican government that it intended to invoke provisions under the BIT with Canada to demand indemnization (Infinito Gold Ltd. and Republic of Costa Rica 2014, 10). The minister of the environment then voided SETENA's first finding and, with a new team in place, launched a second round of environmental impact review. Meanwhile, Infinito promoted a series of community development initiatives, seeking the elusive "social license" that comes with community approval (Soto 2013, 160–167). As the SETENA review dragged on, Infinito acted on its legal threats and submitted a formal request for arbitration under ICSID's Additional Facility Rules in 2005 (Infinito Gold Ltd. and Republic of Costa Rica 2014, 13).

Under pressure, SETENA reversed itself on December 12, 2005, and now announced that the proposed mine was environmentally viable. Crucitas was thus cleared for development, and the company was given two years to initiate operation. As the company advanced through the permitting process and its financing mechanisms were tested, the proposed construction plan underwent a major modification. The new project design, presented as the two-year window was closing, reduced the surface area of the mine by 60%, from 126 hectares to 50 hectares, but increased the proposed mine depth from 20 meters to 60 meters, allowing extraction of gold from the underlying hard rock in addition to the surface saprolite.[12] On February 4, 2008, this change was likewise approved by SETENA, only weeks after the new design was submitted. This bureaucratic accommodation wound up having a cost for the Arias administration, albeit not immediately.

Mining and the Arias Administration

As the Crucitas mine proposal passed through regulatory hoops, activists concerned about issues of environmental sustainability, social inclusion, and

---

[12] Canadian securities regulatory agencies regarded projections of gold quantities to be extracted from superficial saprolite through chemical leaching as less reliable than those derived from tests on underlying hard rock, and the company's financial metrics improved under the new plan (Infinito Gold Ltd. 2014).

MINING SKEPTICS: COSTA RICA   157

market regulation shifted their attention to other pressing struggles. The national debate about CAFTA, Central America's free trade agreement with the United States, took center stage in Costa Rica through 2005–2007 (Spalding 2014, 141–151). This agreement, signed in 2004, required legislative approval in the signatory countries before it could enter into effect. After more than three years in which little headway was made on CAFTA ratification, President Óscar Arias, now newly returned to the presidency for a second term (2006–2010), shifted the venue for ratification out of the legislature and into a national referendum, in the country's first use of this newly established participatory mechanism.

The "no" vote gained momentum across the course of the referendum campaign, but this coalition was narrowly defeated, 51.6% to 48.4%, in the October 2007 referendum. Following months of intense coordination and grassroots campaigning, anti-CAFTA forces then fragmented into diverse political camps.[13] Disenchantment and "political grief" led some activists to temporarily retreat from the institutional battlefield (Mora Solano 2016, 168–179, 270). During this period of activist distraction followed by fragmentation and disengagement, pro-mining actors advanced toward their objective.

Infinito executives found a powerful political ally in President Arias, who had long embraced market opening and foreign investment as the preferred economic development strategy for Costa Rica. Coming into office for the first time during the turbulent and debt-ridden 1980s, Arias had supported the country's pro-market turn as its only viable alternative (Spalding 2014). Now returning to office in 2006, Arias proved a steadfast defender of market-friendly advances, supporting both CAFTA approval and the mining advance. CAFTA-mandated reforms included tariff reductions, strengthened intellectual property protections, investment dispute guarantees, the opening of the state-run telecommunications sector to private competition, and the streamlining of regulations on investments in infrastructure and the extractive sector. However, a persistent thicket of

---

[13] Mora Solano (2016) notes the "re-interest in the political" that emerged in Costa Rica in the 2000s and the challenge that social activism posed to the "technocratic authoritarianism" of the Arias era. Based on in-depth interviews with twenty-two social movement activists and a review of four cycles of collective action between 1995 and 2010, Mora Solano identified multiple currents into which "no" activists transferred following the 2007 CAFTA referendum defeat, including newly emerging parties (PAC, Frente Amplio) and social movements (pp. 168–170).

158 BREAKING GROUND

legal and regulatory constraints designed to protect forests from encroachment still impeded the implementation of Infinito's mine development plan.[14] To break through these restrictions, Arias now took a definitive pro-mining step.

On October 13, 2008, Arias, along with his environmental minister, Roberto Dobles Mora, issued an executive decree declaring the Crucitas mining investment to be of "public interest" (Decreto No. 34801-MINAET 2008), thus lifting the project out of the bureaucratic doldrums. This decree lauded the project as the source of nearly US$65 million in initial investments, 253 direct jobs, an estimated US$8.8 million in annual taxes, and payments to the community of 2% of net profits, which would provide an estimated US$1.4 million per year for the projected eight years the mine would operate. In return, it noted, the company pledged to participate in a reforestation project, planting fifty trees for each one it felled. This decree allowed the company to circumvent legal restrictions on forest cutting and changes in authorized land use—legal tentacles that had prevented construction from getting under way. Within hours of securing the permits, the forest clearing began.

To remove the forest cover and begin the digging, large swaths of trees were downed over the next three days. This action, in a country where forest protection had become part of the national brand and source of local pride, proved catalytic for social mobilization. Telenoticias Canal 7 sent in a helicopter crew to film the result and broadcast visual footage of the downed forest on national television. These images were, according to anti-Crucitas activist Edgardo Araya, "the beginning of the end" (CR1814). With national attention now focused on the case, mining opponents rushed to file for another round of injunctions in the courts. Once again, this troubled project was delayed through judicial action.

---

[14] Legal opinions requested by officials in the Área de Conservación Arenal, the local agency in charge of processing the final paperwork, indicated that reclassification of the land from agriculture to mining would require a presidential declaration that the Crucitas project was of "public interest," an action that would thereby suspend normal regulatory protocols (Soto 2013, 492–494). Decreto #34801-MINAET (2008) notes that articles 13 and 14 of the 1996 Forest Law prohibit changes in designated land use and forest clearing except for public and private projects declared to be of public interest in an executive decree.

Anti-Mining Mobilization: Building a
Decentralized Coalition

Social movement analysts repeatedly note how new movements build on those that came before (Almeida 2014; Rossi 2017). Whether through examination of the threshold effects found in long-term slow-moving mobilization processes and the construction of repertoires of contention (McAdam, Tarrow, and Tilly 2001), the pulsating diffusion processes that extend movements across time and space (Givan, Roberts, and Soule 2010; Bosi, Giugni, and Uba 2016), or the power of "master frames" that "articulate and align a vast array of events and experiences so that they hang together in a relatively unified and meaningful fashion" (Snow and Benford 1992, 137–138), social movement theory recognizes the importance of tracking legacies and understanding how separate instances of mobilization connect into coherent sequences. Prior mobilization is seen to forge shared meanings, entrench vocabularies, and create personal ties that allow movement leaders to draw on previous experience as they filter choices and make informed calculations about alternative frames and tactics. As Heaney and Rojas (2014, 1053) note:

> Movements must be understood in terms of their relationships to past, contemporaneous, and future social movements. Past social movements train activists for current struggles, pass on know-how that becomes the content of tactical repertoires, and leave a cultural legacy that opens and closes doors to current movements.

While building on precedent may facilitate contention and promote successful outcomes, it may also discourage contentious action and promote quiescence. Movements that are captured by their founders and yoked to the agenda of dominant leaders, as in Nicaragua, for example, may find it difficult to adapt to new developments or to respond to grassroots initiatives. A legacy of repression, as we saw in Guatemala, often undermines mobilization or delays its development. Repeated defeat, as seen in both cases, can be demoralizing and lend activism a discontinuous, flickering quality. But previous mobilization can also be an accelerant, leaving in place "abeyance structures" that permit rapid remobilization (Taylor 1989) and "strategic capital" (Almeida 2014) in the form of knowledge and experience that guide informed decision-making.

160   BREAKING GROUND

In the Costa Rican case, anti-mining resistance entered a new and more consequential phase in the wake of Arias's 2008 "national interest" decree, building on prior experiences of mobilization but adapting their repertoire. Consistent with the "intermovement dependency model" of social movement networking (Heaney and Rojas 2014), this expanding coalition rearticulated activist nodes and organizations that had mobilized previously for struggles with resonant goals or concerns. Costa Rica's multisectoral anti-mining movement linked community, environmentalist, religious, and epistemic actors in a broad, loosely networked national coalition that layered new mobilizations on top of prior campaigns and organizational precedents. Anti-mining activists interviewed for the present study made frequent reference to participation in prior mobilizations, most commonly in the movement against telecommunications privatization (Combo del ICE) and the anti-CAFTA campaign, but also in prior struggles over mining issues.

Anti-mining networks operating at the regional (Northern Union for Life, UNOVIDA), and national (the Open Pit Mining National Opposition Front) levels in the late 1990s and early 2000s remobilized after 2008 to serve as the anchors of the mining resistance movement's new wave (CR0514).[15] Anti-mining activists connected with brokers from organizations in the affected region, including Catholic religious activists affiliated with the Pastoral Social de Pavón, and with previously existing networks of environmentalists who had begun organizing nationally, including FECON, APREFLOFAS, and COECO-CEIBA, among others.

Environmentalists also joined forces with the ombudsman (Defensoría de los Habitantes) to mount a human rights challenge to the mining interests. Strong support for the cause emerged at the public universities in and around San José. Academic leaders organized Urgent Call (Llamado Urgente), a network of university affiliates that was designed to diffuse information and coordinate responses. The University Council (Consejo Universitario 2009) of the University of Costa Rica (UCR), drawing on the scientific and technical expertise of the faculty, undertook a six-month investigation of the Crucitas that culminated in a call for the revocation of Arias's presidential decree.

Anti-mining advocates connected with a new generation of internet-savvy followers who used social media networks, NGO websites, blogs, and

---

[15] Describing the goals of UNOVIDA, anti-Crucitas lawyer Edgardo Araya explained: "UNOVIDA wanted to do something different than what the other groups were already doing—we wanted to articulate the groups. The thinking of the individual groups was 'each one to their own struggle.' But we wanted to coordinate, to transfer learning from one to the other" (CR1814).

MINING SKEPTICS: COSTA RICA 161

Facebook pages to reach new audiences.[16] In post after post, internet activists pounded home the message about the risks associated with chemical mining, frequently citing a network of Costa Rican scientists including Allan Astorga (UCR geologist), Jorge Lobo (UCR biologist), and Yamileth Astorga (water resource specialist), who played a critical role as epistemic advisers. Graphic artists depicted the tensions between the national image of Costa Rica as an environmental haven and its prospective despoilment as a depleted wasteland. Dismissing company claims about "green mining," these activists sowed doubt about the safety of the proposed mine and the adequacy of the government's technical review.

This point was brought home to environmental observers in a made-in-Hollywood moment when a mudslide buried the Bellavista mine in 2007. That mine had been the first to open under the new mining regime, despite waves of conflict at the local level. Its leach pad rupture, followed by a major mud inundation, set off alarm bells in the activist community, bringing home their point about the country's regulatory limitations and environmental vulnerability (Isla 2015; Álvarez 2012).[17] The closing down of this mine after only two years of operation sent a powerful message about the viability of gold mining in Costa Rica.

The anti-mining campaign fueled a coordinated but decentralized and homegrown network in which constituent parts engaged in separate actions without a central clearinghouse. As Heidy Murillo, who served as president of both UNOVIDA and FECON during this protest cycle, observed:

We decided that we couldn't leave any stone unturned [descuidar por ningún lado]. Everyone added themselves in according to their own abilities. Some knew how to lobby; others knew activism. Some didn't want us to focus on street-level politics; some didn't want judicial remedies. There were diverse styles. In the end, we used everything—all the strategies. And this was done without any money. If a total of $50,000 was spent, that would be a high estimate. We had lawyers, biologists, engineers,

[16] During the height of the mobilization, key social media sources included Fuera de Crucitas, http://fueradecrucitas.blogspot.com/; http://kioscosambientales.ucr.ac.cr/quienes-somos.html; Llamado Urgente por el País, http://llamadourgenteporelpais.blogspot.com/; UNOVIDA's Facebook page, https://www.facebook.com/Unovida-1554138118161807/; and reports on FECON's website, https://feconcr.com/, among others.

[17] The Bellavista mine had also encountered procedural delays but received a permit under the less restrictive Plan de Gestión Ambiental mechanism and had finally opened in 2005 (Álvarez 2012, 7–11).

162 BREAKING GROUND

economists, geologists . . . and none of them were paid. Everyone donated their time and labor. (CR0514)

Marco Tulio Araya, an UNOVIDA activist and communications specialist, noting the strategic utility of this decentralized model, offered a similar observation:

> We learned to be a hydra-headed organization [*culebra de muchas cabezas*], operating with not just one leader. When there are many organizations, each doing a different thing, the companies don't know whom to attack. We were born decentralized, but later we saw the benefit of this kind of organization, and that centralization wasn't appropriate [*conveniente*]. (CR2014)

Using this decentralized but thematically networked model, Costa Rican activists maintained pressure on the Crucitas project. In addition to the routine repertoire of declarations, demonstrations, fora, and vigils, a sector of the anti-mining network organized a weeklong *caminata* in 2010. The route of this march allowed protesters to physically connect the Casa Presidencial in San José, where the march began, to the rural communities in the vicinity of the proposed mine in the north (Díaz González 2013; Núñez 2010). Young, urban activists from the Central Valley encountered older, religiously oriented rural activists, some of whom had joined this movement back in the 1990s (CR1914). An advance team of resistance organizers prepared the way, meeting with local officials and school groups to encourage a friendly reception and promote positive media visuals (CR0417). One observer noted:

> The people of the towns were very organized. They prepared meals for the marchers and found a place for them to sleep. I asked how they came to be involved, and they told me that they had been organizing against the mine for sixteen years. They were part of the Frente Norte Contra la Minería, which developed in the first protest epoch and was tied to religious communities. (CR1914)

Back in San José, another small group launched a hunger strike outside the presidential office in late 2010, a strategy that added urgency to their call.[18]

---

[18] Although Díaz González's (2013) study of media coverage found that the legal process in the Crucitas case was discussed in ten times as many news articles in the national media as the

MINING SKEPTICS: COSTA RICA   163

The mining company's official account of the movement characterized it dismissively as a "big show" (Soto 2013). Still, this campaign resonated broadly in Costa Rica, as public opinion poll results suggest. As this decentralized, multidimensional movement built in 2009 and 2010, disapproval of open pit mining registered in poll after poll. A CID-Gallup national survey (2010a) conducted in April and May 2010 found that respondents overwhelmingly expressed strong opposition to open pit mining. When asked "Do you agree with having open pit mining in the country?," 75% responded "not at all" (*nada*), the most negative option available, and another 9% responded "little" (*poco*). Only 10% responded that they were in favor, either "strongly" (*mucho*) (5%) or "somewhat" (*algo*) (5%). Opposition was solid even among supporters of the PLN, the political party of Óscar Arias. In CID Gallup's (2010b) September 2010 survey, 60.5% of those who identified with the PLN expressed opposition to open pit mining. Those who identified with other parties were even more sharply resistant; among those who identified with the newly established Citizen Action Party (PAC), more than 86% rejected open pit mining. Disapproval cut across gender and age lines, although it varied somewhat with education; opposition among those with a secondary-plus level of education was 9 percentage points higher than among those who had completed only primary school (CID Gallup 2010b, table 34).

The Crucitas battle kicked off a protest cycle that continued through the Chinchilla administration (2010–2014). The number of collective actions reported in the national media ticked upward in 2011–2014, driven in part by a surge in activism around environmental defense (PEN 2017, 284–285).[19]

---

demonstrations and marches were, his database of Crucitas coverage in four news sources (*La Nación, Diario Extra, Semanario Universidad,* and *El País*) in the year between May 8, 2010, and May 7, 2011, identified 138 articles in *El País* and 28 in *Diario Extra* that referred to the *caminata* and/or hunger strike.

[19] Using news reports of collective actions from *La Nación, Diario Extra,* and *Semanario Universidad,* researchers at the Programa Estado de la Nación have developed a database of over 200,000 protest actions between January 1992 and March 2017, and classified them by issue and type of protest (PEN 2017, 284–285). Their data indicate that whereas the total number of protests rose sharply in 2011 through mid-2014 and declined thereafter, the number of protests about environmental issues increased in the 2010–2016 period relative to historical pattern for the 1992–2009 period (p. 222), indicating that environmental themes had become an increasingly important area of political contention in Costa Rica, both absolutely and relative to other protests.

From Movement to Policy: Two-Track Docking

The activation of social movement networks and the favorable alignment of public opinion can create a propitious environment for public policy change, but the translation of social movement pressure into formal law and regulation is neither automatic nor inevitable. Indeed, some analysts argue that social movements play little role in the policymaking process since large-scale campaigns occur too infrequently to shape most routine policy decisions in modern states. One of the more difficult tasks in policy analysis involves establishing the linkages among these various processes and teasing out information about the impact of one set of variables on another (Silva 2017; Bosi, Giugni, and Uba 2016, 3–37).

I explore the movement-policy relationship by tracing the sequence of interventions by anti-extractivist activists as they engaged with state policymaking processes. My work gives particular attention to the docking points, or the institutional spaces in which social movement and civil society actors can inculcate their concerns in the formal political system and attempt to influence the behavior of state actors. Activists may take a well-trodden path that is commonly employed when citizens appeal for relief, or they may identify or create new institutional access points, carving out fresh space for policy action.

To pursue policy goals with regard to open pit mining in Costa Rica, the mining resistance movement followed a two-track model. First, the immediate risks associated with the opening up of chemical mining led opponents to launch a series of court actions designed to block mine construction by those who currently held mining permits. Second, opponents pursued legislative and regulatory policy changes that would close down the permitting process and prohibit new open pit metallic mining companies from receiving licenses in the future. The next two sections trace these interventions.

Judicialized Environmentalism

Social movement research in Latin America traditionally gave short shrift to the role of courts and litigation as an arena of contestation, focusing instead on activities such as protests, roadblocks, and occupations, where participant numbers and intensity could be made to count. The transformative potential of a disruptive challenge in the streets tended to draw the attention of both

MINING SKEPTICS: COSTA RICA 165

activists and analysts alike, whereas the weakness of the court system led to its neglect.

Recent research, however, has given greater attention to the intersection of social movements and legal processes in Latin America. As noted in the discussion of Guatemalan mining resistance in Chapter 4, social movements have increasingly availed themselves of legal instruments in their struggle for expanded rights. This work suggests a new arena for activist intervention, at least in cases where the courts have developed responsive capacity and are perceived as legitimate. Paralleling the discussion of "political opportunities" in social movement theory, socio-legal scholars have focused on the role of "legal opportunities," which open space for adding legal strategies to social movement repertoires (Hilson 2002; Wilson and Rodríguez-Cordero 2006; Andersen 2006; Helmke and Ríos-Figueroa 2011; Wilson 2011; Vanhala 2011).

Courts may, of course, serve as an impediment to social mobilization rather than a mechanism for its advance (Rosenberg 1991; Sarat and Schiengold 1998; Kolb 2007, 86–89). Institutionally distanced from the electoral competition processes that govern the selection of other occupants of public office, courts may function as countermajoritarian institutions that resist responsiveness to public preferences and popular initiatives (Kramarz, Cosolo, and Rossi 2017). Even when courts are relatively open to citizen demands (i.e., assign low court costs and display judicial receptiveness in terms of standing and filing requirements), the outcomes that are attainable through court action may not reflect movement priorities. Dependence on legal mechanisms to pursue claims may serve to distort the carefully constructed framing negotiated by movement coalitions and to deradicalize the quest, as movement leaders attempt to reshape their objectives in terms of narrow legal categories and viable legal strategies.

In spite of these limitations, activists may view litigation as a "significant but partial tactic—one that works in conjunction with other tactics and aids rather than displaces other forms of mobilization" (NeJaime 2013, 888). Legal mobilization can include diverse tactics and objectives, ranging from public legal education and consciousness-raising to lobbying for a change in law and strategic case litigation (Vanhala 2011, 6).

These possibilities have drawn the attention of numerous activists in Costa Rica, where courts have long been independent and influential actors.[20]

---

[20] Of court systems in eighteen Latin American countries analyzed in da Sousa (2010, 94), Costa Rican courts were ranked number one in 1975 and number two in 2005 in terms of judicial independence.

166 BREAKING GROUND

Use of the judicial system became increasingly common following the creation of Sala IV, the Constitutional Chamber of the Supreme Court, in 1989 (CR1214). Designed to make the chamber accessible, the operating rules allowed citizens and noncitizens alike to file a claim "without formalities, lawyers, fees, or an understanding of the point of law on which the claimant is appealing" (Wilson 2011, 59). As the number of filings soared, the court provided protection for several marginalized groups, including HIV/AIDS patients seeking coverage for antiretroviral drugs and labor unions (Wilson and Rodríguez-Cordero 2006). Costa Ricans reported a relatively high level of trust in their judicial system, which ranked second only to the Catholic Church.[21]

Courts are contested territory, of course, and Costa Rica's highly accessible court system provided opportunities for both sides of the mining conflict. Sala IV was used repeatedly by Infinito Gold to protect its business interests and force the removal of obstacles to mine development. At the same time, the anti-mining activists also used litigation to stay the implementation of mine development, and strategic legal interventions played a critical role in halting construction of the Crucitas mine. Nor was the Crucitas case the only example of judicialized environmentalism in Costa Rica. Using the PEN database of 1994–2013 collective actions, Chacón and Merino (2014, 10) document a pattern of judicialization of environmental protest over a twenty-year period. They found that 17.5% of environmental conflicts resulted in a *denuncia* (legal claim) before a national or international body, whereas only 6.4% of all protests led to this result. Environmental activism in Costa Rica displayed an elective affinity for judicialization, suggesting a legal and cultural context with well-marked tendencies.

While the rest of the government often faced gridlock, with policy deliberations and disputes extending for years, the courts tended to produce definitive findings and to mandate relief relatively quickly, using a simple, low-cost process that allowed anyone to file a claim. The number of cases presented to Sala IV rose from 2,296 in 1990 to 18,850 in 2009, and then stabilized.[22] For anti-mining activists, the juridical process provided an early,

---

[21] Courts received a trust level score of 52.9 points in 2014, second only to the Catholic Church at 62.6 points (Alfaro-Redondo, Seligson, and Zechmeister 2015, 46).

[22] For the 2014–2019 period, Sala IV's average annual case load was 21,299. See https://salaconstitucional.poder-judicial.go.cr/index.php.

critical complement to political struggle in the electoral arena. According to a manager of Infinito whom I interviewed in 2014, a total of twenty-two requests for legal injunctions had been filed against the company by mining opponents (CR0914).

Environmental activists had responded to President Rodríguez's 2001 proclamation granting mining rights to Infinito with the first of several interventions designed to use the court system to protect their constitutional right to a healthy environment. Activists filed a request for an *amparo* (injunction) with the Costa Rican Constitutional Court, challenging the right of the president and environmental minister to authorize exploitation without the company having first submitted and secured approval of its environmental impact statement (EIS) (Soto 2013). In 2004, the court agreed with the claimants and canceled Infinito's mining rights, but it allowed the company to proceed with an EIS process without prejudice to the outcome.[23]

As the judicialization of contention advanced, Costa Rica experienced the development of a small network of "cause lawyers," trained professionals who could wield legal instruments in the defense of social movements.[24] As in Guatemala, where courts provided the means to suspend mine operations, the courts in Costa Rica were an available resource for strategic litigation. Enjoying a widespread perception of legitimacy, and functioning as a protector of guaranteed rights, the Costa Rican court system provided a critical venue for action. The anti-mining movement in Costa Rica became well-schooled in the practice of filing for injunctions.

Anti-mining activists pursued their claims in two different jurisdictions— in Sala IV, which addressed constitutional issues and had long been used by environmental activists to pursue environmental rights, and in Sala I,

---

[23] Prior to 2001, Costa Rican law allowed for the grant of extraction rights, pending EIS approval, before an EIS process was undertaken, a regulatory process that was at odds with best practice in the field. The Mining Code was amended in March 2001 to require successful completion of the EIS process before an extraction permit could be issued.

[24] See discussion of cause lawyers and their role in social movements in Tarrow 2011, 271–272; Sarat and Scheingold 1998; and Rhode 2013. In Costa Rica, movement-aligned lawyers who organized in opposition to mining included Edgardo Araya, Alvaro Sagot, and Nicolás Boeglin. These three lawyers, along with two members of the national assembly, were subsequently charged with defamation by Infinito representatives. Diagnosed by Boeglin (2014) as a SLAPP (strategic lawsuit against public participation), a legal concept defined in the work of Pring and Canan (1996), these defamation charges were eventually dismissed by the courts, with the company required to provide compensation to the defendants for harm done by the company's unsubstantiated claims.

168   BREAKING GROUND

which oversaw administrative law and had not been widely used by social movements. In a process that is noteworthy for its expansion of an institutional docking point, anti-mining activists added this second jurisdiction as a new legal venue in 2008 when they launched their case against Arias before the Administrative Litigation Tribunal (Tribunal Contencioso Administrativo, TCA).

This lower court was responsible for reviewing charges related to administrative adherence to the law and regulatory statutes. Alleging that mine representatives and officials in key government agencies had failed to adhere to the legal requirements for approving mining permits, the environmental organization APREFLOFAS (represented by association member and lawyer Bernal Gamboa) and UCR biologist Jorge Lobo Segura (represented by UCR law professor Alvaro Sagot) filed a claim with the TCA. APREFLOFAS leaders report that the idea for this initiative came from Gamboa, a legally blind lawyer whose prior experience with disability claims and the TCA allowed him to imagine novel ways to process their case (CR0317; CR0417; CR0517). Gamboa's familiarity with administrative court procedures helped him to anticipate the ways in which a 2006 reform of the administrative code to reduce bottlenecks and delays would soon expand the pool of judges reviewing administrative claims and restructure court operations, making this court less entrenched and more agile, and its decisions more timely.

As their case advanced, these claimants were joined in their petition by the regional anti-mining movement based in San Carlos, UNOVIDA (represented by San Carlos attorney and local council member Edgardo Araya). Together they brought charges against Infinito, the National System of Conservation Areas (Sistema Nacional de Áreas de Conservación, SINAC), and the Procuraduría General de la República, alleging that those actors had failed to adhere to administrative requirements for the issuance of a mining permit (TCA 2010; Soto 2013, 338). Further claiming that Arias and his environment minister had not followed the procedures required for authorizing a state of exception related to the "public interest" declaration, they called on the court to cancel the Crucitas permit.

Preparing their legal brief for the TCA case, mine opponents identified an array of discrepancies to support their claim that the EIS review had been flawed and/or incomplete. They demanded an investigation of whether the newly authorized deepening of the pit, which had not been fully assessed in the permit process, would affect the underlying aquifers, including a cross-border aquifer shared with Nicaragua, raising major international concerns. They further claimed that the potential risks posed by seismic activity had not been adequately examined, questioned the adequacy of the geochemical report on toxic waste processing, and exposed SETENA's reliance on technical evaluations produced by and for the company. These and other issues, they contended, could not be dismissed on the legal grounds that they had been previously addressed (*cosa juzgada*) by Sala IV. Instead, they argued, these charges covered administrative law issues, which were appropriately under the purview of the judicial system's administrative wing (Sala I).

Following fifty days of testimony in a "marathon of interrogation" (Soto 2013, 353) through October and November 2010, the TCA announced its finding that major administrative errors had been committed during the Crucitas review. On the basis of this finding, the tribunal annulled SETENA's 2005 and 2008 certifications of environmental viability, Arias's 2008 "public interest" decree, and the extraction permit previously granted to Infinito. In a move that surprised even mining opponents, the TCA ruling called on the public prosecutor (Ministerio Público) to investigate whether this permitting process had involved criminal actions by President Arias, his environment minister, and other key officials involved in the review process.[25]

Although the company and government representatives appealed the TCA decision to the administrative chamber of the Supreme Court (Sala I), and returned once more to Sala IV after they lost their appeal in Sala I, they were unable to secure a reversal of the TCA findings (Soto 2013; Infinito Gold Ltd. and Republic of Costa Rica 2014).[26] Defeat occurred in spite of a lobbying visit to Costa Rica by Infinito owner Ronald Mannix in December 2010 and a visit by Canadian prime minister (and Mannix ally) Stephen Harper in August 2011 (Soto 2013, 387). Crucitas mine officials and home state representatives were obviously troubled by the Costa Rican outcome, as they watched the price of gold rise and potential profits evaporate.

---

[25] According to APREFLOFAS litigants (CR0317, CR0417), their success resulted in part from the confluence of a series of fortuitous developments, including the assignment of the case, by lottery, to a court section with three relatively young and politically independent judges.

[26] Infinito representatives brought their case to Sala IV repeatedly in 2011–2013, but after Sala I upheld the decision of the TCA, Sala IV declined to reopen the case, basing their ruling on technical grounds.

The 2010 Legislative Ban

The second policy initiative pursued by Costa Rican activists involved the promotion of a legal ban on open pit mining. This section focuses on the direct and indirect impact of social movement mobilization on the policymaking activities of elected and appointed officials. It involves deployment of what Felix Kolb (2007, 80–85) calls the "political access mechanism," one of five processes he identified through which social movements impact policy. This process concerns the actions taken by activists who wade into the electoral arena in order to influence the discourse of official representatives, impact the legislative agenda, and help shape the language of the law and regulatory protocols.

Research on the Costa Rican political system generally describes it as a "good" or "high-quality" democracy; quantitative scores breaking down performance by democratic indicators frequently rank Costa Rica in the highest category (see, for example, Altman and Pérez-Liñan 2002; O'Donnell, Vargas Cullell, and Iazzetta 2004).[27] Over the years, Costa Rican governing officials have introduced several initiatives designed to improve transparency and strengthen citizen participation, including the well-regarded Programa Estado de la Nación reports,[28] the previously mentioned popular referendum used in the CAFTA ratification, and a 2006 law that allowed citizens to present their own bills to the legislature based on citizen petition (Carballo Madrigal 2013; OECD 2016, 83).[29]

Despite this evidence of democratic capacity and social movement engagement, the Costa Rican political system has been faulted for numerous soft spots and limitations. Costa Rica's relatively high levels of citizen disengagement compared to other Latin American countries, restrictions on

---

[27] Freedom House, for example, routinely classifies Costa Rica as "free," and gave it a total freedom score of 91 out of 100 in 2017, a third-place ranking in Latin America, behind Uruguay (98) and Chile (94). https://freedomhouse.org/sites/default/files/FH_FIW_2017_Report_Final.pdf.

[28] The State of the Nation Project (Programa Estado de la Nación, PEN), a research initiative coordinated by Costa Rica's public universities, ombudsman (Defensoría de los Habitantes), and national comptroller, promotes rigorous research on the performance of state institutions and provides regular public reporting on quantitative trends.

[29] This citizen initiative law has been used successfully by environmentalists to initiate legislation against sports hunting, in favor of integrated management of water resources, and against mistreatment of animals. To activate the bill, APREFLOFAS launched a national campaign in 2006 and recruited over 1,000 people to collect the 5% of registered voter signatures required to place a wildlife protection bill on the legislative docket. Once the bill was submitted to the legislature in 2008, APREFLOFAS worked with members of the Environment Commission to refine the text, securing unanimous legislative approval in December 2012 and presidential endorsement in December 2013, after seven years of effort (Carballo Madrigal 2013).

public access to information, and limits on the development of genuinely participatory consultation practices have drawn criticism from domestic and outside evaluators (Raventós Vorst et al. 2012; Mora Solano 2016; OECD 2016). Organized civil society and movement activists have faced lingering obstacles as they attempted to influence legislation and regulations.

In spite of the barriers that commonly impede docking even in functioning democracies, activists regularly seek to cross the "permeable barrier" (Goldstone 2003) that separates the informal politics of social movement contention from the formal politics of elections and government institutions. This crossover effort often draws movements into closer contact with political parties, reducing the distance in a number of possible ways. Hanagan (1998, 53), for example, identifies five kinds of processes that affect social movement–political party linkages: articulation (the adoption of a movement position by a party), permeability (infiltration of a party by movement activists), alliance (collaboration on specific issues while maintaining separate organizational identities), independence (adopting an oppositional stance to press for change from the outside), and transformation (in which movements convert themselves into political parties and attempt to channel movement energies into electoral contention without succumbing to institutional routinization). Under propitious conditions, these forms of connection permit activist participation in the development of party platforms and electoral strategies. They may even lead to the placement of movement leaders into political campaigns as candidates for public office, and allow direct incorporation of activists into official roles in the policymaking process in the event of electoral victory.[30]

In the Costa Rican case, several new political parties emerged in the 2000s and sought an alignment with activist networks, with greater or lesser success. Some prominent participants in the Combo del ICE and anti-CAFTA campaigns, for example, went on to assume leadership in the PAC, attaining positions in the legislature and administrative appointments. Others aligned with the Frente Amplio (FA), an electorally volatile party on the left, which elected nine *diputados* in 2014, up from one in the previous electoral period. (See Appendix 5.1.)[31] This spillover of social mobilization momentum into

---

[30] Piccio (2016) discusses three conditions generally found to explain successful movement-party interaction: when there is strong identity coherence, during periods of electoral vulnerability, and following cycles of members' cumulative involvement.

[31] Of the FA deputies elected in 2014, all but one had a well-established history of social movement participation, generally in a leadership capacity (Rosales-Valladares 2017, 69–70), and several, including Edgardo Araya, played a visible role in the campaign against Crucitas.

172 BREAKING GROUND

the electoral arena helped to advance the mining issue on Costa Rica's legislative agenda.

A proposal to reform the mining code and ban open pit mining was introduced in Costa Rica's Legislative Assembly in 2005 by *diputado* Gerardo Vargas Leiva, a founding member of the newly established PAC. The PAC had been created in 2000 when the country's traditional parties entered into crisis and duopoly control over electoral politics began to erode.[32] Formed initially by dissidents from the PLN and PUSC, the PAC advertised itself as an alternative to the heterodox neoliberalism embraced by the old powerhouse parties, which were riddled with bouts of corruption and which had failed to ameliorate entrenched poverty and rising inequality.[33]

The 2005 draft bill called for a reform of the 1982 mining law that would ban the use of cyanide and prohibit open pit forms of mining, noting, "Historically, mining has been one of the human activities with the highest environmental, social and cultural costs" (Asamblea Legislativa [Costa Rica] 2005). The proposal was assigned to the legislature's environmental commission, where it completed the required round of technical review, but it languished in committee as the struggle over Crucitas slowly unfolded.

By 2010, times had changed. The recurring mobilizations and legal battles over mining had raised the profile of this issue, and three out of every four poll respondents now expressed strong opposition to open pit mining (CID Gallup 2010a). In this new political climate, the first act of President Laura Chinchilla (2010–2014) upon taking the oath of office was to decree a ban on new open pit mines (AFP 2010). Chinchilla's decree aligned state policy with clear public preferences. Responding to public sentiment, protecting Costa Rica's image as an environmental haven, and avoiding future conflicts between prospective investors and the country's now energized anti-mining movement, Chinchilla proclaimed Latin America's first national open pit mining ban on May 8, 2010. This step also allowed her to make a mark as

[32] In 1998, fifty of the fifty-seven deputies were from either the PLN or PUSC. By 2006, this figure had dropped to thirty, and the upstart PAC held seventeen seats. See the Universidad de Salamanca's Legislatina, http://americo.usal.es/oir/legislatina/costa_rica.htm#esultados_de_las_elecciones_le gislativas_(1994-2006).

[33] PAC founder and presidential candidate Ottón Solís aligned with the anti-CAFTA movement, calling for renegotiation of the agreement, and gave Óscar Arias stiff competition in the 2006 presidential race. Arias's 40.9% of the vote allowed him to squeak by Solís on a first-round ballot; Tribunal Supremo de Elecciones, "Estadísticas de procesos electorales," https://www.tse.go.cr/esta disticas_elecciones.htm. According to Solís, PAC founders embraced environmental principles and considered calling their new party the "Green Party" before settling on the name they registered under (CR0214).

an independent actor, publicly differentiated from her mentor and sponsor, Óscar Arias—a breach that would widen over time.[34]

The inherent instability of an executive decree, which can be reversed at will and overturned by subsequent presidents, fueled efforts by activists to secure legal codification of the measure through legislative action. Mounting evidence that metal mining had become politically toxic encouraged the incoming crop of *diputados* to publicly repudiate the industry and put this policy debate to rest. Approval of a legislated ban would require completion of a complicated sequence of steps that had become more difficult to manage as the era of dominance by two parties gave way to a multiparty system.[35]

The 2010–2014 legislature included several prominent environmental activists, two of whom, Claudio Monge Pereira (PAC) and José María Villalta (FA), were named to the Environment Commission's subcommittee on mining. Following months of meetings with environmental organizers and state administrative officials, and in the middle of a spate of mobilizations, marches, and media coverage in June and July 2010, these activist-oriented legislators, along with three other colleagues from the Environment Commission, issued a favorable *dictamen* (finding) regarding the proposed ban. Concluding that open pit forms of mining destroy the vegetation cover, including primary forests, and all forms of life that depend on it, along with surface water, reservoirs, and subterranean water flows, they called for a ban on future projects as part of a "repositioning of the image of our country as a nation that respects its environmental legislation and opts for a form of development that is socially just, economically profitable, and environmentally sustainable" (Asamblea Legislativa [Costa Rica] 2010b, 11).

After spending five years under review, the proposal for a mining ban now advanced quickly through the legislative process. Chinchilla placed the mining issue at the top of the legislative agenda for the extraordinary session, the period in the legislative cycle when the president is empowered to

---

[34] Chinchilla's executive decree built on the Arias administration's low-profile abandonment of new mining projects in the final weeks of his administration. Arias continued to be associated with open pit mining, however, by virtue of his 2008 national interest declaration in favor of mining and his enduring support for the Crucitas project.

[35] The Costa Rican legislative process required submission of a draft bill; assignment to committee; solicitation of comment by relevant state and nonstate actors; review by a specialized subcommittee; additional review and the issuance of a finding (*dictamen*) by the full legislative committee; review by technical staff; review, amendment, and approval by the full legislature in the first vote; constitutional review by Sala IV; and approval in a second vote by the full legislature. The constitutional prohibition on consecutive reelection, which extended to the legislature as well as the president, meant that any bill not approved within one legislative term would face further delay and renewed scrutiny by a new legislature in the next (Asamblea Legislativa [Costa Rica] 2012; CR0917).

174 BREAKING GROUND

determine legislative priorities. This measure was voted on and approved unanimously by the Environment Commission only three months after the 2010–2011 legislative session began. Two weeks later it was added to the calendar of the full chamber. Between August 18 and November 3, additional amendments were proposed and discussed, many of which dealt with the question of artisanal gold mining.

The completed bill stated simply that "Neither permits nor concessions for exploration and extraction activities for open pit metallic mining will be granted in national territory." Mining of all types was to be prohibited in national parks, biological reserves, forest reserves, and wildlife refuges. An eight-year transition process was established for artisanal miners, who were to be provided with state assistance as they shifted to other forms of livelihood. The rights of those who had acquired extraction permits would be preserved, but all concession holders whose applications were in process would now have their files archived. All current exploration permits would lapse at the end of their authorized period, and they would not be available for renewal.

With minor modifications in the commission's August 5 proposal, the bill received a unanimous vote of support in the full legislature on November 3, followed by the required second vote six days later. On November 9, 2010, all forty-nine members present (out of fifty-seven total) cast a concluding vote in favor of the open pit mining ban.

Mining Outcomes in Costa Rica: Post-Extractivism Challenges

The mining ban brought the question of industrial-scale gold mining to a policy conclusion in Costa Rica, after over a decade of contention and conflict. With backing from both the president and the legislature, including an executive decree and a unanimous vote of support for a change in the law, the future of open pit mining seemed to finally be settled. Having held off the actual development of the sector with multiple rounds of strategic litigation, achieved strong public support, and seen movement allies achieve pivotal positions as national legislators, including as members of the legislature's environmental committee, the Costa Rican anti-mining movement could now claim victory over the industry.

As summarized in Chapter 2, this outcome responded to three interlaced processes that drove policymaking dynamics. The first was *elite fragmentation on the mining issue.* Unlike what we found in the Nicaraguan and Guatemalan cases, where mining companies organized their domestic supporters and service providers into a business chamber and embedded themselves into the encompassing national business association, mining investors seeking entry into the Costa Rican countryside did not seek that alignment, and received no observable support from the domestic business community. To the extent that mining development ran contrary to the country's "green tourism" brand, the marriage of domestic business and foreign mining interests did not seem promising.

Among political elites, mining support was even more tattered. Although the industry gained strong backing from prominent political leaders, it also drew pointed rejection from others. As public opinion registered strong objections to open pit mining, even established political parties evidenced growing skepticism. New left and center-left political parties experienced electoral gains, and the political balance shifted away from the pro-market forces of old, settling into the prohibition camp.

Critical to this process was the second element: *the development of a sustained and multisectoral anti-mining movement.* Resistance networks built up in waves, drawing on and expanding Costa Rica's complex and ideologically diverse environmental movement. Bolstered by national policy initiatives in favor of environmental regulation, protection of forests and biodiversity, and environmental education, opposition to development projects that challenged the country's "green" commitments proved recurring and robust. Environmentalists of different hues converged with ecologically oriented religious activists and nostalgic traditionalists opposed to deepening neoliberalism to build a broad, decentralized network that connected local actors in impacted communities with national-level actors in San José.

But protest alone does not change policy, as we have seen repeatedly in the preceding chapters. For protest to be consequential in a policy sense, activists need a third element: *the opportunity to engage with state institutions and policymakers, who follow their own institutional processes and logics as they process policy debates.* The Costa Rican case demonstrates how space can open for activist engagement both within the court system and in the electoral process. Legal filings placed the courts inside the political brambles and provided opportunities for strategic litigation. Analysis of the intersection between the movement and the courts illustrates the roles that the judicial system can play in the policy process and the constraints under which

176   BREAKING GROUND

it operates. As the court cases advanced and public attention to mining sharpened, activists engaged the electoral system and brought pressure to bear on candidates and officeholders. The Costa Rican case shows how activists can contribute to the development of new political parties that challenge the dominance of the prior strongholds and advance policy innovation in an area of national interest. The result of successful institutional docking was both the erosion of prior pro-mining certification and the blockage of new forays, as Costa Rica took a distinctive policy turn.

The adoption of an open pit ban did not mean that mining debate was permanently foreclosed in Costa Rica. The development vision that inspired the recruitment of mining investment has not disappeared; the fiscal pressures that long motivated policy adjustments remain; the gold in the ground continues to allure. Costa Rica's open pit mining ban did not resolve the issue of how to eliminate the *coligalleros* (the Costa Rican label for artisanal and small miners), an issue that returned with a vengeance in 2017 when hundreds of informal miners illegally invaded the land once owned by Infinito and were forcibly removed by the police (Alfaro 2017). Nor did it address the issue of "acquired rights" held by mine investors with preexisting concessions, who could challenge state efforts to restrict their operations and claim the legal right to advance into production.[36] It did not take up the issue of international investment disputes, one of which would soon be launched against the country by Infinito Gold, owner of the Crucitas project, as discussed in Chapter 7.[37] The 2020 pandemic-induced economic crisis in Costa Rica, exacerbated by the country's heavy dependence on tourism, intensified the search for new revenue streams.

In this context, discussion has reemerged about the possibilities for a return to mining in Costa Rica. High on the agenda is the improved formalization and regulation of artisanal gold mining, made all the more urgent by the presence of organized crime in the sector. The fiscal losses associated with illegal extraction and the country's signing of the Minamata Convention requiring government control over mercury emissions both call for new state action (Cabrera Medaglia 2019). But slipped in alongside is the pitch for a return to industrial mining, an idea that enjoys support in some corners of

---

[36] Álvarez (2012) reports that the MINAE juridical assessment unit identified eight concessions that had previously acquired extraction permits for mining projects.

[37] Using provisions in the 1998 BIT, which allowed Canadian corporations to bring claims against the Costa Rican government at ICSID, Infinito Gold filed its long-threatened claim in February 2014. As its other legal, economic, and political strategies failed, the company demanded a US$1 billion

the legislature and the bureaucracy.[38] This discussion has predictably ignited a new round of proposals to govern small and "medium-sized" extraction as the mining debate continues (Gamboa Mora 2020).

Costa Rica's national commitment to environmental protection, with all of its limitations (Silva 2003; Honey 2008; Isla 2015; Cabrera Medaglia 2019), raised a green wall against industrial mining. Along with the national commitment to develop a more diversified energy matrix (Feoli 2021) and to become carbon neutral (Flagg 2019), Costa Rica continued its push for a sustainable approach to development. The implications for extractive industries, including mining, are not entirely clear, but the larger dynamics of elite division, social movement networking, and institutional access suggest that significant constraints, at least on large-scale mining, are likely to persist.

payment from the Costa Rican government in compensation for lost investments, a demand they subsequently reduced to US$93.9 million before raising it to US$321 million in 2017 (Infinito Gold Ltd. 2014; Infinito Gold Ltd. and Republic of Costa Rica 2014; Rojas 2017). See Chapter 7 for discussion of this ICSID case.

[38] With support from the Costa Rican School of Geology, new mining proposals were presented to the Costa Rican legislature in 2020. One draft bill, entitled the Ley de Minería Crucitas, called for the establishment of five new medium-sized mines in the Crucitas area, with royalties divided 40/60 between the *municipios* in the region and the Costa Rican social security fund (Consejo Universitario 2021).

178 BREAKING GROUND

Appendix 5.1 Costa Rican Legislature, Composition by Party and Legislative Session (Number of Seats)

Party	1982	1986	1990	1994	1998	2002	2006	2010	2014	2018
PLN	33	29	25	28	23	17	25	24	18	17
PUSC*	18	25	29	25	27	19	5	6	8	9
PAC						8	17	11	14	10
FA								1	9	1
ML					1	5	6	9	3	–
Other	6	3	3	4	6	8	4	6	5	20
Total	57	57	57	57	57	57	57	57	57	57

* Unidad in 1982.

Compiled from Universidad de Salamanca's Legislatina, http://americo.usal.es/oir/legislatina/costa_rica.htm#esultados_de_las_elecciones_legislativas_(1994-2006), and IFES's Election Guide, https://www.electionguide.org/.

Appendix 5.2 Costa Rica: List of Cited Interviews

Code	Affiliation	Sector	Interview date	Location
CR0117	COMEX	Government—executive	November 6, 2017	San José
CR0217	UCR	Academic	November 3, 2017	San José
CR0317	APREFLOFAS	Civil society—environment	November 2, 2017	San José
CR0417	APREFLOFAS	Civil society—environment	November 2, 2017	San José
CR0517	APREFLOFAS	Civil society—environment	November 2, 2017	San José
CR0717	Business company	Business	November 3, 2017	San José
CR0917	Legislature, staff	Government—legislature	November 2, 2017	San José
CR1217	UCR	Academic	November 6, 2017	San José
CR1417	APREFLOFAS	Civil society—environment	September 8, 2017	Washington, DC
CR0214	PAC	Government—political party	July 22, 2014	San José
CR0514	UNOVIDA/FECON	Civil society—environment	July 17, 2014	San José
CR0614	FA	Government—political party	July 17, 2014	San José
CR0914	Infinito	Business—mining company	July 18, 2014	San José

Appendix 5.2 Continued

Code	Affiliation	Sector	Interview date	Location
CR1214	Sala IV	Government—judicial	July 11, 2014	San José
CR1314	FECON	Civil society—environment	July 11, 2014	San José
CR1714	UCR	Academic	July 3, 2014	San José
CR1814	UNOVIDA Legislator, FA	Civil society—environment Government—legislature	July 12, 2014	San José
CR1914	UCR	Academic	July 4, 2014	San José
CR2014	Legislature, staff	Government—legislature	July 22, 2014	San José
CR0110	AMCHAM	Business association	November 4, 2010	San José
CR0210	UCR	Academic	October 31, 2010	San José
CR0510	PAC	Government—political party	November 5, 2010	San José

6

Mining Free

Mining Prohibition in El Salvador

In 2017, El Salvador became the first country to legislate a national ban on all forms of metallic mining. This remarkable development followed twelve years of anti-mining mobilization that opened new spaces in the policymaking process. The Salvadoran mining conflict, which began brewing under Nationalist Republican Alliance (ARENA) president Antonio "Tony" Saca (2004–2009), escalated following the election of Mauricio Funes (2009–2014). Funes was the first successful presidential candidate running under the banner of the Farabundo Martí National Liberation Front (FMLN), a party founded by former revolutionaries in postwar El Salvador. As a candidate, Funes pledged to oppose the licensing of gold mining.

After Funes administration officials moved into their government offices and renewed their commitment to prevent mine development, the assassination of anti-mining leaders in Cabañas began. Marcelo Rivera, environmental activist and director of the Casa de la Cultura in San Isidro, Cabañas, at the time of his murder in June 2009, led the local campaign against the proposed El Dorado gold mine under development nearby. His murder was the first of three assassinations of anti-mining leaders in Cabañas in 2009. Intimidation practices reminiscent of the civil war era reappeared, taking an additional toll on activists in the years that followed.

Six weeks after Funes's election, Canadian mining junior Pacific Rim filed an investment dispute claim against the government of El Salvador at the World Bank's International Centre for the Settlement of Investment Disputes.[1] At issue was the government's delay in issuing gold extraction

---

[1] Pacific Rim was legally incorporated under the name Pac Rim Cayman LLC and filed its investment dispute claim under that name. The parent company in Vancouver operated under the name Pacific Rim Mining Corporation, and its local office in El Salvador registered as Pacific Rim El Salvador. Following the general pattern adopted in its corporate communication and in media reports, the present study refers to the company as Pacific Rim and uses Pac Rim Cayman to reference documents filed in the ICSID case.

Breaking Ground. Rose J. Spalding, Oxford University Press. © Oxford University Press 2023.
DOI: 10.1093/oso/9780197643150.003.0006

MINING FREE: EL SALVADOR 181

permits.[2] This external legal pressure provided an additional tool in the mining companies' arsenal as they pressed forward toward extraction.

In spite of the violence taking place at the local level and the legal threat exerted in the international arena, mining resisters ultimately emerged victorious. This chapter traces the arc of this transition by providing a longitudinal analysis of anti-mining mobilization and policy change in El Salvador. It maps the ways in which the anti-mining movement connected with formal institutions and official policymaking to drive a significant mining policy shift. As such, it brings together two fields of study that have often been separated along disciplinary lines—the study of informal, non-institutional, "street-level" politics of social movements and the study of formal, institutional politics and policymaking by government officials. It plots the path from policies that opened up mining investment to legislation that formally shut the sector down.

As in the other cases examined in this book, the outcome is found to respond to the interplay of three sets of features: *levels of elite consensus, variations in opposition networking,* and *access to docking points within the state apparatus.* That argument, laid out in detail in Chapter 2, is briefly summarized below in relation to the Salvadoran case.

Elite consensus: El Salvador's elite split along the mining fault line. Unlike elites in Nicaragua and Guatemala, who provided a unified front in support of mining, those in El Salvador followed the Costa Rican pattern and revealed visible fissures. Most obviously, the Salvadoran political elite was split into two wings located across the postwar ideological divide. A coalition on the right was anchored by ARENA, the pro-business political party that won four consecutive terms in the aftermath of the 1980s civil war. Typically electing prominent business leaders, ARENA secured the presidencies of Alfredo Cristiani (1989–1994), Armando Calderón Sol (1994–1999), Francisco Flores (1999–2004), and Saca (2004–2009), and dominated the government for twenty years as El Salvador's market transition unfolded. Opposing ARENA was a coalition on the left, led by the FMLN, which successfully advanced the candidacy of Funes (2009–2014) and, in the following term, Salvador Sánchez Cerén (2014–2019). Its decade in office provided the FMLN with opportunities to adjust directions on policy initiatives.

---

[2] This ICSID case, along with those filed by gold mining companies against the governments of Guatemala and Costa Rica, is discussed more fully in Chapter 7.

182   BREAKING GROUND

Operating in close alignment with the anti-mining movement, the FMLN took up its call to prohibit gold extraction, and ultimately won that battle.

Elite support for mining had begun to erode during the Saca administration, as some ARENA leaders stepped back from the neoliberal orthodoxy they had embraced earlier, at least in this politically sensitive area. This internal fissure was related both to electoral dynamics, as evidence mounted that ARENA's lock on power could be successfully challenged in the 2009 election, and to differences emerging within the business sector itself. The Salvadoran business elite, while initially indiscriminate in support of foreign investment, became less uniform regarding mine development as the collective costs and sectoral rivalries associated with extraction became more apparent.

Unlike Nicaragua and Guatemala, where foreign mining investors took on membership in domestic business associations and persuaded colleagues that local investors, construction companies, and service providers would share in the gains, foreign mining investors in El Salvador failed to interlace their projects effectively with those of local elites. A handful of prominent economic leaders continued to lobby for mining investment, but most of the business representatives stepped away from active support. The National Association of Private Enterprise (ANEP), El Salvador's encompassing business association, slowly went silent on the mining question as the anti-mining coalition gained momentum and political costs rose. When foreign mining investors proved unable to galvanize a base of domestic allies, even within El Salvador's highly politicized business sector, the pro-mining policy preferences of the early postwar years unraveled, revealing fissures that expanded opportunities for mining critics.

Opposition Networks: In their struggle against metallic mining, Salvadoran activists constructed a broad, multisectoral, and multiscalar network, and kept it engaged in the fight for a dozen years. This movement played a critical role in connecting diverse sectors of society and coordinating their issue framing. Unlike the Nicaraguan case, where mining disputes generated three different kinds of conflicts, each with their own set of actors and goals, in El Salvador the movement created a single national coordinating group, the National Roundtable on Metallic Mining (Mesa Nacional Frente a la Minería Metálica, henceforth the Mesa), which presented a powerful and unifying message. By emphasizing the protection of water rights in a country experiencing widespread water stress and water quality problems, this movement focused attention on the collective risks associated with large-scale mining. The country's history of environmental disaster (earthquakes, mudslides, tropical storms, etc.), and the shared dependence of much of the population on water from a single river system brought home the message of heightened vulnerability. As in the Costa Rican case, growing attention to climate impacts helped to consolidate a broad movement for change.

This network linked up local communities, national environmental and human rights organizations, and religious activists at both the base and leadership levels. Using processes of bridging, bonding, and brokerage, the Salvadoran mobilization expanded from its community origins to fashion a national movement. Anti-mining activists drew on their own prior histories of organizing, some dating back to the civil war era, to locate reliable allies and build bridges that extended their reach. New forms of *lateral transnationalism* (Spalding 2015), fueled by the experiences of Salvadoran activists as war refugees sheltering in Honduras, forged cross-border relationships that connected anti-mining activists in El Salvador with similar others in nearby Honduras and Guatemala, where mining projects, and resistance to them, had developed in the previous decade. Postwar connections in struggles against privatization provided another layer of interaction on which subsequent coalitions could build. Reserves of previously accumulated "strategic capital" (Almeida 2014) facilitated cross-sectoral coordination and linkages across local, national, and transnational scales by seeding interpersonal connections and adapting frames that could be reactivated as new policy issues emerged.

Docking Points: Not only did the resistance prove capable of building a broad network, it also achieved multiple forms of state penetration. The Salvadoran political system provided mechanisms through which activists could connect with state institutions and exert leverage over the policy process. Unlike the Nicaraguan case, where the putative party of the left rejected the anti-mining message, El Salvador's FMLN facilitated a ready crossover between protest mobilization and electoral work. Its candidates drew heavily on the party's social movement base and carried its message into the halls of power. This link to institutional politics allowed the movement to move beyond resistance and enter the territory of policy response.

Salvadoran courts proved less available for strategic litigation than those in Guatemala and Costa Rica, but anti-mining activists identified other points of entry into policy deliberations. Electoral success of the movement-aligned FMLN allowed access to the legislative process, which proved increasingly responsive as support for the movement broadened. Bureaucratic actors

184 BREAKING GROUND

in the newly created Environmental Ministry also provided an opening, raising technical questions about the advisability of mine promotion given the country's limited regulatory capacity as they slowed the licensing process to a crawl. Activists also deployed the newly established consultation mechanisms embedded in the Municipal Code, which permitted them to call referenda in *municipios* in the "gold belt" region. Although advancement toward policy reform was deterred by the regulatory freeze that set in following the filing of Pacific Rim's international investment dispute claim, activists added this legal maneuver to their list of reasons for opposing mining investments. The threat that the country would be found in violation of international investment protocols and forced to pay compensation to prospectors seeking extraction licenses brought home the legal risks the country faced, and stiffened the spine of Salvadoran lawmakers. Once the investment dispute was resolved (in El Salvador's favor), the reform process advanced quickly toward a legislative ban.

The chapter is organized into six sections. It begins with an overview of mining advocacy by political and economic elites in postwar El Salvador and describes the early advance of the industry. It then turns to the emergence of an opposition movement and examines the bridging and bonding processes that shaped movement expansion. The third section traces the policy contestation unfolding in elections, bureaucratic agencies, and local communities. The fourth describes the erosion of elite support, and the fifth follows the interactive processes that culminated in the official mining ban. The sixth section reviews the findings and concludes.[3]

Elite Positions on Mining in Postwar El Salvador

After a decade of civil war, El Salvador's postwar negotiations left the newly created ARENA party firmly in control. The 1992 peace agreement gave legal status and the opportunity to compete for power to the recently demobilized

---

[3] To trace the processes that ultimately led to the ban, this chapter draws on seventy-eight semistructured interviews conducted in El Salvador and the United States between 2010 and 2017. See Appendix 6.2 for a list of the interviews cited in this chapter. This chapter also incorporates documents from websites and blogs of the Mesa and its affiliates; recorded testimony and legal briefs from the investment dispute between Pac Rim Cayman LLC and the Republic of El Salvador; public opinion data from the Instituto Universitario de Opinión Pública (IUDOP) at the Universidad Centroamericana (UCA) in El Salvador and from CID Gallup; and reports on legislative processes posted at the website for El Salvador's Asamblea Legislativa. For additional information about the research methodology, see the "Argument and Methods" section in Chapter 1.

FMLN, but ARENA consistently won the presidency and, with allied parties, controlled the main institutions of government for the following two decades. Its policies favored the interests of a transnationalized sector of the economic elite, which had acquired a strong position in banking and finance during the postwar transition (Segovia 2002; Schneider 2012; Bull, Castellacci, and Kasahara 2014; ICEFI 2015b; Robles Rivera 2017). As Bull (2014) argues, the elite combined four sources of power—money, force, information, and ideas—to maintain its leverage over the political system. Policymaking relied heavily on the planning proposals of the Salvadoran Social and Economic Development Foundation (FUSADES), a USAID-funded think tank that designed the market transition process and helped to staff the technical ministries (Vidal 2010; Spalding 2014).

Achieving four consecutive presidential terms, ARENA leaders had the opportunity to oversee the neoliberal transformation of El Salvador's economic model. Reforms included privatization of the banking and telecommunications systems, trade liberalization, expansion of the export processing zones, deregulation, and, in 2001, the Law on Monetary Integration, which officially introduced dollarization. To promote foreign investment, ARENA president Calderón Sol signed a new Investment Law in 1999, which allowed foreign investors to bring cases to international tribunals in the event of an investment dispute. Bilateral investment agreements and free trade agreements, including DR-CAFTA, consolidated the new regimen.

As elsewhere in the region, El Salvador revised its mining law during this period of neoliberal reform (see Table 6.1). New legislation, published in the *Diario Oficial* in January 1996, incentivized investment flows toward this largely undeveloped sector by providing additional legal protections and tax exemptions.[4] Exploration by junior mining companies progressed in the early 2000s under Francisco Flores, when the government adopted a yet more investor-friendly amendment to the mining law, reducing the royalties from 4% to 2% and increasing the size limit on concessions (Henríquez 2008, 28; TAU 2011, 33). The new rules attracted investor attention; twenty-nine

---

[4] As in other Central American countries, gold mining in El Salvador developed in the colonial era and lost its dynamism relative to the new agro-export products in the early twentieth century. In 1913, the value of precious metals exports from El Salvador was the highest in the region, but equaled only one-fifth that of coffee exports (Bulmer-Thomas 1987, 8). Gold became a significant export for El Salvador in the decade after the depression (p. 78). Value added for mining and quarrying (metallic and nonmetallic mining) in El Salvador peaked in 1942 at $5.8 million (1970 prices) before declining to around one-third that level in the 1960s (pp. 320–321). Gold mining collapsed during the 1980s civil war.

186 BREAKING GROUND

Table 6.1 Salvadoran Mining Policy Timeline

Mining Policies and Related Actions (Year)	Presidential Administration and Political Party/Coalition	Term
Mining Law adopted (1996) Environment Law adopted, MARN created (1998)	Calderón Sol, ARENA	1994–1999
Investment Law adopted (1999) Mining Law revised (2001) Law on Monetary Integration (dollarization) adopted (2001)	Flores, ARENA	1999–2004
Pacific Rim submitted EIA for El Dorado mine to MARN (2004) MINEC and MARN announced suspension of mine licensing (2007)	Saca, ARENA	2004–2009
Pacific Rim filed ICSID case against El Salvador (2009) Strategic Environmental Assessment report completed by TAU (2011) MINEC and MARN proposed official mining moratorium (2012)	Funes, FMLN	2009–2014
Pacific Rim case dismissed by ICSID (2016) Metallic Mining Prohibition Law approved (2017)	Sánchez Cerén, FMLN	2014–2019

companies held exploration licenses in 2006 (TAU 2011, 39), as a regional "gold belt" of potential projects was identified.

The most advanced gold belt project in 2004 was the El Dorado mine, where the Canadian mining company Pacific Rim had acquired an existing concession through merger in 2002. Testimony of Pacific Rim executives in the ICSID investment dispute demonstrates the many ways in which the government attempted to accommodate mining companies during these early years. Concessions were granted with little more than signatures and fees, and deadlines became flexible devices that were routinely postponed in deference to company needs. The legislative assembly altered the rules governing the duration of concessions several times at the request of investors, first approving an emergency extension and later lengthening the concession period by law (Pac Rim Cayman 2013, 33–47). Pacific Rim's president at the time, Catherine McLeod Seltzer, concluded in 2004 that the country had "very friendly mining laws," noting that the company "'had a hand in helping the Government draft' the 2001 amendment to the 1995 Mining Law 'so that El Salvador would be open and receptive to mining investment and allow deposits to be developed in a timely way'" (Pac Rim Cayman 2013, 39–40).

The clock was ticking for the expiration of the El Dorado concession when Pacific Rim acquired it, and the new management moved quickly to seek an extraction permit in December 2004. Pacific Rim proposed a subterranean mine in Cabañas, one of the country's poorest departments. This project envisioned a ten-year production timeline, with two years to start up, six years of operation, and two years to close down. The projected value of gold exports from Cabañas mines topped US$1 billion, with a formal sector workforce of 2,818 in what was projected to become six mines (TAU 2011, 41–42, 45), making this envisioned mining complex one of the largest (albeit short-lived) enterprises in the country. According to a highly optimistic economic projection commissioned by Pacific Rim from former finance minister Manuel Hinds (2007), the El Dorado mine would produce an 8.4% increase in the GDP of Cabañas, leading to a 23% drop in the department's extreme poverty levels.

As the process for reviewing the company's environmental impact assessment (EIA) got under way at the newly established Ministry of Environment and Natural Resources (MARN), the mining policy tide began to turn. Internal discussion within the MARN and the Ministry of Economy (MINEC) in 2005 and 2006 intersected with the rise of an antimining movement, and, faced with technical questions sown by mining critics, state officials in the MARN identified a series of deficiencies in both the EIA and their own regulatory processes (Nadelman 2018, 222–225; Broad and Cavanagh 2021, 86–87). Technical questions aligned with political ones; as ARENA's electoral hold on power softened during the Saca administration, the president reportedly verbalized concerns about the potential impact of this issue on ARENA's vote tally (Shrake 2010, 44–45). With Saca's support, MINEC and MARN ministers jointly announced the suspension of the mining licensing process in June 2007, pending completion of a strategic environmental assessment (SEA).[5] The SEA pointed out additional deficiencies and regulatory gaps, leading MARN and MINEC ministers to call for a formal moratorium in 2012. After additional discussion and movement recalibration, as described in the section "Adoption

---

[5] The World Bank defines SEAs as "analytical and participatory approaches to strategic decision-making that aim to integrate environmental considerations into policies, plans and programmes, and evaluate the inter linkages with economic and social considerations" (Loayza 2012, 4).

188 BREAKING GROUND

of a Formal Legislative Ban," the country took a formal policy U-turn. The Metallic Mining Prohibition Law was approved in 2017.

The Mining Opposition Network in El Salvador

The outcomes of national resource conflicts depend not just on the extent of elite support but also on the characteristics of resistance organizing and the permeability of state institutions. This section turns our attention to the organizational aspects of the mining opposition network in El Salvador. As I argued in Chapter 2, mining resistance is more likely to be consequential in policy terms when the movement achieves broad scope and unity. When resistance erodes, falters, or fragments, activist ability to achieve policy objectives likewise diminishes.

Studies of social movements frequently find that prior experiences with mobilization contribute to protest durability, recurrence, and escalation. This occurs through the creation of "strategic capital," which Almeida (2014, 25) defines as "repositories of collective knowledge about which strategic and organizational elements in their localities are best employed to generate joint action." Eckstein (2001, 33–37) identifies "popular cultures of resistance" as a factor contributing to recurring bouts of defiance and protest in Latin America. Previous mobilizing can generate both enduring organizational forms and "abeyance structures" (Taylor 1989) that fade during periods of inactivity but spring quickly to life when new opportunities arise.

Rossi (2015) elaborates on the role of historical experience in shaping strategic choice with his concept of "stock of legacies," defined as "the concatenation of past struggles, which, through the sedimentation of what is lived and perceived to be lived as well as what is intentionally learned, produces an accumulation of experience that adds or eliminates specific strategies from the repertoire of strategies as both a self-conscious and oblivious process" (p. 31). The stock of legacies tends to be historically grounded and recursive, as successful strategies are replicated and adapted. Changes are made possible through intentional processes of emulation and teaching, "resignification" (which adapts a strategy by fitting it with new meaning), and transnationalism, which is understood as mutually influential (pp. 34–37).

Contemporary movements may connect across scales and intersect with transnational allies that share elements of a normative or strategic framework (Tarrow 2005). Transnational activism was traditionally understood in terms of the "boomerang" effect (Keck and Sikkink 1998), in which local groups operating in authoritarian regimes aligned with international allies in hope of persuading powerful international actors to exert external pressure on an unresponsive state, pushing it to heed the call of local activists. With the advance of formal democratization, transnational alliances increasingly work to strengthen domestic actors so that they may more effectively pressure their home states directly (downward scale shift), or to assist local groups who bypass engagement with their home state and push directly for change in the behavior of powerful international actors (upward scale shift) (Silva 2013). Transnationalism may foster global connections, linking actors in the global South and global North, or it may mobilize lateral connections, building cross-border networks in similarly situated contexts (sometimes neighboring countries). Because they emerge in roughly parallel settings, lateral forms of transnationalism provide a ready transfer of experiences and produce forms of knowledge that are relatively easy to assimilate (Spalding 2015).

Transnationalization can provide informational access, technical and financial resources, validating research, and new venues for struggle. By allowing local activists to invoke international standards, transparency guidelines, and scientific findings, and by providing financing to cover operational costs and support the dissemination of their story, international linkages promote the strategic dexterity that may be required for long struggle against formidable opponents. In the context of mining conflicts accompanied by criminalization and repression, international allies may assist in outreach to mining company stockholders, legislators in corporate home countries, and international nongovernmental organizations (INGOs) with specialization in international human rights, corporate regulation, and environmental law. Although transnational alliance structures raise the risk of external co-optation and de-radicalization (Petras 1997; Bob 2005) and create challenges for activists seeking authentic local grounding (Lewis 2016), they may also raise a movement's profile and help resisters break through domestic constraints (Spalding 2015; Broad and Cavanagh 2021).

In the end, the ability of social movements to influence public policy depends not just on the resources provided by transnational allies but also on the ability of local and national activists to achieve relational connections and social penetration at home. As noted in Chapter 2, this requires the development of *spatial reach* (ability to connect across local and national scales), *sectoral breadth* (ability to link across sectors), and *frame alignment* (ability to define congruent interpretations and overlapping objectives). Movement

190 BREAKING GROUND

networks can disseminate information through interconnected clusters built on common identities and shared experiences (*bonding*). They can also extend connective tissue by linking sectors across social and political divides (*bridging*) (Putnam 2000).

Bonding, a form of networking that mobilizes *close ties*, builds linkages based on familiar, routine, and trust-based connections. Bridging, a networking form based on *weak ties*, provides opportunities to connect with less familiar others, beyond the parameters of routine experiences. Bridging processes may be particularly important if durable policy change requires the construction of alliances that overcome partisan polarization by transcending insular community ties. As the literature on the strength of weak ties suggests (Granovetter 1982; Marsden and Campbell 2012; Biggs and Andrews 2015), bridging permits mobilization beyond the redundant forms of communication that characterize in-group networking, and supports the diversification of repertoires and the mobilization of varied forms of expertise that can help to sustain a movement as the political context changes.

The Mesa Nacional Frente a la Minería Metálica

Launched formally in 2005, El Salvador's Mesa Nacional Frente a la Minería built upon solid local grounding at the community level, forged cross-spatial linkages between local and national-level associations, and built cross-sectoral connections of both bonding and bridging varieties. This bundle of ties helped the movement to expand its reach and diversify its strategies, and provided the flexibility needed to adapt to shifting opportunities. Community-level allies brought local knowledge and urgency to the process, as residents mobilized to prevent imminent mining encroachment. National-level allies, although further removed from the mining zones, provided physical proximity to decision-making centers and greater familiarity with policymaking processes, which allowed resistance activists to make strategic choices about alliances, timing, and funding. The movement built on a legacy of mobilization and resistance that dated back to the civil war and postwar transition, leaving an organizational trace on which new rounds of resistance could build.

Local-Level Organizing in the Salvadoran Gold Belt

As elsewhere in Latin America, ground zero for mining resistance in El Salvador was in the communities targeted for mine development. The prospective mining zone included communities that had experienced active combat during the 1980s civil war and that emerged with resilient forms of oppositional organization. Having endured massacres and military campaigns, followed by flight, dislocation, and return only a decade before (Rauda, Dimas, and Palacios 2019), communities in concessioned territory proved particularly resistant to the entry of mining prospectors. Some community residents had undergone lengthy relocation in refugee camps in nearby Honduras, where Mesa Grande served as a temporary resettlement camp (Smith-Nonini 2010). The experience of military assault and desperate flight followed by life in the camps left the trace of collective trauma, as victims attempted to cope with the magnitude of their losses. It also left an organizational foundation, as this population constructed various forms of self-governance while displaced. Although formally separated from the military conflict, some refugees had family or community ties to the FMLN and maintained contact with combatants, who preserved an unofficial presence in the camps (Viterna 2015, 94).

Following years of displacement in the 1980s, many Salvadoran refugees returned to the villages in the northern region of El Salvador from which they had fled (Smith-Nonini 2010; ES2417). They formed local and regional organizations like the Refugee and Repopulated Communities Coordinator (CCR, later called the Association of Communities for Chalatenango Development) and the Social and Economic Development Association (ADES) in the repopulated community of Santa Marta in Cabañas. These organizations in turn combined forces under the national umbrella of the Rural Communities Association for Salvadoran Development (CRIPDES), which claimed 100,000 affiliates in 398 communities.[6] Many in the repopulated communities maintained strong ties to the FMLN, which, following its postwar transition into a political party, tended to win local elections there by a large margin (Sprenkels 2018, 143–159). This was the setting into which the mining companies advanced.

Some residents of the gold belt were won over by the prospect of mining jobs or the general economic growth promised by company representatives. Many, however, viewed mining investors as intruders who threatened their communities with renewed displacement and political annihilation. Chalatenango activists tell of residents in the *municipios* of San José Las Flores, Guarjila, Arcatao, and Nueva Trinidad who repeatedly disrupted

---

[6] See CRIPDES, "Historia," http://www.cripdes.net/quienes-somos/historia.

the activities of the company advance teams.[7] Drawing on strategic capital accumulated during prior periods of organizing, residents closely monitored company comings and goings and surreptitiously removed survey markers planted in their fields. As exploration advanced, activists took more forceful steps, blocking company vehicles that attempted to enter their zone, tracking down drilling sites, and threatening to burn equipment if it was not hauled away.

In communities in Cabañas, where the mining opposition was weaker, resisters focused on identifying allies and organizing informational sessions. Local leaders in Cabañas learned, according to one organizer, to "speak without saying" (*hablar sin hablar*), that is, to communicate obliquely, without making explicit statements that would invite rejection and retaliation. Their protest style emphasized artistic and cultural activities, including a Green Walk in Defense of Water (Caminata Verde en Defensa del Agua), for example, instead of a march or protest, terms that local people traditionally identified with leftist discourse (ES0417).

Spatial Reach: Local-National-Transnational Connections

Although community-level resistance can derail particular projects, it has a limited ability to impact policy. To achieve that goal, community movements need to build robust connections to broader national networks. In the Salvadoran case, wartime collaboration and postwar mobilization helped forge organizational links that allowed activists to bridge the local-national divide. Relationships between local and national-level FMLN sympathizers left trust bonds established through shared risk-taking and values, creating a "stock of legacies" (Rossi 2015) on which future organizing could build. Prior experiences with organizing permitted the rapid identification of potential allies whose usefulness and credibility as partners could be reliably assessed. As the prospect of mine development became imminent, community leaders in the emerging anti-mining front reached out to "trustworthy" organizations at the national and international levels for assistance in interpreting and framing the evolving mining debate (ES2017; ES2417; ES2517).[8]

---

[7] Cartagena (2009, 230–231); ES2417; Broad and Cavanagh (2021, 34–35, 55–56); for additional discussion of community confrontation with mining representatives, see the interview with Francisco Pineda, leader of the Environmental Committee of Cabañas (CAC), by Labrador and Meza (2011).

[8] In my interviews with founding Mesa organizers, the individuals and organizations they reached out to for the initial meetings were repeatedly described as "de confianza," suggesting that trustworthiness was a significant criterion for inclusion.

Ten organizations came together to form the Mesa in 2005.[9] This coalition, which combined grassroots community organizations from the mining zone with national-level NGO allies, became the backbone of El Salvador's anti-mining mobilization. In addition to CRIPDES, national network partners included the Salvadoran Ecological Unit (UNES), a national environmental organization; the Foundation for the Study of the Application of Law (FESPAD), a human rights organization; and the Investment and Trade Research Center (CEICOM), an activist-oriented research center. Between the community organizations operating at the local level in territory targeted for mining concessions and their carefully curated national allies with specializations in environmental rights and legal protections, El Salvador's anti-mining front quickly achieved notable spatial and multisectoral reach.

Mesa activists also collaborated with an expanding network of transnational allies, who provided additional resources and support (Spalding 2015; Democracy Center 2017; Broad and Cavanagh 2021). Some of these alliances connected Mesa leaders with similarly situated activists in neighboring Central American countries where mining development was already under way, such as MadreSelva in Guatemala (as discussed in Chapter 4). Cross-border connections with other Central American organizations facilitated lateral forms of transnationalism, where organizational familiarity and similarities in local impacts permit a ready recognition of parallels and the relatively easy diffusion of digestible information (Spalding 2015).

Other allies hailed from the global North. These partners included US solidarity organizations, such as the US–El Salvador Sister Cities network, whose work in El Salvador dated back to the 1980s civil war. Their long-term presence and community-level work permitted movement domestication, characterized by horizontal (nonhierarchical) networking structures and leadership by local staff (Spalding 2015).[10] Assistance also came from

---

[9] Mesa membership rose from the initial ten organizations to thirteen by 2008 (Henríquez 2008, 29; Cartagena 2009, 231, 233). Mesa members in 2006 included ADES, CAC, Cáritas El Salvador, CCR, CEICOM, the Salvadoran Center for Appropriate Technology (CESTA), CRIPDES, FESPAD, Rural Communities North of San Salvador and La Libertad Union (UCRES), and UNES. By 2008, the Association of Alternative Economy Students (ASEAL) of the UCA, the Association of Friends of San Isidro Cabañas (ASIC), and the Franciscan Justice, Peace, and Creation Integrity program (JPIC) had also joined the coalition. Following shifts and reshuffling, membership in 2017, when the Mesa was officially composed of eleven organizations, included Unified Movement Francisco Sánchez 1932 (MUFRAS 32), the Salvadoran Foundation for Cooperation and Community Development (CORDES), Activist Network, and La Maraña, an offshoot of CAC (ES2017).

[10] *Domestication* of international NGOs occurs when external actors are durably embedded in local community structures, staffed to the executive level by local residents, and take direction from locally derived rather than externally driven mandates.

194   BREAKING GROUND

INGOs that operated in global power centers and provided thematic specialization and technical expertise. These non-domesticated international allies included networks like Oxfam America, which provided early financial and logistical support, and helped to connect activists across the region; MiningWatch Canada, which documented the growing number of mining conflicts around the world; and the Center for International Environmental Law (CIEL), which provided strategic support for communities engaged in international investment disputes.[11]

An international support network began to take formal shape following the 2010 creation of the "International Allies," which brought together solidarity groups, human rights organizations, corporate critics, and extractive sector monitors in a loose and expanding alliance (ES0710; Broad and Cavanagh 2021, 113–116). These international supporters provided increased visibility, which supported movement durability and impact, and facilitated funding flows that allowed Mesa organizations to hire full-time staff members and communications specialists.

Mesa leaders report working hard to frame a consistent story about who they were and what they wanted. They adopted a razor-sharp focus on a mining ban as their principal policy objective, a position they adhered to with notable tenacity. They orchestrated a long and growing list of actions that included week-long events carried out simultaneously in several cities; marches flowing from the communities to demonstrations in front of central government buildings in San Salvador; delegations to visit mining communities in neighboring countries; petition and letter-writing drives; mock internment of mining companies; and local festivals in celebration of life and water. To maintain momentum, organizational meetings of Mesa members were scheduled every two weeks (ES2017); affiliates interlaced by cross-posting messages on their social media sites, where these organizations maintained a robust presence.

Their frame of action crystallized around water rights, offering a resonant message that connected communities across the country (Broad and Cavanagh 2021). This message focused on the Río Lempa, which was "the

---

[11] International supporters also included the Institute of Policy Studies and the Council of Canadians, among others. Actively seeking support abroad, Mesa representatives participated in numerous international events and exchanges during the 2005–2017 period (ES0312; ES0717; Democracy Center 2017). ADES leaders, for example, reported attendance at nine international events in 2015 alone. The work of the Mesa was recognized with the Institute for Policy Studies (IPS) Letelier-Moffett Human Rights award in 2009, and Francisco Pineda of then-Mesa-affiliated CAC received the prestigious Goldman Environmental Prize in 2011.

most important freshwater source in El Salvador, providing 50% of the drinking water, 50% of hydroelectric energy, and irrigation for agriculture in more than half of the country" (McKinley 2018). Concern about the Río Lempa, repeatedly described in interviews as the "aortic artery of the country," seeded both local and national alarm given the proximity of the proposed mining zone to this critical water resource. The impact of mining on water access and quality in multiple regions of the country further connected people across the local and national scales, promoting network spatial reach. Growing awareness of the impact of climate change, in a country pummeled by water stress and extreme weather (Odell, Bebbington, and Frey 2018; Bárcena et al. 2020), helped to broaden the growing movement.

Sectoral Breadth: Bonding and Bridging Linkages to Catholic Church Allies
In addition to the sectoral breadth baked into the Mesa at its founding, the anti-mining movement expanded through its alliance with the Catholic Church. Church leaders have been recurring partners in anti-mining mobilizations across Latin America, with local priests often providing religious accompaniment in support of community struggles (Holden and Jacobson 2011; Arellano-Yanguas 2014; Arce 2014; Li 2015). As we saw in Chapter 3, Nicaraguan church officials played a critical role in support of anti-mining organizing in Rancho Grande; Chapter 4 documented the leadership role of Bishop (subsequently Cardinal) Ramazzini in the protest against the Marlin Mine in the Guatemalan Highlands. In the Salvadoran case, diverse church actors became recurring and critical partners, with Catholic leaders and activists operating within the Mesa and beyond it. These linkages contributed to both spatial reach, drawing on connections between the national-level church hierarchy and the local parishes, and sectoral breadth, as previously unaffiliated sectors were incorporated into the network through religious ties. These connections drew on both the bonding ties of familiar, long-term collaborators and the bridging ties between autonomous actors with infrequent and tenuous links.

Close church ties with the Mesa emerged initially through the Catholic Church's social action wing, Cáritas El Salvador, which was a founding member of the Mesa. Cáritas provided a physical office space for the Mesa's coordination activities during the first two years of its operation (ES0817) and supported its popular education campaign in the decade that followed (see Figure 6.1). JPIC, a Franciscan-sponsored peace and justice organization, joined the Mesa soon after its founding, and its representatives became featured contributors and

Figure 6.1 Cáritas El Salvador anti-mining graphic, from cover of Cáritas El Salvador 2016. Reproduced with permission.

emissaries at national and international events (ES0112). These activist church agents enjoyed previously established trust bonds with Mesa affiliates based on prior collaboration, and played a critical role as brokers, linking the anti-mining network with more establishment-oriented church leaders in a classical bridging alliance.

Spatial and sectoral connections thickened in 2007 when Catholic ecclesiastical leaders aligned with the campaign, following their own institutional discourse and processes. Although less consistently engaged with the mining issue and more politically and socially removed from the Mesa core, the upper hierarchy of the Salvadoran Catholic Church entered the fray publicly as the Latin American Catholic Church leaders more generally turned to embrace an environmental message. At the urging of the archbishop of San

MINING FREE: EL SALVADOR   197

Salvador, Fernando Sáenz Lacalle, the Episcopal Conference of El Salvador (CEDES), composed of the country's eleven bishops, issued a joint statement calling on the government to deny permits for metal mining (CEDES 2007).[12] Declaring that "this class of mining causes irreversible damage to the environment and surrounding communities," the bishops concluded that metal mining in El Salvador "should not be permitted."

Although some individual parish priests still preached in support of mine development (Cartagena 2009, 244; ES1517), national church leaders maintained an oppositional stance, facing down weekly pro-mining protests outside the cathedral where the archbishop offered Sunday mass (ES1710; ES3510; McKinley 2020). As mining policy reform continued to stall, CEDES repeated its call three years later under the incoming archbishop of San Salvador, José Luis Escobar Alas (CEDES 2010). Public pronouncements by these widely respected elite actors helped to energize and expand the movement beyond well-worked circuits on the left.[13] In addition to the sectoral variation in its founding membership, the Mesa's growing alliance with church leaders lengthened the movement's reach, allowing it to link up activists across the country's traditional ideological lines.

Docking Points and Policy Impacts

As noted in Chapter 2, resistance alone is not likely to produce significant policy consequences, even when activists achieve national scope and multisectoral breadth. To produce this effect, activists need to locate or create spaces in the political system that can absorb public pressure and produce an institutional response. As the anti-mining network expanded in El Salvador, activists and their allies looked for docking points where they could connect with policymakers and move mining policy reform onto the national agenda. Through iterative engagement with institutional actors, they opened space for fuller debate about mining costs and risks. This process in El Salvador involved the insertion of resistance demands into three sets of institutional

[12] Trained as a chemist at the Universidad de Zaragoza in Spain, Archbishop Sáenz Lacalle rejected claims by Pacific Rim concerning their proposed processes of cyanide detoxification, reportedly finding them unscientific and manipulative (ES3510; Nadelman 2018).

[13] When asked in a 2006 IUDOP public opinion poll, "How much confidence did you have . . . in the following institutions?," 58.2% of respondents said "much" or "some" with respect to the Catholic Church, a confidence level surpassing that expressed for all other institutions listed (Artiga-González 2007, 428).

198 BREAKING GROUND

docking points: political parties, with their affiliated candidates and elected officials; bureaucratic agencies in charge of policy implementation; and municipal governments, where consultation processes could be activated in a carefully curated set of gold belt communities.

Parties and Elections

The close link between the FMLN and Salvadoran social movements, described by Paul Almeida (2006) as "social movement partyism," has drawn repeated attention in the academic literature. Collaboration between movement actors and FMLN organizers has been observed repeatedly in large-scale mobilizations, including the 2000–2003 protests against health care privatization, where up to 200,000 participants dressed in white and turned out in waves to express solidarity with hospital workers (Smith-Nonini 2010; Almeida 2014, 70–78). Guillermo Mata, the president of the national association of physicians and the high-profile leader of that protest wave, went on to become the FMLN's vice presidential candidate in 2004 and, following that defeat, a three-term FMLN deputy. The Salvadoran movements against water privatization and against CAFTA a few years later also linked resistance activists to the FMLN. FMLN legislators, who voted as a bloc against CAFTA ratification in 2004, lost that legislative battle (Haglund 2010, 186–193; Spalding 2014, 130–135) but retained their ties to an activist base.

These connections brought social movements directly into the electoral arena, where FMLN candidates cultivated their allegiance and pledged to support their demands. The FMLN's 2009 presidential candidate, Funes, along with his vice presidential candidate, FMLN leader and former guerrilla Salvador Sánchez Cerén, campaigned on a platform critical of metal mining, while their ARENA rival, Rodrigo Ávila, sidestepped this debate. Launching their campaign in November 2007, the Funes team spent seventeen months bringing their "Caravan of Hope" to municipalities across the country to rally support (Almeida 2014, 82–86). During a stop in Cabañas, Funes declared, "As long as [the mining companies] fail to demonstrate that these projects do not contaminate the environment and [do not damage] the health of our population, we are not going to permit metal mining" (Redacción Diario Co Latino 2008).

Building outward from the FMLN's formal membership of 80,000, Funes's campaign networked with an array of social movement organizations,

MINING FREE: EL SALVADOR 199

including the Mesa, to get out the vote. Although the race tightened in the final lap, Funes emerged victorious with 51.3% of the vote. This alliance was replicated in 2014 when Sánchez Cerén headed the ticket. Sánchez Cerén also embraced an anti-mining position, and his similarly slim victory was celebrated by Mesa leaders.

Bureaucracies and Scientific Activism

Activists used a combination of strategies in an attempt to influence the bureaucracy and derail the mining advance. As we observed in Chapter 4 on Guatemala and Chapter 5 on Costa Rica, resistance leaders recognized that they would need to make their argument on both technical and political grounds, and they collaborated with scientists and environmental consultants to deploy "scientific activism." This form of activism brings together activists and scientists to "co-produce new and alternative knowledge that gives the local organizations visibility and legitimacy, information on how to protect themselves from the impacts, and allows them to engage in practical activism, challenging the manufactured uncertainty and other information produced by the state or companies running the projects" (Marta Conde Puigmal 2015, 67).

In 2005, as Pacific Rim's environmental impact study for the El Dorado mine was undergoing review at the MARN, Mesa affiliate ADES secured international funding to contract US hydrologist and geochemist Robert Moran for an independent assessment. Moran, who had just completed a critical review of the Marlin mine's EIA in Guatemala, as discussed in Chapter 4, was asked to evaluate Pacific Rim's EIA for El Dorado and present his findings to a community gathering.[14] Although Moran had worked for US mining companies to prepare EIAs for more than two decades, he had become "tired of the half-truths" that often characterized these assessments (ES3710). In 1998 he joined a growing community of activist professionals, lending his technical expertise to the critique of those documents (Conde Puigmal 2015, appendices 90–103). His report on the El Dorado EIA (Moran

---

[14] Between 2001 and 2010, Moran carried out EIA reviews in eight Latin American countries and more than two dozen projects elsewhere, calling attention to the weaknesses of these assessments and highlighting the resulting environmental risks (Spalding 2013, 34–36). Critical scientific assessments of mining damage were also presented by Dina Larios de López (López, Guzmán, and Mira 2008), a Salvadoran-US academic specialist in acid mine drainage, who collaborated with a CEICOM team and provided legislative testimony.

200 BREAKING GROUND

2005b) pointed to its inadequate baseline water study, misleading assessment of cyanide detoxification processes, and weak financial guarantees. Since the official public consultation process permitted the release of only one hard copy of the 1,400-page EIA for a ten-day period, and included some annexes presented only in English, with no photocopying permitted, Moran's assessment also called attention to these citizen consultation failings. El Salvador's public comment process, he concluded, "lacked openness and transparency" (ES3710).

This critical appraisal circulated inside the MARN as the ministry took up its review of the El Dorado EIA. While the newly created agency geared up to define the regulatory standards that would be used to evaluate the EIAs, Moran's report triggered internal questions and concerns, including at the ministerial level (ES0312; Pac Rim Cayman 2014b, 103–104; ES0717; Nadelman 2018, 221–223; Broad and Cavanagh 2021, 66–67). Pacific Rim officials, who once reported an array of accommodations, now found permits delayed and paperwork returned for clarification (Shrake 2010; Pac Rim Cayman 2013). Gaps concerning the failure to acquire surface property rights were found in their extraction application. Corporate assurances about cyanide remediation and water safety no longer bought official acquiescence. MARN officials returned the application to the company more than three times in 2005 and 2006, with questions that needed answers and requests for additional information. In the space that opened with application deceleration, officials acquired additional information about mining risks. The more they learned, the more concern they registered.

In mid-2006, Hugo Barrera, the minister of environment and natural resources and ARENA co-founder, publicly expressed personal reservations about mining, and permitting processes ground to a halt. Asked in an interview published in *La Prensa Gráfica* on July 9, 2006, about how MARN would monitor the mines when it already lacked the capacity to monitor the other 24,000 industries in the country, Barrera acknowledged the problem, and then identified a standard to which he thought mining companies should adhere:

> To authorize, we would have to look at international mining norms. If someone could provide a 100% guarantee that there will be no environmental damages, there would be no problem. But I doubt that for these small amounts of gold anyone will want to make the investments needed to guarantee there will be no environmental damage. This means that if they

do not guarantee that they will take these measures, we are not going to authorize anything. (Barrera 2006, 5)

Increasingly alarmed over the rising opposition and the issues the mining resisters raised, the Ministry of Economy hired Peruvian environmental law specialist Manuel Pulgar-Vidal to review El Salvador's mining regulations and identify changes "such that the mining sector develops as an industry that utilizes proper mining practices to avoid environmental degradation" (Pac Rim Cayman 2016, VI-39).[15] Pulgar-Vidal's August 2006 report highlighted gaps and inconsistencies in the Salvadoran regulations and noted the absence of national agreement about mining advancement. He recommended that the government arrange a strategic environmental assessment to produce a full-fledged evaluation of mining costs and benefits. Under instruction from Saca, the Minister of Economy began work on a legislative proposal to declare a three-year moratorium (Pac Rim Cayman 2016, VI-51–52). In May 2007, MARN and MINEC ministers called a meeting with the main concession holders and announced the suspension of the mine licensing process pending the completion of a SEA.

Issues introduced in the mining debate were not just technical; they were also political, and highly charged. As protests sponsored by the Mesa and the FMLN raised the profile of the mining conflict, the electoral risks associated with mine promotion began to grow. The development of a well-organized anti-mining movement, combined with a growing electoral threat to ARENA dominance, encouraged a recalculation of the political costs of mining advocacy by high-level officials (Shrake 2010). After a decade of collaboration with would-be mining investors, the ARENA government slowly backed away. The business subsector that had initially supported mine development failed to lock down broad elite backing, and neither ANEP nor the right-wing media mounted a defense.

With no strong business lobby anchoring the pro-mining side, Saca, the fourth consecutive ARENA president, began detaching from the mining alliance. Facing the country's first truly competitive postwar presidential election, Saca moved official opposition out into the open in March 2008, proclaiming that "in principle, I do not agree with granting these [mining]

---

[15] Pulgar-Vidal served as executive director of the Sociedad Peruana de Derecho Ambiental from 1990 to 2011, and became Peru's minister of environment during the Humala administration (2011–2016).

202 BREAKING GROUND

permits."[16] The following year, just weeks before the March 2009 election, he called in to a live Catholic radio station program on mining and pledged that he would "not grant a single permit" (López Piche 2009, 2). In defiance of Pacific Rim's threat to file an investment dispute claim, Saca continued, "They are about to file an international claim and I want to make this clear: I would prefer to pay the $90 million than to give them a permit" (p. 2).

Activists kept the pressure up as state leadership transferred across party lines to the Funes administration. Buying time and seeking to build a national consensus, the new president finally commissioned the recommended SEA. The Spanish consulting company TAU Consultora Ambiental carried out the assessment, with a blue ribbon oversight committee added to ensure the quality of the report.[17] The SEA identified a long list of environmental vulnerabilities in El Salvador and described in detail the institutional deficiencies in the government's regulatory capacity (TAU 2011). According to this assessment, major policy change and institutional development would be needed in seventeen areas, with sixty-three specific actions identified for change (TAU 2011, table 19, pp. 81–84). Armed with this document, the ministers of the environment and the economy jointly presented a proposal to the legislature in August 2012, calling for a formal mining moratorium. Noting that an outright ban could trigger ICSID demands by any of the twenty-six companies that currently held exploration rights, environment minister Herman Rosa Chávez (2012) concluded, "In reality, [the moratorium] is the only option."

Direct Democracy and Community Consultation

In addition to their campaign and election work and their push for heightened bureaucratic monitoring, mining opponents moved to open new institutional spaces where they could register their views directly. Unlike countries in Latin America where mechanisms of direct democracy became part of the institutional landscape during the period of electoral democratization (Breuer 2007), direct forms of citizen participation remained quite limited in El Salvador. Whereas Nicaragua, Guatemala, and Costa Rica were obliged to

---

[16] As quoted in Pac Rim Cayman 2009, 30.

[17] The four-person international oversight committee was composed of Robert Goodland, Ann Maest, Allan Astorga, and Anthony Bebbington, who chaired its work (Bebbington et al. 2015, 205n24).

ensure indigenous consultation, El Salvador's small indigenous population did not enjoy consultation rights under ILO 169, which El Salvador had not signed.[18] El Salvador lacked a grassroots recall process and most other forms of citizen initiatives and did not provide opportunities for participation in national policy referenda. Citizen groups could not introduce bills for legislative review directly (Artiga González 2007, 335–337; ES0117). Civil society groups with an interest in changing the law had to recruit cabinet officials or legislators to serve as sponsors of their bills.

In spite of these limitations, anti-mining activists identified two mechanisms through which to register community voices in this debate. The first looked to recently approved decentralization laws, focusing on the municipal code. The second involved conducting public opinion polls in areas where mining exploration was under way. These processes demonstrated high levels of local opposition, which challenged the mining companies' narrative of community support.

The first step involved activating a previously unused consultation provision embedded in El Salvador's 2005 Municipal Code. This provision allowed local residents to invoke a variant of the *consulta* process employed by anti-mining movements elsewhere in Latin America (Walter and Urkidi 2016). Under this guideline, if 40% of registered voters in a *municipio* petitioned for a *consulta popular*, the Consejo Municipal was required to call one. If turnout was at least 40% of the vote tally from the previous municipal election, the majority preference was to be regarded as binding.

Between 2014 and 2017, CRIPDES organized five municipal-level consultations on the mining question in gold belt communities (ES1517; ES1617). The towns selected for these consultations were strongholds of the FMLN and politically atypical, even for their departments.[19] The "no" vote was predictably overwhelming in these towns, with opposition to mining ranging from 98% to 100%. Strategically placing the *consultas* in propitious territory, dispersing the costs of running them across the seasons and years, inviting domestic and international observers to witness the process and

---

[18] According to the World Bank assessment of indigeneity in Latin America, only 0.2% of the Salvadoran population was classified as indigenous in the 2007 census (World Bank Group 2015, 25).

[19] *Consultas* regarding approval of local mine development were carried out in San José Las Flores, San Isidro Labrador, Nueva Trinidad, Arcatao, and Cinquera. The 2014 second-round vote for the FMLN presidential candidate Salvador Sánchez Cerén in these five communities ranged from a high of 96% in San José Las Flores to a low of 61% in Cinquera, in all cases running substantially above his national vote tally of 50.1%. For election results, see the Tribunal Supremo Electoral website, https://www.tse.gob.sv/.

align with their struggle, and promoting favorable media coverage of the results, Mesa affiliates kept the message of community opposition to mining on a repeat cycle that bolstered their demand for prohibition.

The second process involved two rounds of public opinion polling in potentially affected communities, the first in 2007 and the second in 2015. These public opinion surveys, carried out by the Universidad Centroamericana (UCA)'s Instituto Universitario de Opinión Pública (IUDOP) in *municipios* where exploration concessions had been granted, revealed that opposition to mining was already the dominant view in those communities in 2007. When asked, "Do you consider El Salvador an appropriate country for mining operations?," 62.5% of respondents in mining communities said no (IUDOP 2008, 1). A repeat survey eight years later found that opposition had become yet more comprehensive, with the proportion saying no increasing to 79.5% (IUDOP 2015, 58). Almost four out of every five respondents in this zone of heightened vulnerability concluded that mining was not an appropriate activity for El Salvador in 2015. Mesa activists disseminated these results widely, countering corporate claims that the industry enjoyed a positive reception in El Salvador and casting doubt on corporate declarations that the companies had acquired a "social license to operate."

Although formal opportunities were few in El Salvador for mining critics to register their views directly through the introduction of local-level initiatives, referenda, and consultations, and the Salvadoran court system did not respond to citizen petitions with the receptiveness found in Costa Rica and Guatemala, activists used direct and indirect means to register local mining opposition, and to demonstrate the gap between popular preferences and mining development.

Elite Fracture and the Loss of Allies

Elite consensus—the first element of the model described in Chapter 2—is easily found to be absent in the Salvadoran mining case. Initially divided across party lines, with ARENA hegemony and pro-market euphoria assuring the mining companies of backing while the FMLN stood in opposition, political elites were already fractured at the outset of the debate over mining. The growing hesitancy in the Saca administration signaled a deepening fissure also emerging within the ARENA front. The election of two consecutive FMLN-backed presidents further eroded official support and put the mining industry on notice. Firm backing from the business sector might have compensated for these political divisions, but economic elites also proved unavailable as the mining debate unfolded. Without solid support from within the local business community, foreign mining company officials found it difficult to advance.

To counter rising resistance, Pacific Rim took a series of steps in rapid succession. As in Costa Rica, the company attempted to improve the image of metallic mining by launching a "green mining campaign," selling the idea that modern mining had overcome its bad-boy past and now operated in an environmentally sound way. Pacific Rim proffered an array of CSR initiatives in hope of building support at the community level, including eye care for children, environmental education programs in the schools, recycling pickup, river solid waste cleanup, and planting over 40,000 trees (Shrake 2010, 37). According to the annual reports filed by Pacific Rim with the Salvadoran government, the company spent $1.1 million on public relations activities between 2007 and August 2008 (Pac Rim Cayman 2014a, 117).

Recognizing the need for business backing and political allies, Pacific Rim hired corporate lobbyists and consultants to mobilize support inside the government and the business community.[20] These high-level hiring decisions were calculated and strategic, and the alliances brought the company close to some prominent political and economic actors. Those approached for collaboration included several members of the legislature, whose support, it was hoped, would secure any needed legal adjustments.

Existing law in El Salvador required applicants for extraction licenses to acquire surface property rights for land above subterranean tunnels, a requirement that Pacific Rim found difficult to meet due to the resistance and bargaining strategies of local property owners. To eliminate that stipulation and address legal problems cropping up in its project proposal, Pacific Rim recruited National Conciliation Party (PCN) legislators to introduce a revised bill in November 2007, making concessions in terms of increased royalties and other guarantees in return for changes in surface rights requirements (Pac Rim Cayman 2016, VI-36). As noted in the ICSID testimony of Pacific

---

[20] According to Pacific Rim's ICSID testimony (Pac Rim Cayman 2016, VI-52), the company's lobbyists during the Saca administration included Fidel Chávez, former Christian Democratic Party presidential candidate and father of Rodrigo Chávez, Pacific Rim–El Salvador's vice president; and Francisco Escobar, brother-in-law of Vice President Ana Vilma de Escobar, whose husband, Patricio Escobar, worked for the Poma Group, one of El Salvador's most important business groups. Rodrigo Chávez was subsequently convicted of murder, further tarnishing the company's image.

206 BREAKING GROUND

Rim managers, the proposed reform bill was elaborated in close consultation with company lawyers (Pac Rim Cayman 2016, VI-36).[21]

A scattering of political and business elites provided behind-the-scenes support for the mining agenda, including, as tensions mounted, Ricardo Poma, head of the powerful Poma Group (Funes 2017; Jimenez 2017; Nadelman 2018, 183–185; Broad and Cavanagh 2021, 81–82).[22] But mining exploration companies that pursued entry in El Salvador may have underestimated the role of rivalries within the business sector and the growing competition among economic elites for access to water.[23] Perhaps depending too much on high-level contacts, corporate representatives failed to construct resilient relationships with broad networks of local elites.

Unlike the mining sector's business allies in Nicaragua and Guatemala, who generally had strategic ties to the mining industry, business associations in El Salvador had little connection to the sector. Mining company managers in El Salvador did not form their own business chamber, where they could combine forces and advance shared interests. Nor did they secure an alliance with the national encompassing association, the National Association of Private Enterprise (ANEP), which represented the collective interests of the Salvadoran business elite. Unlike their counterparts in Nicaragua and Guatemala, who firmly took both of those steps, mining executives pursing investments in El Salvador did not embed themselves in local business networks. Business associations, in turn, did not serve as advocates when the sector hit bumps in the road.

When I asked an ANEP spokesperson, in a 2017 interview, to describe the position the association took on the mining ban, they adopted a stance of studied neutrality, and replied that the association had taken "no position" (ES1917).[24] Unable to identify personal opportunities, and unwilling to take

---

[21] The PCN was an old-line conservative party and frequent ARENA partner in the legislature. This bill languished in 2008 as the Saca administration backed away from mine development and the PCN became increasingly isolated.

[22] In 2017, Auxiliary Bishop Gregorio Rosa Chávez (soon to be named as El Salvador's first cardinal) described pressure exerted on the bishops by an unnamed ARENA financier, who pushed them to withdraw from the anti-mining campaign (Jimenez 2017). Former president Mauricio Funes (2017) tweeted his speculation that Rosa Chávez was referring to Ricardo Poma, who had also lobbied the Funes administration on behalf of mining.

[23] Nadelman (2018, 170–171), for example, points to tensions between Ricardo Poma and Roberto Murray Meza, of the Agrisal Group, over the future of water rights and the Lempa River.

[24] See Broad and Cavanagh (2015, 421–422) on the absence of strong domestic business support for mining in El Salvador and Costa Rica; see also Bebbington et al. (2015, 198) and Nadelman (2018, 144–194). Local actors who appeared publicly in the mining sector's defense generally entered this arena as paid consultants, like the former minister of finance Manuel Hinds, or local managers employed by mining companies, like the former MARN official Ericka Colindres.

on the growing liabilities of the mining companies, most Salvadoran business leaders kept their distance. Operating outside the protective framework designed for collective business coordination, mining companies seeking access to resources in El Salvador became political orphans.

Even skillful pursuit of collaboration with local business interests might have failed, given the rising competition for water rights. El Salvador's precarious position in terms of vulnerability to natural disaster and climate change (Bebbington et al. 2015) made water, already a scarce commodity, a source of growing intra-elite rivalry. New concerns about levels of water consumption by the mining sector deepened the divide for large-scale agricultural producers and local bottling industries (ES1017; Nadelman 2018, 169–171; Broad and Cavanagh 2021, 73). The absence of solid business backing weakened the position of mining sector pioneers, making them vulnerable to the growing push for policy change.

Adoption of a Formal Legislative Ban: A Window of Opportunity

The anti-mining movement had succeeded in getting the mining debate onto the policy agenda in El Salvador by 2006 and halted actual mine development with a de facto license moratorium. Resistance activists had broadened local participatory spaces and put bureaucrats on notice about deficiencies in their institutional practices. When the FMLN won the presidency again in 2014, the movement secured some high-level administrative appointments.[25] But this coalition had not yet translated these achievements into an official mining policy change.

This was not for lack of effort. Activists in the Mesa maintained their call for an outright ban on metal mining, and they worked closely with FMLN legislators to advance that initiative in the National Assembly. First introduced in December 2006, a bill to prohibit metallic mining was presented repeatedly on behalf of the Mesa by a dedicated group of FMLN legislators. According to the online database for the Asamblea Legislativa, this bill or a lightly adapted equivalent was reintroduced between one and

---

[25] During the Sánchez Cerén administration, long-term civil society advocate Lina Pohl became minister of the MARN and Ángel Ibarra, one of the founders of the environmental organization UNES (and Mesa member), served as MARN vice minister.

208 BREAKING GROUND

four times a year over the next eight years, for a total of fifteen submissions between 2006 and 2014. But none of these bills made it out of committee, and the future of the industry remained uncertain.

In 2017, however, after a twelve-year campaign, the situation changed. Within weeks, a new mining law, which prohibited all forms of metallic mining, won unanimous support in the national legislature. Two processes ultimately triggered the adoption of El Salvador's mining ban. First, the regulatory freeze was successfully lifted when the ICSID case was resolved in Washington, DC, with the Republic of El Salvador emerging as the winner. This experience left behind a sense of national vulnerability that added urgency to legislative deliberations, while resolution of the case, making it possible to proceed legislatively without affecting the outcome, now lowered the barriers for policy advancement. Second, the anti-mining movement recalibrated its leadership structure, building on bridging mechanisms to stitch together a reorganized coalition. This final section turns our attention to formal policy catalysts, where sudden changes in the alignment of players opened new territory for policy reform.

Pacific Rim's legal claim against El Salvador argued that the company had been defrauded by the Saca administration, which had arbitrarily denied an extraction permit after the company had completed all requirements. The company's initial $90 million claim soon rose to $314 million (Pac Rim Cayman 2013) before settling at $250 million as the case progressed. This ICSID demand raised the stakes for El Salvador, even as it impeded legislative action (ES2717). Fearful that regulatory change on its part would jeopardize the government's case, subsequent administrations spent years caught in an impasse.

After almost eight years of legal limbo, Pacific Rim lost its ICSID case in October 2016. In a unanimous vote, the ICSID tribunal concluded that the company had never completed the extraction license application process due to its failure to secure permission for underground mine construction from the owners of surface property, as required by Salvadoran law (Pac Rim Cayman 2016). On the basis of this fairly narrow and technical finding, the company's case against the government was dismissed.

Legislative deliberations then entered a new phase in San Salvador. As one legislative observer noted, "With the claim filed in ICSID, we could see that we were unprotected, that any other firm could file a demand against us and we would be vulnerable. We needed to act to prohibit [metal mining] to prevent that from happening again. That [ICSID] decision could have gone the other way" (ES0117). Salvadorans had faced the threat of paying out $250 million to a company that had never fully established its right to mine, or of being required, through external pressure, to authorize the initiation of an industry with well-documented environmental risks, which the country was, on the basis of the best evidence, unprepared to manage. The possibility of a ripple effect, as other similarly situated mining companies filed their own cases against the country, perhaps with greater success, brought the potential costs of inaction into sharp relief.

Ironically, an institution and process that had been designed to promote international investment by increasing protections for investors may have served, at this stage, to accelerate prohibition. As anti-mining mobilization continued and evidence accumulated showing that the country was ill-prepared to regulate the industry, political leaders recognized the need to take definitive action to contain the threat of new legal demands. When the policy freeze imposed by active litigation was lifted, a ban suddenly became a feasible alternative. In the words of one ARENA legislator (ES0317), "This year we found there was a window of opportunity." Even ARENA-aligned voices that had once favored mining were now subdued (ES2617). "After the Pacific Rim case," one observer noted, "no one wanted to defend mining" (ES1017).

During this juncture, a new round of high-profile interventions by Catholic Church leaders drove the process forward. In this final lap, collaboration between the Mesa and the church hierarchy shifted to accent the role of the church. This recalibration of the anti-mining alliance triggered some tensions and indications of mistrust, which are not uncommon in weak-tie relationships. Although reorganization came at a cost, the emphasis on church leadership succeeded in easing the partisan identity of the cause and in giving the process a fresh start. As one Asamblea respondent observed:

> One thing that helped the [Environment and Climate Change] Committee and the Assembly to move forward in 2017 was that the church presented a new proposal. The committee wasn't required to go back to the old proposals that had already been debated and had already generated polarized responses. Instead, it could start fresh with a new proposal that was clear and straightforward. With the earlier ones, sometimes the bills were internally contradictory, or they missed an important issue. With this new one from the church, those problems did not arise. (ES0117)

210   BREAKING GROUND

This realignment involved collaboration among a variety of church-linked institutions and policy strategists, several of which served as bridging agents. The Jesuit-run UCA took the lead on developing a new mining prohibition bill (ES1017; ES1717; McKinley 2020, 239). With assistance from the university's legal team and legal studies faculty, the UCA's mission-driven Social Projection office oversaw a technical analysis of the bills under legislative review and, finding deficiencies, moved to draft a new version in 2016. The new bill prohibited metallic mining both above and below ground, and it set a two-year deadline for the elimination of artisanal gold mining operations.

UCA administrators presented the new proposal to Archbishop Escobar Alas, who embraced it as his own. Under his leadership, a delegation of Catholic authorities formally presented the draft bill to the Asamblea on February 6, 2017, with prearranged sponsorship provided by key legislative leaders.[26] Three weeks later, the archbishop organized a major signature drive in support of the ban. Priests circulated petitions before and after Sunday mass and collected more than 37,000 signatures in a little over a week. Church leaders then gathered several thousand followers to accompany them as they carted boxes of petitions to the entrance of the Asamblea. They were met by a contingent of legislators, including Assembly president Guillermo Gallegos, who promised rapid action. Claiming that mining was a "life or death threat," the archbishop called on the legislators to step away from partisanship and deliver unanimous support (Gómez and Orellana 2017).

The bill was approved quickly in a 69–0 vote on March 29, 2017 (Asamblea Legislativa [El Salvador] 2017). After more than a decade of legislative delay, debate, and dismissal, legislators from all five parties lined up to endorse this new policy. Support was automatic with FMLN lawmakers, who festooned the chamber with banners reading "No a la minería, sí a la vida" (No to mining, yes to life). The Grand Alliance for National Unity (GANA), which had been formed in 2009 following Saca's expulsion from ARENA and which served as the FMLN's frequent legislative partner, also endorsed the measure.[27] The solitary Christian Democrat (PDC) vote had been previously

---

[26] The bill was presented by the archbishop of San Salvador, José Luis Escobar Alas; Auxiliary Bishop Gregorio Rosa Chávez, the president of Cáritas; Andreu Oliva, the UCA rector; and José María Tojeira, the director of the Human Rights Institute of the UCA. Fray Domingo Solís, in representation of the Franciscan JPIC, accompanied the second delegation the following month.

[27] Saca was expelled from ARENA in December 2009 following internal conflicts that led twelve of ARENA's thirty-two legislators to quit the party and create GANA. In 2018, Saca pled guilty to accusations of misappropriation of $300 million from a presidential discretionary fund, and received a ten-year prison sentence.

pledged in support of the ban, providing mining opponents a slim margin of victory. The lingering question, then, concerned legislators from ARENA and the PCN, who controlled the remaining 49% of the seats (see Appendix 6.1).

Legislators in El Salvador traditionally owed their candidacy to their party, not directly to the voting public, and party bloc voting in the Asamblea was the norm (FUSADES-DEL 2017). Changing the voting position of a legislator normally required persuasion at the level of party leaders rather than recruitment of individual members. New election rules governing preferential voting for individual candidates and the option of split-ticket balloting hinted at a possible reconfiguration of legislative voting practices down the road, but change was developing slowly, and disciplined party voting was still the norm.

Reflecting on the unanimity of the prohibition vote, one longtime legislative observer noted that the 2015 legislative election brought into office a number of new representatives, and that ARENA in particular "had diversified" (ES0117). One member of this cohort was John Wright Sol, a US-educated former firefighter in Fairfax County, Virginia, who hailed from a prominent ARENA-founding family. As a newly minted legislator, Wright Sol had volunteered for the Environment and Climate Change Committee, the committee in charge of mining policy deliberations. His decision to throw his weight behind the 2017 mining ban helped move his party toward the emerging legislative consensus.

The biggest surprise was the favorable vote by the PCN legislators, who had a history of support for the mining industry. The PCN was ARENA's most durable legislative coalition partner and was crucial to its ability to secure legislative majorities (FUSADES-DEL 2010, 126). With ARENA's shift toward mining opposition, the PCN legislators were now abandoned. One legislative observer (ES0117) interpreted the PCN vote as an effort to avoid political isolation, which was destined, in any case, to be futile ("Their thinking was, 'We'll be alone in our opposition and lose anyway'"). Another (ES2517) viewed it as an attempt by PCN leaders to avoid public condemnation, not just by Salvadorans but by the numerous international organizations that were now monitoring the case.

This voting pattern suggests that strong "social cascade effects" (Baumgartner 2006, 43) contributed to the legislative sweep, as political parties that had once endorsed pro-mining legislation now moved into the opposition. As in Costa Rica, when mining risks grew more visible and prohibition support accumulated, the ban coalition achieved a tipping point,

212 BREAKING GROUND

and formerly oppositional parliamentary groups tumbled into the swelling anti-mining majority, party by party. For those legislators who were not in agreement, the options were to adhere to party decisions to support the ban, in spite of personal reservations, or to not cast a vote, either through absence or by nonparticipation.[28]

Analysis of national public opinion data collected in the aftermath suggests that the ban enjoyed broad national support, and legislators may have been aligning themselves with shifting popular preferences. In an eight-country poll concerning attitudes toward mining conducted by CID Gallup in 2018, 58% of Salvadoran respondents said that mining company operations should be prohibited, second only to the 59% registered in Costa Rica (CID Gallup 2018; see Chapter 2 for details). Less than a quarter (24%) of the Salvadoran respondents stated that mining company operations should be permitted, the lowest percentage in any of the eight countries. When those who called for prohibition were asked why they opposed mining, 68% of Salvadoran respondents identified environmental damage as their main concern.

Discussion and Conclusions

The shift in El Salvador's mining policy, which transitioned from rules that favored investors to an absolute legislative ban, can be explained by tracing the interactions identified in the three-part framework presented in Chapter 2. The deepening fractures in elite support for the sector, the organizational sweep and cohesion of the anti-mining network, and the availability of entry points that permitted institutional penetration all combined to alter the landscape where mining policy is enacted.

As the Salvadoran case demonstrates, elite support for mining development is not automatic and should not be assumed. Variation occurs depending on alliance structures, the uneven propensity for gain, and the internal rivalries that mining unleashes. Whereas elite support for mining spread across all major parties and permeated the business encompassing associations in Nicaraguan and Guatemala, elites were divided in Costa Rica and El Salvador and business alliances failed to mature. In the absence of cohesive backing by political and economic elites, the opportunities expanded for social movement influence. The anti-mining movement's broad,

---

[28] Five legislators who were registered as attending the session did not cast a vote on the mining ban.

multisectoral outreach, stoked by the Mesa for over a decade, disseminated a resistance message to a growing public, eventually reaching into opposition territory. Social movement networking accelerated the breakdown of elite support and fostered a new anti-mining tilt.

The alliance formed by the Mesa and the leadership of the Catholic Church repeatedly pressed for a mining prohibition, focusing attention on mining's environmental and human rights costs. This coalition drew on bonding and bridging ties to expand the network's spatial reach and multisectoral breadth, combining the Mesa's capacity to connect grassroots activists at the local and national levels with the church leaders' access to both elite and mass publics. Resisters drew on reserves of strategic capital as they renewed linkages that had been forged in previous struggles. And they mobilized transnational alliances through both lateral connections with activists in neighboring countries and global links with allies located in geopolitical power nodes, particularly the United States and Canada.

Social mobilization by itself, however, is "often insufficient to effect changes in public policy" (Amenta 2006, 24). As Marco Giugni (2004, 161) found in his cross-national study of policy reform, there was "no consistent pattern of co-variation" between changes in movement organizational resources, such as increased membership and financial assets, and policy shifts that occurred over time. A spike in protests does not translate easily or automatically into an outpouring of new policies and programs.

To clarify the connection between social movement activities and public policy outcomes, Edwin Amenta (2006) used the tools of historical institutionalism to carefully excavate and sequence primary source material as he analyzed the influence of the Townsend movement on social security policy development in the United States. To respond to the question about "when movements matter," Amenta (2006, 31) closely reviewed the archival record to determine "whether a challenger altered the plans and agendas of political leaders; influenced the content of the proposals as devised by executives, legislators, or administrators; influenced the votes of representatives key to the passage of proposed legislation; or influenced the speed or nature of the implementation of legislation." When movements are found to directly affect the behavior of institutional actors and inform the contents of a policy text, Amenta argues, then their influence can be more confidently asserted.

Using Amenta's guidelines as the standard against which to judge the impact of the anti-mining movement in El Salvador, the evidence presented in this study supports a positive evaluation of movement consequences.

214 BREAKING GROUND

Anti-mining activists identified institutional collaborators and committed to direct political engagement, taking on the risks of formalization and central-ization. Political party connections allowed movement leaders to gain access to candidates who pledged public support, including at the presidential level, and to locate FMLN legislators who sponsored anti-mining bills on their be-half. Collaboration with experts and participation in the public comment phase of the EIA review allowed opponents to access bureaucratic actors, using scientific activism to insert information about mining risks. Public opinion polling and referenda at the community level documented durable forms of local resistance and led officials to question "social license" claims in the public debate.

Corporate strategies bought time, as mining executives hired lobbyists and built CSR projects. Resisters found it difficult to advance when investors shifted the contestation venue to ICSID in Washington, DC. Transferring a hefty piece of the deliberative process to the international scale and encasing it in the strictures of administrative law, the ICSID case disrupted the processes of democratic contention that had permitted social move-ment actors to place this issue on the national policy agenda. International judicialization froze out reform during the long waiting period when the in-vestment dispute impeded the forward movement that the country seemed ready to pursue.

Activists secured a rapid legislative finale, however, once the ICSID ob-stacle was removed. Church leadership shifted the framing of the debate away from partisan identification and toward moral claims related to envi-ronmental and human rights. Broad national agreement in support of a ban made it more difficult for business elites to advocate on behalf of mining, and encouraged political and economic elites to take stock of mining downsides. As elite fissures widened, leaving few to make the case for mining, a growing sense of a national anti-mining consensus brought along the votes of key rep-resentatives who had once been on the opposing side.

It is possible, of course, that the prohibition would have been approved even without the sustained effort of mining opponents. Precise estimation of movement impact requires consideration of such counterfactuals (Amenta 2006, 30–31). El Salvador's small size, heavy dependence on a single river system, and well-documented vulnerability to climate change could have prompted a policy shift away from metallic mining based on technocratic criteria, even in the absence of a movement advocating a ban. But it is un-likely that the Salvadoran government would have taken this step without pressure from and accompaniment by movement actors. Bold technocratic leadership by elected or bureaucratic officials in El Salvador has not been widely observed, nor is it commonly seen in mining policy disputes elsewhere in the region. Only Costa Rica has adopted similar legislation, and in that case as well, the ban followed years of forceful organizing by environmental and community activists.

In sum, the Salvadoran case demonstrates how a multisectoral national movement can develop in opposition to mining and achieve frame alignment around a cohesive policy objective. When accompanied by fissures in the elite, the movement may be able to avoid the most debilitating forms of repression and find high-level allies and champions who can support their campaign. When the state apparatus is permeable enough to absorb pressures and respond to interventions from grassroots social actors, then movement leaders may be able to activate institutional docking points to push policy deliberation along to policy enactment. This interactive process can reshape national policy outcomes, at least for the immediate future.

Achievement of a mining ban did not mean a radical redefinition of El Salvador's development model. Nor did it indicate that this policy change would be irreversible. Much of the pro-market logic embraced by Salvadoran political and economic elites in the postwar era remained intact, and rollback of environmental reforms has been a common problem in Latin America. However, the breadth of mining opposition, as registered in public opinion polling and the unanimity of the legislative vote, suggests that any push for renewal of metallic mining in El Salvador would face significant opposition. The absence of elite consensus in support of mining and the presence of a broad coalition of mining opponents weigh against the reopening of the mining debate, at least if docking points continue to operate and the state apparatus remains open to the influence of public pressure.

216 BREAKING GROUND

Appendix 6.1 El Salvador Legislature, Composition by Political Party and Legislative Session (Number of Seats)

	2003	2006	2009	2012	2015
ARENA	27	34	35	33	35
PCN	16	10	11	6	6
FMLN	31	32	32	31	31
GANA*	–	–	–	11	11
Others	10	8	6	3	1
Total	84	84	84	84	84

Sources: Compiled from Inter-Parliamentary Union, PRALINE database, at www.ipu.org, and the El Salvador Asamblea Legislativa website, https://www.asamblea.gob.sv/.
* Founded after the 2009 election.

Appendix 6.2 El Salvador: List of Cited Interviews

Code	Affiliation	Sector	Interview date	Location
ES0117	Legislature, staff	Government— legislature	October 17, 2017	San Salvador
ES0217	Legislator, FMLN Presidency	Government— legislature Government— executive	October 26, 2017	San Salvador
ES0317	Legislator, ARENA	Government— legislature	October 19, 2017	San Salvador
ES0417	MUFRAS 32	Civil society—community	October 25, 2017	Cabañas
ES0517	Legislator, FMLN	Government— legislature	October 26, 2017	San Salvador
ES0617	MARN	Government— executive	October 23, 2017	San Salvador
ES0717	ADES	Civil society—community	October 25, 2017	Cabañas
ES0817	Cáritas El Salvador	Civil society—religious	October 19, 2017	San Salvador
ES0917	Cáritas El Salvador	Civil society—religious	October 19, 2017	San Salvador
ES1017	UCA	Academic	October 18, 2017	San Salvador
ES1517	ARDM	Civil society—community	October 24, 2017	Cabañas
ES1617	CRIPDES	Civil society—community	October 30, 2017	San Salvador
ES1717	UCA	Academic	October 30, 2017	San Salvador

Appendix 6.2 Continued

Code	Affiliation	Sector	Interview date	Location
ES1817	MINEC	Government—executive	October 30, 2017	San Salvador
ES1917	ANEP	Business association	October 20, 2017	San Salvador
ES2017	FESPAD	Civil society—human rights	October 23, 2017	San Salvador
ES2117	CRS	INGO—religious	October 21, 2017	San Salvador
ES2417	CRIPDES/CCR	Civil society—community	October 27, 2017	San Salvador
ES2517	UNES	Civil society—environment	October 27, 2017	San Salvador
ES2617	Ministry of Finance Consultant	Government—executive Business	October 20, 2017	San Salvador
ES2717	Arbitration lawyer	Government—legal	September 7, 2017	Washington, DC
ES0113	CIEL	INGO—legal and environment	July 23, 2013	Washington, DC
ES0112	JPIC	Civil society—religious	November 14, 2012	Chicago
ES0312	ADES	Civil society—community	December 3, 2012	Cabañas
ES1012	Mesa Nacional	Civil society—anti-mining	May 17, 2012	Chicago
ES0710	Sister Cities	INGO—solidarity	July 19, 2010	San Salvador
ES1710	Oxfam	INGO—development	July 13, 2010	San Salvador
ES3510	CRS	INGO—religious	July 12, 2010	San Salvador
ES3710	EIA consultant	International technical expert	September 3, 2010	Colorado

7

Mining Reform in Latin America

International Regimes and the Challenges of Regulation

Natural resource extraction stands at the center of the modern world project. Mining operations provide a vast array of resources used in global production and build the tracks on which the world system runs—those interconnected highways, ports, supertankers, and automotive fleets that move people and goods around the planet. Our everyday lives depend on information flows streaming through phones, computers, and TV screens, which run, at their core, courtesy of Mother Nature. But what rules should govern the extraction and distribution of subsoil resources? And who should decide what those rules will be? What are the non-market-related costs of these extracted materials? And who should pay those costs?

Answering these questions requires us to unpack a dense cluster of connections that link technology, finance, production, and power. Determining where and how mining takes place, and the distribution of its impacts, involves not just geological assessments and calculations of engineering costs. Estimating the full costs of mining requires a complex set of calculations about the environmental and sociological consequences of alternative development strategies and regulatory regimes. The geolocation of mining operations depends on who absorbs the externalized costs and the social and environmental disruptions associated with extraction. As Stuart Kirsch (2014, 146) notes, "The life of an ore body is therefore as much of a social as a natural fact."

Economic theories to the contrary, mining output does not automatically mirror fluctuating levels of profitability. Not only does the map of global mining fail to align with the planetary distribution of mineral ores, it also fails to respond in a simple way to shifting price signals. Increasing profit margins certainly animate speculators and exploratory juniors, but the rhythm of production is affected by a wide array of interlinked processes and sunk costs. As we have seen in this study, mining activities may be slow to ramp up, even during a commodity boom. And highly productive mines

Breaking Ground. Rose J. Spalding, Oxford University Press. © Oxford University Press 2023.
DOI: 10.1093/oso/9780197643150.003.0007

may be taken out of commission when facing high levels of community resistance and successful legal challenges.

In spite of the economic, social, and cultural significance of extractive sector development in Latin America, and the rise in environmental conflicts leading to deaths, displacement, and migration, the research needed to understand the process of extractive sector development and mining reform remains a work in progress. My attention to policy debates and institutional innovation reflects the urgency of our need to improve natural resource governance. We face the challenge of designing domestic and international agreements that prioritize human rights and environmental protection over the creation of exploitable hinterlands and "sacrifice zones" where local identities are constructed as "underdeveloped, unproductive, or even non-existent for the purpose of extra-local exploitation" (Klinger 2017, 15). New guidelines are needed to move us toward more harmonious forms of living, both with each other and with the natural world, and to prevent the rollback of reforms currently under way.

Restatement of the Model

This book demonstrates how the policies that shape mining sector development emerge in response to three interwoven processes: the extent to which political and economic elites are united or divided regarding mining development; the degree to which mining resistance movements are fragmented, disconnected, and dispersed or are united, cohesive, and nationally networked; and the extent to which civil society actors enjoy or lack docking opportunities. This third component calls attention to the formal and informal characteristics of the political system, particularly access to participatory portals into the policymaking apparatus, whether through political parties, elected officials, state agencies, the courts, popular consultation mechanisms, or local officials operating under decentralized governance arrangements. Table 7.1 summarizes the four sets of dynamics identified in the previous chapters.

In the Nicaraguan case, all three factors supported the adoption of mining-friendly policies and contributed to an acceleration of mining development. Economic and political elites embraced mining for its development potential, and policies that encouraged mining investment were layered across successive administrations, even as the party in power shifted over time. Mining

220 BREAKING GROUND

Table 7.1 Summary of the Results, by Country

	Elite Pro-Mining Cohesion	Resistance Fragmentation	Impediments to Docking	Mining Policy Model
Nicaragua	Yes	Yes	Yes	Sustained promotion
Guatemala	Yes	Yes	Mixed	Intermittent approval
Costa Rica	No	Mixed	No	Resistant authorization > prohibition
El Salvador	No	No	No	Extended moratorium > ban

development was featured in official planning and investment guides, and potential investors received both discursive support and access to top officials, including the president. Mining companies were absorbed into the national business chamber, where they received recognition and assistance as they became a growing part of the national economy. Local-level opposition got swept aside through top-down partisan pressures and policing interventions that constrained the spread of resistance forces and undermined networking. Although public opinion polls indicated substantial opposition to mining, resisters found few allies within the political class. When opponents resisted dislocation or presented demands for collective rights (water, information, local voice), state agencies were either nonresponsive or adversarial.

This dynamic culminated in a *sustained promotion* package that combined fiscal incentives, light regulation, legal and political favor, and security guarantees—an arrangement that encouraged recurring rounds of mining investment. As in other mining hotspots in Latin America such as Chile and Peru, where political and economic elites have traditionally circled their wagons in favor of mine expansion and where mining resisters are organizationally fragmented and have limited access to state institutions, Nicaragua experienced rapid growth in its mining sector, and it is unlikely to undergo significant policy recalibration.

Guatemalan elites also provided support for mining, and they succeeded in advancing the sector's development during the commodity boom. As in Nicaragua, foreign mining companies were incorporated into the country's powerful business chamber and enjoyed domestic accompaniment as they negotiated a supportive investment climate. Guatemalan business elites

MINING REFORM IN LATIN AMERICA 221

built commercial ties to foreign mining companies, serving as mine representatives, suppliers, and junior partners. Business-friendly political parties embraced mining as a promising sector and produced a string of high-level elected and appointed officials who provided license access and military support. Mining resistance developed, but opponents failed to construct a national coalition or advance through the tough work of coordinating mobilization and frame alignment across affected communities. Although polls indicated substantial opposition to mining, the fissures and localisms that had impeded development of a cohesive coalition on the left or a powerful national-level indigenous rights movement continued to constrain network development among anti-mining activists. Mining resistance clustered in the shadow of proposed mines but did not scale up to the national level.

But unlike in Nicaragua, where protesters faced difficulties inserting their claims into the state apparatus, resistance forces in Guatemala were able to gain traction by proceeding through the judicial track. Strategic litigation, which propelled legal disputes onto the dockets of the Supreme Court of Justice and the Constitutional Court, pushed magistrates to nullify licensing practices that did not meet legal obligations. Egregious violations of indigenous consultation requirements proved to be a potent sticking point. As a national political crisis over corruption and impunity expanded openings for judicial activism, court rulings resulted in a cascade of mining license suspensions and brought metallic mining to a temporary halt. Continued elite support and resistance fragmentation, however, along with limited movement access to political parties, legislators, and state agencies in charge of regulation, suggest that the mining disruption could prove short-lived in Guatemala. The *intermittent approval* model, characterized by stop-and-go cycles, may persist due to the seesaw effect that tugs Guatemala back and forth between elite insistence and resistance demands. This policy volatility could also emerge elsewhere in the region, in countries such as Ecuador and Colombia, where Constitutional Court rulings and local referenda have placed significant constraints on mining development.

Costa Rica, in contrast, underwent a full-scale mining policy shift. Not only did the Costa Rican government halt the entry of new investment, but it also closed down ventures that were already under way. After launching a bid for mining development and securing high-level presidential support, including a "national interest" declaration that cleared out a thicket of environmental regulations impeding license acquisition, gold mining investors got set for a wave of growth. But unlike elites in Nicaragua and Guatemala,

222   BREAKING GROUND

Costa Rican elites remained divided on the mining question. A sequence of switchbacks in presidential discourse and declarations signaled divergence within the political leadership. Foreign mining companies did little to align with Costa Rican business chambers, and the domestic business elite did not come to their defense. This absence of elite consensus created opportunities for mining adversaries.

A decade of prior organization on behalf of environmental objectives in Costa Rica left a legacy of activists who took up the mine resistance call. Although anti-mining networks never merged into a single resistance front, two large coalitions collaborated on oppositional organizing, each contributing based on their own repertoire. Costa Rica's relatively open and well-developed institutions provided multiple points of access for mining resisters. In response to complaints filed by environmental activists, the courts undertook rigorous review of the administrative process by which mining licenses were granted, and found a series of regulatory failings. As public opinion registered widespread anti-mining views, both the established parties and emerging challengers embraced a critical perspective on open pit mining. Under these conditions, policy reversal gained both presidential and legislative support. In this model, *resistant authorization* transitioned into *prohibition*, and plans for open pit mining came to an end.

Like most of Latin America, El Salvador began the new century with mine-friendly legislation. Early regulatory accommodations to company needs pointed to the government's eagerness to support the industry. But Salvadoran political elites, divided between ARENA, the hegemonic pro-business party, and the FMLN, the party forged from a demobilized revolutionary movement, split into competing camps on the issue. As political competition intensified and FMLN victories became more likely, ARENA backing for mine development also ruptured, leaving only a thin layer of elite support. Foreign mining companies failed to network broadly with local business elites, and enjoyed only limited and episodic support from lone business figures.

In contrast to this division within the elite, mining opponents maintained a united front. A grassroots opposition movement, anchored in the former wartime conflict zone, organized a single, multisectoral resistance network that quickly scaled up to the national level. Resisters gained access to policymakers through party alliances and interactions with like-minded *diputados* and legislative commissions. Resistance to mine development

MINING REFORM IN LATIN AMERICA   223

intensified as expert assessments confirmed the country's environmental vulnerabilities. Opposition broadened beyond party lines as Catholic Church officials aligned with and eventually assumed leadership of the anti-mining coalition. This network configuration, which led in the initial phase to an *extended moratorium*, ultimately facilitated adoption of a *mining ban*, which, like Costa Rica's prohibition, was approved with unanimous legislative support.

Formalization of a ban was not easily achieved in either of these cases. This change took over a decade to unfold, in part due to the counterpressures that the mining companies and their supporters brought to bear. In addition to their ability to hire public relations teams, secure favorable media coverage, provide campaign support for allies, soften opposition with social investments, and obtain diplomatic backing from home countries, foreign mining corporations enjoyed investment protections embedded in a host of international treaties and agreements. These protections raised the costs of imposing new constraints on mining activity and left an imprint on the domestic-level processes that are featured in this book. The remainder of this chapter examines the deployment of these mechanisms and assesses their impacts on national-level mining policies in Central America.

International Investment Regimes

As part of the corporate push for increased protection of foreign investments, international trade agreements since the 1990s have tended to include investor-state dispute settlement clauses that encourage the regulatory diffusion of dominant state norms (Schneiderman 2008; Wilske and Raible 2009; Tienhaara 2011; Van Harten 2013; Franck 2019). These provisions allow foreign investors to bring claims against host states in international arbitration tribunals rather than rely on courts and mediation processes in their countries of operation. Eager to gain access to foreign investment, governments have signed bilateral investment treaties and free trade agreements that routinely incorporate these features.[1] Claims of expropriation by the state or the

---

[1] This belief in the signaling power of investment agreements appears to be apocryphal. Empirical analysis of the relationship between signing a bilateral investment treaty and subsequent foreign direct investment flows has found the link to be "marginal" (Schneiderman 2008, 42). Subsequent research has concluded that "there is no strong evidence that international investment agreements (IIAs), much less ISDS, impact investment flows" (Johnson and Sachs 2016, 10; see also Haslam 2010, 1183).

224 BREAKING GROUND

loss of expected profits due to changes in state policies or laws ("indirect expropriation" or "regulatory takings") led increasingly to dispute adjudication under the terms of these international investment rules (Tienhaara 2011; Fach Gomez 2011; Orellana, Baños, and Berger 2015).[2]

The construction of standardized rules to govern the global marketplace has given rise to a new set of boundaries constraining the development of public policy. Schneiderman (2008, 2–3) notes the establishment of an "investment rules regime" that serves to "insulate economic policy from majoritarian politics" and places "substantive limits on state capacity in matters related to markets." Labeling this process a *new constitutionalism*, he focuses on ISDS processes embedded in free trade agreements and bilateral investment treaties and enforced by international institutions. The emerging constitutionalization of economic globalization limits the ability of democratic elections to shape economic policy and balance competing interests through domestic dispute adjudication. Instead, rulings in ISDS cases are made by international tribunals composed of expert arbitrators far removed from the local political arena.[3]

Gus Van Harten (2013), in his content analysis of 243 publicly available international investor-state arbitration cases, found a tendency "for the arbitrators to assert explicitly or implicitly an expansive role for themselves" rather than exercising restraint or demonstrating deference to state-level institutions. Based on a detailed quantitative analysis of keywords in the filings and reasons provided to explain the awards, Van Harten raised questions about the quality of many arbitration decisions and concluded that arbitrators frequently

> appeared reluctant to acknowledge their own governing role, suspicious of the democratic or political origins of state decisions; sceptical of discretion in government; unprepared to accredit party autonomy and sanctity of contract where these principles called for restraint; or unwilling to acknowledge the superior independence, specialization, or legitimacy of another adjudicative forum. (p. 162)

---

[2] Indirect expropriation is defined by Haslam (2010, 1196) as the "application of regulations that may not, ostensibly, be aimed at expropriating the investment, but which effectively deprive the investor of his or her investment."

[3] ICSID tribunals are made up of three international investment experts who serve as arbitrators, one selected by each of the disputing parties and the third, who presides, selected by mutual agreement.

MINING REFORM IN LATIN AMERICA   225

These externally imposed rulings impeded national-level decision-making, even in response to democratic processes that would seem to require policy flexibility (Tienhaara 2011; Orellana, Baños, and Berger 2015; Cotula 2017).

The principal investment dispute tribunal that emerged under these new rules was the International Centre for the Settlement of Investment Disputes, an affiliate of the World Bank and housed in Washington, DC. As of December 31, 2021, ICSID had registered a total of 869 cases of investment disputes since 1972, with the numbers rising sharply after 2000.[4] Twenty-eight percent of these cases involved countries in South America, Central America, and the Caribbean (ICSID 2022, 12). Perhaps not surprisingly, the economic sector with the largest number of claims was oil, gas, and mining, which represented 25% of the total (p. 12).

ICSID arbitration processes sparked an array of criticisms, raising questions about pro-investor bias in the awards, lack of transparency, inconsistent decision-making, limitations in the appeals process, inadequate responsiveness to economic crisis, problems with enforcement of awards, and the overall expense of the process.[5] Concerns also emerged about the ways that investment treaties reduce the policy space for signatory states and how US investor protection policies have migrated into contexts where they may be detrimental to development (Fach Gómez 2011; Eberhardt and Olivet 2012; Wilske and Raible 2009; Pellegrini et al. 2020). These questions fueled a backlash against ICSID and led three "pink tide" governments in Latin America to withdraw from the organization (Bolivia in 2007, Ecuador in 2009, and Venezuela in 2012).[6]

---

[4] For the five-year period between 1996 and 2000, the average annual number of new ICSID cases was nine. The average increased to twenty-four for 2001–2005, twenty-six for 2006–2010, forty-four for 2011–2015, and fifty-one for 2016–2020 (ICSID 2022, 7). The total number of ISDS cases being processed by all international tribunals through the end of 2021 was 1,190 (UNCTAD database, https://investmentpolicy.unctad.org/, accessed July 28, 2022).

[5] To assess "microlevel decision-making processes of individual arbitrators," Sergio Puig and Anton Strezhnev (2017, 257) sent questionnaires regarding a fictitious set of investment disputes to a pool of international arbitrators. They got back 257 responses, which showed that arbitrators did make one decision that favored the poor countries: if arbitrators decided that the claimant was in the wrong, they were more likely to find that the claimant should pay the legal fees for the case if the respondent was a low-income country rather than one that was better off. Debate about arbitration biases continues; see Franck 2019 for discussion.

[6] Ecuador re-signed the ICSID agreement in June 2021 following a change in administration. Controversy about the way ISDS agreements favor foreign investors, who can pursue these claims before international tribunals, over domestic investors, who cannot, has affected new investment treaty negotiations, including those involving the United States and Canada. The United States–Mexico–Canada Agreement (USMCA), which replaced NAFTA in 2020, diluted ISDS guarantees (Casey and Villarreal 2020).

226   BREAKING GROUND

ICSID critics have argued that the distance, costs, power relations, and cultural barriers involved in presenting a successful defense kept states in an unfavorable position in these legal battles and produced a tendency for corporations to win (Wilske and Raible 2009; Fach Gómez 2011; Moore and Pérez Rocha 2019; Remmer 2019).[7] Analysts of international investment disputes have described the "regulatory chill" that emerges when states, attempting to regulate investment practices on environmental or social grounds, face claims against them that allege discriminatory treatment or indirect expropriation (Tienhaara 2011). The length of the process and the highly specialized nature of this legal subfield meant assuming substantial legal fees in the event that the state is targeted. With average costs per case in the $8–10 million range (Remmer 2019, 798), responding to an ISDS claim places an extra burden on low- and middle-income countries, even when they ultimately win. Dealing with multiple, simultaneous claims raises the burden still further.

Karen Remmer (2019) found that Latin American and Caribbean (LAC) countries have been disproportionately targeted in these disputes. Although states in this region had signed only 19% of the international investment agreements and received only 13% of global foreign direct investment, they had been cited in 31% of the investment disputes registered in the 2016 UNCTAD database. The outcomes were also less favorable for LAC countries than for other lower- and middle-income countries. Whereas tribunals found in favor of the state in 43% of the cases involving other lower- and middle-income countries, they ruled in favor of LAC states in only 30% of the cases (p. 797). A critical review of the ISDS process by Jen Moore and Manuel Pérez Rocha (2019, 6) found that cases brought against Latin American countries often involved "staggering amounts," with claims, and even awards, topping US$1 billion. Latin American countries that experienced economic crisis or restructuring have faced a steady hammering of ISDS cases. A growing number have been named as respondents in more than a dozen cases, with Argentina (62), Venezuela (55), Mexico (38), Ecuador (25), Peru (31), Bolivia (19), Colombia (19), and Panama (16) facing an onslaught of challenges by disgruntled foreign corporations.[8]

---

[7] Other sources report less tilt in favor of investors. See the UNCTAD Database, https://investmentpolicy.unctad.org/, accessed July 28, 2022.

[8] UNCTAD Database as of December 31, 2021, https://investmentpolicy.unctad.org/, accessed July 28, 2022. This tally includes all cases (pending, settled, discontinued, and decided).

MINING REFORM IN LATIN AMERICA   227

Most significant for our purposes are the questions that have arisen about the impact of ISDS on citizen movements that are attempting to secure indigenous and environmental rights and build more participatory democratic practices (Orellana 2011; Orellana, Baños, and Berger 2015; Cotula 2017; Pellegrini et al. 2020). As Remmer (2019) points out, this question has special resonance in Latin America, a region that underwent a wave of formal democratization in recent decades, and where political leaders have strong incentives to respond to widespread public preferences. Pressures imposed by ISDS arbitration tend to disconnect political leaders from their citizenry, in contradistinction to the requirements of democratic governance. Given the growing tendency of disgruntled foreign investors to seek international arbitration, community movements in opposition to gold mining face a serious barrier when they attempt to halt an investment, particularly one that previous national leaders had cultivated and encouraged. Even when mining resisters are successful in challenging the legality of the licensing process or persuading officials to affirm constitutional rights and raise regulatory standards, external pressure exercised by dissatisfied investors through international tribunals serves as a counterforce that undermines enforcement.

Investor-State Dispute Settlement Cases in Central American Mining Conflicts

Investors in Latin American gold mines have repeatedly used threats of international arbitration to force through license authorizations and accelerate mine construction. Looking at just the countries analyzed in this study, mining companies seeking resource access have filed ICSID claims in three of the four cases (El Salvador, Costa Rica, and Guatemala). Even in Nicaragua, where mining has progressed with little interruption and no investor dispute claim has been filed, the possibility of such action has been used to deter elite defection and undermine resistance organizing.[9]

Beginning in 2009, Canadian mining company Pacific Rim filed an ICSID claim against the government of El Salvador, contending that, after

---

[9] During the struggle against the Pavón mine in Nicaragua, a state official informed protesters in Rancho Grande that since the state had already given out an exploration license for this concession, it was obliged to allow extraction (see discussion in Chapter 3). According to this framework, the state had no choice but to permit the advance from exploration to extraction, regardless of local preferences or environmental concerns. National leaders used this discourse to stifle resistance and encourage acquiescence by local officials.

228 BREAKING GROUND

the company had spent years developing an underground gold mine project and millions of dollars completing the preparatory work, the government had declared a de facto mining moratorium, leaving the company with major losses (Pac Rim Cayman 2009). Five years later, Canadian mining company Infinito Gold followed suit, filing an ICSID claim against the government of Costa Rica, where Infinito had lost its license after an administrative court determined in 2010 that technical procedures required in licensing regulations had not been followed (Infinito Gold Ltd. and Republic of Costa Rica 2014). In 2018, US investor Daniel Kappes and his company, Kappes, Cassiday & Associates (KCA), joined the fray, filing a claim against the government of Guatemala and arguing that their company had been the victim of a "travesty of justice" due to a suspension of their mining license (*Kappes/KCA v. Guatemala* 2020a, 2). El Salvador, Costa Rica, and Guatemala faced cumulative demands for US$1–1.5 billion in compensation if authorization to mine was not forthcoming.[10] These cases are briefly reviewed below.

Pac Rim Cayman LLC v. Republic of El Salvador

The first of these disputes occurred in El Salvador, as the political and environmental costs of developing a gold mining industry became more apparent and mining policy was reconsidered by state officials (see Chapter 6).[11] Pacific Rim described the Salvadoran government as a helpful partner when the company made its initial investments in 2002 (Pac Rim Cayman 2013).[12] Government officials made repeated accommodations to move the project forward, and they designed creative work-arounds so that the project could meet legal requirements. As the plan passed from the exploratory stage into construction preparation in 2005, however, a resistance movement began to organize and bureaucratic gatekeepers became more attentive. The costs,

---

[10] This total is based on a $314 million demand presented in *Pacific Rim Cayman LLC v. Republic of El Salvador* (Pac Rim Cayman 2013, 226); an estimate of $321 million against Costa Rica based on a 2016 report from a consulting firm employed by Infinito Gold (*Tico Times* 2016); and a claim for $405–450 million presented by Kappes and KCA against Guatemala in the company's ICSID brief (*Kappes/KCA v. Guatemala* 2020a, 185).

[11] The US gold mining company Commerce Group also filed an ICSID claim against El Salvador in 2009, but that claim was initially rejected because the company had a parallel case under way in Salvadoran domestic court, and it was later discontinued due to nonpayment of fees. That claim is not discussed in this chapter.

[12] Pacific Rim was acquired by Oceana Gold in 2013, but the ICSID case proceeded under the original company name.

both political and technical, of developing a metallic mining industry became more apparent, as did the environmental risks. State officials, particularly in the environmental ministry (MARN), reportedly became unresponsive to company overtures, failing to meet their own deadlines or deliver on explicit promises.

Pacific Rim managers initially viewed the inaction as a byproduct of high turnover in the ministry and its lack of experience in processing applications for this new and complex industry. A large backlog of applications at the MARN had been observed in reports by the World Bank and USAID, and delay seemed to be part of the cost of doing business in El Salvador. Positive interactions with other high-level state officials reportedly persuaded the company to continue exploratory work, in spite of these delays, until 2008, when President Tony Saca made public pronouncements expressing his personal opposition to mining, as discussed in Chapter 6.

This new turn, according to the company, constituted evidence of an illegal, de facto mining ban. According to a witness statement provided by Pacific Rim president Thomas Shrake, President Saca informed him on June 25, 2008, at a high-level meeting arranged by US ambassador Charles T. Glazer, "that he was worried that issuing permits to [Pacific Rim El Salvador] would cost his ARENA party votes in the upcoming election" (Pac Rim Cayman 2013, 191). Although Saca reportedly reassured Shrake that all permissions would be granted in April 2009, after the election was over (Shrake 2010), the president continued making proclamations against the industry and publicly pledged to withhold all permits. Following extended bureaucratic delays and ongoing presidential criticism, Pacific Rim managers concluded that their project had failed and began dismissing employees in late 2008. They then filed a notice of intent to pursue an investment dispute at ICSID. Following the election of FMLN candidate Mauricio Funes, who had also publicly declared his opposition to mining, Pacific Rim moved forward and filed a notice of arbitration in April 2009, citing violations of investment protections included in the Central American Free Trade Agreement (DR-CAFTA) and El Salvador's 1999 Investment Law.

To defend itself against the company's argument that the investment breakdown resulted from whimsical, discriminatory, or illegal actions by a personalistic president who fomented disinformation during election season and ignored his legal obligations, the Salvadoran government hired a Washington, DC, legal team that specialized in international disputes. Luis Parada, a West Point–trained Salvadoran military officer turned international litigation and arbitration lawyer, served as the government's lead attorney. The case advanced through three stages: the jurisdictional phase, which determined whether the company had a right, under the terms of its investment agreements, to present an ICSID claim against the Salvadoran government; the merits stage, in which Pacific Rim's claims were presented and contested through the mobilization of evidence and testimony; and the awards stage, in which the three-person tribunal announced its decision and set each party's required payments.

Lawyers for the Salvadoran government effectively challenged Pacific Rim's claim to DR-CAFTA protection, demonstrating that the company's corporate presence in the United States amounted to little more than a post office box in Reno and showing that guarantees provided to US corporations under the agreement did not apply. El Salvador's 1999 Investment Law, however, did provide legal authorization for the ICSID arbitration to advance, in spite of the discarded DR-CAFTA claim. Written during the heyday of neoliberal reform in El Salvador, the 1999 law allowed foreign investors to have investment dispute claims adjudicated abroad, giving preference to foreign over domestic investors and opening the country to international arbitration.

When the ICSID case moved to the merits phase, the Salvadoran government argued that it had applied only a temporary moratorium on mine licensing, not a ban, and that the suspension was based on external expert advice (Pulgar-Vidal's report) confirming the inadequacy of the country's legal and regulatory structure in the mining sector (Pac Rim Cayman 2014b). Furthermore, the government claimed, Pacific Rim did not merit compensation because it had never acquired legal permission to mine. The deficits in its application (failure to acquire surface property ownership, absence of a full feasibility study, and no official approval of its environmental impact assessment) meant that the company had not met clearly stipulated requirements under Salvadoran law. In addition, it argued, the company had never acquired the community support needed for a "social license" to operate.

Efforts to introduce community views into international arbitration processes increased as this venue for dispute settlement became more active. To open the investment dispute process to a wider array of participants, including those civil society and grassroots organizations that had historically been excluded from these international proceedings, resistance networks sought to use "friend of the court" (amicus curiae) briefs and join the lawsuit as a third party (Orellana, Baños, and Berger 2015; ES1012; ES0312; ES2017;

ES2717).[13] Pointing to the April 2006 ICSID rule amendments that permitted amicus curiae submissions under certain narrowly defined conditions, the Mesa petitioned and gained partial access to the proceedings.[14] With approval of the parties, support from the International Allies, and assistance from the DC-based Center for International Environmental Law (CIEL), Mesa leaders added a statement to the case documents in which they claimed that "real opposition to Pac Rim's mining plans was not generated at the level of government ministries, but rather at the level of the local, potentially affected communities" (CIEL 2011, 2).[15] As they framed the issue:

> Local communities and NGOs, including amici, in reflection of their hard-fought empowerment and awareness of their own rights, and in a legitimate exercise of the democratic process in the post–Civil War political environment, refused to accept Pac Rim's plans to dig mines under their own lawfully owned land, build dangerous waste ponds, and otherwise threaten the continuity of their environment, livelihoods, and way of life. (CIEL 2011, 3)

Local communities, they argued, had a legitimate right of self-protection, which included the right to prohibit mining encroachment.

The company dismissed the Mesa's efforts to incorporate "soft law" concepts into the proceedings, claiming the issues of democratic consultation and international human rights did not address binding obligations under international investment law. In a common corporate maneuver, Pacific Rim's response questioned the representativeness and good faith of Mesa affiliates, and claimed strong local support, calling attention to the company's public relations outreach in the area of the proposed mine (Pac Rim Cayman 2014a).

When the ICSID tribunal finally rendered its findings in October 2016 (Pac Rim Cayman 2016), it put aside the amicus filing by the Mesa and, not surprisingly, did not address the larger set of issues that movement actors had raised. It also put aside the company's claims about the illegality of actions

---

[13] Interviews referenced in this chapter are included in Appendix 5.2 and Appendix 6.2.

[14] Many documents entered into evidence were regarded as privileged and not released to third-party participants. In addition to these limitations on access, there was no requirement that their brief be considered in the ruling.

[15] CIEL became involved in preparation of amicus curiae briefs for environmental organizations in ICSID cases in 2005, beginning with *Suez, Sociedad General de Aguas de Barcelona, S.A. and Vivendi Universal v. Argentina Republic*, ISCID Case No. ARB/03/18, the first case in which such a brief was accepted.

232 BREAKING GROUND

undertaken by Saca and MARN officials. Instead of addressing the many substantive issues that had been raised by the case, the arbitrators issued a finding based on the one area in which they were all in agreement—that the company's extraction application was incomplete and that, consequently, Pacific Rim had not acquired a legal right to mine.[16] Specifically, the company had failed to meet the legal obligation to secure access to surface property above its planned underground mine, in spite of repeated communications pointing out that requirement under Salvadoran law. Pacific Rim's unwillingness or inability to meet that stipulation or to get the law modified to remove that requirement caused its application to fail, giving it no legal basis on which to file for compensation or to demand authorization to mine. The Pacific Rim case was ultimately decided in favor of the Salvadoran government based on a technicality after a legal process that extended more than seven years and generated legal fees of US$12.6 million.

This outcome, which Luis Parada described as a "dry victory" (ES2717), left questions about the interface between corporate rights, environmental protection, and democratic deliberation unresolved.[17] But the finding was not without consequence in the push toward improved environmental policymaking in El Salvador. Although adjustments away from the neoliberal bargain can be difficult to achieve, in part because of the policing function played by international institutions, investor overreach may sometimes be challenged using the stature of the institutions designed to protect them. Even partial victories can contribute to political recalibration, all the more so when they take place on the global stage. The fact that the company failed in its bid to force a payout and was ultimately required to assume 62% of the government's legal fees created a perception of vincibility regarding corporate power. The government's success, in contrast, encouraged a sense of vindication among the mining critics. This dynamic increased the political space available for a new round of discussion about the future of mining in El Salvador. The resulting recalibration of elite perspectives, resistance network leadership, and docking prerogatives permitted a rapid advance toward a mining ban, as described in Chapter 6.

[16] Unanimity meant that even the arbitrator selected by the company concurred, an outcome that presumably required concessions on other matters from the arbitrator selected by the government. One consequence of a unanimous outcome is that it reduces the likelihood of an appeal or reversal.

[17] In our subsequent email correspondence on April 4, 2018, Parada elaborated on this view: "For me it was dry instead of sweet because the tribunal declined to decide some issues that would have resulted in full vindication for El Salvador and [would have] awarded the entire amount the country spent to defend itself ($12.6 million) instead of the $8 million it did."

Infinito Gold Ltd. v. the Republic of Costa Rica

The actual filing of an ISDS claim may not be necessary in order to induce compliance from vulnerable state leaders. The mere threat of an ISDS dispute can remind elites of the potential costs of neoliberal abdication and be a deterrent to government action. As noted in Chapter 5, the threat of an ICSID claim by Infinito Gold led the Pacheco administration (2002–2006) to step back from the mining moratorium that the president had boldly proclaimed. Risk mitigation encouraged decision-makers to classify Infinito as a current concession holder even though its claim to that designation was weak, allowing the company to sidestep Pacheco's moratorium declaration and advance toward permit authorization for the Crucitas mine.

Arbitration threats appeared repeatedly throughout the permitting process in Costa Rica. Canadian mining company Vannessa Ventures, owner of Infinito Gold, filed a notice of dispute with the Ministry of Commerce in 2003 after the National Environmental Technical Secretariat (SETENA) rejected Infinito's initial environmental impact assessment (*Infinito v. Costa Rica* 2017, 21). After SETENA reopened the review but continued to delay approval, Infinito took the next step and filed its first request for arbitration in June 2005. SETENA then approved the EIA on December 12, 2005. Recurring bouts of legal pressure from corporate lawyers, in both domestic and international venues, pushed the Costa Rican government to open the gates and allowed the company to advance through the regulatory process, in spite of clear concern about the environmental consequences expressed by both elected leaders and national regulators.

Costa Rican laws governing biodiversity and controlling against forest loss still impeded mine development, leading President Óscar Arias and his environment minister to issue their "national interest" declaration in 2008. This executive prerogative allowed top state officials to clear a way through the thicket of laws protecting forests and biodiversity and issue the permits allowing immediate forest clearing and the initiation of mine construction. Environmental organizations and activists moved quickly to disrupt the advance, bringing *amparo* petitions to multiple courts.[18] In November 2010, they succeeded in a previously untested legal venue, a lower-level administrative court, based on the failure of officials to adhere

---

[18] While the UNOVIDA and FECON petitions, which were designed to prevent the required forest clearing on constitutional grounds, were rejected by the Constitutional Court, the filing by APREFLOFAS in the TCA was accepted because it focused on technical and administrative criteria.

234   BREAKING GROUND

to Costa Rican administrative requirements during the license application review. The finding meant that the license had been granted inappropriately and it now lacked legal weight. The lower court's ruling was upheld by the Administrative Chamber of the Supreme Court (Sala I) in 2011, a decision that was recognized as definitive by the Supreme Court's Constitutional Chamber (Sala IV) in 2013. In the meantime, Costa Rican president Laura Chinchilla had declared a new mining moratorium in 2010, and the legislature had approved the 2010 ban on new open pit mining, closing the door on future large-scale mining.

Infinito Gold president and CEO John Morgan presented a notice of breach of agreement in a letter to the minister of commerce on April 4, 2013, claiming the company was being unlawfully deprived of an asset whose value, "if it is able to be fully developed, is in excess of US $1 billion." The company, he continued, "has not been treated fairly, transparently, or consistently, and finds itself in a situation of complete legal insecurity" (Infinito Gold 2013). When the Costa Rican government continued to uphold the domestic court rulings, Infinito made good on its long-standing threat, filing an official request for arbitration with ICSID on February 6, 2014. At that point the company dropped its compensation claim to at least US $94 million, in keeping with its declared actual investment in development of the project (Infinito Gold Ltd. and Republic of Costa Rica 2014, 27).

Infinito claimed that its Crucitas investments were "expropriated by court and executive measures without due process and payment of adequate compensation" (Infinito Gold Ltd. and Republic of Costa Rica 2014, 19). The claim was filed under the Agreement for the Promotion and Protection of Investments, a bilateral investment agreement signed by Canada and Costa Rica in 1998. Beginning in 2016, the costs for Infinito's legal defense were covered through third-party financing, an increasingly common tactic that allows corporations to share arbitration risks and opportunities with a network of independent financial agents who speculate on the outcome. This process permits corporations that face the prospect of default to maintain litigation under a modified financial arrangement that parcels out prospective gains.

As in the Pacific Rim case, anti-mining activists sought to join the legal battle. A local environmental organization, APREFLOFAS, mobilized to enter a third-party submission into the dispute process. As initiators of the case wherein the TCA annulled Infinito's license, APREFLOFAS members now struggled to prevent a reversal of their legal victory when the case moved to the international scale. They were particularly concerned that the corruption allegations that had been lodged against Arias and his environmental minister in the lower court case be brought to light in this new venue, where the successful insertion of corruption claims would preclude the use of arbitration (CR0317; CR0417; CR0517; CR1417). In spite of Infinito's forceful opposition to their participation (APREFLOFAS, Infinito claimed, has "no interest in this arbitration, let alone a significant one"), the tribunal authorized APREFLOFAS to file a written brief (*Infinito v. Costa Rica* 2016).[19]

In June 2021, after seven years in arbitration, the tribunal ultimately denied Infinito Gold's demand and found on behalf of the state (*Infinito v. Costa Rica* 2021). As with the Pacific Rim claim, this tribunal also put aside the amicus statement and decided the case on narrow grounds. Concluding that Arias had granted the license before the 2002 moratorium had been formally lifted, and that the TCA and the administrative chamber of the Supreme Court had not violated the BIT when ruling that the license was granted in violation of administrative regulations, the tribunal found that Infinito Gold had established no rights that were capable of expropriation in Costa Rica. Although the tribunal majority concluded that Costa Rica had acted inappropriately in legislating a mining ban that made no accommodation for companies in the process of securing a license, the company could not claim damages since its "approvals had been vitiated by an absolute nullity" (p. 211).[20] The company's belief that their asset had value, the tribunal concluded, was "premised on an illusion" (p. 213). Although the country ultimately escaped the full impact of a punitive ruling in the Crucitas case, it spent seven years in arbitration and was required to assume the full costs of its defense ($3.8 million) (pp. 229–230).

The government of Costa Rica had been named as a respondent in twelve ISDS cases as of December 31, 2021, with all of the attendant financial obligations and uncertainties this entails.[21] Disputes over the ICSID process inspired an "ir o no ir" (go or don't go) debate in Costa Rica, with a prominent group of Crucitas critics calling for a refusal to participate in this form

---

[19] APREFLOFAS's access to ICSID documents was restricted and they were denied access to participation in the tribunal hearings, but they were granted permission to present submissions in both the jurisdictional and merits phases.

[20] The tribunal concluded that the application of the legislated mining ban to the Crucitas project violated the "fair and equitable treatment" requirements of the investment agreement. But since Infinito held only an exploration permit and was already prevented from pursuing an extraction permit by the May 2010 moratorium, their concession was not directly affected by this legislation.

[21] See UNCTAD Database, https://investmentpolicy.unctad.org/, accessed July 28, 2022.

236 BREAKING GROUND

of international arbitration. These controversies have led to a move in Costa Rica for jurisdiction over investment disputes to be returned to domestic courts, but concerns about potential investment losses and local court neutrality leave this demand unresolved.

Daniel W. Kappes and Kappes, Cassiday & Associates v. Republic of Guatemala

As elsewhere in the region, mining companies in Guatemala have repeatedly used the threat of an ICSID claim as a tool to induce government cooperation. According to Manuel Pérez-Rocha (2016), when the Colom administration indicated that it would suspend operations of the Marlin mine, in compliance with the precautionary recommendation of the Inter-American Human Rights Commission in 2010, official concerns that Goldcorp would file an investment claim against the government prompted speedy reconsideration (p. 238). Faced with the prospect of being required to pay damages based on an unfavorable finding by an arbitration tribunal, the Guatemalan government retreated, allowing the mine to continue operation while the IACHR investigation advanced.

ISDS pressure rose again when the La Puya protest at the El Tambor gold mine project disrupted mining construction in 2012. Community activists, citing concerns about the impact of mining on water quality in an area with high levels of naturally occurring arsenic, and the absence of a meaningful consultation process, mounted an around-the-clock roadblock that prevented the completion of the mine construction. In response, KCA's lawyers in Washington, DC, sent a letter to the Guatemalan minister of energy and mines, with a copy to the Guatemalan president, threatening an international lawsuit if the government did not intervene to open the road.[22] The prospect of an ICSID claim by the US mining company, under investment guarantees included in DR-CAFTA, reportedly prompted the Pérez Molina government to order the forcible removal of the protesters following a two-year standoff.

Kappes and KCA claimed that the company had followed all laws related to securing a mining license, including public presentation of the project

---

[22] Ryan Adams, KCA representative, as quoted in Reeves 2014, after the La Puya roadblock was broken in 2014.

in local towns and villages, where no objections were raised (*Kappes/KCA v. Guatemala* 2020a, 12–17). They highlighted their social responsibility initiatives, which included building health service and sports facilities. The MARN and MEM had both confirmed the company's compliance with requirements, and an extraction license had been issued in 2011. According to the company, protests were led by people from outside the communities, including leaders from the Unidad Revolucionaria Nacional Guatemalteca (URNG), a party established by former revolutionaries, and from environmental NGOs (p. 18). The unwillingness or inability of the police to protect the mine from roadblocks had halted construction for two years and had required assertive legal action on their part, including the filing of a legal claim against the director general of the national police (p. 20). Only after forceful police intervention in 2014 was the company able to complete mine construction and begin to see returns.

The conflict with La Puya soon turned to the domestic courts, as described in Chapter 4. The legal-environmental advocacy organization CALAS filed a request for an injunction against the MEM for granting the El Tambor zone mining license without conducting a community consultation. Since Guatemala, as a signatory to ILO 169, was required to ensure consultations with indigenous populations regarding projects that could affect their territory, the absence of such processes put Guatemala out of compliance with its own legal obligations. In a series of dramatic decisions in 2015 and 2016, the Supreme Court ruled that the license had been granted without the required community consultation, a ruling that was upheld by the Constitutional Court. The El Tambor license was then definitively suspended in 2016, with production halted until the MEM prepared and completed the required community consultation.

KCA's legal team claimed that the license suspension, forced closure of the mine, and subsequent impound of company gold concentrate stockpiles en route to export constituted a form of expropriation that had "rendered the investment worthless" (*Kappes/KCA v. Guatemala* 2020a, 79). They denounced the suspension as "arbitrary, unlawful and discriminatory" (p. 83).[23] Even though the Tambor project license was suspended,

---

[23] A 2017 Constitutional Court decision had allowed a hydroelectric project whose license was similarly defective to continue operating as the consultation process was carried out. These cases differed, according to the government's response, because hydroelectric power generation has "constitutional urgency" since access to electricity affects national well-being and because the social conflict around dam development had been better managed through negotiation (*Kappes/KCA v. Guatemala* 2020d).

238 BREAKING GROUND

not revoked or rescinded, the Kappes and KCA lawyers described the economic impact as "devastating" (p. 79). When the company filed its merits brief in 2020, following the ICSID tribunal's acceptance of jurisdiction under DR-CAFTA, the forced closure had lasted over four years and the MEM had still not initiated a community consultation, making the losses persistent and cumulative.[24] Guatemala, in this telling, had engaged in unlawful expropriation and had failed to provide "fair and equitable treatment" and "full protection and security," again falling short of DR-CAFTA obligations. Based on the proclaimed losses the company had experienced, Kappes and KCA filed for US$403–450 million in compensation (p. 185).

The Guatemalan government responded that the company had committed a series of transgressions that undermined its claim to compliance with legal requirements, and that the state had acted correctly in suspending licenses until the indigenous community consultation was complete (*Kappes/KCA v. Guatemala* 2020d). Kappes and KCA, it argued, had provided false or misleading information in order to secure the license and open up the operation, and had used force and abusive tactics in their dealings with local protesters. The government alleged multiple deficiencies in the company's environmental impact assessment, including inadequate consultation ("social studies") with local communities. Arguing that the Guatemalan Constitutional Court had developed clear and coherent jurisprudence and mandated indigenous consultation in a uniform and nondiscriminatory fashion, the Guatemalan government challenged the claim that it had violated the terms of the investment treaty. It continued:

> Even assuming that there were acts of interference with Claimants' property rights or interests, whatever those may be, that are attributable to the State of Guatemala, such interference was the result of a non-discriminatory regulatory action designed and applied to protect the legitimate public welfare objective of protecting the rights of indigenous

---

[24] In the decades that had passed since Guatemala ratified ILO 169, the Guatemalan legislature had failed to approve an indigenous consultation law, in spite of several false starts. Indigenous right organizations, noting that ILO 169 calls for consultation that respects indigenous cultural traditions, resisted state efforts to define and control the process. Without legislated guidelines, MEM officials argued that the ministry had no legal grounds on which to carry out the process. This unresolved struggle over how to define and conduct indigenous consultation left a legal vacuum that added to Guatemala's vulnerability to ISDS challenges. See discussion in Chapter 4. Delays in legislating and implementing indigenous consultation have been common in Latin America and contribute to extractive sector conflict in much of the region (see Jaskoski 2022).

peoples in Guatemala. The state has a margin of discretion to determine public welfare objectives. (p. 184)

As in the other cases described above, community activists opposed to the mine attempted to insert their views into the ICSID process. La Puya mining resisters applied repeatedly for authorization to submit an amicus curiae brief, offering to provide additional information about the critical expert reports they had commissioned and the violence and intimidation they had faced. Asked by the tribunal for their response to this request, Kappes and KCA rejected La Puya's participation bid, arguing that the movement's identity and independence had not been established and implying that La Puya might actually represent or be funded by foreign NGOs or governments (*Kappes/KCA v. Guatemala* 2020b). Claiming that the organization had not demonstrated special expertise in the subject matter of the arbitration, Kappes and KCA called on the tribunal to deny the request.

This ISDS case, which is unresolved as of mid-2022, challenged the government's effort to fulfill human rights commitments and improve official responsiveness to public demands. Guatemala's court-mandated requirement that indigenous consultation be carried out is a potential achievement that could open discussion of mining to broader debate and add marginalized voices to that deliberation. Judicial activism in support of indigenous rights could bring mining development into line with the country's international obligations and with its own constitutional principles. Although experience elsewhere in Latin America indicates that indigenous consultation offers limited benefits, these efforts create new participatory practices that could embed community consultation into deliberations about future development. Laws and regulations, including international investment protections that were written for an earlier period, when market reform was ascendant and consultation rights were dismissed, need public review and reformulation. To the extent that ISDS rules and award processes complicate the strengthening of democratic processes and weaken the protection of indigenous rights, these strictures will also need to be adapted or abolished.

Final Reflections and Conclusions

International mining companies, their home states, and their host-state allies have eagerly pursued extraction opportunities across Latin America, using

240 BREAKING GROUND

an array of tools to pressure governments in propitious terrain for authorization and protection. They offer jobs, tax revenues, and a spate of corporate social responsibility projects for local communities, some of which have high poverty levels and are much in need of additional resources. This combination has proved attractive, particularly for national-level leaders whose territorial frames of reference are far removed from these "sacrifice zones" and who may have limited appreciation for any alternative development vision emerging in affected communities. Mining investors, who face high risks and insecure returns, lock in guarantees under international investment regimes that reduce legal uncertainty and enhance regulatory predictability, making rule changes costly and more difficult to achieve.

The ICSID case summaries presented in this chapter show how mining companies used investment dispute mechanisms to pressure elected governments to maintain pro-mining protocols, even as the externalities related to mining became increasingly apparent in the host country and preexisting mining bargains began to obsolesce. Government officials are left with the struggle between prior obligations to provide propitious territory for corporate transactions, on the one hand, and their need to improve environmental protection, provide essential life services, and comply with human rights commitments embedded in law and constitutions, on the other. Mining disputes pitted government officials against strongly held public views, and antagonized the democratic principles of popular representation and accountability.

In keeping with the logic of this book, ISDS processes are understood in terms of their impact on the three features that shape mining policy in the domestic arena—elite preferences, resistance organization, and state permeability. In case after case, ISDS mechanisms served as a tool to shore up pro-mining elite views, to disassemble and disarticulate resistance networks, and to narrow the space for civil society docking inside domestic political institutions. We see mining companies and their political allies leveraging the prospect of an ICSID claim to pressure the government to authorize licenses, as in El Salvador; to whittle down the impact of presidential moratorium declarations and elude regulations by environmental agencies, as in Costa Rica; to get the authorities to control protests, break up roadblocks, and limit consultation, as in Guatemala; and to restrict the exercise of municipal autonomy and nip back resistance organizational efforts, as in Nicaragua.

State actors may pursue policy reforms that affect investor interests, but they do so facing high potential costs and constraints. In El Salvador, growing public concern about the impact of gold mining on water access and quality, combined with the desire of officials to avoid electoral penalty, led to official reconsideration of the country's approach to mine regulation beginning in 2006. Corporate pressure, in the form of ISDS claims, served to freeze the regulatory arrangement in place during a long de facto moratorium and deterred the advancement of formal policy reform until 2017.

In Costa Rica, threats of international litigation served to force open a mine licensing process that many elected officials, regulators, and citizens wanted to close, impeding the process of policy reform for almost a decade. Anti-mining elites were forced to back down as pro-mining elites slashed environmental restrictions and issued favorable declarations. The ISDS claim that followed the eventual license annulment threatened the country with hefty penalties for upholding administrative standards and pursuing development policies that aligned with both popular preferences and environmental priorities.

In Guatemala as well, the threat of an investment dispute slowed the effort to address well-known deficiencies in the mining law and regulatory policies, defects that concerned both the quality of environmental protection and consultation rights for indigenous communities. The ISDS process complicated the effort of the Constitutional Court to remedy Guatemala's long history of ethnic exclusion and to improve enforcement of constitutional guarantees.

The legal and archival record points to repeated instances in which the threat of an investor dispute and the heavy costs that could be inflicted is used as a deterrent to action that would strengthen democratic responsiveness and promote environmental sustainability. Clauses in international investment agreements, free trade agreements, and even domestic investment law functioned as an invisible straitjacket that constrained public deliberations and policymakers' options. They strengthened the hand of the elite coalition that favored mining investments and other forms of market opening by raising the costs of intervention. Opposition to the easy entry and exit of foreign capital and investor-friendly regulatory regimes was derided as not just wrongheaded but an act of lawless irresponsibility that was harmful to the nation. This framing limits the space for diverse perspectives among parties and potential leaders, and even among business elites, who may not ipso facto be uniform in their assessment of development priorities.

This constraint can also affect the way the state reacts to mining resistance movements. With so much perceived to be at stake, officials may resort to repression to break up civil society protests, particularly those that elicit investor complaints and in countries where civil liberties protections are weak. Such interventions can deter grassroots organizing and undermine multisectoral connections. Although hardly the only factor that impedes robust national networking, this kind of external threat can become an element in a larger matrix.

ISDS threats also play a role in shaping the operation of the general political system and determining the level of participatory penetrability. Perceptions of ISDS obligations can discourage honest debate in the legislature about the pros and cons of metallic mining and the best ways to mitigate risks. They can make it difficult to engage the courts and seek rights-based interventions at the domestic scale. They can promote bureaucratic insularity and unresponsiveness when protesters are depicted as ideologues and outsiders rather than citizens with something to say. ISDS processes can also undermine the development of iterative and dialogic forms of community consultation, in which locals, whether indigenous-identified or not, are authorized to weigh in on decisions that directly affect their lives.

But constraint is not destiny, as we have seen repeatedly in this book. Mining project plans have been upended by protests and roadblocks in countries across the region. Resisters have challenged these projects in court, based on violations of the law by managers in charge or failures by state officials to implement requirements related to permit or monitoring protocols. Formally declared suspensions and official mining moratoria have halted or redirected many mining investments. Licenses have been cancelled, as in the landmark decision of Ecuador's Constitutional Court to cancel the mining concessions in the Los Cedros protected area in 2021. *Municipios* have declared themselves off-limits, as in Cuenca, Ecuador, where residents voted in 2021 to prohibit future large-scale mines in five watershed zones. States and provinces in the United States, Argentina, and the Philippines have prohibited different kinds of metallic mining, responding to local risk perceptions regarding environmental harm. Whole countries have approved national mining bans, as in the case of Costa Rica and El Salvador.

While external pressure can penalize deviations from neoliberal rules and slow the process of regulatory reform, investor disputes have not prevented a move to greater state control over mining, including even prohibition, when conditions are ripe. When elite support fractures due to growing recognition of mining's costs and trade-offs, when resistance groups create multisectoral networks that prove capable of frame alignment and scale up to the national level, and when political institutions open up docking points where public demands can be inserted and state actors can be compelled to respond, then significant mining policy reform becomes feasible. Whether this takes the form of a temporary or a permanent ban, becomes manifest in a localized or national prohibition, or emerges as heightened regulation and the rebalancing of rents will depend on the particular configuration found in the case. Continuing struggles over mining policy in affected areas raise the prospects for significant shifts in these underlying elements and for ongoing policy reform to strengthen community voice and attenuate environmental risks.

References

Abers, Rebecca Neaera. 2019. "Bureaucratic Activism: Pursuing Environmentalism Inside the Brazilian State." *Latin American Politics and Society* 61, no. 2 (May): 21–44.

Abers, Rebecca Neaera, and Luciana Tatagiba. 2015. "Institutional Activism: Mobilizing for Women's Health from Inside the Brazilian Bureaucracy." In *Social Movement Dynamics: New Perspectives on Theory and Research from Latin America,* edited by Federico M. Rossi and Marisa von Bülow, 73–101. Burlington, VT: Ashgate.

Acosta, Alberto. 2013. "Extractivism and Neoextractivism: Two Sides of the Same Curse." In *Beyond Development: Alternative Visions from Latin America,* edited by Miriam Land and Dunia Mokrani, 61–86. Amsterdam: TNI.

ADDAC. 2010. "Rancho Grande: Intervención de ADDAC." Asociación para la Diversificación y el Desarrollo Agrícola Comunal. Accessed June 12, 2015. http://www.addac.org.ni/paginas/rancho-grande.

ADES. 2016. "Memoria de labores 2015." Asociación de Desarrollo Económico y Social-Santa Marta. http://www.adessantamarta.sv/docs/memoriasdelabores/memoria2015.pdf.

AFP. 2010. "Chinchilla declara moratoria de minería a cielo abierto." *El Nuevo Diario,* May 8, 2010.

Aguilar-Støen, Mariel. 2015. "Staying the Same: Transnational Elites, Mining and Environmental Governance in Guatemala." In *Environmental Politics in Latin America,* edited by Benedicte Bull and Mariel Aguilar-Støen, 131–148. London: Routledge.

Aguilar-Støen, Mariel, and Benedicte Bull. 2016. "Protestas contra la minería en Guatemala ¿Qué papel juegan las élites en los conflictos?" *Anuario de Estudios Centroamericanos* 42: 15–44.

Aguilar-Støen, Mariel, and Cecilie Hirsch. 2017. "Bottom-up Responses to Environmental and Social Impact Assessments: A Case Study from Guatemala." *Environmental Impact Assessment Review* 62: 225–232. https://doi.org/10.1016/j.eiar.2016.08.003.

Aldana, Raquel, and Randall S. Abate. 2016. "Banning Metal Mining in Guatemala." *Vermont Law Review* 40: 597–671.

Alfaro, Josué. 2017. "Sorprenden a 100 personas extrayendo oro en Crucitas." *Semanario Universidad,* October 25, 2017. https://semanariouniversidad.com/pais/sorprenden-100-personas-extrayendo-oro-crucitas/.

Alfaro-Redondo, Ronald, Mitchell A. Seligson, and Elizabeth J. Zechmeister. 2015. *Cultura política de la democracia en Costa Rica y en las Américas, 2014.* San José, Costa Rica: PEN.

Ali, Saleem. 2021. "The Science and Politics of Moratoria." Springer Nature Sustainability Community. July 10, 2021. https://sustainabilitycommunity.springernature.com/posts/the-science-and-politics-of-development-moratoria.

Almeida, Paul D. 2006. "Social Movement Unionism, Social Movement Partyism, and Policy Outcomes: Health Care Privatization in El Salvador." In *Latin American Social Movements,* edited by Hank Johnston and Paul Almeida, 57–73. Lanham, MD: Rowman and Littlefield.

246 REFERENCES

Almeida, Paul D. 2014. *Mobilizing Democracy: Globalization and Citizen Protest.* Baltimore: Johns Hopkins University Press.

Almeida, Paul D. 2015. "The Role of Threats in Popular Mobilization in Central America." In *Social Movement Dynamics: New Perspectives on Theory and Research from Latin America,* edited by Federico M. Rossi and Marisa von Bülow, 105–126. Burlington, VT: Ashgate.

Altman, David, and Aníbal Pérez-Liñan. 2002. "Assessing the Quality of Democracy: Freedom, Competitiveness and Participation in Eighteen Latin American Countries." *Democratization* 9, no. 2 (Summer): 85–100.

Altomonte, Hugo, and Ricardo J. Sánchez. 2016. *Hacia una nueva gobernanza de los recursos naturales en América Latina y el Caribe.* Santiago: CEPAL.

Álvarez, Mauricio. 2012. "Estudio de casos de proyectos en operación, suspendidos y cancelados." Radiografía minera de proyectos e intereses mineros M4, Costa Rica. Unpublished.

Álvarez, Rolando. 2015. "Decimos un NO radical a la minería." *Revista Envío* no. 400 (July).

Amenta, Edwin. 2006. *When Movements Matter: The Townsend Plan and the Rise of Social Security.* Princeton, NJ: Princeton University Press.

Amenta, Edwin. 2016. "Raising the Bar for Scholarship on Protest and Politics: Review Essay." *Contemporary Sociology* 45, no. 5: 566–570.

Amenta, Edwin, Neal Caren, Elizabeth Chiarello, and Yang Su. 2010. "The Political Consequences of Social Movements." *Annual Review of Sociology* 36: 287–307. https://doi.org/10.1146/annurev-soc-070308-120029.

Amnesty International. 2016. "We Are Defending the Land with Our Blood: Defenders of the Land, Territory and Environment in Honduras and Guatemala." https://www.amnesty.org/en/documents/amr01/4562/2016/en/.

Anaya, James. 2011. "Report of the Special Rapporteur on the Situation of Human Rights and Fundamental Freedoms of Indigenous People. Addendum: Observations on the Situation of the Rights of Indigenous People of Guatemala with Relation to the Extraction Projects, and Other Types of Projects, in Their Traditional Territories." UN General Assembly, A/HRC/18/35/Add.3. https://digitallibrary.un.org/record/709557?ln=en.

Andersen, Ellen Ann. 2006. *Out of the Closet and into the Courts: Legal Opportunity Structure and Gay Rights Litigation.* Ann Arbor: University of Michigan Press.

Anderson, Leslie E. 2010. "Poverty and Political Empowerment: Local Citizen Political Participation as a Path Toward Social Democracy in Nicaragua." *Forum on Public Policy* 2010, no. 4. https://www.forumonpublicpolicy.co.uk/_files/ugd/553e83_c1ef20813c1f41c2870bcd1c907b20fa.pdf.

Anderson, Leslie E., and Won-Ho Park. 2018. "International Contributions to Nicaraguan Democracy: The Role of Foreign Municipal Donations for Social Development." *Foreign Policy Analysis* 14, no. 2: 276–297.

Anria, Santiago. 2013. "Social Movements, Party Organization and Populism: Insights from the Bolivian MAS." *Latin American Politics and Society* 55, no. 3: 19–46.

Araya, Marco Tulio. 2010. "Costa Rica." In *Ecología política de la minería en América Latina,* edited by Gian Carlo Delgado-Ramos, 306–318. Mexico City: Universidad Nacional Autónoma de México.

Arce, Moisés. 2014. *Resource Extraction and Protest in Peru.* Pittsburgh: University of Pittsburgh Press.

Arce, Moisés, Michael S. Hendricks, and Marc S. Polizzi. 2022. *The Roots of Engagement: Understanding Opposition and Support for Resource Extraction.* New York: Oxford University Press.

REFERENCES 247

Arce, Moisés, and Roberta Rice, eds. 2019. *Protest and Democracy*. Calgary: University of Calgary Press.

Arellano-Yanguas, Javier. 2014. "Religion and Resistance to Extraction in Rural Peru: Is the Catholic Church Following the People?" *Latin American Research Review* 49: 61–80.

Artiga González, Álvaro. 2007. *Gobernabilidad y democracia en El Salvador*. San Salvador: UCA.

Asamblea Legislativa [Costa Rica]. 2005. "Proyecto de ley adición de un artículo 8 bis y modificación del inciso K) del artículo 103 del Código de Minería." Ley no. 6797 de 4 de octubre de 1982 y sus reformas. Ley para declarar a Costa Rica país libre de minería de metales pesados a cielo abierto, expediente no. 15.948, July 5, 2005. http://www.asamb lea.go.cr/Centro_de_informacion/Consultas_SIL/SitePages/ConsultaProyectos.aspx.

Asamblea Legislativa [Costa Rica]. 2010a. Ley para declarar a Costa Rica país libre de minería metálica a cielo abierto, ley no. 8904, November 9, 2010. http://www.asamblea. go.cr/Centro_de_informacion/Consultas_SIL/SitePages/ConsultaLeyes.aspx.

Asamblea Legislativa [Costa Rica]. 2010b. Comisión Permanente Especial de Ambiente, sesión ordinaria no. 12, 5 de agosto de 2010 [minutes]. http://www.asamblea.go.cr/.

Asamblea Legislativa [Costa Rica]. 2012. *Reglamento de la Asamblea Legislativa de Costa Rica*. San José: Imprenta Nacional.

Asamblea Legislativa [El Salvador]. Various years. Comisión de Medio Ambiente y Cambio Climático. Expedientes. Accessed December 17, 2017. https://www.asamb lea.gob.sv/comisiones-legislativas/permanentes/comision-de-medio-ambiente-y-cam bio-climatico/legislatura-2012-2015/expedientes-en-estudio/LISTA%20DE%20EXPE DIENTES%20EN%20ESTUDIO%20-%20COMISION%20DE%20MEDIO%20A MBIENTE%20Y%20CAMBIO%20CLIMATICO.pdf.

Asamblea Legislativa [El Salvador]. 2017. Ley de prohibición de la minería metálica. Decreto no. 639, March 29, 2017. https://www.asamblea.gob.sv/sites/default/files/ documents/decretos/171117_073735928_archivo_documento_legislativo.pdf.

Asamblea Nacional [Nicaragua]. 1990. "Ley de creación de la Junta General de las Corporaciones Nacionales del Sector Público." *La Gaceta* 94. http://digesto.asamblea. gob.ni/consultas/normas/shownorms.php?idnorm=Mzg5.

Asamblea Nacional [Nicaragua]. 2001. Ley especial sobre exploración y explotación de minas, no. 387. http://digesto.asamblea.gob.ni/consultas/normas/shownorms.php?idn orm=NjY3NA==.

Asamblea Nacional [Nicaragua]. 2017. Ley creadora de la Empresa Nicaragüense de Minas (ENIMINAS). No. 953. http://legislacion.asamblea.gob.ni/normaweb.nsf/9e314 815a08d4a6206257265005d21f9/a73c80196e1ef245062581520061e4b7.

ASIES. 2010. "Estudio de opinión pública sobre la minería de metales en Guatemala: Informe de resultados." Asociación de Investigación y Estudios Sociales. http://asies.org.gt/downl oad.php?get=201007opinionmineriagtdice.pdf.

Associated Press. 1987. "Contras Attack in East Nicaragua." *New York Times,* December 21, 1987. https://www.nytimes.com/1987/12/21/world/contras-attack-in-east-nicara gua.html.

Avendaño Castellón, Néstor M. 2017. "Análisis de la actividad minera en Nicaragua: 2006–2016." http://caminic.com/wp-content/uploads/2017/08/analisis-actividad-min era-nicaragua-2006-2016.pdf.

B2Gold. 2017a. "Responsible Mining Report 2016." http://www.b2gold.com/_resources/ reports/B2Gold_ResponsibleMiningReport2016_Web_2_13July2017.pdf.

B2Gold. 2017b. "Trabajando juntos: Cómo la minería industrial coexiste con la minería artesanal." Departamento de Asuntos Corporativos, Managua.

248 REFERENCES

B2Gold. 2018. "Políticas y estándares corporativos: El compromiso de B2Gold con las prácticas empresariales responsables." Gerencia de Asuntos Corporativos, Managua.

Babinia, María Luisa, and Isabel Marina Sirias. 2010. "Instrumentos de seguimiento al proceso de descentralización en Nicaragua." Centro de Estudios y Análisis Político, Managua.

BCN. 2011. "Anuario de estadísticas macroeconómicas 2010." Banco Central de Nicaragua, Managua.

BCN. 2014. "Nicaragua en cifras 2013." Banco Central de Nicaragua, Managua.

BCN. 2018. "Macroeconomic Statistics Yearbook 2017." Banco Central de Nicaragua, Managua.

BCN. 2021. "Informe anual 2020." Banco Central de Nicaragua, Managua.

Baracco, Luciano, ed. 2019. *Indigenous Struggles for Autonomy: The Caribbean Coast of Nicaragua*. Lanham, MD: Lexington Books.

Baraybar Hidalgo, Viviana, and Eduardo Dargent. 2020. "State Responses to the Gold Rush in the Andes (2004–2018): The Politics of State Action (and Inaction)." *Studies in Comparative International Development* 55: 516–537.

Bárcena, Alicia. 2018. "Gobernanza de los recursos naturales en América Latina y el Caribe para el desarrollo sostenible." PowerPoint presentation at CEPAL seminar "La minería en América Latina y el Caribe: interdependencias, desafíos y oportunidades para el desarrollo sostenible," Lima, November 19, 2018. https://www.cepal.org/sites/default/files/presentation/files/181119-final_final_corta-giz_revisada_alicia_barcen a_ministros_mineria_limarev.pdf.

Bárcena Ibarra, Alicia, Joseluis Samaniego, Wilson Peres, and José Eduardo Alatorre. 2020. *The Climate Emergency in Latin America and the Caribbean: The Path Ahead—Resignation or Action?* ECLAC Books, No. 160 (LC/PUB.2019/23-P). Santiago: ECLAC.

Barrera, Hugo. 2006. "Sin garantías no habrá permiso." Interview by Metzi Rosales Martel. *La Prensa Gráfica*, July 9, 2006. http://www.commercegroupcorp.com/images/cafta/SEP16/Response%20to%20Preliminary%20Objection/2.%20Exhibits/C-1%20Interv iew%20With%20Hugo%20Barrera.pdf.

Bastos, Santiago, and Roddy Brett. 2010. *El movimiento maya en la década después de la paz (1997–2007)*. Guatemala City: F&G.

Baumgartner, Frank R. 2006. "Punctuated Equilibrium Theory and Environmental Policy." In *Punctuated Equilibrium and the Dynamics of U.S. Environmental Policy*, edited by Robert Repetto, 24–46. New Haven, CT: Yale University Press.

Bebbington, Anthony, Abdul-Gafaru Abdulai, Denise Humphreys Bebbington, Marja Hinfelaar, and Cynthia A. Sanborn. 2018. *Governing Extractive Industries: Politics, Histories, Ideas*. Oxford: Oxford University Press.

Bebbington, Anthony, and Jeffrey Bury, eds. 2013. *Subterranean Struggles: New Dynamics of Mining, Oil, and Gas in Latin America*. Austin: University of Texas Press.

Bebbington, Anthony J., Jeffrey Bury, Nicholas Cuba, and John Rogan. 2015. "Mining, Risk and Climate Resilience in the 'Other' Pacific: Latin American Lessons for the South Pacific." *Asia Pacific Viewpoint* 56, no. 2 (August): 189–207.

Bebbington, Anthony, Benjamin Fash, and John Rogan. 2019. "Socio-Environmental Conflict, Political Settlements, and Mining Governance: A Cross-Border Comparison, El Salvador and Honduras." *Latin American Perspectives* 46, no. 2 (March): 84–106.

Bebbington, Anthony, Denise Humphreys Bebbington, Leonith Hinojosa, María-Luisa Burneo, and Jeffrey Bury. 2013. "Anatomies of Conflict: Social Mobilization and New

REFERENCES 249

Political Ecologies of the Andes." In *Subterranean Struggles: New Dynamics of Mining, Oil, and Gas in Latin America*, edited by Anthony Bebbington and Jeffrey Bury, 241–266. Austin: University of Texas Press.

Becker, Marc. 2014. "Ecuador: Correa, Indigenous Movements, and the Writing of a New Constitution." In *Rethinking Latin American Social Movements: Radical Action from Below*, edited by Richard Stahler-Sholk, Harry E. Vanden, and Marc Becker, 267–284. Lanham, MD: Rowman and Littlefield.

Bell, Fred G., and Laurence J. Donnelly. 2006. *Mining and Its Impact on the Environment*. New York: Taylor and Francis.

Beltrán, Adriana. 2020. "Behind the Fight to Hijack Guatemala's Justice System." Commentary. Washington Office on Latin America, July 10, 2020.

Bickham Mendez, Jennifer. 2005. *From the Revolution to the Maquiladoras: Gender, Labor and Globalization in Nicaragua*. Durham, NC: Duke University Press.

Biggs, Michael, and Kenneth T. Andrews. 2015. "Protest Campaigns and Movement Success: Desegregating the U.S. South in the Early 1960s." *American Sociological Review* 80, no. 2: 416–443.

Biondi-Morra, Brizio N. 1993. *Hungry Dreams: The Failure of Food Policy in Revolutionary Nicaragua, 1979–1990*. Ithaca, NY: Cornell University Press.

Bloomfield, Michael John. 2017. *Dirty Gold: How Activism Transformed the Jewelry Industry*. Cambridge, MA: MIT Press.

Bob, Clifford. 2005. *The Marketing of Rebellion*. Cambridge: Cambridge University Press.

Boeglin, Nicolás. 2014. "Contextualizando el CIADI." Presentation at UCR conference "Arbitraje de Crucitas, ir o no ir." Accessed September 5, 2014. http://kioscosambienta les.ucr.ac.cr/documentos/ironoir/IronoirNBoeglin.pdf.

Bolaños, Enrique. 2003. "Propuesta de Plan Nacional de Desarrollo." http://sajurin.enr iquebolanos.org/docs/Plan%20Nacional%20de%20desarrollo.pdf.

Bolaños, Rosa María. 2016. "MEM no suspenderá proyecto minero en San José del Golfo y San Pedro Ayampuc." *La Prensa Libre*, March 1, 2016.

Bosi, Lorenzo, Marco Giugni, and Katrin Uba. 2016. "The Consequences of Social Movements: Taking Stock and Looking Forward." In *The Consequences of Social Movements*, edited by Lorenzo Bosi, Marco Giugni, and Katrin Uba, 3–37. Cambridge: Cambridge University Press.

Bowen, Rachel E. 2017. *The Achilles Heel of Democracy: Judicial Autonomy and the Rule of Law in Central America*. Cambridge: Cambridge University Press.

Brett, Roddy. 2011. "Confronting Racism from Within the Guatemalan State: The Challenges Faced by the Defender of Indigenous Rights of Guatemala's Human Rights Ombudsman's Office." *Oxford Development Studies* 39, no. 2 (June): 205–228.

Breuer, Anita. 2007. "Institutions of Direct Democracy and Accountability in Latin America's Presidential Democracies." *Democratization* 14, no. 4: 554–579.

Brinks, Daniel M., and Abby Blass. 2018. *The DNA of Constitutional Justice in Latin America*. New York: Cambridge University Press.

Broad, Robin. 2014. "Responsible Mining: Moving from a Buzzword to Real Responsibility." *The Extractive Industries and Society* 1, no. 1: 4–6.

Broad, Robin, and John Cavanagh. 2015. "Poorer Countries and the Environment: Friends or Foes?" *World Development* 72: 419–431.

Broad, Robin, and John Cavanagh. 2021. *The Water Defenders: How Ordinary People Saved a Country from Corporate Greed*. Boston: Beacon Press.

250 REFERENCES

Bull, Benedicte. 2014. "Toward a Political Economy of Weak Institutions and Strong Elites in Central America." *European Review of Latin American and Caribbean Studies* 97 (October): 117–128.

Bull, Benedicte, and Mariel Cristina Aguilar-Støen, eds. 2015. *Environmental Politics in Latin America: Elite Dynamics, the Left Tide and Sustainable Development.* New York: Routledge.

Bull, Benedicte, Fulvio Castellacci, and Yuri Kasahara. 2014. *Business Groups and Transnational Capitalism in Central America: Economic and Political Strategies.* New York: Palgrave Macmillan.

Bulmer-Thomas, Victor. 1987. *The Political Economy of Central America Since 1920.* Cambridge: Cambridge University Press.

Burnett, Henry G., and Louis-Alexis Bret. 2017. *Arbitration of International Mining Disputes: Law and Practice.* Oxford: Oxford University Press.

Bury, Jeffrey, and Anthony Bebbington. "New Geographies of Extractive Industries in Latin America." In *Subterranean Struggles: New Dynamics of Mining, Oil, and Gas in Latin America*, edited by Anthony Bebbington and Jeffrey Bury, 27–66. Austin: University of Texas Press.

Cabanas, Andrés. 2014. "Las consultas como expresión de las comunidades ante las industrias extractivas." Fundación Rigoberta Menchú Tum, Guatemala City. https://issuu.com/memorialguatemala/docs/las_consultas_como_expresi__n_de_la.

Cabrera Medaglia, Jorge. 2019. "Normativa e institucionalidad ambiental en Costa Rica." *Informe Estado de la Nación en Desarrollo Humano Sostenible 2019.* http://repositorio.conare.ac.cr/handle/20.500.12337/7811.

CACIF. 2017a. "Falta de certeza jurídica repercute seriamente en crecimiento del país y la atracción de inversiones." *Prensa Libre, campo pagado*, October 30, 2017. Comité Coordinador de Asociaciones Agrícolas, Comerciales, Industriales y Financieras. https://cacif.org.gt/noticias.

CACIF. 2017b. "El sector empresarial organizado manifiesta." Comité Coordinador de Asociaciones Agrícolas, Comerciales, Industriales y Financieras. September 1, 2017. https://cacif.org.gt/noticias.

CACIF. 2018. "Sobre la situación que enfrenta el empresario Max Quirin, el Sector Privado Organizado manifiesta." Comité Coordinador de Asociaciones Agrícolas, Comerciales, Industriales y Financieras. August 1, 2018. https://cacif.org.gt/noticias.

CACIF. 2019. "CACIF se pronuncia por decisión de la CC." Press release, Comité Coordinador de Asociaciones Agrícolas, Comerciales, Industriales y Financieras. October 4, 2019. https://cacif.org.gt/noticias.

CALAS. 2016. "Criminalización de defensores y defensoras de derechos humanos ambientales que resisten a la imposición de proyectos mineros: Dos estudios de caso." Centro de Acción Legal-Ambiental y Social de Guatemala, Guatemala City.

Calibre Mining Corp. 2021. "Annual Information Form for the Year Ended December 31, 2020." https://www.calibremining.com/site/assets/files/6007/cxb_aif_december_31_2020.pdf.

Call, Charles T., and Jeffrey Hallock. 2020. "Too Much Success? The Legacy and Lessons of the International Commission Against Impunity in Guatemala." CLALS Working Paper Series no. 24. Center for Latin American and Latino Studies, American University, Washington, DC.

REFERENCES 251

Cameron, Maxwell A. 2021. "Pathways to Inclusion in Latin America." In *The Inclusionary Turn in Latin American Democracies*, edited by Diana Kapiszewski, Steven Levitsky, and Deborah J. Yashar, 401–433. New York: Cambridge University Press.

Campbell, Lisa M. 2002. "Conservation Narratives in Costa Rica: Conflict and Co-Existence." *Development and Change* 33, no. 1: 29–56.

Camus, Manuela, Santiago Bastos, and Julián López García, eds. 2015. *Dinosaurio Reloaded: Violencias Actuales en Guatemala*. Guatemala City: Facultad Latinoamericana de Ciencias Sociales and Fundación Constelación.

CAO. 2005. "Assessment of a Complaint Submitted to CAO in Relation to the Marlin Mining Project in Guatemala." Compliance Advisor Ombudsman. https://www.cao-ombudsman.org/sites/default/files/downloads/CAO-Marlin-assessment-English-7Sep05.pdf.

CAO. 2019. "Compliance Appraisal: Summary of Results, Condor Gold (IFC Project # 32519) Nicaragua." Compliance Advisor Ombudsman. https://www.cao-ombudsman.org/sites/default/files/downloads/CAOComplianceAppraisalCondorGold-01Nicaragua_ENG.pdf.

Carballo Madrigal, Arturo. 2013. "Democracia participativa y legislación en función de la naturaleza, la experiencia de la primera iniciativa popular en Costa Rica." *Revista REDpensar* 2: 1–21.

Cárdenas, Julián. 2016. "Why Do Corporate Elites Form Cohesive Networks in Some Countries, and Do Not in Others: Cross-National Analysis of Corporate Elite Networks in Latin America." *International Sociology* 31, no. 3: 341–363.

"Cardinal Accuses Canadian Firm of Destroying Honduras." 2001. Vincentian Family Information Network. July 7, 2001. Accessed July 18, 2018. https://famvin.org/en/2001/07/07/cardinal-accuses-canadian-firm-of-destroying-honduras/.

Cáritas El Salvador. 2016. *Las mentiras de la minería*. San Salvador: Cáritas.

Cáritas El Salvador. 2017. "Iglesia llama a diputados a aprobar ley contra minería." https://www.caritas.sv/nuestro-trabajo/noticias/120-iglesia-llama-a-diputados-a-aprobar-ley-contra-mineria.

Carrera, Fernando. 2017. "Guatemala's International Commission Against Impunity: A Case Study on Institutions and Rule of Law." Background Paper, World Development Report. World Bank Group, Washington, DC.

Cartagena Cruz, Rafael E. 2000. "El público vs. Placer Dome: Comunicación y conflicto ambiental en el espacio público." MA thesis, Universidad de Costa Rica.

Cartagena Cruz, Rafael E. 2009. "Metabolismo socio-natural y conflictos ambientales en Costa Rica y El Salvador, 1992–2007." PhD thesis, FLACSO-Costa Rica.

Casaús Arzú, Marta Elena. 2006. *Guatemala, linaje y racismo*. Guatemala City: F&G Editores.

Casey, Christopher A., and M. Angeles Villarreal. 2020. "USMCA: Investment Provisions." *Congressional Research Service: In Focus*, January 8, 2020. https://crsreports.congress.gov/product/pdf/IF/IF11167.

CECON-USAC and CODIDENA. 2019. "Desigualdad, extractivismo y desarrollo en Santa Rosa y Jalapa." Centro de Estudios Conservacionistas–Universidad de San Carlos and Comisión Diocesana de la Defensa de la Naturaleza, Guatemala City.

CEDES. 2007. "Cuidemos la casa de todos: pronunciamiento de la Conferencia Episcopal de El Salvador sobre la explotación de minas de oro y plata." Conferencia Episcopal de El Salvador, May 3, 2007. https://caritas.sv/nuestro-trabajo/documentos/otros/

252 REFERENCES

49-pronunciamientos-de-los-obipos-de-el-salvador-sobre-la-mineria-metalica-cuide mos-la-casa-de-todos-y-defendamos-la-vida-y-el-bien-comun/file.

CEDES. 2010. "Defendamos la vida y el bien común." Conferencia Episcopal de El Salvador, November 12, 2010. https://caritas.sv/nuestro-trabajo/documentos/otros/ 49-pronunciamientos-de-los-obipos-de-el-salvador-sobre-la-mineria-metalica-cuide mos-la-casa-de-todos-y-defendamos-la-vida-y-el-bien-comun/file.

CEH. 1999. *Guatemala Memoria del Silencio*. Comisión para el Esclarecimiento Histórico, Oficina de Servicios para Proyectos de las Naciones Unidas, Guatemala City.

CELAM. 2007. "Concluding Document." Fifth General Conference of the Latin American and Caribbean Bishops' Conference, Consejo Episcopal Latinoamericano, May 13–31, 2007, Aparecida, Brazil. http://www.celam.org/aparecida/Ingles.pdf.

Cementos Progreso S.A. 2014. "Two Views of Consulta Previa in Guatemala: A View from the Private Sector." *Americas Quarterly,* April 24, 2014.

CEN. 2013. "Comunicado de la diócesis de Matagalpa ante instalación de minas extranjeras." Conferencia Episcopal de Nicaragua, March 6, 2013. Accessed December 25, 2014. http://www.cen-nicaragua.org/index.php?subaction=showfull&id=1362534 948&ucat=1,3&,

CEN. 2014. "En búsqueda de nuevos horizontes para una Nicaragua mejor." Conferencia Episcopal de Nicaragua, May 21, 2014. https://www.envio.org.ni/articulo/4856.

CENIDH. 2013a. "Informe del CENIDH sobre proyecto minero: El Pavón en Rancho Grande, Matagalpa." Centro Nicaragüense de Derechos Humanos. www.cenidh.org/ noticias/534/.

CENIDH. 2013b. "Violencia y represión contra población del municipio de Santo Domingo, Chontales." Centro Nicaragüense de Derechos Humanos. http://www.cen idh.org/noticias/404/.

Centro Humboldt. 2008. "Informe sistema productivo minería: Monitoreo ambiental de sistemas productivos." Centro Humboldt, Managua.

Centro Humboldt. 2014. "Estado actual del sector minero y sus impactos socio-ambientales en Nicaragua, 2012–2013." Centro Humboldt, Managua.

Centro Humboldt. 2015. "Valoración de riesgos e impactos socio-ambientales de la minería metálica en Nicaragua 2013–2015." Centro Humboldt, Managua.

Centro Humboldt and IEEPP. 2017. "La minería industrial en Nicaragua: Una mirada desde la óptica fiscal." Centro Humboldt and Instituto de Estudios Estratégicos y Políticas Públicas, Managua.

Chacón, Karen, and Leonardo Merino. 2014. "Veinte años de conflictividad ambiental en Costa Rica. 1994–2013." Ponencia. Vigésimo Informe Estado de la Nación en Desarrollo Humano Sostenible 2013. PEN, San José, Costa Rica.

Chaloping-March, Minerva. 2014. "The Mining Policy of the Philippines and 'Resource Nationalism' Toward Nation Building." *Journal de la Société des Océanistes* 138–139: 93–106.

CID Gallup. 2010a. "Costarricenses opuestos a la minería a cielo abierto." Encuesta de opinión pública, Costa Rica, May.

CID Gallup. 2010b. Opinión pública nacional Costa Rica no. 126, September.

CID Gallup. 2018. Estudio de opinión pública (various countries), January.

CID Gallup, Costa Rica por Siempre, and the Nature Conservancy. 2009. "Encuesta Nacional sobre Opinión Ambiental: Principales Resultados," December.

CIEL. 2011. "Application for Permission to Proceed as Amici Curiae." Center for International Environmental Law. *Pac Rim Cayman LLC v. Republic of El Salvador.*

REFERENCES 253

ICSID Case No. ARB/09/12, March 2, 2011. https://www.italaw.com/sites/default/files/case-documents/ita0609.pdf.

CIG. 2015. "Directorio industrial 2015." Cámara de Industria de Guatemala.

CIPRES. 1992. "El proyecto económico de los trabajadores." Cuadernos del CIPRES no. 12. Centro para la Investigación, la Promoción y el Desarrollo Rural y Social, Managua.

Close, David. 2016. *Nicaragua: Navigating the Politics of Democracy*. Boulder, CO: Lynne Rienner.

Close, David. 1999. *Nicaragua: The Chamorro Years*. Boulder, CO: Lynne Rienner.

Close, David, Salvador Martí i Puig, and Shelley McConnell, eds. 2012. *The Sandinistas and Nicaragua Since 1979*. Boulder, CO: Lynne Rienner.

Colectivo MadreSelva. 2006. *Manual de Resistencia Ecologista*. 2nd edition. Guatemala City: Colectivo MadreSelva.

"Comandante Daniel Ortega preside acto del 36 aniversario del Ministerio de Gobernación." 2015. *La Voz del Sandinismo*, October 14, 2015. https://www.lavozdelsandinismo.com/nicaragua/2015-10-14/comandante-daniel-ortega-preside-acto-del-36-aniversario-del-ministerio-de-gobernacion-13102015-texto-integro/.

Comisión Municipal de Minería Artesanal Bonanza–Región Costa Caribe Norte Nicaragua. 2018. "Sesión especial: Aniversario de la CMMA Bonanza." PowerPoint presentation.

"Comunicado ante la represión a la libre movilización." 2014. Press release by seventeen Central American anti-mining organizations, August 13, 2014, Managua.

Conde, Marta. 2014. "Activism Mobilising Science." *Ecological Economics* 105: 67–77.

Conde Puigmal, Marta. 2015. "Resistance to Mining: Enabling Factors and Control of Knowledge in Uranium Mining Conflicts in Africa." PhD thesis, Environmental Sciences, Universitat Autònoma de Barcelona.

Condor Gold. 2018. "Permitting Update, Mina La India." February 26, 2018. http://www.condorgold.com/sites/default/files/news/Permitting%20Update%20Mina%20La%20India%20Redesigned%20Open%20Pit%2C%20No%20Resettlement.pdf.

Congreso de la República de Guatemala. 1997. Ley de minería. Decreto no. 48-97. https://www.mem.gob.gt/wp-content/uploads/2015/06/1._Ley_de_Mineria_y_su_Reglamento.pdf.

Consejo del Pueblo Maya-CPO. 2016a. "Criminalización: la respuesta del Estado de Guatemala a las acciones de los pueblos en defensa de su territorio." Consejo del Pueblo Maya-CPO. https://www.escr-net.org/sites/default/files/informe_sentencias_criminaliz acion_1.pdf.

Consejo del Pueblo Maya-CPO. 2016b. "Sentencias de la Corte de Constitucionalidad sobre licencias mineras." Consejo del Pueblo Maya-CPO, April 27, 2016. https://cpo.org.gt/2019/?p=150.

Consejo Universitario, Universidad de Costa Rica. 2009. "Informe especial: Minería química a cielo abierto: El caso de Las Crucitas." Presented at Sesión No. 5354 Extraordinaria, May 21, 2009. https://www.cu.ucr.ac.cr/actas/2009/5354.pdf.

Consejo Universitario, Universidad de Costa Rica. 2021. "Criteria de la Universidad de Costa Rica sobre la ley de minería Crucitas." Expediente no. 22.007, August 4, 2021. https://documentos.cu.ucr.ac.cr/Ley_de_mineria_Crucitas.pdf.

Copeland, Nicholas. 2019a. "Defending Consultation: Indigenous Resistance against the Escobal Mine in Guatemala." *NACLA Report on the Americas*, May 23, 2019.

Copeland, Nicholas. 2019b. *The Democracy Development Machine: Neoliberalism, Radical Pessimism and Authoritarian Populism in Mayan Guatemala*. Ithaca, NY: Cornell University Press.

254 REFERENCES

Copelovitch, Mark S. 2010. *The International Monetary Fund in the Global Economy: Banks, Bonds and Bailouts*. Cambridge: Cambridge University Press.

Corrales-Pérez, Daniel, and Francisco Martín Romero. 2013. "Evaluación de la peligrosidad de jales de zonas mineras de Nicaragua y México y alternativas de solución." *Boletín de la Sociedad Geológica Mexicana* 65, no. 3: 427–446.

Corte de Constitucionalidad [Guatemala]. 1995. "Opinión consultiva relativa al Convenio 169 sobre pueblos indígenas y tribales en países independientes." Expediente 199-95. May 18, 1995. https://www.elaw.org/content/guatemala-opinion-consultiva-relativa-al-convenio-n%C3%BAm-169-sobre-pueblos-ind%C3%ADgenas-y-tribales.

Corte de Constitucionalidad [Guatemala]. 2018. Expediente 4785-2017. Issued September 3, 2018. https://cc.gob.gt/2018/09/04/resolucion-4785-2017-caso-min era-san-rafael/.

Corte de Constitucionalidad [Guatemala]. 2020a. Expedientes acumulados 3207-2016 and 3344-2016. Issued June 11, 2020. https://consultajur.cc.gob.gt/wcJur/Portal/wfNu mExpediente.aspx.

Corte de Constitucionalidad [Guatemala]. 2020b. Expediente 697-2019. Issued June 18, 2020. https://consultajur.cc.gob.gt/wcJur/Portal/wfNumExpediente.aspx.

Corte Suprema de Justicia [Guatemala]. 2015. Amparo 1592-2014. Issued November 11, 2015. http://www.ghrc-usa.org/wp-content/uploads/2016/05/Amparo-calas-LaPuya.pdf.

COSEP. 2012. "Gestión anual 2011." Consejo Superior de la Empresa Privada, Managua.

COSEP. 2016. *Revista del Consejo Superior de la Empresa Privada: Nicaragua Empresaria*, vol. 44, Consejo Superior de la Empresa Privada, Managua.

Costanza, Jennifer Noel. 2016. "Mining Conflict and the Politics of Obtaining a Social License: Insight from Guatemala." *World Development* 79: 97–113.

Cotula, Lorenzo. 2017. "Democracy and International Investment Law." *Leiden Journal of International Law* 30: 351–382.

Couso, Javier, Alexandra Huneeus, and Rachel Sieder. 2010. *Cultures of Legality: Judicialization and Political Activism in Latin America*. New York: Cambridge University Press.

CPO. N.d. Consultas comunitarias [database]. Consejo de Pueblos de Occidente. Accessed September 12, 2015. http://www.cpo.org.gt/mapa/prueba13.php.

CPO. 2012. "Acción de inconstitucionalidad general total contra la ley de minería." Consejo de Pueblos de Occidente, March 12, 2012. https://drive.google.com/file/d/0B31fnGLtBsbMMkZyalN1OGlRejJtdThheDcweFh2dw/view.

Cuffe, Sandra. 2017. "Nicaragua's Golden Rule?" *NACLA Report on the Americas* 49, no. 4: 436–440.

Da Sousa, Mariana Magaldi. 2010. "How Courts Engage in the Policymaking Process in Latin America: The Different Functions of the Judiciary." In *How Democracy Works: Political Institutions, Actors and Arenas in Latin American Policymaking*, edited by Carlos Scartascini, Ernesto Stein, and Mariano Tommasi, 77–118. Washington, DC: IDB.

Damonte, Gerardo Hector. 2018. "Mining Formalization at the Margins of the State: Small-Scale Miners and State Governance in the Peruvian Amazon." *Development and Change* 49, no. 5: 1314–1335.

Dary Fuentes, Claudia. 2017. "Diagnóstico situación de la cultura Xinka." Ministerio de Cultura y Deporte, Guatemala. https://mcd.gob.gt/wp-content/uploads/2017/02/Diag nostico-Xinca.pdf.

REFERENCES   255

Dashwood, Hevina S. 2012. *The Rise of Global Corporate Social Responsibility: Mining and the Spread of Global Norms*. Cambridge: Cambridge University Press.

Davis, Jeffrey, and Edward H. Warner. 2007. "Reaching Beyond the State: Judicial Independence, the Inter-American Court of Human Rights, and Accountability in Guatemala." *Journal of Human Rights* 6, no. 2: 233–255.

Dawson, Casey. 2014. "Why Honduras Should Not Jump on the Ban Wagon: A Study of Open Pit Mining Bans and their Pitfalls." *Suffolk Transnational Law Review* 37 (Winter): 67–108.

de Castro, Fábio, Barbara Hogenboom, and Michiel Baud, eds. 2016. *Environmental Governance in Latin America*. New York: Palgrave Macmillan.

De Echave, José. 2017. "Entrevista a José De Echave por Stephany Calisaya." *Politai*, año 8, segundo semestre, no. 15: 133–143. http://revistas.pucp.edu.pe/index.php/politai/arti cle/view/19591/19689.

De Fazio, Gianluca. 2012. "Legal Opportunity Structure and Social Movement Strategy in Northern Ireland and Southern United States." *International Journal of Comparative Sociology* 53, no. 1: 3–22.

de Franco, Mario A. 1996. "La economía política de la privatización en Nicaragua." Serie Reformas de Política Pública #44. CEPAL, Santiago, Chile.

de la Torre, Armando. 2018. "CICIG and the Rule of Law." https://ligapropatria.com/wp-content/uploads/2018/04/CICIG-AND-THE-RULE-OF-LAW.pdf.

Decreto no. 30477-MINAE [Costa Rica]. 2002. "Declara moratoria nacional por plazo indefinido para la actividad de minería metálica de oro a cielo abierto en el territorio nacional." June 5, 2002. http://www.pgrweb.go.cr/scij/Busqueda/Normativa/Normas/nrm_texto_completo.aspx?param1=NRTC&nValor1=1&nValor2=48710&nValor3=72615&strTipM=TC#ddown.

Decreto no. 34801-MINAET [Costa Rica]. 2008. "Declara de interés público y conveniencia nacional el Proyecto Minero Crucitas." October 13, 2008. http://www.pgr web.go.cr/scij/Busqueda/Normativa/Normas/nrm_texto_completo.aspx?nValor1=1&nValor2=64157.

Delgado-Ramos, Gian Carlo, ed. 2010. *Ecología Política de la Minería en América Latina*. Mexico City: Universidad Nacional Autónoma de México.

della Porta, Donatella, and Mario Diani. 2006. *Social Movements: An Introduction*. 2nd edition. Malden, MA: Blackwell.

Democracy Center. 2017. Video Conference—International Solidarity Campaign with Anti-Mining Struggle in El Salvador. Interviews with Jen Moore, Manuel Pérez Rocha, Pedro Cabezas, Robin Broad. https://terra-justa.org/resource/video-conference-international-solidarity-campaign-with-the-anti-mining-struggle-in-el-salvador/.

Deonandan, Kalowatie. 2015. "Evaluating the Effectiveness of the Anti-Mining Movement in Guatemala: The Role of Political Opportunities and Message Framing." *Canadian Journal of Latin American and Caribbean Studies* 40, no. 1: 27–47.

Deonandan, Kalowatie, and Michael L. Dougherty, eds. 2016. *Mining in Latin America: Critical Approaches to the New Extraction*. New York: Routledge.

Diani, Mario. 2015. *The Cement of Civil Society: Studying Networks in Localities*. New York: Cambridge University Press.

Diani, Mario, and Doug McAdam. 2003. *Social Movements and Networks: Relational Approaches to Collective Action*. Oxford: Oxford University Press.

256 REFERENCES

Díaz, Guillermo. 2016. "Oligarquía y élite económica guatemalteca: Un análisis de redes sociales." *Sociedad y Discurso* 30 (December): 50–70.

Díaz González, José Andrés. 2013. "De caminatas a los juzgados: análisis del discurso de los medios de prensa sobre el proyecto minero Crucitas." *Polis* 12, no. 36: 315–341. https://www.scielo.cl/pdf/polis/v12n36/art14.pdf.

Dietz, Kristina. 2019. "Direct Democracy in Mining Conflicts in Latin America: Mobilising Against the *La Colosa* Project in Colombia." *Canadian Journal of Development Studies* 40, no. 2: 145–162. https://doi.org/10.1080/02255189.2018.1467830.

Doan, David B. 1996. "The Mineral Industry of Nicaragua." US Geological Survey. https://minerals.usgs.gov/minerals/pubs/country/1996/9517096.pdf.

Dosal, Paul. 1995. *Power in Transition: The Rise of Guatemala's Industrial Oligarchy, 1871–1994*. Westport, CT: Praeger.

Dougherty, Michael L. 2011. "The Global Gold Mining Industry, Junior Firms, and Civil Society Resistance in Guatemala." *Bulletin of Latin American Research* 30 (October): 403–418.

Dougherty, Michael L. 2019a. "Boom Time for Technocrats? How Environmental Consulting Companies Shape Mining Governance." *The Extractive Industries and Society* 6: 443–453.

Dougherty, Michael L. 2019b. "How Does Development Mean? Attitudes toward Mining and the Social Meaning of Development in Guatemala." *Latin American Perspectives* 46, no. 2 (March): 161–181.

Dupuy, Kendra E. 2014. "Community Development Requirements in Mining Laws." *The Extractive Industries and Society* 1: 200–215.

Durand, Francisco, and Eduardo Silva, eds. 1998. *Organized Business, Economic Change, Democracy in Latin America*. Miami: North-South Center Press.

Earthworks, IPS-Global Economy Program, and Maritimes-Guatemala Breaking the Silence Network. 2020. "Advances in the Escobal Mine Consultation Overshadowed by Constitutional Crisis." https://earthworks.org/wp-content/uploads/2020/12/ConsultationAtRisk_FinalEnglish-1.pdf.

Eberhardt, Pia, and Cecilia Olivert. 2012. "Profiting from Injustice: How Law Firms, Arbitrators and Financiers Are Fueling an Investment Arbitration Boom." Brussels and Amsterdam: Corporate Europe Observatory and Transnational Institute.

Ebus, Bram, and Thomas Martinelli. 2021. "Venezuela's Gold Heist: The Symbiotic Relationship between the State, Criminal Networks and Resource Extraction." *Bulletin of Latin American Research*, May 26. https://doi.org/10.1111/blar.13246.

Eckstein, Susan. 2001. "Power and Popular Protest in Latin America." In *Power and Popular Protest: Latin American Social Movements*, edited by Susan Eckstein, 1–60. Berkeley: University of California Press.

Eisenstadt, Todd A., and Karleen Jones West. 2019. *Who Speaks for Nature? Indigenous Movements, Public Opinion, and the Petro-State in Ecuador*. New York: Oxford University Press.

EITI. 2014. "Segundo Informe Nacional de Conciliación EITI-GUA. Años 2012–2013." Extractive Industry Transparency Initiative. https://eiti.org/sites/default/files/attachments/2012-2013_guatemala_eiti_report_es.pdf.

"Empresa Minera Promete, Pero . . ." 2006. *Última Hora Electrónico* 19, no. 2 (July 31, 2006). Accessed July 27, 2018. http://www.bio-nica.info/biblioteca/UltimaHoraElectr%C3%B3nico19.pdf.

REFERENCES   257

Epp, Charles R. 1998. *The Rights Revolution: Lawyers, Activists, and Supreme Courts in Comparative Perspective*. Chicago: University of Chicago Press.

España-Nájera, Annabella. 2018. "Party Manifestos in Newer Party Systems: El Salvador and Guatemala." *Party Politics* 24, no. 3: 307–313.

Esquirol, Jorge L. 2020. *Ruling the Law: Legitimacy and Failure in Latin American Legal Systems*. Cambridge: Cambridge University Press.

Evans, Sterling. 1999. *The Green Republic: A Conservation History of Costa Rica*. Austin: University of Texas Press.

"Ex-ministro Barrera reitera oposición a la minería." 2008. *Revista La Macana* [Sensuntepeque], September 24, 2008. http://revistalamacana.blogspot.com/2008/09/ex-ministro-barrera-reitera-oposicin-la.html.

Fach Gómez, Katia. 2011. "Latin America and ICSID: David vs. Goliath?" *Law and Business Review of the Americas* 195: 216–221.

Fach Gómez, Katia. 2012. "Rethinking the Role of Amicus Curiae in International Investment Arbitration: How to Draw the Line Favorably for the Public Interest." *Fordham International Law Journal* 35: 510–564.

Fairfield, Tasha. 2015. *Private Wealth and Public Revenue in Latin America: Business Power and Tax Politics*. New York: Cambridge University Press.

Fairfield, Tasha, and Candelaria Garay. 2017. "Redistribution Under the Right in Latin America: Electoral Competition and Organized Actors in Policymaking." *Comparative Political Studies* 50, no. 14: 1871–1906.

Falleti, Tulia G., and Thea N. Riofrancos. 2018. "Endogenous Participation: Strengthening Prior Consultation in Extractive Economies." *World Politics* 70, no. 1: 86–121.

Feoli, Ludovico. 2021. "Social Mobilization and the Implementation of a New Policy Vision in Costa Rica's Electricity Sector." Paper presented at the Latin American Studies Association Meeting, May 26–29, 2021.

Fischer, Karin, and Harald Waxenecker. 2020. "Redes de poder: Consideraciones sobre la élite neoliberal de poder y conocimiento en Guatemala." *Revista CIDOB d'Afers Internacionals* 126 (December): 89–115.

Flagg, Julia A. 2019. "From Symbol to (Some) Substance: Costa Rica's Carbon Neutral Pledge." *Human Ecology Review* 25, no. 1: 23–42.

Flemmer, Riccarda, and Almut Schilling-Vacaflor. 2016. "Unfulfilled Promises of the Consultation Approach: The Limits to Effective Indigenous Participation in Bolivia's and Peru's Extractive Industries." *Third World Quarterly* 37, no. 1: 172–188.

Fonseca L., Roberto. 2018. "Nicaragua: El 70% de la población demanda la renuncia de Ortega." *Estrategia y Negocios*, June 11, 2018. http://www.estrategiaynegocios.net/lasc lavesdeldia/1186398-330/nicaragua-el-70-de-la-poblaci%C3%B3n-demanda-la-renun cia-de-ortega.

Fontana, Lorenza B., and Jean Grugel. 2016. "The Politics in Indigenous Participation Through 'Free Prior Informed Consent': Reflections from the Bolivian Case." *World Development* 77: 249–261.

Franck, Susan D. 2019. *Arbitration Costs: Myths and Realities in Investment Treaty Arbitration*. Oxford: Oxford University Press.

Franks, Daniel M., Rachel Davis, Anthony J. Bebbington, Saleem H. Ali, Deanna Kemp, and Martin Scurrah. 2014. "Conflict Translated Environmental and Social Risk into Business Costs." *PNAS* 111, no. 21: 7576–7581.

Fuentes Knight, Juan Alberto. 2016. "State Capture and Fiscal Policy in Latin America." *Plaza Pública*, June 15, 2016.

258 REFERENCES

Fulmer, Amanda M., Angelina Snodgrass Godoy, and Philip Neff. 2008. "Indigenous Rights, Resistance, and the Law: Lessons from a Guatemala Mine." *Latin American Politics and Society* 50, no. 4: 91–121.

FUNDESA and CACIF. 2016. *Revista Mejoremos Guate #15.* Fundación para el Desarrollo de Guatemala and Comité Coordinador de Asociaciones Agrícolas, Comerciales, Industriales, y Financieras. https://issuu.com/fundesaguatemala/docs/mejoremos_guate_fundesa_2016baja.

Funes, Mauricio. 2017. "Seguro que gran empresario que menciona Rosa Chávez fue Poma. A mi gobierno también intentó convencerlo. Esos son los intereses que defiende." Twitter, April 18, 2017.

Fung, Archon. 2011. "Reinventing Democracy in Latin America." *Perspectives on Politics* 9, no. 4: 857–871.

Fung, Archon, and Erik Olin Wright, eds. 2003. *Deepening Democracy: Institutional Innovations in Empowered Participatory Governance.* Princeton, NJ: Princeton University Press.

FUNIDES. 2014. "La minería en Nicaragua: importancia, desafíos y oportunidades." PowerPoint presentation by Juan Sebastián Chamorro, Executive Director, Fundación Nicaragüense para el Desarrollo Económico y Social, at Congreso Internacional de Minería, Managua, Nicaragua, August 12–14, 2014. https://issuu.com/congresomin ero/docs/beneficios_e_impacto_del_sector_min.

FUNIDES. 2016. "Impacto Económico y Social de la Minería en Nicaragua." Fundación Nicaragüense para el Desarrollo Económico y Social. http://caminic.com/wp-content/uploads/2017/10/CAMFUN_II.pdf.

FUSADES. 2010. "Las instituciones democráticas en El Salvador II: Valoración de rendimientos y plan de fortalecimiento." Fundación Salvadoreña para el Desarrollo Económico y Social, Departamento de Estudios Legales, San Salvador.

FUSADES. 2017. "El Salvador: Año político. junio de 2016 a mayo de 2017." Fundación Salvadoreña para el Desarrollo Económico y Social, Departamento de Estudios Legales, San Salvador.

Gamboa Mora, Bernal. 2020. "Minería metálica en Costa Rica: Análisis jurídico del nuevo proyecto Crucitas en la Zona Norte." *El País* [Costa Rica], November 28, 2020. https://www.elpais.cr/2020/11/28/mineria-metalica-en-costa-rica-analisis-juridico-del-nuevo-proyecto-crucitas-en-la-zona-norte/.

García, Jody. 2018. "Jimmy, Baldizón y estos mega-empresarios organizaron el lobby contra Todd y la CICIG (parte 1)." *Nómada*, October 11, 2018. https://nomada.gt/pais/entender-la-politica/jimmy-baldizon-y-estos-mega-empresarios-organizaron-el-lobby-contra-todd-y-la-cicig-parte-1/.

García Peralta, Mónica. 2015. "Vida en El Limón." *La Prensa* [Nicaragua], October 25 2015. https://www.laprensa.com.ni/2015/10/25/suplemento/la-prensa-domingo/1924 769-16419.

GHRC. 2014. "The Peaceful Environmental Justice Movement at 'La Puya.'" Guatemala Human Rights Commission, November 12, 2014. www.ghrc-usa.org/wp-content/uplo ads/2014/11/Puya-report-final.pdf.

GIEI. 2018. "Nicaragua: Informe sobre los hechos de violencia ocurridos entre el 18 de abril y el 30 de mayo de 2018." Grupo Interdisciplinario de Expertos Independientes, December 21, 2018. https://gieinicaragua.org/giei-content/uploads/2019/02/GIEI_IN FORME_DIGITAL_07_02_2019_VF.pdf.

Giugni, Marco. 2004. *Social Protest and Policy Change: Ecology, Antinuclear, and Peace Movements in Comparative Perspective.* Lanham, MD: Rowman and Littlefield.

REFERENCES   259

Giugni, Marco. 2007. "Useless Protest? A Time-Series Analysis of the Policy Outcomes of Ecology, Antinuclear, and Peace Movements in the United States, 1977–1995." *Mobilization* 12, no. 1: 53–77.

Givan, Rebecca Kolins, Kenneth M. Roberts, and Sarah A. Soule. 2010. "Introduction: The Dimensions of Diffusion." In *The Diffusion of Social Movements*, edited by Rebecca Kolins Givan, Kenneth M. Roberts, and Sarah A. Soule, 1–18. Cambridge: Cambridge University Press.

Godoy, Angelina Snodgrass. 2013. *Medicines and Markets: Intellectual Property and Human Rights in the Free Trade Era.* Stanford, CA: Stanford University Press.

Goldfrank, Benjamin. 2011. *Deepening Local Democracy in Latin America: Participation, Decentralization and the Left.* University Park: Pennsylvania State University Press.

Goldstone, Jack A., ed. 2003. *States, Parties, and Social Movements.* Cambridge: Cambridge University Press.

Gómez, Elder, and Gloria Silvia Orellana. 2017. "FMLN anuncia apoyo a ley contra la minería metálica." *Diario Co Latino*, March 9, 2017. https://www.diariocolatino.com/fmln-anuncia-apoyo-ley-la-mineria-metalica/.

Goodland, Robert. 2011. "Best Practice Mining in Colombia." Paper presented at Best Practice Mining Forum, December 2011. https://studylib.net/doc/7507176/best-practice-mining-in-colombia.

Goodwin, Jeff, and James M. Jasper. 1999. "Caught in a Winding, Snarling Vine: The Structural Bias of Political Process Theory." *Sociological Forum* 14: 27–54.

Graef, Dana J. 2013. "Negotiating Environmental Sovereignty in Costa Rica." *Development and Change* 44, no. 2: 285–307.

Granovetter, Mark S. 1982. "The Strength of Weak Ties: A Network Theory Revisited." In *Social Structure and Network Analysis*, edited by Peter V. Marsden and Nan Lin, 201–233. Beverly Hills, CA: SAGE.

Granovsky-Larsen, Simon. 2018. "Land and the Reconfiguration of Power in Post-Conflict Guatemala." In *Dominant Elites in Latin America*, edited by Liisa L. North and Timothy D. Clark, 181–204. Cham, Switzerland: Springer.

GRUN. 2018. "Empresa Nicaragüense de Minas (ENIMINAS)." PowerPoint presentation. Gobierno de Reconciliación y Unidad Nacional, Secretario Privado para Políticas Nacionales, Presidencia de la República. Unpublished.

Gudynas, Eduardo. 2018. "Extractivisms: Tendencies and Consequences." In *Reframing Latin American Development*, edited by Ronaldo Munck and Raúl Delgado Wise, 61–82. New York: Routledge.

Gurva Lavalle, Adrian, and Marisa von Bülow. 2015. "Institutionalized Brokers and Collective Actors: Different Types, Similar Challenges." In *Social Movement Dynamics: New Perspectives on Theory and Research from Latin America*, edited by Federico M. Rossi and Marisa von Bülow, 157–180. Burlington, VT: Ashgate.

Gustafsson, Maria-Therese. 2018. *Private Politics and Peasant Mobilization: Mining in Peru.* New York: Palgrave Macmillan.

Gutiérrez, Edgar. 2017. "Actores y contextos de la crisis política de 2015." In *Transformaciones de la cultura política en Guatemala*, edited by Instituto Nacional Demócrata, 75–143. Guatemala City: Serviprensa.

Gutiérrez Elizondo, Hilda María. 2015. "Mining and Resource Mobilization for Social Development: The Case of Nicaragua." UNRISD Working Paper 2015-9. http://www.unrisd.org/80256B3C005BCCF9/(httpAuxPages)/1524AC2902E8323DC1257E310031BA2E/$file/Gutierrez.pdf.

260 REFERENCES

Haglund, LaDawn. 2010. *Limiting Resources: Market-Led Reform and the Transformation of Public Goods*. University Park: Pennsylvania State University Press.

Hale, Charles R. 2002. "Does Multiculturalism Menace? Governance, Cultural Rights and the Politics of Identity in Guatemala." *Journal of Latin American Studies* 34, no. 3: 485–524.

Hanagan, Michael. 1998. "Social Movements: Incorporation, Disengagement, and Opportunities-A Long View." In *From Contention to Democracy*, edited by Marco Giugni, Doug McAdam, and Charles Tilly, 3–30. Lanham, MD: Rowman and Littlefield.

Harvey, David. 2004. "The 'New' Imperialism: Accumulation by Dispossession." *Socialist Register* 40: 63–87.

Haslam, Paul Alexander. 2010. "The Evolution of the Foreign Direct Investment Regime in the Americas." *Third World Quarterly* 31: 1181–1203.

Haslam, Paul Alexander. 2018. "Beyond Voluntary: State-Firm Bargaining over Corporate Social Responsibilities in Mining." *Review of International Political Economy* 25, no. 3: 418–440. https://doi.org/10.1080/09692290.2018.1447497.

Haslam, Paul Alexander, and Pablo Heidrich, eds. 2016. *The Political Economy of Natural Resources and Development*. New York: Routledge.

Haslam, Paul Alexander, and Nasser Ary Tanimoune. 2016. "The Determinants of Social Conflict in the Latin American Mining Sector: New Evidence with Quantitative Data." *World Development* 78: 401–419.

Heaney, Michael T., and Fabio Rojas. 2014. "Hybrid Activism: Social Movement Mobilization in a Multimovement Environment." *American Journal of Sociology* 119, no. 4 (January): 1047–1103.

Helmke, Gretchen, and Julio Ríos-Figueroa, eds. 2011. *Courts in Latin America*. Cambridge: Cambridge University Press.

HEMCO. 2018. "Gerencia de minería artesanal." PowerPoint presentation. Unpublished.

HEMCO and Mineros S.A. 2016. "Modelo Bonanza: La minería industrial y la minería artesanal pueden y deben trabajar juntas." https://hemco.com.ni/wp-content/uploads/HEM_ModeloBonanza050816.pdf.

Hendricks, Michael, and Mario Sánchez González. 2021. "Minería: ¿El elixir de la vida o la fruta prohibida? Un examen empírico de las oportunidades y amenazas de la minería en Santo Domingo, Nicaragua: Una comunidad dividida sobre la minería." *Quid 16* 14: 239–268.

Henríquez, Katia. 2008. *Perspectiva de la industria minera de oro en El Salvador*. San Salvador: Ediciones CEICOM.

Hertel, Shareen. 2019. *Tethered Fates: Companies, Communities and Rights at Stake*. New York: Oxford University Press.

Hessbruegge, Jan Arno, and Carlos Fredy Ochoa García. 2011. "Mayan Law in Post-Conflict Guatemala." In *Customary Justice and the Rule of Law in War-Torn Societies*, edited by Deborah Isser, 77–118. Washington, DC: United States Institute of Peace Press.

Higley, John, and Richard Gunther, eds. 1992. *Elites and Democratic Consolidation in Latin America and Southern Europe*. Cambridge: Cambridge University Press.

Hilson, Chris. 2002. "New Social Movements: The Role of Legal Opportunity." *Journal of European Public Policy* 9, no. 2: 238–255.

Hilson, Gavin, Tara Rava Zolnikov, Daisy Ramirez Ortiz, and Cynthia Kumah. 2018. "Formalizing Artisanal Gold Mining under the Minamata Convention: Previewing the Challenge in Sub-Saharan Africa." *Environmental Science and Policy* 85: 123–131.

Hinds, Manuel Enrique. 2007. "La minería de oro en El Salvador: Costos y beneficios." Unpublished.

Hinton, Jennifer J. 2005. *Communities and Small-Scale Mining: An Integrated Review for Development Planning.* Washington, DC: CASM. http://artisanalmining.org/Reposit ory/01/The_CASM_Files/CASM_Publications/CASM%20Book%20draft%20v091 505.pdf.

Hochstetler, Kathryn, and Margaret E. Keck. 2007. *Greening Brazil: Environmental Activism in State and Society.* Durham, NC: Duke University Press.

Hochstetler, Kathryn, and Ricardo Tranjan. 2016. "Environment and Consultation in the Brazilian Democratic Developmental State." *Comparative Politics* 48, no. 4 (July): 497–516.

Holden, William N., and R. Daniel Jacobson. 2011. "Ecclesial Opposition in Nonferrous Metals Mining in Guatemala and the Philippines: Neoliberalism Encounters the Church of the Poor." In *Engineering Earth: The Impact of Megaengineering Projects,* edited by Stanley D. Brunn, 383–411. Dordrecht: Springer.

Holland, D. Lynn. 2018. "'New Extractivism' in Mexico: Hope and Deception." *Journal of Politics in Latin America* 10, no. 2: 123–138.

Holloway, John. 2002. *Change the World Without Taking Power.* New York: Pluto.

Honey, Martha. 2008. *Ecotourism and Sustainable Development: Who Owns Paradise?* 2nd edition. Washington, DC: Island Press.

Hopkins, Jack W. 1995. *Policymaking for Conservation in Latin America: National Parks, Reserves, and the Environment.* Westport, CT: Praeger.

Horton, Lynn R. 2007. *Grassroots Struggles for Sustainability in Central America.* Boulder: University of Colorado Press.

Horton, Lynn R. 2013. "From Collectivism to Capitalism: Neoliberalism and Rural Mobilization in Nicaragua." *Latin American Politics and Society* 55, no. 1: 119–140.

Huber, Evelyne, and John D. Stephens. 2010. "Successful Social Policy Regimes? Political Economy, Politics, and Social Policy in Argentina, Chile, Uruguay, and Costa Rica." In *Democratic Governance in Latin America,* edited by Scott Mainwaring and Timothy R. Scully, 155–209. Stanford, CA: Stanford University Press.

Hudson, Andrew, and Alexandra W. Taylor. 2010. "The International Commission Against Impunity in Guatemala: A New Model for International Criminal Justice Mechanisms," *Journal of International Criminal Justice* 8, no. 1: 53–74. https://dx.doi. org/mqq003.

IACHR. 2014. "Report No. 20/14, Petition 1566-07 Report on Admissibility, Communities of the Sipakepense and Mam Mayan People of the Municipalities of Sipacapa and San Miguel Ixtahuacán, Guatemala." Inter-American Commission on Human Rights. www.oas.org/en/iachr/decisions/2014/GTAD1566-07EN.pdf.

IACHR. 2020. "Persons Deprived of Liberty in Nicaragua in Connection with the Human Rights Crisis That Began on April 18, 2018." Inter-American Commission on Human Rights. https://www.oas.org/en/iachr/reports/pdfs/Nicaragua-PPL-en.pdf.

IACHR. 2021. "IACHR Expresses Concern over Impeachment Proceedings Brought Against Members of Guatemala's Constitutional Court." Press release, Inter-American Commission on Human Rights, March 18, 2021. https://www.oas.org/en/IACHR/jsF orm/?File=/en/iachr/media_center/PReleases/2021/065.asp.

ICEFI. 2014a. "Diagnóstico de la situación minera de Honduras, 2002–2012." Instituto Centroamericano de Estudios Fiscales, Guatemala City. https://icefi.org/sites/default/

262 REFERENCES

files/diagnostico_de_la_situacion_minera_en_honduras_2007-2012_version_para_sitio_web.pdf.

ICEFI. 2014b. "La minería en Guatemala: realidad y desafíos frente a la democracia y el desarrollo. Guatemala." Instituto Centroamericano de Estudios Fiscales, Guatemala City. http://icefi.org/sites/default/files/la_mineria_en_guatemala_-_2da_edicion.pdf.

ICEFI. 2015a. "Buenas prácticas internacionales de transparencia fiscal en industrias extractivas: Aplicaciones para Guatemala." Instituto Centroamericano de Estudios Fiscales, Guatemala City. http://icefi.org/sites/default/files/estudio_buenas_practicas_de_transparencia_fiscal_-_para_web_nva_version.pdf.

ICEFI. 2015b. *Política fiscal: Expresión del poder de las elites centroamericanas.* Instituto Centroamericano de Estudios Fiscales. Guatemala City: F&G Editores.

ICEFI. 2016. "Lineamientos de políticas públicas en industrias extractivas." Instituto Centroamericano de Estudios Fiscales, Guatemala City. https://icefi.org/sites/default/files/lineamientos_de_politicas_publicas_en_industrias_extractivas.pdf.

ICMM, UNEP, and PRI. 2020. "Global Industry Standard on Tailings Management." International Council on Mining and Metals, United Nations Environment Programme, and Principles for Responsible Investment. https://wedocs.unep.org/bitstream/handle/20.500.11822/36139/GISTM_En.pdf.

ICSID. 2022. *The ICSID Caseload—Statistics*, Issue 2022-1. International Centre for the Settlement of Investment Disputes. https://icsid.worldbank.org/sites/default/files/documents/The_ICSID_Caseload_Statistics.1_Edition_ENG.pdf.

IFC. 2014a. "Condor Gold Plc. Summary of Investment Information." Project Investment Portal, International Finance Corporation. https://disclosures.ifc.org/#/projectDetail/SII/32519.

IFC. 2014b. "A Strategic Approach to Early Stakeholder Engagement: A Good Practice Handbook for Junior Companies in the Extractive Industries." International Finance Corporation. https://documents.worldbank.org/pt/publication/documents-reports/documentdetail/784051524469298172/a-strategic-approach-to-early-stakeholder-engagement-a-good-practice-handbook-for-junior-companies-in-the-extractive-industries.

IGF. 2017. "Global Trends in Artisanal and Small-Scale Mining (ASM): A Review of Key Numbers and Issues." Intergovernmental Forum on Mining, Minerals, Metals and Sustainable Development, Winnipeg.

IGF. 2019. "Insights on Incentives: Tax Competition in Mining." Intergovernmental Forum on Mining, Minerals, Metals and Sustainable Development, Ottawa. https://www.iisd.org/sites/default/files/publications/insights-incentives-tax-competition-mining.pdf.

ILO. 1989. C169—Indigenous and Tribal Peoples Convention, 1989 (No. 169). International Labor Organization. http://www.ilo.org/dyn/normlex/en/f?p=NORMLEXPUB:12100:0::NO::P12100_ILO_CODE:C169.

Imai, Shin, Leah Gardner, and Sarah Weinberger. 2017. "The 'Canada Brand': Violence and Canadian Mining Companies in Latin America." Osgoode Legal Studies Research Paper no. 17.

Infinito Gold Ltd. 2013. "Notice of Intent to Arbitrate." Letter from John Morgan, president and CEO, to Anabel González Campabadal, Costa Rican minister of foreign trade, April 3, 2013. https://www.italaw.com/sites/default/files/case-documents/italaw3016.pdf.

REFERENCES   263

Infinito Gold Ltd. 2014. "Crucitas Chronology." [No longer available]. Accessed March 25, 2014. www.infinitogold.com/s/LasaCrucitasChronology.asp.

Infinito Gold Ltd. and Republic of Costa Rica. 2014. "Request for Arbitration to the Secretary-General of the International Centre for Settlement of Investment Disputes." February 6, 2014. http://www.italaw.com/sites/default/files/case-documents/italaw3 118.pdf.

Infinito v. Costa Rica. 2016. "Procedural Order No. 2." *Infinto Gold Ltd. v. Republic of Costa Rica*. ICSID Case No. ARB14/5, June 1, 2016. http://icsidfiles.worldbank.org/icsid/ICS IDBLOBS/OnlineAwards/C3384/DC8372_En.pdf.

Infinito v. Costa Rica. 2017. "Decision on Jurisdiction." *Infinto Gold Ltd. v. Republic of Costa Rica*. ICSID Case No. ARB14/5, December 4, 2017. http://icsidfiles.worldbank. org/icsid/ICSIDBLOBS/OnlineAwards/C3384/DS10811_En.pdf.

Infinito v. Costa Rica. 2021. "Award." *Infinto Gold Ltd. v. Republic of Costa Rica*. ICSID Case No. ARB14/5, June 3, 2021. http://icsidfiles.worldbank.org/icsid/ICSIDBLOBS/Onlin eAwards/C3384/DS16472_En.pdf.

Instituto Nacional de Estadística Guatemala. 2019. "Resultados Censo 2018." https:// www.censopoblacion.gt/documentacion.

Inter-American Court of Human Rights. 2001. *Case of the Mayagna (Sumo) Awas Tingni Community v. Nicaragua*. August 31, 2001. http://www.corteidh.or.cr/docs/casos/ articulos/seriec_79_ing.pdf.

Invest in Guatemala. 2014. "7. Mining." www.investinguatemala.org/sites/default/files/7-mining_engl.pdf.

IPADE. 2012. "Catálogo estadístico de elecciones en Nicaragua 1990–2011." Instituto para el Desarrollo y la Democracia, Managua.

Isaacs, Anita. 2021. "Traditional Guatemalan Elites Must Change Now. Here Is Where to Start." *Plaza Pública*, April 19, 2021. https://plazapublica.com.gt/multimedia/disiden cia-y-disciplina/traditional-guatemalan-elites-must-change-now-here-is-where-to-start.html.

Isla, Ana. 2015. *The "Greening" of Costa Rica: Women, Peasants, Indigenous Peoples, and the Remaking of Nature*. Toronto: University of Toronto Press.

IUDOP. 2008. "Conocimientos y percepciones hacia la minería en zonas afectadas por la incursion minera." Instituto Universitario de Opinión Pública, Universidad Centroamericana José Simeón Cañas, San Salvador, January 22, 2008. http://www.uca. edu.sv/publica/iudop/Web/2008/Resumen-IUDOP-Mineria.pdf.

IUDOP. 2015. "Encuesta sobre conocimientos y percepciones hacia el medio ambiente y la minería metálica en El Salvador." Serie de informes EP. Instituto Universitario de Opinión Pública, Universidad Centroamericana José Simeón Cañas, San Salvador, June 2015. http://www.uca.edu.sv/iudop/wp-content/uploads/INFORME-MINER%C3%8DA-2015.pdf.

Janíková, Pavlína, Jaromír Starý, Radúz Klika, Pavel Kavina, Jakub Jirásek, and Martin Sivek. 2015. "Gold Deposits of the Czech Republic from a Mineral Policy Perspective." *Mineral Resources Management* 31, Issue 4: 35–50. https://doi.org/10.1515/ gospo-2015-0041.

Jaskoski, Maiah. 2022. *The Politics of Extraction: Territorial Rights, Participatory Institutions, and Conflict in Latin America*. New York: Oxford University Press.

Jastrzembski, Benjamin. 2016. "Historia de Siuna, Nicaragua. 1905–2009." *Revista Universitaria del Caribe* 16, no. 1: 33–64.

264 REFERENCES

Jiménez, Mirna. 2017. "Financista de ARENA intentó que iglesia cambiara posición sobre la minería." *Diario Co Latino*, April 18, 2017. https://www.diariocolatino.com/financista-arena-intento-iglesia-cambiara-posicion-la-mineria/.

Johnson, Lise, and Lisa Sachs. 2016. "The Outsized Costs of Investor-State Dispute Settlement." *AIB Insights* 16, no. 1: 10–13.

Jones, Mark P. 2011. "Weakly Institutionalized Party Systems and Presidential Democracy: Evidence from Guatemala." *International Area Studies Review* 14, no. 4: 3–30.

Juárez, Tulio. 2015. "Empresarios exigen inmediata renuncia del presidente Otto Pérez Molina." *El Periódico* [Guatemala], August 21, 2015. https://elperiodico.com.gt/nacionales/2015/08/21/empresarios-exigen-inmediata-renuncia-del-presidente-otto-perez-molina/.

Justice and Corporate Accountability Project. 2016. "Request to Investigate Tahoe Resources for Failure to Disclose Material Information." http://miningwatch.ca/sites/default/files/sec_disclosure_sent.pdf.

Kapiszewski, Diana. 2013. "Economic Governance on Trial: High Courts and Elected Leaders in Argentina and Brazil." *Latin American Politics and Society* 55, no. 4: 47–73.

Kapiszewski, Diana, Steven Levitsky, and Deborah J. Yashar, eds. 2021. *The Inclusionary Turn in Latin American Democracies*. New York: Cambridge University Press.

Kapiszewski, Diana, Gordon Silverstein, and Robert A. Kagan, eds. 2013. *Consequential Courts: Judicial Roles in Global Perspective*. New York: Cambridge University Press.

Kappes/KCA v. Guatemala. 2020a. "Claimants' Memorial." *Daniel W. Kappes and Kappes, Cassiday & Associates v. Republic of Guatemala*. ISCID Case No. ARB/18.43. July 20, 2020. https://jusmundi.com/en/document/other/en-daniel-w-kappes-and-kappes-cassidy-associates-v-republic-of-guatemala-claimants-memorial-monday-20th-july-2020#other_document_17976.

Kappes/KCA v. Guatemala. 2020b. "Claimants' Response to La Puya Amicus Curiae Petition." *Daniel W. Kappes and Kappes, Cassiday & Associates v. Republic of Guatemala*. ISCID Case No. ARB/18.43. September 25, 2020. https://jusmundi.com/en/document/other/en-daniel-w-kappes-and-kappes-cassidy-associates-v-republic-of-guatemala-letter-from-claimant-to-the-tribunal-on-amicus-curiae-participation-by-la-puya-friday-25th-september-2020#other_document_19205.

Kappes/KCA v. Guatemala. 2020c. "Decision on Respondent's Preliminary Objections." *Daniel W. Kappes and Kappes, Cassiday & Associates v. Republic of Guatemala*. ISCID Case No. ARB/18.43. March 13, 2020. https://www.italaw.com/cases/6611.

Kappes/KCA v. Guatemala. 2020d. "Guatemala's Counter-Memorial." *Daniel W. Kappes and Kappes, Cassiday & Associates v. Republic of Guatemala*. ISCID Case No. ARB/18.43. December 7, 2020. https://jusmundi.com/en/document/other/en-daniel-w-kappes-and-kappes-cassidy-associates-v-republic-of-guatemala-guatemalas-counter-memorial-monday-7th-december-2020#other_document_19200.

Kappes/KCA v. Guatemala. 2021. "Claimants' Reply." *Daniel W. Kappes and Kappes, Cassiday & Associates v. Republic of Guatemala*. ISCID Case No. ARB/18.43. June 11, 2021. https://jusmundi.com/en/document/other/en-daniel-w-kappes-and-kappes-cassidy-associates-v-republic-of-guatemala-claimants-reply-friday-11th-june-2021#other_document_20848?su=/en/search?query=kappes.

Keck, Margaret E., and Kathryn Sikkink. 1998. *Activists Beyond Borders*. Ithaca, NY: Cornell University Press.

REFERENCES   265

King, Brayden G., Keith G. Bentele, and Sarah A. Soule. 2007. "Protest and Policymaking: Explaining Fluctuation in Congressional Attention to Rights Issues, 1960–1986." *Social Forces* 86, no. 1: 137–163. https://doi.org/10.1353/sof.2007.0101.

Kinzer, Stephen. 1999. *Blood of Brothers: Life and War in Nicaragua*. New York: Anchor.

Kirsch, Stuart. 2014. *Mining Capitalism: The Relationship Between Corporations and Their Critics*. Oakland: University of California Press.

Klinger, Julie Michelle. 2017. *Rare Earth Frontiers: From Territorial Subsoils to Lunar Landscapes*. Ithaca, NY: Cornell University Press.

Kolb, Felix. 2007. *Protest and Opportunities: The Political Outcomes of Social Movements*. Chicago: University of Chicago Press.

Kramarz, Teresa, David Cosolo, and Alejandro Rossi. 2017. "Judicialization of Environmental Policy and the Crisis of Democratic Accountability." *Review of Policy Research* 34, no. 1: 31–49.

Kröger, Markus. 2020. *Iron Will: Global Extractivism and Mining Resistance in Brazil and India*. Ann Arbor: University of Michagan Press.

Le Billon, Philippe, and Nicholas Middeldorp. 2021. "Empowerment or Imposition? Extractive Violence, Indigenous Peoples, and the Paradox of Prior Consultation." In *Our Extractive Age: Expressions of Violence and Resistance*, edited by Judith Shapiro and John-Andrew McNeish, 71–93. London: Routledge.

Labrador, Gabriel, and Frederick Meza. 2011. "A las amenazas de que me van a matar ni caso les hago ya." Interview with Francisco Pineda. *El Faro*, June 9, 2011. https://elfaro.net/es/201106/el_agora/4269/A-las-amenazas-de-que-me-van-a-matar-ni-caso-les-hago-ya.htm?st-full_text=all&tpl=11.

Laitos, Jan G. 2012. "The Current Status of Cyanide Regulations." *Engineering and Mining Journal*, February. https://www.e-mj.com/features/the-current-status-of-cyanide-regulations/.

Langford, Malcolm, César Rodríguez-Garavito, and Julieta Rossi, eds. 2017. *Social Rights Judgments and the Politics of Compliance: Making It Stick*. New York: Cambridge University Press.

LaPlante, J. P., and Catherine Nolin. 2014. "*Consultas* and Socially Responsible Investing in Guatemala: A Case Study Examining Maya Perspectives on the Indigenous Right to Free, Prior, and Informed Consent." *Society and Natural Resources* 27: 231–248.

Lazenby, Henry. 2014. "Nicaragua an Attractive Mining Destination, Says 'Open for Business.'" *Mining Weekly Online*, March 11, 2014. http://www.miningweekly.com/article/nicaragua-an-attractive-mining-destination-says-open-for-business-2014-03-11.

LeCoq, Jean-François, Geraldine Froger, Denis Pesche, Thomas Legrand, and Fernando Saenz. 2015. "Understanding the Governance of the Payment for Environmental Services Programme in Costa Rica: A Policy Process Perspective." *Ecosystem Services* 16: 253–265.

Lée L., Sigfrido, and María Isabel Bonilla de Anzueto. 2009. "Contribución de la industria minera al desarrollo de Guatemala." CIEN, Guatemala City. https://cien.org.gt/wp-content/uploads/2013/10/mineria2009.pdf.

Leifsen, Esben, Maria-Therese Gustafsson, María A. Guzmán-Gallegos, and Almut Schilling-Vacaflor. 2017. "New Mechanisms of Participation in Extractive Governance: Between Technologies of Governance and Resistance Work." *Third World Quarterly* 38, no. 5: 1043–1057.

Lewis, Tammy L. 2016. *Ecuador's Environmental Revolutions: Ecoimperialists, Ecodependents, and Ecoresisters*. Cambridge, MA: MIT Press.

266 REFERENCES

Li, Fabiana. 2015. *Unearthing Conflict: Corporate Mining, Activism, and Expertise in Peru.* Durham, NC: Duke University Press.

Loayza, Fernando, ed. 2012. *Strategic Environmental Assessment in the World Bank: Learning from Recent Experience and Challenges.* Washington, DC: World Bank Group. http://documents.worldbank.org/curated/en/729811468331017746/Strategic-environmental-assessment-in-the-World-Bank-learning-from-recent-experience-and-challenges.

López, Dina Larios de, Herbert Guzmán, and Edgardo Mira. 2008. "Riesgos y posibles impactos de la minería metálica en El Salvador." *Revista ECA* 63, nos. 711–712: 77–91.

López, Petronilo, and Elorgio Davila. 2014. "We're Going to Defend Our Paradise Against Mining." *Revista Envío* no. 399 (October).

López Piche, Keny. 2009. "No a la minería: Saca cierra puertas a exploración de metales." *La Prensa Gráfica*, February 26, 2009, 2–3.

Mahoney, James, and Kathleen Thelen, eds. 2015. *Advances in Comparative Historical Analysis.* Cambridge: Cambridge University Press.

MARN [El Salvador]. 2010. "Informe de labores: 01 de junio de 2009 al 31 de mayo de 2010." Ministerio de Medio Ambiente y Recursos Naturales, San Salvador.

MARN [Guatemala]. 2015. "Reglamento de evaluación, control, y seguimiento ambiental." Acuerdo Gubernativo, número 60-2015. Ministerio de Ambiente y Recursos Naturales, Guatemala.

Marroquín, Andrés, and Fritz Thomas. 2015. "Classical Liberalism in Guatemala." *Econ Journal Watch* 12, no. 3: 460–478.

Marsden, Peter V., and Karen E. Campbell. 2012. "Reflections on Conceptualizing and Measuring Tie Strength." *Social Forces* 91, no. 1: 17–23.

Martí i Puig, Salvador. 2010. "The Adaptation of the FSLN: Daniel Ortega's Leadership and Democracy in Nicaragua." *Latin American Politics and Society* 52, no. 4 (Winter): 79–106.

Martí i Puig, Salvador. 2018. "El regimen patrimonial de Nicaragua y las elecciones de 2016." In *Elecciones y Partidos en América Latina en el Cambio de Ciclo,* edited by Manuel Alcántara, Daniel Buquet and María Laura Tagina, 303–326. Madrid: CIS.

Martínez-Alier, Joan. 2003. *The Environmentalism of the Poor: A Study of Ecological Conflicts and Valuation.* Northampton, MA: Edward Elgar.

Martínez-Alier, Joan, Michiel Baud, and Héctor Sejenovich. 2016. "Origins and Perspectives of Latin American Environmentalism." In *Environmental Governance in Latin America*, edited by Fábio de Castro, Barbara Hogenboom and Michiel Baud, 29–57. New York: Palgrave Macmillan.

Martínez Cuenca, Alejandro. 1992. *Sandinista Economics in Practice: An Insider's Critical Reflections.* Boston: South End Press.

Martínez M., Luis Eduardo. 2013. "Clero dice 'no' a minería." *La Prensa* [Nicaragua], March 6, 2013.

Mash-Mash and José Guadalupe Gómez. 2014. "Two Views of Consulta Previa in Guatemala: A View from Indigenous People." *Americas Quarterly*, April 17.

Mayén, Guisela, and Carlos Fredy Ochoa. 2018. "Manual de diálogo social intercultural." Cuaderno Estado y Derecho 3, year 1, no. 1, December. https://www.kas.de/docume nts/275611/275660/Cuaderno+3+Di%C3%A1logo+Social+Intercultural.pdf/ed14a 09a-9c87-587e-50a6-eb1359929ced?version=1.0&t=1592971329801.

Mayer, Joshua L. 2019. "Negotiating Consultation: The Duty to Consult and Contestation of Autonomy in Nicaragua's Rama-Kriol Territory." In *Indigenous Struggles for*

Autonomy: The Caribbean Coast of Nicaragua, edited by Luciano Baracco, 99–129. Lanham, MD: Lexington Books.

Mazzuca, Sebastián. 2013. "The Rise of Rentier Populism in South America." *Journal of Democracy* 24, no. 12: 108–122.

McAdam, Doug, and Hilary Schaffer Boudet. 2012. *Putting Social Movements in Their Place: Explaining Opposition to Energy Projects in the United States, 2000–2005.* New York: Cambridge University Press.

McAdam, Doug, Sidney Tarrow, and Charles Tilly. 2001. *Dynamics of Contention.* Cambridge: Cambridge University Press.

McAllister, Carlota, and Diane M. Nelson, eds. 2013. *War by Other Means: Aftermath in Post-Genocide Guatemala.* Durham, NC: Duke University Press.

McCammon, Holly J., and Allison R. McGrath. 2015. "Litigating Change? Social Movements and the Court System." *Sociology Compass* 9, no. 2: 128–139.

McCleary, Rachel M. 1999. *Dictating Democracy: Guatemala and the End of Violent Revolution.* Miami: University Press of Florida.

McGinley, Kathleen A., and Frederick W. Cubbage. 2012. "Governmental Forest Policy for Sustainable Forest Management in Costa Rica, Guatemala, and Nicaragua: Regulation, Implementation, and Impact." *Journal of Sustainable Forestry* 31: 355–375.

McKinley, Andrés. 2018. "¿Y ahora qué pasará con la ley antiminera en El Salvador?" Radio news, May 4, 2018.

McKinley, Andrés. 2020. *For the Love of the Struggle: Memoirs from El Salvador.* Ottawa: Daraja Press.

McNeill, J. R., and George Vrtis. 2017. *Mining North America: An Environmental History Since 1522.* Berkeley: University of California Press.

McNeish, John-Andrew. 2017. "A Vote to Derail Extraction: Popular Consultation and Resource Sovereignty in Tolima, Colombia." *Third World Quarterly* 38, no. 5: 1128–1145.

MEM [Guatemala]. 2020. "Dirección General de Minería." *Anuario Estadístico Minero 2019.* Ministerio de Energía y Minas. https://mem.gob.gt/wp-content/uploads/2020/11/Anuario-Estad%C3%ADstico-Minero-2019-Final02.pdf.

MEM [Nicaragua]. 2014a. "Estadísticas Mineras." Ministerio de Energía y Minas, Dirección General de Minas. September 2014.

MEM [Nicaragua]. 2014b. "El Sector Minero de Nicaragua." PowerPoint presentation by Ing. Carlos Zarruk, director general de minas, Ministerio de Energía y Minas, Dirección General de Minas, at Congreso Internacional de Minería, Managua, Nicaragua, August 12, 2014. https://issuu.com/congresominero/docs/sector_minero_de_nicaragua/1.

MEM [Nicaragua]. 2015. "Estadísticas Mineras." Ministerio de Energía y Minas, Dirección General de Minas.

MEM [Nicaragua]. 2020. PowerPoint presentation, Ministerio de Energía y Minas, Dirección General de Minas.

MEM [Nicaragua]. 2021. "Principales indicadores sector minero 2007–2020." PowerPoint presentation, Ministerio de Energía y Minas, Dirección General de Minas. http://www.mem.gob.ni/wp-content/uploads/2021/02/Principales-Indicadores-Sector-Minero-2007-2020_020221.pdf.

Mesa Nacional Frente a la Minería Metálica de El Salvador. 2014. "Submission of Amicus Curiae Brief on the Merits of the Dispute." Pac Rim Cayman LLC v. Republic of El Salvador, ICSID Case No. ARB/09/12. https://www.italaw.com/sites/default/files/case-documents/italaw4195.pdf.

268 REFERENCES

Mill, John Stuart. 1843. *A System of Logic: Ratiocinative and Inductive*, vol. 1. London: John W. Parker.

Miller, Michael. J. 2006. "Biodiversity Policy Making in Costa Rica: Pursuing Indigenous and Peasant Rights." *Journal of Environment and Development* 15: 359–381.

MIPLAN [Nicaragua]. 1980. "Programa de reactivación ecónomica en beneficio del pueblo." FSLN, Ministerio de Planificación, Managua.

Miranda Aburto, Wilfredo, and Julio César Chavarría. 2014. "Policía impide que mineros protesten en Managua." *Confidencial*, August 13, 2014.

Mische, Ann. 2015. "Partisan Performance: The Relational Construction of Brazilian Youth Activist Publics." In *Social Movement Dynamics: New Perspectives on Theory and Research from Latin America*, edited by Federico M. Rossi and Marisa von Bülow, 43–72. Burlington, VT: Ashgate.

Mische, Ann. 2007. *Partisan Publics: Communication and Contention Across Brazilian Youth Activist Networks*. Princeton, NJ: Princeton University Press.

Moore, Jen, and Manuel Pérez Rocha. 2019. "Extraction Casino." Institute for Policy Studies, Washington, DC. https://ips-dc.org/wp-content/uploads/2019/07/ISDS-Mining-Latin-America-Report-Formatted-ENGLISH.pdf.

Moore, Jen, Roch Tassé, Chris Jones, and Esperanza Moreno. 2015. "In the National Interest? Criminalization of Land and Environment Defenders in the Americas: Full Discussion Paper." MiningWatch Canada and International Civil Liberties Monitoring Group, Ottawa. http://miningwatch.ca/sites/default/files/inthenationalinterest_full paper_eng_1.pdf.

Moore, Jennifer, and Teresa Velásquez. 2013. "Water for Gold: Confronting State and Corporate Mining Discourses in Azuay, Ecuador." In *Subterranean Struggles: New Dynamics of Mining, Oil, and Gas in Latin America*, edited by Anthony Bebbington and Jeffrey Bury, 119–148. Austin: University of Texas Press.

Mora Solano, Sindy. 2016. *La política de la calle: organización y autonomía en la Costa Rica contemporánea*. San José: Universidad de Costa Rica.

Moran, Robert E. 2005a. "New Country, Same Story: Review of the Glamis Gold Marlin Project EIA, Guatemala." https://remwater.org/wp-content/uploads/2015/10/Moran-Robert-E.-2005-February-New-Country-Same-Story-Review-of-the-Glamis-Gold-Marlin-Project-EIA-Guatemala.pdf.

Moran, Robert E. 2005b. "Technical Review of the El Dorado Mine Project Environmental Impact Assessment (EIA), El Salvador." https://miningwatch.ca/sites/default/files/technical_review_el_dorado_eia_0.pdf.

Moran, Theodore H. 1975. *Multinational Corporations and the Politics of Dependence: Copper in Chile*. Princeton, NJ: Princeton University Press.

Moran, Theodore H. 2011. *Foreign Direct Investment and Development: Launching a Second Generation of Policy Research*. Washington, DC: Peterson Institute for International Economics.

Moreno-Brid, Juan Carlos, and Alicia Puyana. 2016. "Mexico's New Wave of Market Reform and Its Extractive Industries." In *The Political Economy of Natural Resources and Development*, edited by Paul A. Haslam and Pablo Heidrich, 141–157. New York: Routledge.

Murillo, Rosario. 2015. "Rosario en Multinoticias. 12 de Octubre 2015." *El 19 Digital*, October 13, 2015. http://www.el19digital.com.

REFERENCES 269

Nadelman, Rachel. 2015. "'Let Us Care for Everyone's Home': The Catholic Church's Role in Keeping Gold Mining Out of El Salvador." CLALS Working Paper Series, no. 9. http://papers.ssrn.com/sol3/papers.cfm?abstract_id=2706819.

Nadelman, Rachel. 2018. "Sitting on a Gold Mine: The Origins of El Salvador's De Facto Moratorium on Metals Mining. 2004–2008." PhD thesis, School of International Service, American University.

NeJaime, Douglas. 2013. "Constitutional Change, Courts, and Social Movements." *Michigan Law Review* 111: 877–902.

Niesenbaum, Richard A., and Joseph E. B. Elliott. 2019. *In Exchange for Gold: The Legacy and Sustainability of Artisanal Gold Mining in Las Juntas de Abangares, Costa Rica.* Champaign, IL: Common Ground Research Networks.

Núñez, María José. 2010. "Harán caminata de San Carlos a San José: Lucha contra minería en Crucitas toma fuerza." *Semanario Universidad*, August 25, 2010.

Oakland Institute. 2020. "Nicaragua's Failed Revolution: The Indigenous Struggle for Saneamiento."

OAS. 2015. "Electoral Observation Mission—Guatemala. Presidential, Legislative, Municipal, and Central American Parliamentary Elections September 6 and October 25, 2015." Organization of American States. http://aceproject.org/ero-en/regions/americas/GT/guatemala-report-presidential-legislative/view.

OAS. 2017. "Preliminary Report of the Electoral Observation Mission of the Organization of American States in Nicaragua." Organization of American States. November 7, 2017. http://www.oas.org/documents/eng/press/preliminary-report-electoral-observation-mission-nicaragua-2017.pdf.

Ochoa García, Carlos Fredy. 2015. "La valoración social del diálogo y la buena fe." In *Entre las buenas y malas prácticas en la Consulta Previa-Casos de América Latina,* edited by Marco Mendoza, Thiago Almeida García, Guisela Mayén, Carlos Freddy Ochoa and Guillermo Vidalón, 109–136. Guatemala City: Konrad Adenauer Stiftung.

Odell, Scott D., Anthony Bebbington, and Karen E. Frey. 2018. "Mining and Climate Change: A Review and Framework for Analysis." *The Extractive Industries and Society* 5: 201–214.

O'Donnell, Guillermo. 2003. "Horizontal Accountability: The Legal Institutionalization of Mistrust." In *Democratic Accountability in Latin America,* edited by Scott Mainwaring and Christopher Welna, 34–54. Oxford: Oxford University Press.

O'Donnell, Guillermo, Jorge Vargas Cullell, and Osvaldo M. Lazzetta. 2004. *The Quality of Democracy.* Notre Dame, IN: University of Notre Dame Press.

OECD. 2014. *OECD Foreign Bribery Report: An Analysis of the Crime of Bribery of Foreign Public Officials.* Organisation for Economic Cooperation and Development. Geneva: OECD Publishing.

OECD. 2016. *Open Government in Costa Rica.* Organisation for Economic Cooperation and Development. Paris: OECD Publishing.

OHCHR. 2016. "Informe anual del Alto Comisionado de las Naciones Unidas para los Derechos Humanos sobre las actividades de su oficina en Guatemala." A/HRC/31/3/Add.1. Oficina del Alto Comisionado de las Naciones Unidas para los Derechos Humanos, February 19, 2016. http://www.acnur.org/t3/fileadmin/Documentos/BDL/2016/10308.pdf.

270 REFERENCES

OHCHR-Guatemala. 2014. "Maya Programme: New Paths Towards the Fulfilment of Indigenous Peoples' Rights in Guatemala." Oficina del Alto Comisionado de las Naciones Unidas para los Derechos Humanos. http://www.ohchr.org/EN/NewsEvents/Pages/MayaProgramme.aspx#sthash.KRi0zHGc.dpuf.

On Common Ground Consultants. 2010. "Human Rights Assessment of Goldcorp's Marlin Mine." Vancouver, Canada. https://ilas.sas.ac.uk/research-projects/legal-cultures-subsoil/human-rights-impact-assessment-goldcorps-marlin-mine-2010.

Ondetti, Gabriel. 2021. *Property Threats and the Politics of Anti-Statism.* New York: Cambridge University Press.

Open Society Justice Initiative. 2016. "Against the Odds: CICIG in Guatemala." https://www.opensocietyfoundations.org/sites/default/files/against-odds-cicig-guatemala-20160321.pdf.

Orantes, Patricia. 2010. "Comprendiendo el Conflicto sobre Minería en Guatemala." Instituto Regional de Altos Estudios Políticos, Guatemala City.

Orellana, Marcos A. 2011. "The Right of Access to Information and Investment Arbitration." *ICSID Review: Foreign Investment Law Journal* 26, no. 2 (Fall): 59–106.

Orellana, Marcos A., Saúl Baños, and Thierry Berger. 2015. "Bringing Community Perspectives to Investor-State Arbitration: The *Pac Rim* Case." International Institute for Environment and Development, London. https://www.iied.org/sites/default/files/pdfs/migrate/12579IIED.pdf.

Ortega, Daniel. 2010. Comments at ceremony to reopen La Libertad Gold Mine [speech]. May 11, 2010. [No longer available]. Accessed December 10, 2014. tortillaconsal.com/tortilla/es/note/5943.

Otto, James, Craig Andrews, Fred Cawood, Michael Doggett, Pietro Guj, Frank Stermole, John Stermole, and John Tilton. 2006. *Mining Royalties A Global Study of Their Impact on Investors, Government, and Civil Society.* Washington, DC: World Bank. http://documents1.worldbank.org/curated/en/103171468161636902/pdf/372580Mining0r101OFFICIAL0USE0ONLY1.pdf.

Owen, John R., Deanna Kemp, Eléonore Lèbre, Kamila Svobodova, and Gabriel Pérez Murillo. 2019. "Catastrophic Tailings Dam Failures and Disaster Risk Disclosure." *International Journal of Disaster Risk Reduction* 12 (October): 101361. https://doi.org/10.1016/j.ijdrr.2019.101361.

Özkaynak, Begüm, Beatriz Rodríguez-Labajos, and Cem Iskender Aydin. 2015. "Towards Environmental Justice Success in Mining Resistances: An Empirical Investigation." *Ejolt Report* 14 (April). http://www.ejolt.org/2015/04/towards-environmental-justice-success-mining-conflicts/.

Pac Rim Cayman. 2009. "Notice of Arbitration." *Pac Rim Cayman LLC v. Republic of El Salvador.* ICSID Case No. ARB/09/12, April 30, 2009. https://www.italaw.com/sites/default/files/case-documents/ita0591_0.pdf.

Pac Rim Cayman. 2013. "Claimant Pac Rim Cayman LLC's Memorial on the Merits and Quantum." *Pac Rim Cayman LLC v. Republic of El Salvador.* ICSID Case No. ARB/09/12, March 29, 2013. https://www.italaw.com/sites/default/files/case-documents/italaw1425.pdf.

Pac Rim Cayman. 2014a. "Claimant Pac Rim Cayman LLC's Response to the Amicus Curiae Submission Dated 25 July 2014." *Pac Rim Cayman LLC v. Republic of El Salvador.* ICSID Case No. ARB/09/12, September 2, 2014. https://www.economia.gob.sv/download/2014-09-02-claimants-response-to-amicus-curiae-c/.

REFERENCES 271

Pac Rim Cayman. 2014b. "The Republic of El Salvador's Rejoinder on the Merits." *Pac Rim Cayman LLC v. Republic of El Salvador*. ICSID Case No. ARB/09/12, July 11, 2014. https://www.italaw.com/sites/default/files/case-documents/italaw3321.pdf.

Pac Rim Cayman. 2016. "Award." *Pac Rim Cayman LLC v. Republic of El Salvador*. ICSID Case No. ARB/09/12. https://www.italaw.com/sites/default/files/case-documents/itala w7640_0.pdf.

Pacheco Cueva, Vladimir. 2017. *An Assessment of Mine Legacies and How to Prevent Them*. Cham, Switerland: Springer.

Pacheco de la Espriella, Abel. 2002. "Mensaje inaugural de toma de posesión del Presidente de la República para el período constitucional Mayo 2002—Mayo 2006." *La Nación*, May 8, 2002. http://wvw.nacion.com/ln_ee/2002/mayo/08/discursoabel.html.

Paige, Jeffrey M. 1998. *Coffee and Power: Revolution and the Rise of Democracy in Central America*. Cambridge, MA: Harvard University Press.

Pallister, Kevin. 2013. "Why No Mayan Party? Indigenous Movements and National Politics in Guatemala." *Latin American Politics and Society* 55, no. 3: 117–137.

Pallister, Kevin. 2017. *Election Administration and the Politics of Voter Access*. New York: Routledge.

Paredes Marín, Ana Eugenia. 2016. "Industria minera y represión en Guatemala. Los casos del Comité en Defensa de la Vida y la Paz de San Rafael Las Flores y La Resistencia Pacífica La Puya." M.A. thesis, Instituto Mora, Mexico.

Parsons, J. J. 1955. "Gold Mining in the Nicaragua Rain Forest." *Yearbook of the Association of Pacific Coast Geographers* 17: 49–55.

PDH. 2018. "Derecho de Consulta Previa, Libre e Informada (Borrador)." Procurador de los Derechos Humanos [Guatemala], February 20, 2018. Unpublished.

Pedersen, Alexandra. 2014. "Landscapes of Resistance: Community Opposition to Canadian Mining Operations in Guatemala." *Journal of Latin American Geography* 13, no. 1: 187–214.

Pellegrini, Lorenzo. 2018. "Imaginaries of Development Through Extraction: The 'History of Bolivian Petroleum' and the Present View of the Future." *Geoforum* 90: 130–141.

Pellegrini, Lorenzo, Murat Arsel, Marti Orta-Martínez, and Carlos F. Mena. 2020. "International Investment Agreements, Human Rights, and Environmental Justice: The Texaco/Chevron Case from the Ecuadorian Amazon." *Journal of International Economic Law* 23, no. 2: 455–468.

PEN. 2014. *Estadísticas de Centroamérica 2014*. Pavas, Costa Rica: Programa Estado Nación en Desarrollo Humano Sostenible.

PEN. 2016. *Informe Estado de la Región*. 5th edition. San José: Programa Estado Nación en Desarrollo Humano Sostenible.

PEN. 2017. *Informe Estado de la Nación*. San José: Programa Estado Nación en Desarrollo Humano Sostenible.

Pérez Baltodano, Andrés. 2012. "Democracia Electoral sin Consenso Social." *Revista de Ciencia Política* 32, no. 1 (April–May): 211–228.

Pérez González, Teresa. 2015. "Minería y Desarrollo en Nicaragua: Una Mirada Feminista del Caso de Rancho Grande." M.A. thesis, Facultad de Ciencias Sociales, Universidad Centroamericana, Nicaragua.

Pérez-Rocha, Manuel. 2016. "Free Trade's Chilling Effects." *NACLA Report on the Americas* 48, no. 3: 233–238.

Pérez Soza, Nomel. 2013. "En seis años se habrán llevado todo el oro." *Revista Envío* no. 373 (April).

272 REFERENCES

Petras, James. 1997. "Imperialism and NGOs in Latin America." *Monthly Review* 49, No. 7. http://www.monthlyreview.org/1297petr.htm.

Picado, Francisco, Alfredo Mendoza, Steven Cuadra, Gerhard Barmen, Kristina Jakobsson, and Goran Bengtsson. 2010. "Ecological, Groundwater, and Human Health Risk Assessment in a Mining Region of Nicaragua." *Risk Analysis* 30, no. 6: 916–933.

Piccio, Daniela R. 2016. "The Impact of Social Movements on Political Parties." In *The Consequences of Social Movements*, edited by Lorenzo Bosi, Marco Giugni, and Katrin Uba, 263–284. Cambridge: Cambridge University Press.

Picq, Manuela. 2016a. "'Lawfare' Against Maya Authorities in Guatemala." *Intercontinental Cry*, April 28, 2016. https://intercontinentalcry.org/lawfare-maya-authorities-guatemala/.

Picq, Manuela. 2016b. "Nim Ajpu Indigenous Lawyers Who Are Changing the Face of Guatemala." *NACLA Report on the Americas*, August 24, 2016.

Pitán, Edwin, and Glenda Sánchez. 2016. "CSJ escucha argumentos a favor y en contra de la Puya." *Prensa Libre*, May 16, 2016. http://www.prensalibre.com/guatemala/justicia/pobladores-de-la-puya-se-encaran-por-minera.

Polanyi, Karl. 2001 [1944]. *The Great Transformation: The Political and Economic Origins of Our Time*. Boston: Beacon Press.

Ponce, Aldo F., and Cynthia McClintock. 2014. "The Explosive Combination of Inefficient Local Bureaucracies and Mining Production: Evidence from Localized Societal Protests in Peru." *Latin American Politics and Society* 56, no. 3 (Fall): 118–140.

Porras, Gloria. 2021. "Guatemala's Justice System Is at a Breaking Point." *Americas Quarterly*, April 20, 2021.

Potter, Rachel Augustine. 2019. *Bending the Rules: Procedural Politicking in the Bureaucracy*. Chicago: University of Chicago Press.

Prado Ortiz, Silvio. 2020. "La autonomía municipal y la cigarra." In *Anhelos de un nuevo horizonte. Aportes para una Nicaragua democrática*, edited by Alberto Cortés Ramos, 287–302. San José: FLACSO.

Prado, Silvio, and Raquel Mejía. 2009. *CSM y CPC: Modelos participativos: rutas y retos*. Managua: Centro de Estudios y Análisis Políticos.

Pring, George W., and Penelope Canan. 1996. *SLAPPs: Getting Sued for Speaking Out*. Philadelphia: Temple University Press.

PRONicaragua. 2013. "Nicaragua: Discover the Mining Opportunities." PRONicaragua, Managua.

PRONicaragua. 2014. "Nicaragua: ¡Crezcamos Juntos!" PowerPoint presentation by Javier Chamorro, Executive Director of PRONicaragua, Congreso Internacional de Minería, Managua, Nicaragua, August 12, 2014. https://issuu.com/congresominero/docs/presentaci__n_general_de_pa__s/13.

PRONicaragua. 2018a. "Guía del inversionista 2018." PRONicaragua, Managua.

PRONicaragua. 2018b. "Nicaragua ¡Crezcamos Juntos! Let's Grow Together." PowerPoint presentation. PRONicaragua, Managua.

Przeworski, Adam, and Michael Wallerstein. 1988. "Structural Dependence of the State on Capital." *American Political Science Review* 82, no. 1 (March): 11–29. https://doi.org/10.2307/1958056.

Puig, Sergio, and Anton Strezhnev. 2017. "The David Effect and ISDS." *European Journal of International Law* 28, no. 3: 731–761.

Putnam, Robert D. 2000. *Bowling Alone: The Collapse and Revival of American Community*. New York: Simon and Schuster.

REFERENCES 273

Quesada A., Gabriel. 2010. "Nacimiento del movimiento ecologista y ALCOA." *Semanario Universidad*. May 12, 2010. https://historico.semanariouniversidad.com/opinion/nacimiento-del-movimiento-ecologista-y-alcoa/.

Rabchevsky, George A. 1994. "The Mineral Industry of Nicaragua." USGS Report. https://www.usgs.gov/centers/national-minerals-information-center/latin-america-and-canada-north-america-central-america.

Radius Gold Inc. 2012. "Radius Gold Sells Interest in Guatemala Gold Property." Cision PR Newswire, August 31, 2012. https://www.prnewswire.com/news-releases/radius-gold-sells-interest-in-guatemala-gold-property-168167006.htm.

Rasch, Elisabet Dueholm. 2012. "Transformations in Citizenship: Local Resistance Against Mining Projects in Huehuetenango (Guatemala)." *Journal of Developing Societies* 28: 159–184.

Rauda, Nelson, Andrés Dimas y Claudia Palacios. 2019. "La masacre ignorada del río Lempa." *El Faro*, December 8, 2019. https://los-olvidados.elfaro.net/inicio.

Raventós Vorst, Ciska, Marco Vinicio Fournier Facio, Diego Fernández Montero, and Ronald Alfaro Redondo. 2012. *Respuestas ciudadanas ante el malestar con la política: Salida, voz y lealtad*. San José: Instituto de Formación y Estudios en Democracia and Universidad de Costa Rica.

Recurso de Amparo. 2015. "Recurso de Amparo a la Honorable Sala Civil y Laboral del Tribunal de Apelaciones de la Circunscripción Norte." January 28. https://ia801308.us.archive.org/33/items/150128RecursoAmparoRanchoGrande/150128-Recurso-Amparo_RanchoGrande.pdf.

Redacción Diario Co Latino. 2008. "Mauricio Funes anuncia en Cabañas que no permitirá proyectos contra el medio ambiente." *Diario Co Latino*, March 11, 2008. http://izotenews.blogspot.com/2008/03/mauricio-funes-anuncia-en-cabaas-que-no.html.

Redacción UH. 2017. "Mons. Rosa Chávez indica que millonario pidió a la iglesia abortar lucha contra la minería." *Última Hora*, April 18, 2017. https://ultimahora.sv/rosa-chavez-indica-que-millonario-pidio-a-la-iglesia-abortar-lucha-contra-la-mineria/.

Reeves, Benjamin. 2014. "Guatemala's Anti-Mining La Puya Protesters Are Under Siege." Vice News, April 12, 2014. https://news.vice.com/article/guatemalas-anti-mining-la-puya-protesters-are-under-siege.

Remmer, Karen L. 2019. "Investment Treaty Arbitration in Latin America." *Latin American Research Review* 54, no. 4: 795–811.

República de Guatemala. 1985. Constitución política de 1985. https://pdba.georgetown.edu/Parties/Guate/Leyes/constitucion.pdf.

Reuters Staff. 2012. "PDAC-Canada's B2Gold Bets on Nicaragua." Reuters, March 6, 2012. https://www.reuters.com/article/canada-mining-pdac-b2gold/pdac-canadas-b2gold-bets-on-nicaragua-idUSL2E8E5BLU20120306.

Revenga, Alvaro, dir. 2005. *Sipakapa No Se Vende*. Documentary film. Producciones Caracol.

Rey Rosa, Magalí. 2018. "A Diary of Canadian Mining in Guatemala, 2004–2013." In *Human and Environmental Justice in Guatemala*, edited by Stephen Henighan and Candace Johnson, 87–117. Toronto: University of Toronto Press.

Rhode, Deborah L. 2013. *Lawyers as Leaders*. New York: Oxford University Press.

Rich, Jessica A. J., Lindsay Mayka, and Alfred P. Montero. 2019. "The Politics of Participation in Latin America: New Actors and Institutions." *Latin American Politics and Society* 61, no. 2: 1–20.

274 REFERENCES

Riofrancos, Thea N. 2020. *Resource Radicals: From Petro-Nationalism to Post-Extractivism in Ecuador*. Durham, NC: Duke University Press.

Ríos, Sergio. 2012. "CAMINIC Government-Private Sector Relations." PowerPoint presentation. Unpublished.

Robles Rivera, Francisco. 2017. "Elites en El Salvador: Cambios y Continuidades, 2000–2016." *Anuario de Estudios Centroamericanos* 43: 99–124.

Robles Rivera, Francisco. 2019. "Media Captured: Elites' Cohesion and Media Networks in Costa Rica and El Salvador." Ph.D. dissertation, Freie Universität Berlin.

Rodríguez E., Tania. 2009. "Conflictos socioambientales en zonas de frontera, los casos de Osa y Crucitas durante el año 2008." Ponencia. *Decimoquinto Informe Estado de la Nación en Desarrollo Humano Sostenible: Informe Final*. San José: PEN.

Rodríguez-Garavito, César, and Diana Rodríguez-Franco. 2015. *Radical Deprivation on Trial: The Impact of Judicial Activism on Socioeconomic Rights in the Global South*. New York: Cambridge University Press.

Rodríguez Quiroa, Luisa Fernanda. 2018. "Empresarios con poder: Al menos 58 instancias del Estado en las que las cámaras tienen voto o voz." *Plaza Pública*, January 30, 2018. https://www.plazapublica.com.gt/content/empresarios-con-poder-58-instancias-del-estado-en-las-que-las-camaras-tienen-voz-y-voto

Rogers, Chris. 2017. "Reconstituting Xinkan: Translating a Marginalized Culture on the Brink of Extinction." *Georgetown Journal of International Affairs*, September 19, 2017.

Rojas, Pablo. 2017. "Industrias Infinito pide $321 milliones a Costa Rica por fallida mina en Crucitas." *CR Hoy*, April 7, 2017. https://www.crhoy.com/nacionales/industrias-infinito-pide-321-millones-a-costa-rica-por-fallida-mina-en-crucitas/.

Rosa Chávez, Herman. 2012. "No hay condiciones para el desarrollo de la minería metálica con garantías ambientales." Interview with Gabriel Labrador Aragón. *El Faro*, August 20, 2012. https://elfaro.net/es/201208/noticias/9401/No-hay-condiciones-para-el-desarrollo-de-la-miner%C3%ADa-met%C3%A1lica-con-garant%C3%ADas-ambientales.htm.

Rosales, Antulio. 2019. "Statization and Denationalization Dynamics in Venezuela's Artisanal and Small Scale-Large-Scale Mining Interface." *Resources Policy* 63: 101422. https://doi.org/10.1016/j.resourpol.2019.101422.

Rosales-Valladares, Rotsay. 2017. "Estado del arte y enfoques metodológicos para el estudio de los partidos-movimientos, su utilidad para el estudio de un caso: El Frente Amplio de Costa Rica." https://www.ciep.ucr.ac.cr/images/InvestigacionesyProyectos/ESTADO-DEL-ARTE-Y-ENFOQUES-METODOLGICOS-PARA-EL-ESTUDIO-DE-LOS-PARTIDOS-MOVIMIENTOS.pdf.

Rosario, Joana, and Steven K. Ault. 1997. "Reducing the Environmental and Health Impacts of Mercury and Cyanide in Gold-Mining in Nicaragua." Activity Report No. 33. Prepared for the USAID Mission to Nicaragua. http://pdf.usaid.gov/pdf_docs/pnaca500.pdf.

Rosenberg, Gerald N. 1991. *The Hollow Hope: Can Courts Bring About Social Change?* Chicago: University of Chicago Press.

Rosenblatt, Fernando. 2018. *Party Vibrancy and Democracy in Latin America*. Oxford: Oxford University Press.

Rossi, Federico M. 2015. "Conceptualizing Strategy Making in a Historical and Collective Perspective." In *Social Movement Dynamics: New Perspectives on Theory and Research from Latin America*, edited by Frederico M. Rossi and Marisa von Bülow, 15–42. Burlington, VT: Ashgate.

REFERENCES 275

Rossi, Federico M. 2017. *The Poor's Struggle for Political Incorporation: The Piquetero Movement in Argentina*. Cambridge: Cambridge University Press.

Rossi, Federico M., and Marisa von Bülow, eds. 2015. *Social Movement Dynamics: New Perspectives on Theory and Research from Latin America*. Burlington, VT: Ashgate.

Saade Hazin, Miryam. 2013. "Desarrollo minero y conflictos socioambientales: Los casos de Colombia, México y el Perú." Macroeconomía del Desarrollo #137. CEPAL, Chile.

Sáenz de Tejada, Ricardo. 2017. "La crisis política de 2015: procesos, actores y repertorios de acción política." In *Transformaciones de la cultura política en Guatemala*, edited by Instituto Nacional Demócrata, 147–192. Guatemala: Serviprensa.

Sanborn, Cynthia A., Verónica Hurtado, and Tania Ramírez. 2016. "Consulta Previa in Peru: Moving Forward." Report for the Americas Society/Council of the Americas, April 20, 2016. http://www.as-coa.org/sites/default/files/2015_CP_P ERU_June_29.pdf.

Sánchez Albavera, Fernando, Georgina Ortiz, and Nicole Moussa. 2001. *Mining in Latin America in the Late 1990s*. Santiago: CEPAL.

Sánchez González, Mario. 2016. "Los Recursos en Disputa: El Caso del Conflicto Minero en Rancho Grande, Nicaragua." *Anuario de Estudios Centroamericanos* 42: 93–131.

Sánchez, Mario. 2017. *Extractivismo y lucha campesina en Rancho Grande: La expresión de un ecologismo político en Nicaragua*. Managua: Centro de Análisis Socio Cultural, UCA.

Sánchez, Mario. 2018. Rancho Grande survey. Unpublished data.

Sánchez, Mario, and Hloreley Osorio Mercado. 2020. "Abril 2018, Nicaragua: El desafío de la democracia frente al autoritarismo." In *Nicaragua 2018: La insurrección cívica de abril*, edited by Manuel Ortega Hegg, Irene Agudelo Builes, Jessica Martínez Cruz, Mario Sánchez, Hloreley Osorio Mercado, Jessica Pérez Reynosa, Sergio Ramírez, Hellen Castillo Rodríguez, Juan Pablo Gómez, and Oscar Navarrete, 73–116. Managua: UCA Publicaciones.

Sánchez-Sibony, Omar. 2016. "Guatemala's Predicament: Electoral Democracy without Political Parties." In *Guatemala: Gobierno, Gobernabilidad, Poder Local y Recursos Naturales*, edited by Gemma Sánchez Medero and Rubén Sánchez Medero, 121–150. Valencia: Tirant Humanidades.

Santos, Boaventura de Sousa, and César A. Rodríguez-Garavito. 2005. "Law, Politics, and the Subaltern in Counter-Hegemonic Globalization." In *Law and Globalization from Below: Towards a Cosmopolitan Legality*, edited by Boaventura de Sousa Santos and César A. Rodríguez-Garavito, 1–26. Cambridge: Cambridge University Press.

Sarat, Austin, and Stuart Scheingold, eds. 1998. *Cause Lawyering: Political Commitments and Professional Responsibilities*. New York: Oxford University Press.

Schedler, Andreas. 2006. *Electoral Authoritarianism: The Dynamics of Unfree Competition*. Boulder, CO: Lynne Rienner.

Schneider, Aaron. 2012. *State-Building and Tax Regimes in Central America*. New York: Cambridge University Press.

Schneider, Ben Ross. 2004. *Business Politics and the State in Twentieth-Century Latin America*. Cambridge: Cambridge University Press.

Schneider, Ben Ross. 2013. *Hierarchical Capitalism in Latin America: Business, Labor, and the Challenges of Equitable Development*. New York: Cambridge University Press.

Schneiderman, David. 2008. *Constitutionalizing Economic Globalization: Investment Rules and Democracy's Promise*. Cambridge: Cambridge University Press.

276 REFERENCES

Schwartz, Rachel A. 2021. "How Predatory Informal Rules Outlast State Reform: Evidence from Postauthoritarian Guatemala." *Latin American Politics and Society* 63, no. 1: 48–71.

Seccatore, Jacopo, Marcello Veiga, Chiara Origliasso, Tatiane Marin, and Giorgio De Tomia. 2014. "An Estimation of the Artisanal Small-scale Production of Gold in the World." *Science of the Total Environment* 496 (October 15): 662–667.

Segovia, Alexander. 2002. *Transformación estructural y reforma económica en El Salvador.* Guatemala City: F&G Editores.

Segovia, Alexander. 2005. *Integración real y grupos de poder económico en América Central.* San José: Fundación Friedrich Ebert.

Segovia, Alexander. 2019. "Las guatemaltecas, las élites centroamericanas menos dispuestas al cambio social." Interview by Enrique Naveda. *Plaza Pública*, May 7, 2019. https://www.plazapublica.com.gt/content/segovia-las-guatemaltecas-las-elites-centr oamericanas-menos-dispuestas-al-cambio-social.

Selee, Andrew, and Enrique Peruzzotti. 2009. *Participatory Innovation and Representative Democracy in Latin America.* Baltimore: Johns Hopkins University Press.

Seligson, Mitchell, and Juliana Martínez Franzoni. 2010. "Limits to Costa Rica Heterodoxy: What Has Changed in 'Paradise'?" In *Democratic Governance in Latin America,* edited by Scott Mainwaring and Timothy R. Scully, 307–337. Stanford, CA: Stanford University Press.

Sequeira-León, Yasica, Inti Luna-Avilés, and Jorge Huete-Pérez. 2011. "Mercury Pollution in La Libertad, a Gold Mining Town in Central Nicaragua. Uncontrolled Mining. Economic Crisis, and Climate Effects—A Dangerous Mixture." *Epidemiology* 22, 1 Abstracts (January supp.): 291–292.

Shapiro, Judith and John-Andrew McNeish. 2021. *Our Extractive Age: Expressions of Violence and Resistance.* London: Routledge.

Shrake, Thomas C. 2010. "Witness Statement of Thomas C. Shrake." *Pac Rim Cayman LLC v. Republic of El Salvador*, December 2, 2010. ICSID Case No. ARB/09/12. https://www.italaw.com/sites/default/files/case-documents/ita0605.pdf.

Sibrián, Anabella, and Chris van der Borgh. 2014. "La Criminalidad de los Derechos: La Resistencia a la Mina Marlin." *Oñati Socio-Legal Series* 4, no. 1: 63–84.

Sieder, Rachel. 2007. "The Judiciary and Indigenous Rights in Guatemala." *International Journal of Constitutional Law* 5, no. 2: 211–241.

Sieder, Rachel. 2010. "Legal Cultures and the (Un)Rule of Law: Indigenous Rights and Juridification in Guatemala." In *Cultures of Legality,* edited by Javier A. Couso, Alexandra Huneeus, and Rachel Sieder, 161–181. Cambridge: Cambridge University Press.

Sieder, Rachel. 2011. "Contested Sovereignties: Indigenous Law, Violence and State Effects in Postwar Guatemala." *Critique of Anthropology* 31, no. 3: 161–184.

Sieder, Rachel. 2016. "Indigenous Peoples' Rights and the Law in Latin America." In *Handbook of Indigenous People's Rights,* edited by Corinne Lennox and Damien Short, 414–423. New York: Routledge.

Sieder, Rachel, Line Schjolden, and Alan Angell. 2005. *The Judicialization of Politics in Latin America.* New York: Palgrave Macmillan.

Silva, Eduardo. 2003. "Selling Sustainable Development and Shortchanging Social Ecology in Costa Rican Forest Policy." *Latin American Politics and Society* 45, no. 3: 93–127.

Silva, Eduardo. 2009. *Challenging Neoliberalism in Latin America.* Cambridge: Cambridge University Press.

REFERENCES 277

Silva, Eduardo. 2013. *Transnational Activism and National Movements in Latin America: Bridging the Divide*. New York: Routledge.

Silva, Eduardo. 2017. "Pushing the Envelope? Mega-Projects, Contentious Action, and Change." Research Group Mega Working Paper No. 1. https://stonecenter.tulane.edu/uploads/RGM_Working_Paper_1b-1502998235.pdf.

Silva, Eduardo, and Federico Rossi. 2018. *Reshaping the Political Arena in Latin America: From Resisting Neoliberalism to the Second Incorporation*. Pittsburgh: University of Pittsburgh Press.

Silva, Eduardo, Maria Akchurin, and Anthony Bebbington. 2018. "Policy Effects of Resistance Against Mega-Projects in Latin America: An Introduction." Special Collection: Mega-Projects, Contentious Action, and Policy Change in Latin America. *European Review of Latin American and Caribbean Studies* 106 (July–December): 25–46. http://doi.org/10.32992/erlacs.10397.

Silva, José Adán, and Luis E. Martínez. 2013. "Rancho Grande contra minería." *La Prensa*, March 23, 2013.

Simmons, Erica S. 2016. *Meaningful Resistance: Market Reform and the Roots of Social Protest in Latin America*. New York: Cambridge University Press.

Slack, Keith. 2009. "Digging Out from Neoliberalism: Responses to Environmental (Mis)governance of the Mining Sector in Latin America." In *Beyond Neoliberalism in Latin America?*, edited by John Burdick, Philip Oxhorn, and Kenneth M. Roberts, 117–134. New York: Palgrave Macmillan.

Slater, Dan, and Daniel Ziblatt. 2013. "The Enduring Indispensability of the Controlled Comparison." *Comparative Political Studies* 46, no. 10: 1301–1327.

Smith-Nonini, Sandy. 2010. *Healing the Body Politic: El Salvador's Popular Struggle for Health Rights from the Civil War to Neoliberal Peace*. New Brunswick, NJ: Rutgers University Press.

Snow, David A., and Robert D. Benford. 1992. "Master Frames and Cycles of Protest." In *Frontiers in Social Movement Theory*, edited by Aldon Morris and Carol McClurg Mueller, 133–155. New Haven. CT: Yale University Press.

Solano, Luis. 2013. "Development and/as Dispossession: Elite Networks and Extractive Industry in the Franja Transversal del Norte." In *War by Other Means: Aftermath in Post-Genocide Guatemala*, edited by Carlota McAllister and Diane M. Nelson, 119–142. Durham, NC: Duke University Press.

Solano, Luis. 2015. "Under Siege: Peaceful Resistance to Tahoe Resources and Militarization in Guatemala." https://miningwatch.ca/sites/default/files/solano-under seigereport2015-11-10.pdf.

Solís Miranda, Regina, ed. 2016. *La Fuerza de Las Plazas: Bitácora de la Indignación Ciudadana en 2015*. Guatemala City: Friedrich-Ebert Stiftung FED.

Sosa, Tania. 2015. "Rancho Grande, una herencia natural y productiva amenazada por la minería." Centro Humboldt, Managua.

Soto, Gerardo J. 2011. "Metal Mining in Central America (Early 1500s–Late 1800s)." In *History of Research in Mineral Resources*, edited by José Eugenio Ortiz, Octavio Puche, Isabel Rábano, and Luis F. Mazadiego, 89–97. Madrid: Instituto Geológico y Minero de España.

Soto, Yokebec. 2013. "La verdad a cielo abierto: Más de 20 años de historia de la mina Crucitas." San José, Costa Rica.

Soule, Sarah A., and Brayden G. King. 2006. "The Stages of the Policy Process and the Equal Rights Amendment, 1972–1982." *American Journal of Sociology* 111, no. 6: 1871–1909.

278 REFERENCES

Spalding, Rose J., ed. 1987. *The Political Economy of Revolutionary Nicaragua.* Boston: Allen & Unwin.

Spalding, Rose J. 1994. *Capitalists and Revolution in Nicaragua, Opposition and Accommodation.* Chapel Hill: University of North Carolina Press.

Spalding, Rose J. 2013. "Transnational Networks and National Action: El Salvador's Antimining Movement." In *Transnational Activism and National Movements in Latin America: Bridging the Divide,* edited by Eduardo Silva, 23–55. New York: Routledge.

Spalding, Rose J. 2014. *Contesting Trade in Central America: Market Reform and Resistance.* Austin: University of Texas Press.

Spalding, Rose J. 2015. "Domestic Loops and Deleveraging Hooks: Transnational Social Movements and the Politics of Scale Shift." In *Social Movement Dynamics: New Perspectives on Theory and Research from Latin America,* edited by Federico M. Rossi and Marisa Von Bülow, 181–214. Burlington, VT: Ashgate.

Spalding, Rose J. 2017. "Los empresarios y el Estado posrevolucionario: El reordenamiento de las élites y la nueva estrategia de colaboración en Nicaragua." *Anuario de Estudios Centroamericanos* 43: 149–188.

Spalding, Rose J. 2018. "From the Streets to the Chamber: Social Movements and the Mining Ban in El Salvador." *European Review of Latin American and Caribbean Studies* 106 (July–December): 47–74. https://doi.org/10.32992/erlacs.10377.

Spalding, Rose J. 2022. "FPIC and Megaprojects: Community Consultation and Megaproject Development in Guatemala." Paper presented at the XL International Congress of the Latin American Studies Association, May 5–8.

Spalding, Rose J. 2023. "Network Approaches to Latin American Social Movements." In *The Oxford Handbook of Latin American Social Movements,* edited by Federico M. Rossi, 85–104. New York: Oxford University Press.

Sprenkels, Ralph. 2018. *After Insurgency: Revolution and Electoral Politics in El Salvador.* Notre Dame: University of Notre Dame Press.

Stahler-Sholk, Richard, Harry E. Vanden, and Marc Becker, eds. 2014. *Rethinking Latin American Social Movements: Radical Action from Below.* Lanham, MD: Rowman and Littlefield.

Stedman, Ashley, and Kenneth P. Green. 2019. "Fraser Institute Annual Survey of Mining Companies 2018." https://www.fraserinstitute.org/sites/default/files/annual-survey-of-mining-companies-2018.pdf.

Stein, Ernesto, et al. 2006. *The Politics of Policies.* Washington, DC: Inter-American Development Bank and David Rockefeller Center for Latin American Studies, Harvard University.

Steiner, Richard. 2010. "El Salvador—Gold, Guns, and Choice." Report for the International Union for the Conservation of Nature and the Commission on Environmental, Economic and Social Policy. https://miningwatch.ca/sites/default/files/gold_guns_and_choice-el_salvador_report_0.pdf.

Stuart Almendárez, Roberto. 2010. "Consejos del poder ciudadano y gestión pública en Nicaragua." Centro de Estudios y Análisis Políticos, Managua.

Studnicki-Gizbert, Daviken. 2017. "Exhausting the Sierra Madre: Mining Ecologies in Mexico over the Longue Durée." In *Mining North America: An Environmental History Since 1522,* edited by J. R. McNeill and George Vrtis, 19–46. Berkeley: University of California Press.

Svampa, Maristella. 2019. *Neo-Extractivism in Latin America.* Cambridge: Cambridge University Press.

Sveinsdottir, Anna G., Mariel Aguilar-Støen, and Benedicte Bull. 2021. "Resistance, Repression and Elite Dynamics: Unpacking Violence in the Guatemalan Mining Sector." *Geoforum* 118: 117–129. https://doi.org/10.1016/j.geoforum.2020.12.011.

Tahoe Resources. 2013. "Guatemalan President Visit to Minera San Rafael Signals Support for Escobal Project." *Nosotros: Our Community*, July 12, 2013.

Tarrow, Sidney. 2005. *The New Transnational Activism*. Cambridge: Cambridge University Press.

Tarrow, Sidney. 2011. *Power in Movement: Social Movements and Contentious Politics*. 3rd edition. New York: Cambridge University Press.

TAU. 2011. "Servicios de consultoría para la Evaluación Ambiental Estratégica (EAE) del sector minero metálico de El Salvador: Informe final." No. CPI-02/AECIA/2010. TAU Consultora Ambiental. https://ilas.sas.ac.uk/sites/default/files/reports/EAE_minero_metalico_informe%20final%20OIR%20MARN-2021-00106.pdf.

Taylor, Verta. 1989. "Social Movement Continuity: The Women's Movement in Abeyance." *American Sociological Review* 54, no. 5: 761–775. https://doi.org/10.2307/2117752.

TCA [Costa Rica]. 2010. Sentencia No. 4399-2010, Expediente No. 08-001282-1027-CA, December 14, 2010. Tribunal Contencioso Administrativo, Costa Rica. https://nexu spj.poder-judicial.go.cr/document/sen-1-0034-552000.

Temper, Leah, Federico Demaria, Arnim Scheidel, Daniela Del Bene, and Joan Martínez Alier. 2018. "The Global Environmental Justice Atlas (EJATLAS): Ecological Distribution Conflicts as Force for Sustainability." *Sustainability Science* 13: 573–584.

Tico Times. 2016. "Canadian Mining Company Reorganizes to Seek Damages from Costa Rica." *Tico Times*, January 21, 2016. https://ticotimes.net/2016/01/21/canadian-min ing-company-reorganizes-seek-damages-costa-rica.

Tienhaara, Kyla. 2011. "Regulatory Chill and the Threat of Arbitration: A View from Political Science." In *Evolution in Investment Treaty Law and Arbitration*, edited by Chester Brown and Kate Miles, 606–628. Cambridge: Cambridge University Press.

Tolvanen, Anneli. 2001. "Interviews in La Libertad and Bonanza, Nicaragua." http://mini ngwatch.ca/sites/default/files/Nicaragua_interviews.pdf.

Tolvanen, Anneli. 2003. "The Legacy of Greenstone Resources in Nicaragua." http://mini ngwatch.ca/sites/default/files/Nicaragua_studies_0.pdf.

Torres Wong, Marcela. 2019. *Natural Resources, Extraction and Indigenous Rights in Latin America: Exploring the Boundaries of State Corporate Crime in Bolivia, Peru and Mexico*. London: Routledge.

Tzul Tzul, Gladys. 2018. *Gobierno comunal indígena y estado guatemalteco*. Guatemala: Instituto Amaq.

UCCAEP. 2011. "Informe de Labores." Unión Costarricense de Cámaras y Asociaciones del Sector Empresarial Privado. https://www.uccaep.or.cr/images/content/informe-de-labores/2010-2011.pdf.

UNCTAD. 2011. *Investment Policy Review: Guatemala*. United Nations Conference on Trade and Development. New York and Geneva: United Nations. https://unctad.org/system/files/official-document/diaepcb201009_en.pdf.

UNCTAD. 2016. *World Investment Report 2016*. United Nations Conference on Trade and Development. http://unctad.org/en/PublicationsLibrary/wir2016_en.pdf.

UNEP. 2017. Minamata Convention on Mercury. United Nations Environment Programme. https://www.unep.org/resources/report/minamata-convention-mercury.

Ungar, Mark. 2017. "Prosecuting Environmental Crime: Latin America's Policy Innovation." *Latin American Policy* 8, no. 1: 63–92.

280 REFERENCES

United Nations General Assembly. 2007. United Nations Declaration on the Rights of Indigenous Peoples (UNDRIP). https://www.un.org/esa/socdev/unpfii/documents/DRIPS_en.pdf.

Urkidi, Leire, and Mariana Walter. 2011. "Dimensions of Environmental Justice in Anti-Gold Mining Movements in Latin America." *Geoforum* 42: 683–695.

USGS. Various years. *Minerals Yearbook Volume III: Area Reports—International—Latin America and Canada.* [Database.] Washington, DC: US Department of the Interior and US Geological Survey. https://www.usgs.gov/centers/nmic/latin-america-and-canada-north-america-central-america-and-caribbean.

Valdez, José Fernando. 2015. *El gobierno de las élites globales: Cómo se organiza el consentimiento, la experiencia del triángulo norte.* Guatemala City: Universidad Rafael Landívar, Editorial Cara Parens.

Van Cott, Donna Lee. 2005. *From Movement to Parties in Latin America.* New York: Cambridge University Press.

Van de Sandt, Joris. 2009. "Mining Conflicts and Indigenous Peoples in Guatemala." Cordaid, The Hague. https://www.cordaid.org/nl/wp-content/uploads/sites/2/2012/12/Mining_Conflicts_and_Indigenous_Peoples_in_Guatemala.pdf.

Van den Hombergh, H. G. M. 2004. *No Stone Unturned: Building Blocks of Environmentalist Power versus Transnational Industrial Forestry in Costa Rica.* Amsterdam: Dutch University Press.

Van Harten, Gus. 2013. *Sovereign Choices and Sovereign Constraints: Judicial Restraint in Investment Treaty Arbitration.* Oxford: Oxford University Press.

Vanden, Harry E., and Gary Prevost. 1993. *Democracy and Socialism in Sandinista Nicaragua.* Boulder, CO: Lynne Rienner.

Vanhala, Lisa. 2011. *Making Rights a Reality? Disability Rights Activists and Legal Mobilization.* Cambridge: Cambridge University Press.

Vargas, José P. Mauricio, and Santiago Garriga. 2015. "Explaining Inequality and Poverty Reduction in Bolivia." IMF Working Paper, WP/15/265. https://www.imf.org/external/pubs/ft/wp/2015/wp15265.pdf.

Veiga, Marcello M., Gustavo Angeloci, Michael Hitch, and Patricio Colón Velásquez-López. 2014. "Processing Centres in Artisanal Gold Mining." *Journal of Cleaner Production* 64: 535–544.

Veiga, Marcello, and Henrique Morais. 2015. "Backgrounder: Artisanal and Small-Scale Mining (ASM) in Developing Countries." Canadian International Resources and Development Institute. https://static1.squarespace.com/static/5bb24d3c9b8fe8421e87bbb6/t/5c2a832988251b499681df64/1546289962450/CIRDI-ASM-Backgrounder_2015Apr10.pdf.

Velásquez Nimatuj, Irmalicia. 2013. "'A Dignified Community Where We Can Live': Violence, Law, and Debt in Nueva Cajola's Struggle for Land." In *War by Other Means,* edited by Carlota McAllister and Diane M. Nelson, 170–191. Durham, NC: Duke University Press.

Veltmeyer, Henry, and James Petras. 2014. *The New Extractivism: A Post-Neoliberal Development Model or Imperialism of the Twenty-First Century?* London: Zed.

Vernon, Raymond. 1971. *Sovereignty at Bay.* New York: Basic Books.

Viales Hurtado, Ronny J., and Juan José Marín Hernández. 2012. "Los conflictos ecológico-distributivos en Puntarenas: El caso de la Mina Bellavista de Miramar. Una aproximación inicial." *Diálogos: Revista Electrónica de Historia,* October, 243–286.

REFERENCES   281

Vidal, Juan Héctor. 2010. *De la ilusión al desencanto: Reforma económica en El Salvador, 1989–2009*. San Salvador: Universidad Tecnológica de El Salvador.

Vieyra, Juan Cruz, and Malaika Masson. 2014. *Transparent Governance in an Age of Abundance: Experiences from the Extractive Industries in Latin America and the Caribbean*. Washington, DC: Inter-American Development Bank.

Viterna, Jocelyn S. 2015. "Women's Mobilization into the Salvadoran Guerrilla Army." In *The Social Movement Reader: Cases and Concepts*, edited by Jeff Goodwin and James M. Jasper, 83–100. 3rd edition. West Sussex, UK: Wiley Blackwell.

Vogt, Manuel. 2015. "The Disarticulated Movement: Barriers to Maya Mobilization in Post-Conflict Guatemala." *Latin American Politics and Society* 57, no. 1: 29–50.

Vogt, Manuel. 2019. *Mobilization and Conflict in Multiethnic States*. Oxford: Oxford University Press.

Voss, Marianne, and Emily Greenspan. 2012. "Community Consent Index: Oil, Gas and Mining Company Public Positions on Free, Prior, and Informed Consent (FPIC)." Oxfam America Research Backgrounder. https://s3.amazonaws.com/oxfam-us/www/static/oa4/community-consent-index.pdf.

Walker-Said, Charlotte, and John D. Kelly, eds. 2015. *Corporate Social Responsibility? Human Rights in the New Global Economy*. Chicago: University of Chicago Press.

Wall, Elizabeth. 2015. "Working Together: How Large-Scale Mining Can Engage with Artisanal and Small-Scale Miners." International Council on Mining and Metals, IFC CommDev, and Communities and Small-Scale Mining Program. https://www.commdev.org/wp-content/uploads/pdf/publications/Working-together-How-large-scale-mining-can-engage-with-artisanal-and-small-scale-miners.pdf.

Walter, Mariana, and Leire Urkidi. 2016. "Community Consultation: Local Response to Large-scale Mining in Latin America." In *Environmental Governance in Latin America*, edited by Fábio de Castro, Barbara Hogenboom, and Michiel Baud, 287–325. New York: Palgrave Macmillan.

Walters, Jonah. 2019. "The Sandinista Labor Paradox." *NACLA Report on the Americas*, September 16.

Wampler, Brian, and Leonardo Avritzer. 2005. "The Spread of Participatory Budgeting in Brazil: From Radical Democracy to Participatory Good Government." *Journal of Latin American Urban Studies* 17: 737–752.

Warnaars, Ximena S. 2013. "Territorial Transformations in El Pangui, Ecuador: Understanding How Mining Conflict Affects Territorial Dynamics, Social Mobilization, and Daily Life." In *Subterranean Struggle: New Dynamics of Mining, Oil, and Gas in Latin America*, edited by Anthony Bebbington and Jeffrey Bury, 149–171. Austin: University of Texas Press.

WOLA. 2019. "Fact Sheet: The CICIG's Legacy in Fighting Corruption in Guatemala." Commentary. Washington Office on Latin America.

WOLA. 2021. "International Organizations Demand End to Criminalization of Justice Officials and Human Rights Defenders in Guatemala." Joint Statement, June 8, 2021. Washington Office on Latin America.

Willis, Eliza, and Janet Seiz. 2012. "The CAFTA Conflict and Costa Rica's Democracy: Assessing the 2007 Referendum." *Latin American Politics and Society* 54, no. 3: 123–156.

Wilske, Stephan, and Martin Raible. 2009. "The Arbitrator as Guardian of International Public Policy? Should Arbitrators Go Beyond Solving Legal Issues?" In *The Future of*

Investment Arbitration, edited by Catherine A. Rogers and Roger P. Alford, 249–272. New York: Oxford University Press.

Wilson, Bruce M. 2011. "Enforcing Rights and Exercising an Accountability Function: Costa Rica's Constitutional Chamber of the Supreme Court." In *Courts in Latin America,* edited by Gretchen Helmke and Julio Ríos-Figueroa, 55–80. Cambridge: Cambridge University Press.

Wilson, Bruce M., and Camila Gianella-Malca. 2019. "Overcoming the Limits of Legal Opportunity Structures: LGBT Rights' Divergent Paths in Costa Rica and Colombia." *Latin American Politics and Society* 61, no. 2 (May): 138–163.

Wilson, Bruce M., and Juan Carlos Rodríguez-Cordero. 2006. "Legal Opportunity Structures and Social Movements: The Effects of Institutional Change on Costa Rican Politics." *Comparative Political Studies* 39, no. 3: 325–351.

Wo Ching, Eugenia. 2014. "Costa Rica: The First Latin American Country Free of Open-Pit Gold Mining." In *The Earth Charter, Ecological Integrity and Social Movements,* edited by Laura Westra and Miriam Vilela, 216–229. New York: Routledge.

World Bank. 1996. "A Mining Strategy for Latin America and the Caribbean." World Bank Technical Paper No. 345. Washington, DC: World Bank. http://documents1.worldb ank.org/curated/en/650841468087551845/pdf/multi0page.pdf.

World Bank. 2007. "Implementation Completion and Results Report." Report No. ICR0000342. http://documents.worldbank.org/curated/en/851141468053331757/ pdf/ICR0000342.pdf.

World Bank. 2008. "An Evaluation of Bank Support for Decentralization in Client Countries." IEG Fast Track Brief. Washington, DC: World Bank. https://openknowle dge.worldbank.org/handle/10986/10595.

World Bank. 2009. *Mining Together: Large-Scale Mining Meets Artisanal Mining, A Guide for Action.* Washington, DC: World Bank. https://openknowledge.worldbank.org/han dle/10986/12458.

World Bank Group. 2015. *Indigenous Latin America in the 21st Century.* Washington, DC: World Bank Group. https://openknowledge.worldbank.org/bitstream/handle/ 10986/23751/Indigenous0Lat0y000the0first0decade.pdf?sequence=1&isAllowed=y.

Wright, Michael. 2018. "Yes or No in I-186: 20 Years After Cyanide Ban, Will Voters Approve Another Measure Strengthening Mining Regulations?" *Bozeman Daily Chronicle,* September 23, 2018. https://www.bozemandailychronicle.com/news/envi ronment/yes-or-no-on-i—years-after-cyanide-ban/article_390dec0d-5025-51ef-b58e-22f3fa16183e.html.

Wyss, Jim, and Kyra Gurney. 2018. "Dirty Gold Is the New Cocaine in Colombia—and It's Just as Bloody." *Miami Herald,* January 23, 2018 [updated version]. http://www. miamiherald.com/news/nation-world/world/americas/colombia/article194188 034.html.

Xiloj Cuin, Lucía Inés. 2016. "Sistematización del proceso de implementación del derecho a la consulta a los pueblos indígenas establecido en el Convenio 169 de la Organización Internacional del Trabajo (OIT) en Guatemala." Oxfam, Guatemala City. https://www. plazapublica.com.gt/sites/default/files/oxfam_sistematizacion_1.pdf.

Yagenova, Simona Violetta, ed. 2012. *La industria extractiva en Guatemala: Políticas públicas, derechos humanos, y procesos de resistencia popular en el período 2003–2011.* Guatemala: FLACSO.

Yagenova, Simona. 2014. *La Mina El Tambor Progreso VII derivada y la Resistencia de la Puya.* Guatemala City: MadreSelva.

Yagenova, Simona. 2016. "Guatemala: El Estado y procesos de resistencia popular frente a la industria extractiva 2003–2013." In *Política minera y sociedad civil en América Latina*, edited by Paúl Cisneros, 95–146. Quito: Instituto de Altos Estudios Nacionales.

Yagenova, Simona, José Cruz, Jorge Grijalva, Julio González, Ana González, and Gerardo Paiz. 2015. "Cuatro casos de gestión de seguridad ambiental y humana." Cordaid and Aso-Seprodi, Guatemala City.

Yashar, Deborah J. 2018. *Homicidal Ecologies: Illicit Economies and Complicit States in Latin America*. Cambridge: Cambridge University Press.

Zaremberg, Gisela, and Marcela Torres Wong. 2018. "Participation on the Edge: Prior Consultation and Extractivism in Latin America." *Journal of Politics in Latin America* 10, no. 3: 29–58.

Zechmeister, Elizabeth J., and Dinorah Azpuru. 2017. "What Does the Public Report on Corruption, the CICIG, the Public Ministry, and the Constitutional Court in Guatemala?" Latin American Public Opinion Project, Topical Brief #29. https://www.vanderbilt.edu/lapop/insights/ITB029en.pdf.

Zimmerer, Karl S. 2011. "'Conservation Booms' with Agricultural Growth? Sustainability and Shifting Environmental Governance in Latin America, 1985–2008 (Mexico, Costa Rica, Brazil, Peru, Bolivia)." *Latin American Research Review* 46 (Special Issue): 82–114.

Selected Databases

AmericasBarometer. https://www.vanderbilt.edu/lapop/

Compliance Advisor Ombudsman for the IFC. http://www.cao-ombudsman.org/cases/

EJATLAS, Global Atlas of Environmental Justice. https://ejatlas.org/

ISCID cases. https://icsid.worldbank.org/cases

IFC projects. https://disclosures.ifc.org/#/landing

OCMAL Database of Mining Conflicts. https://mapa.conflictosmineros.net/ocmal_db-v2/

UNCTAD Investment Dispute Settlement Navigator. https://investmentpolicy.unctad.org/investment-dispute-settlement

World DataBank, Worldwide Governance Indicators. http://databank.worldbank.org/data/reports.aspx?source=worldwide-governance-indicators

Index

For the benefit of digital users, indexed terms that span two pages (e.g., 52–53) may, on occasion, appear on only one of those pages.

Tables and figures are indicated by *t* and *f* following the page number

Abers, Rebecca Neaera, 56
abeyance structures, 159, 188
Academia de Centroamérica (Costa Rica), 145–46
accountability mechanisms, 66–67
accumulation by dispossession, 92–93
acquired rights, 176
acronyms, list of, xiii–xvii
ADDAC (Asociación para la Diversificación y Desarrollo Agrícola Comunal, Nicaragua), 84
ADES (Social and Economic Development Association, El Salvador), 191, 199
Administrative Chamber of the Supreme Court (Sala I, Costa Rica), 167–68, 169, 233–34
Administrative Litigation Tribunal (Tribunal Contencioso Administrativo, TCA, Costa Rica), 167–69, 234–35
adverse governmental actions, 16
AECO (Asociación Ecologista de Costa Rica), 149
Agreement for the Promotion and Protection of Investments. *See* Canada-Costa Rica Agreement for the Promotion and Protection of Investment
agriculture, mining conflicts in productive agricultural zones, 19–20
ALCOA (Aluminum Company of America), 150–51
Aldana, Thelma, 132–33
Alemán, Arnoldo, 65, 72–73, 94
Alianza País (Ecuador), 53
Almeida, Paul, 7, 38–39, 45, 188, 198
Álvarez Lagos, Rolando José, 86, 87–88

Amenta, Edwin, 3–4, 26–27, 213
American Chambers of Commerce (AmChams), 47
amicus curiae (friend of the court) briefs, 230–32, 234–35, 239
amparo (injunction), 167, 233–34
Anderson, Leslie E., 94
ANEP (National Association of Private Enterprise, El Salvador), 182, 201, 206
APREFLOFAS (Asociación Preservacionista de Flora y Fauna Silvestre, Costa Rica), 149, 150*f*, 168, 170n.29, 234–35
Araya, Edgardo, 158, 160n.15, 168, 171n.31
Araya, Marco Tulio, 162
Arbenz, Jacobo, 111n.4
arbitration. *See* investor-state dispute settlement cases
Arce, Moisés, 4, 41–42, 52, 82, 84–85
ARENA. *See* Nationalist Republican Alliance
Arévalo, Juan José, 111n.4
Argentina
  ISDS cases against, 226
  mining bans, 22, 242
  mining conflicts, 7
  natural resource rents, 8, 9*f*
Arias, Óscar
  CAFTA, actions on, 156–57
  Chinchilla and, 172–73
  Crucitas mine and, 156
  Infinito Gold mining license, approval of, 235
  legal actions against, 168, 169
  mine development under, 153

286 INDEX

Arias, Óscar (cont.)
mining, actions on, 156–58, 160
mining, support for, 50–51
"national interest" declaration, 50–51,
153, 158, 160, 173n.34, 221–22,
233–34
open pit mining, association with, 173n.34
arsenic and mining, 123–24
artisanal and small-scale mining (ASM)
in brownfield sites, 44
child labor in, 90–91
coligalleros, 176
in Costa Rica, 174, 176
economic and environmental issues
with, 42–44, 88, 90
in El Salvador, 210
guiriseros, 89
impact of large-scale mining on, 92–93
lack of sufficient research on, 81
in Nicaragua, 88–91
regulatory control of, 20
See also scale conflicts
Arzú, Álvaro, 108, 113
Asamblea Legislativa (National Assembly,
El Salvador), mining ban, actions on,
207–8, 210–12
ASIES (Asociación de Investigación
y Estudios Sociales, Research
and Social Studies Association,
Guatemala), 116
ASM. See artisanal and small-scale mining
Asociación Ecologista de Costa Rica
(AECO), 149
Asociación para la Diversificación y
Desarrollo Agrícola Comunal
(ADDAC, Nicaragua), 84
Asociación Preservacionista de Flora
y Fauna Silvestre (APREFLOFAS,
Costa Rica), 149, 150f, 168, 170n.29,
234–35
Astorga, Allan, 160–61
Astorga, Yamileth, 160–61
Attractiveness Index (Fraser Institute),
9–10
authoritarian populism, 127–28
autoconsultas (good faith community
consultations, consultas comunitarias
de buena fe), 120–21

autoconvocados (self-convened), 97
Ávila, Rodrigo, 198
Ayau, Manuel, 112–13

Baldetti, Roxana, 134–35
bans
in Argentina, 22, 242
in Costa Rica, 22, 25, 221–22, 242
in Czech Republic, 22
de facto and temporary (provisional
bans), 23–24
discussion of, 22–26
in Ecuador, 24
in El Salvador, 22–23, 25, 142, 180, 208,
242
as focus of reform proposals, 15–16
in Germany, 22
in Honduras, 24
legal challenges to, 23
of national scope, legal and permanent
(full bans), 25–26
in Philippines, 22, 242
territorial (partial bans), 24–25
in United States, 22, 242
See also investor-state dispute
settlement cases (ISDS)
barren regions, mining conflicts in,
19–20
Barrera, Hugo, 200–1
Bebbington, Anthony, 5–6, 16, 48
Bellavista mining project, 151, 155, 161
Berger, Óscar, 50–51, 113, 118–19, 132
Best Practices Mineral Potential Index
(Fraser Institute), 9–10
bilateral investment treaties (BITs), 154–55,
156, 223–24, 234
Biodiversity Law (1998, Costa Rica),
146–48
bishops, on mining
in Costa Rica, 152
in El Salvador, 196–97, 206n.22
in Guatemala, 79–80, 123, 125
in Honduras, 79–80
in Nicaragua, 80, 86, 87–88
statement from 2007 meeting, 79–80
BITs (bilateral investment treaties), 154–55,
156, 223–24, 234
Bolaños, Enrique, 46–47, 65, 73–75, 84

INDEX   287

Bolivia
  ASMs in, 42–43
  cash transfers for social programs, 14
  Hydrocarbons Law #3058 (2005), 14
  ICSID, withdrawal from, 225
  ISDS cases against, 226
  Mining Law #3787 (2007), 14
  natural resource rents, 8, 9f
  resource nationalism, 14
  Supreme Decree #28701 (2006), 14
  top-down community consultations, 59
  water wars, 38–39
Bonanza mine (Nicaragua)
  artisanal and small-scale mining in,
    88–89, 89f
  contra attacks on, 70
  discussion of, 64
  HEMCO and distributive conflicts over, 83
  local capital investment in, 71
  unions, lack of, 83
bonding-based networks, 39, 40, 189–90
boomerang effect, 188–89
bottom-up consultation processes, 58
Brazil
  ASMs in, 42–43
  Brumadinho disaster, 6–7
  business associations, 47–48
  electricity projects, number of conflicts
    over, 15
  mining conflicts, 7
  natural resource rents, 8, 9f
Brenes, Leopoldo, 80
Breuer, Anita, 57
bridging-based networks, 39–40, 189–90
brownfield sites, 44
Brumadinho disaster (Brazil), 6–7
B2Gold, 50, 83, 84
buffer zones (zonas de amortiguamiento),
  78–79
Bull, Benedicte, 184–85
bureaucracies and bureaucratic politics
  in Costa Rica, docking and, 55–57, 143
  in Costa Rica, support for mining, 176–77
  docking and, 32, 54, 55–57, 60
  in El Salvador, docking and, 199–202
  importance of, 20
  in policymaking cycle, 55–56
  revolving door and, 55–56

  scientific activism and, 199–202
  in United States, 55n.9
Bury, Jeffrey, 5–6
business associations
  in Costa Rica, 221–22
  in El Salvador, 182, 206
  in Guatemala, 104–5, 114, 220–21
  impact of perceived class-based threats
    to, 111
  in Nicaragua, 174–75, 219–20
  See also ANEP; CACIF; CAMINIC;
    CIG; COSEP; Gremial de Industrias
    Extractivas; UCCAEP
business (economic) elites
  in Costa Rica, 221–22
  discussion of, 46–48
  in El Salvador, 181–82, 204–5, 206, 214, 222
  in Guatemala, 110–16, 220–21
  in Nicaragua, 74–75, 219–20
  possible divisions among, 51
business policy research centers
  Academia de Centroamérica (Costa
    Rica), 145–46
  Fundación Nicaragüense para el
    Desarrollo Económico y Social
    (FUNIDES, Nicaragua), 81–82, 90
  Fundación para el Desarrollo de
    Guatemala (Guatemalan Development
    Foundation, FUNDESA), 115
  Salvadoran Social and Economic
    Development Foundation
    (FUSADES), 46–47, 184–85

Cabañas, El Salvador
  assassination of anti-mining leaders
    in, 180
  Funes in, 198
  mining resistance in, 192
  Pacific Rim's proposed mine in, 187–88
Cabrera Ovalle, Julio Edgar, 123n.21
CACIF (Comité Coordinador de
    Asociaciones Agrícolas, Comerciales,
    Industriales y Financieras, Coordinating
    Committee of Agricultural,
    Commercial, Industrial, and Financial
    Associations, Guatemala), 110–12,
    113–14, 115, 135–36, 137
  See also FUNDESA

288   INDEX

CAFTA (Central American Free Trade
    Agreement), 57, 156–58, 198
    See also DR-CAFTA
CALAS (Centro de Acción Legal-
    Ambiental y Social, Environmental
    and Social Legal Action Center,
    Guatemala), 130–31, 135, 237
Calderón Sol, Armando, 181–82, 185
Calibre Mining Corp., 64–65, 87–88
Cámara Minera de Nicaragua (Nicaraguan
    Mining Chamber, CAMINIC),
    49–50, 75, 96–97, 98
Cameron, Maxwell A., 127–28
caminatas (marches), 162
Caminata Verde en Defensa del Agua
    (Green Walk in Defense of Water), 192
CAMINIC (Cámara Minera de Nicaragua,
    Nicaraguan Mining Chamber),
    49–50, 75, 96–97, 98
Canada-Costa Rica Agreement for
    the Promotion and Protection of
    Investment, 154–55, 156, 234
Canadian Centre for International Justice,
    132
CAO (Compliance Advisor Ombudsman,
    World Bank), 12, 123–24
Cáritas El Salvador, 195–96, 196*f*
Castillo Armas, Carlos, 111
Castro, Xiomara, 24
Catholic Church, views and actions on
    mining
    in Costa Rica, 160
    Diocesan Committee in Defense of
        Nature, 125
    in El Salvador, 51, 195–97, 209–10, 213,
        214, 222–23
    in Guatemala, 123, 125
    Laudato Si' encyclical, 79–80
    in Nicaragua, 78, 80, 85, 86
    resistance movements, participation
        in, 195
    See also bishops, on mining
cause lawyers, 167
CCR (Refugee and Repopulated
    Communities Coordinator, El
    Salvador), 191
CEDES (Episcopal Conference of El
    Salvador), 196–97
CEICOM (Investment and Trade Research
    Center, El Salvador), 193

Cementos Progreso (Guatemala), 114–15
CENIDH (Centro Nicaragüense de los
    Derechos Humanos), 86, 96
Center for International Environmental
    Law (CIEL), 132, 193–94, 230–31
Central America
    gold output by country and year, 110*f*
    mining conflicts in, 7
Central American Free Trade Agreement
    (CAFTA), 57, 156–58, 198
    See also DR-CAFTA
Centro de Acción Legal-Ambiental y Social
    (CALAS, Environmental and Social
    Legal Action Center, Guatemala),
    130–31, 135, 237
Centro Humboldt (Humboldt Center),
    78–79, 79n.16, 86
Centro Nicaragüense de los Derechos
    Humanos (CENIDH), 86, 96
Cerro Blanco mining project, 109–10
Chacón, Karen, 166
Chamber of Industry (CIG, Guatemala),
    49–50, 113
Chamorro, Violeta, 65, 70–71
change, proposals for. *See* reform
    alternatives and proposals for change
chemical extraction processes, toxicity of,
    40–41
children
    child labor, 90–91
    as participants in local consultations,
        120–21
Chile
    business associations in, 47–48
    factors shaping mining sector
        development, 220
    mining conflicts in, 7
    natural resource rents in, 8, 9*f*
Chinchilla, Laura, 1, 153, 163, 172–74, 233–34
Christian Democrat (PDC, El Salvador),
    210–11
CICIG (International Commission
    Against Impunity in Guatemala),
    54–55, 132–33, 134–35
CID-Gallup national survey on open pit
    mining (Costa Rica), 163
    See also public opinion: on mining
CIEL (Center for International
    Environmental Law), 132, 193–94,
    230–31

CIG (Chamber of Industry, Guatemala), 49–50, 113
CINDE (Costa Rican Investment Promotion Agency), 145
Citizen Action Party (PAC, Costa Rica), 163, 171–72
Citizen Participation Law (#475, 2003, Nicaragua), 94
Citizens Power Councils (CPCs, Nicaragua), 94–95
Ciudad Quesada, Costa Rica, proposed open pit mine in, 152
Coates, Maurice Eugene, 151–52
Código Municipal de Guatemala (Municipal Code, 2002, Guatemala), 121
COECE-CIEBA (Costa Rica), 149n.5
coexistence conflicts (*conflictos de convivencia*), 41
coligalleros. See artisanal and small-scale mining (ASM)
Colom, Álvaro, 134, 236
Colombia
  ASMs in, 42–43
  Constitutional Court, 25
  courts and docking in, 54–55
  ISDS cases against, 226
  mining conflicts, 7
  natural resource rents, 8, 9f
  possible policy volatility, 221
  territorial prohibitions, recommendations for, 24–25n.22
colonial era, extractivism during, 106
COMEX (Ministry of Foreign Trade, Costa Rica), 145
Comisión Municipal de Minería Artesanal Bonanza, 90–91
Comité Coordinador de Asociaciones Agrícolas, Comerciales, Industriales y Financieras (CACIF, Coordinating Committee of Agricultural, Commercial, Industrial, and Financial Associations, Guatemala), 110–12, 113–14, 115, 135–36, 137
Committee in Defense of Life and Peace (Guatemala), 125
commodities consensus, 14
community consultation
  autoconvocado (self-convened), 97
  in Costa Rica, lack of, 155

docking and, 57–60
in El Salvador, 203–4
good faith community consultations (*consultas comunitarias de buena fe*), 120–21
in Guatemala, demands for, 120–22
in Guatemala, lack of, 108
of indigenous populations, 59–60
limitations on, 12
in Nicaragua, lack of, 100
question of validity of, 21
right to, 21
territorial bans and, 25
top-down and bottom-up processes, 58–59
See also direct participation; free, prior, and informed consent processes; ILO; indigenous peoples and communities; municipal codes
compensation contests, 18–19
Compliance Advisor Ombudsman (CAO, World Bank), 12, 123–24
Concertación Económica y Social (Nicaragua), 70–71
concertación processes, 71n.7
Conde, Marta, 119
Condor Gold, scale conflicts and, 91–92
conflictos de convivencia (coexistence conflicts), 41
conflictos de resistencia (resistance conflicts), 41
Consejo de Pueblos de Occidente (CPO, People's Council of the Western Highlands, Guatemala), 121–22, 131
Consejo Superior de la Empresa Privada (COSEP, Nicaragua), 74–75, 76–77
consent processes, free, prior, and informed, 20–21, 58, 135, 138–39
See also community consultation
Constitutional Chamber of the Supreme Court (Sala IV, Costa Rica), 154n.10, 165–66, 169
Constitutional Court (Ecuador), 242
Constitutional Court (Guatemala), 132n.31, 135, 136–37, 138, 237
consulta process, 121–22, 203–4
consultas comunitarias de buena fe (good faith community consultations, *autoconsultas*), 120–21
controlled comparison methodology, 27

290 INDEX

Convention on Biodiversity, 146–48
Coordinating Committee of Agricultural, Commercial, Industrial, and Financial Associations (Comité Coordinador de Asociaciones Agrícolas, Comerciales, Industriales y Financieras, CACIF, Guatemala), 110–12, 113–14, 115, 135–36, 137
COPAE (Pastoral Commission for Peace and Ecology), 123
Copeland, Nicholas, 127–28
Corporaciones Nacionales del Sector Público (CORNAP, Nicaragua), 71
corporate social responsibility (CRS), 10, 11–13, 239–40
Correa, Rafael, 24, 50–51
corruption and bribery charges, 18, 134–35
COSEP (Consejo Superior de la Empresa Privada, Nicaragua), 74–75, 76–77
Costa Rica (in general), 142–77
acronym list, xiii–xiv
cited interviews, list of, 178t
corporate pressure and government vacillation, 153–56
decentralized anti-mining mobilization, 95–96, 116–17, 159–63
docking, two-track, 164–74
introduction to, 142–45
judicialized environmentalism, 164–69
market reform and environmental initiatives, 145–51
mining sector debates, 151–58
overview of, 31, 32
post-extractivism challenges, 174–77
social movement organizing and environmental activism, 149–51
summary of factors shaping mining sector development, 220t, 221–22
Costa Rica (details)
bureaucracies and docking, 56
Canada-Costa Rica Agreement for the Promotion and Protection of Investment, 154–55, 156, 234
courts and docking, 54–55
elite fracture and recombination, 62
El Salvador, comparison with, 27–28, 143–44

forest cover, 149t, 233–34
gold and silver export value in 1913, 68–69
gold output (2004–2016), 110f
Infinito Gold Ltd. v. the Republic of Costa Rica, 233–36
investment dispute claim against, 227–28
investment disputes, impact of threats of, 241
legislature, composition of, 178t
mining bans, 22, 25, 172–74, 221–22, 242
mining policy timeline, 147t
National Assembly vote on mining, 1
natural resource rents, 8, 9f
open pit mining ban (2010), 1, 142, 170–74
political leaders, 142, 153–54, 175, 221–22
public opinion on mining, 35t, 36
referenda, 57
resistant authorization and prohibition of mining development, 222
rule of law, 130t
structural adjustment by, 145, 152
tourism, 152–53, 174–75, 176
wildlife protection legislation, 57
See also cause lawyers; Sala I; Sala IV
Costa Rican Investment Promotion Agency (CINDE), 145
Council of the Xinka People of Guatemala, 131
courts and judicial systems
cause lawyers, 167
in Costa Rica, 175–76, 222
in Costa Rica, Administrative Litigation Tribunal (Tribunal Contencioso Administrativo, TCA), 167–69
in Costa Rica, judicialized environmentalism, 164–69
in Costa Rica, Sala I (Administrative Chamber of the Supreme Court), 167–68, 169, 233–34
in Costa Rica, Sala IV (Constitutional Chamber of the Supreme Court), 154n.10, 165–66, 169
in Costa Rica, use of, 144–45, 155, 158, 164–69, 170–74

INDEX 291

denuncias (legal claims), 166
docking and, 54–55
in El Salvador, 204
in Guatemala, Constitutional Court, 132n.31, 135, 136–37, 138, 221
in Guatemala, court cases and mining cases, 133–35
in Guatemala, judicial docking, 136–37
in Guatemala, judicial institutions and processes, 129–35, 221
in Guatemala, resistance movements' use of, 127, 128
in Guatemala, Supreme Court of Justice, 132n.31, 134, 135
judicial independence, 132–33, 165–66
legal opportunity structure, 54–55
legal rights infrastructure, 130–33
in Nicaragua, 95, 100
strategic litigation, 54–55, 105, 128, 165–69
See also law; rule of law
CPCs (Citizens Power Councils, Nicaragua), 94–95
CPO (Consejo de Pueblos de Occidente, People's Council of the Western Highlands, Guatemala), 121–22, 131
criminalization
of mining protesters, 50–51
of protests in Guatemala, 117–18, 119, 128
CRIPDES (Rural Communities Association for Salvadoran Development), 191, 193, 203–4
Cristiani, Alfredo, 181–82
CRS (corporate social responsibility), 10, 11–13, 239–40
Crucitas mining project (Costa Rica)
actions against, 162, 166
arbitration process for, 234–35
conflicts over, 155–57
initial stages of, 151–52
investigation of, 160
"national interest" proclamation for, 50–51, 153, 158, 160, 173n.34, 221–22, 233–34
permit cancellation, 153
See also Industrias Infinito S.A.

CSJ (Sala Constitucional de la Corte Suprema de Justicia, Nicaragua), 95
Cuenca, Ecuador, mining prohibitions in, 241
Custer, Teodoro, 85
Cutris, Costa Rica, anti-mining organizing in, 150–51
Czech Republic, mining bans in, 22

Daniel W. Kappes and Kappes, Cassiday & Associates v. Republic of Guatemala, 236–39
Dashwood, Hevina S., 13
Da Sousa, Mariana Magaldi, 165n.20
decentralization
of Costa Rican anti-mining campaign, 159–63
decentralization initiatives, 57
decentralization laws in Guatemala, 121
in El Salvador, 203–4
local referenda, 95–96, 100, 221
in Nicaragua under Bolaños, 94
Decreto #30477-MINAE (2002, Costa Rica), 154
Decreto #34801-MINAET (2008, Costa Rica), 158
De Echave, José, 41, 42
de facto and temporary prohibitions (provisional bans), 23–24
Defenders of the Yaoska River (Guardianes de Yaoska, Nicaragua), 85–86
Defensoría de los Habitantes (Costa Rica), 160
Defensoría del Pueblo (Peru), 7n.10
definitional conflicts, 42, 66, 81, 84–88, 100, 116, 138
deforestation, 148
della Porta, Donatella, 39
democratic systems, docking points in, 66–67
denuncias (legal claims), 166
derecho de picaporte (right to knock and be received), 113
DGM (Dirección General de Minas, Nicaragua), 76
Diani, Mario, 39

292 INDEX

dictamen (finding), 173
Dietz, Kristina, 58
Diocesan Committee in Defense of Nature (CODIDENA, Guatemala), 125
Dirección General de Minas (DGM, Nicaragua), 76
direct participation
  direct democracy, in El Salvador, 202–3
  local referenda, 95–96, 100, 221
  participatory budgeting, 57
  public comment, 12, 29–30, 199–200, 213–14
  public hearings, 10–11, 85
  See also community consultation
distributive conflicts, 18, 42, 66, 81–83, 100
docking and docking points
  bureaucracies and, 55–57
  community consultation and, 57–60
  in Costa Rica, 175–76, 222
  definition and description of, 30–31, 37–38, 51–52
  direct participation and, 57
  domains comprising opportunities for, 52
  elections and, 56
  in El Salvador, 183–84, 197–204, 215, 222–23
  in Guatemala, 104, 105, 127–37, 221
  importance of, 143
  institutional engagement and, 54–57
  ISDS processes' impact on, 240, 242
  local governments and, 57–58
  in Nicaragua, 66–67, 93–98, 100, 101
  policy deliberation and, 51–60
  political parties and, 53–54
  See also community consultation; courts; decentralization; elites and elite cohesion; social resistance movements
Dominican Republic, public opinions on mining, 35t, 36
DR-CAFTA (Dominican Republic Central American Free Trade Agreement), 185, 229, 230, 236, 237–38
  See also CAFTA

earth movement, in mining, 6–7
Eckstein, Susan, 188

ecodependents, 15
ecoentrepreneurs, 15
ecoimperialists, 15
economic elites. *See* business elites
ecoresisters, 15
ecotourism, in Costa Rica, 152–53
Ecuador
  ASMs in, 42–43
  environmental actors, clusters of, 15
  ICSID, withdrawal from, 225
  ISDS cases against, 226
  Mining Mandate (2008), 24
  natural resource rents, 8, 9f
  possible policy volatility, 221
  temporary mining bans, 24
EIAs. *See* environmental impact assessments
Eisenstadt, Todd A., 38–39, 59–60
EJOLT (Environmental Justice Organizations, Liabilities and Trade) database, 34–35
El Dorado mine project (El Salvador), 12, 180, 186–87
  See also Pacific Rim
El Escobal silver mine (Guatemala), 109–10
elites and elite cohesion
  in Costa Rica, 142–43, 152–53, 174–75, 221–22
  in Costa Rica, political elites, 154, 175
  discussion of, 45–51
  elite fragmentation, 35–49, 62, 181–82, 204–5
  elite power, sources of, 184–85
  elites, definition of, 45–46
  in El Salvador, 62, 181–82, 184–88, 204–7, 212–13
  in Guatemala, 104–5, 114, 135–36, 138, 220–21
  importance of, 26–27, 37
  ISDS processes' impact on, 240, 241
  mining and, 49–51
  in Nicaragua, 65–66, 99–100
  overview of, 37
  See also docking and docking points; social resistance movements
El Limón mine (Nicaragua), 64–65, 71, 81–83

El Pavón mine (Rancho Grande, Nicaragua), 50, 84–88, 96–97
El Salvador (in general), 180–215
  acronym list, xiv–xv
  bureaucracies and scientific activism, 199–202
  cited interviews, list of, 216t
  direct democracy and community consultation, 202–4
  discussion and conclusions on, 212–15
  docking points and policy impacts, 197–204
  elite fracture in, 62, 204–7
  elite positions on mining, 184–88
  Gold Belt, local-level organizing in, 190–92
  introduction to, 180–84
  legislature, composition of, 216t
  mining ban, adoption of formal, 207–12
  mining opposition network, 188–97
  mining policy timeline, 186t
  overview of, 31, 32
  political parties and elections, 198–99
  summary of factors shaping mining sector development, 220t, 222–23
El Salvador (details)
  anti-mining movement, 95–96, 116–17
  bureaucracies and docking, 56
  civil war, refugee camps during, 190–91
  Costa Rica, comparison with, 27–28, 143–44
  El Dorado mine project, limitations on community comments on, 12
  extended moratorium and mining ban, 222–23
  Foreign Investment Law (1999), 185
  forest cover, 149t
  gold and silver export value during revolutionary period, 68–69
  gold output (2004–2016), 110f
  investment dispute claim against, 180–81, 183–84, 208, 227–28
  investment disputes, impact of threats of, 240–41
  Investment Law (1999), 229, 230
  local-level plebiscites, 96–97
  Mesa Nacional Frente a la Minería Metálica, 182–83, 190–97, 198–99

Metallic Mining Prohibition Law (2017), 187–88
mining bans, 22–23, 25, 142, 180, 208, 242
Mining Law, revisions to, 185–86
moratorium, de facto, 201, 207, 227–28
Municipal Code (2005), 203
natural resource rents, 8, 9f
Nicaragua, comparison with, 27–28
Nicaraguan organizers' visit to, 96–97
Pac Rim Cayman LLC v. Republic of El Salvador, 180–81, 208, 214, 228–32
political leaders, 182, 185, 198, 202, 209, 211, 213
precious metal production, 106
public opinion on mining, 35t, 36
royalty rates, 72–73
rule of law, 130t
See also Pacific Rim
El Tambor gold mining project, 236
El Tambor zone, Guatemala, 124
Empresa Nicaragüense de Minas (ENIMINAS), 77–78
"En búsqueda de nuevos horizontes para una Nicaragua mejor" (Conferencia Episcopal de Nicaragua), 80
environment
  environmental activism in Costa Rica, 166
  environmental controls, 19–20
  environmental destruction, 38–39
  environmental harms, association with ASM, 43
  environmentalism of the poor, 15
  environmentalisms, 15
  environmental legislation in Guatemala, 115
  environmental organizations in Costa Rican civil society, 149–50
  environmental protections in Costa Rica, 146
  environmental sustainability, shifts in corporate attitudes toward, 13
  judicialized environmentalism in Costa Rica, 164–69
  judicialized environmentalism in Guatemala, 133–35
  See also environmental impact assessments

294 INDEX

Environmental and Social Legal Action Center (Centro de Acción Legal-Ambiental y Social, CALAS, Guatemala), 130–31, 135, 237
environmental impact assessments (EIAs)
in Costa Rica, 167, 168–69
critical reviews of, 119–20
demand for, 19
for El Dorado Mine (El Salvador), 199–200
IFC recommendations on, 11
limitations on community comments on, 12
for Marlin Mine (Guatemala), 133–34
in Nicaragua, 72–73
for Progreso VII Derivada (Guatemala), 119–20
Environmental Justice Organizations, Liabilities and Trade (EJOLT) database, 34–35
Environmental Ministry (El Salvador), 183–84
Episcopal Conference of El Salvador (CEDES), 196–97
Ernst and Young, 12n.15
Escobal mine (Guatemala), 125–26, 133n.32, 135, 136, 137
Escobar Alas, José Luis, 197, 210
Espinoza, Pablo, 86
Executive Order 79 (Philippines), 22
Executive Order 13851 (US), 98n.35
Exploraciones Mineras de Guatemala (EXMINGUA), 109–10
extraction and extractivism, 6–7, 106–16
extractive sector conflict, traditional focus of research on, 34

FA (Frente Amplio, Costa Rica), 171–72
Fairfield, Tasha, 46n.5, 74
family capitalism, 46
Farabundo Martí National Liberation Front (FMLN, El Salvador)
attitudes toward mining, summary of, 222
civil war refugees' association with, 190–91
docking points and, 183–84
elites and, 181–82
Funes and, 180

link with social movements, 198
local-level resistance and, 192
mining, opposition to, 204–5, 213–14
on mining ban, 210–11
as movement-based political party, 53
Federación Costarricense para la Conservación del Ambiente (FECON, Costa Rica), 149–50
FESPAD (Foundation for the Study of the Application of Law, El Salvador), 193
Flores, Francisco, 181–82, 185–86
FMLN. See Farabundo Martí National Liberation Front
Foreign Investment Law (1993, Mexico), 10–11
Foreign Investment Law (1999, El Salvador), 185
Foreign Investment Promotion Law #344 (2000, Nicaragua), 72–73
Forest Law (1996, Costa Rica), 148, 157–58, 158n.14
Foundation for the Study of the Application of Law (FESPAD, El Salvador), 193
FPIC (free, prior, and informed consent) processes, 20–21, 58, 135, 138–39
frame alignment (in resistance movement analysis), 37, 189–90
framework summary, factors leading to divergent outcomes, 61t
Francis, Pope, 79–80
Fraser Institute, 9–10
free, prior, and informed consent (FPIC) processes, 20–21, 58, 135, 138–39
free trade agreements (FTAs)
CAFTA, 57, 156–58, 198
See also DR-CAFTA
dispute settlement clauses, 223–24
DR-CAFTA, 185, 229, 230, 236, 237–38
See also CAFTA
NAFTA, 10–11
Frente Amplio (FA, Costa Rica), 171–72
Frente Norte Contra la Minería (Costa Rica), 162
Frente Sandinista de Liberación Nacional (FSLN, Sandinista National Liberation Front, Nicaragua), 67, 68–69, 70, 87, 99

INDEX 295

friend of the court (amicus curiae) briefs,
230–32, 234–35, 239
FTAs. *See* free trade agreements
Fundación Nicaragüense para el
Desarrollo Económico y Social
(FUNIDES, Nicaragua), 81–82, 90
Fundación para el Desarrollo de
Guatemala (Guatemalan
Development Foundation,
FUNDESA), 115
FUNDESA (Fundación para el Desarrollo
de Guatemala, Guatemalan
Development Foundation), 115
Funes, Mauricio, 180, 181–82, 198–99,
202, 228–32
FUSADES (Salvadoran Social
and Economic Development
Foundation), 46–47, 184–85

Gallegos, Guillermo, 210
Gamboa, Bernal, 168
GANA (Grand Alliance for National
Unity, El Salvador), 210–11
Garay, Candelaria, 74
García, Alan, 50–51
Germany, mining bans in, 22
Gesellschaft für Internationale
Zusammenarbeit (GTZ), 72
Giammattei, Alejandro, 113, 139
Giugni, Marco, 3, 26–27, 213
Glamis Gold, 109
Glazer, Charles T., 229
Global Magnitsky Human Rights
Accountability Act, 98n.35
gold and gold mining
ASMs in production of, 42–43
in Costa Rica, protests against, 150–51
in El Salvador, history, 185n.4
in Guatemala, history, 106
importance, 5
mercury use in gold mining, 43, 43n.4,
72, 88, 89, 89*f*
in Nicaragua, history, 64, 68–70
output by country and year, 110*f*
Gold Belt (El Salvador), local-level
organizing in, 190–92
Goldcorp, 109, 123–24
González, Díaz, 162–63n.18

good faith community consultations
(*consultas comunitarias de buena fe,
autoconsultas*), 120–21
Goodland, Robert, 24–25n.22
Governmental Accord 499-2007
(Guatemala), 50–51
Gran Canal project (Nicaragua), 59
Grand Alliance for National Unity
(GANA, El Salvador), 210–11
green criminology, 20
green mining, 160–61, 205
Greenstone Resources, 71
Green Walk in Defense of Water
(Caminata Verde en Defensa del
Agua), 192
Gremial de Industrias Extractivas
(GREMIEXT, Union of Extractive
Industries, Guatemala), 49–50, 113
Grupo Estratégico contra la Minería
(Strategic Group Against Mining,
Matagalpa, Nicaragua), 86
GTZ (Gesellschaft für Internationale
Zusammenarbeit), 72
Guardianes de Yaoska (Defenders of the
Yaoska River, Nicaragua), 85–86
Guatemala (in general), 104–39
acronym list, xv–xvi
business elites, organization and
advocacy, 110–16
court cases and mining conflicts,
133–35
elite support and extractivist
ascendance in, 106–16
introduction to, 104–6
judicial institutions and processes,
129–35
legal rights infrastructure, building of,
130–33
mining outcomes, 135–39
mining policy timeline, 107*t*
mining sector development, summary
of factors shaping, 220–21, 220*t*
overview of, 31–32
resistance in, 116–27
resistance strategies and tactics, 118–22
Guatemala (details)
anti-mining activists, 183
anti-mining mobilization, 95–96

296 INDEX

Guatemala (details) (*cont.*)
  business associations, 47–48
  cited interviews, list of, 140*t*
  constitution (1985), on mining, 106–8
  Daniel W. Kappes and Kappes,
    Cassiday & Associates v. Republic of
    Guatemala, 236–39
  docking in, 127–35
  elites, 220–21
  forest cover, 149*t*
  gold output (2004–2016), 110*f*
  Guatemalan Revolution, 111
  Guatemala Spring, 134–35
  intermittent approval model for mining
    development, 221
  international investment dispute claim
    against, 227–28
  investment disputes, impact of threats
    of, 241
  local-level plebiscites, 96–97
  Marlin mine, limitations on community
    comments on, 12
  mining conflicts, 7
  Mining Law (1997), 108–9, 133, 135–36
  mining promotion, 62
  natural resource rents, 8, 9*f*
  peace accord, 108
  politics, 127–28
  public opinions on mining, 35*t*, 36
  royalty rates, 72–73
  strategic litigation, 127
  tax revenues, CACIF and, 111–12
  See also community consultation; El
    Escobal silver mine; Marlin Mine;
    Progreso VII Derivada open pit mine
Guatemala City, Guatemala, protests in,
    134–35
Guatemalan Chamber of Industry (CIG),
    113
Guatemalan Development Foundation
    (Fundación para el Desarrollo de
    Guatemala, FUNDESA), 115
Guatemalan Human Rights Commission
    (GHRC), 132
guiriseros. See artisanal and small-scale
    mining
Gunther, Richard, 45
Gustafsson, Maria-Therese, 13

hablar sin hablar (speak without saying),
    192
Hanagan, Michael, 171
Harper, Stephen, 169
Harvey, David, 92–93
Haslam, Paul Alexander, 15, 84–85, 224n.2
Heaney, Michael T., 159
HEMCO mining company (Hunt
    Exploration and Mining Company),
    64, 71, 83, 88–89
Higley, John, 45
Hinds, Manuel, 187
Hochstetler, Kathryn, 15
Honduras
  anti-mining activists, 183
  extractivism, 106
  forest cover, 149*t*
  natural resource rents, 8, 9*f*
  public opinions on mining, 35*t*, 36
  temporary bans, 24
Humboldt Center (Centro Humboldt),
    78–79, 79n.16, 86
hunger strikes, 162
hungry mines, 87–88
Hunt, Bunker, 71
Hunt Exploration and Mining Company
    (HEMCO mining company), 64, 71,
    83, 88–89
Hurricane Mitch, 72

IACHR (Inter-American Commission on
    Human Rights), 55, 97, 133–34, 236
IACtHR (Inter-American Court for
    Human Rights), 55
Ibarra, Ángel, 207n.25
ICMM (International Council on Mining
    and Metals), 42–43
ICSID. *See* International Centre for the
    Settlement of Investment Disputes
IFC (International Finance Corporation,
    World Bank), 11–12, 42–43, 91, 109
ILO 169 (Indigenous and Tribal Peoples
    Convention), 21, 25, 94–95, 108,
    120–21, 237
IMF (International Monetary Fund), 145,
    148
indigenous peoples and communities
    buen vivir principle, 15

INDEX   297

community consultation in, 59–60
consultation rights for, 58
in El Salvador, 202–3
in Guatemala, 221
in Guatemala, anti-mining movement
and, 117–18, 134
in Guatemala, consultations with, 108,
109, 120, 121–22, 237–39
in Guatemala, destruction of, 106
Maya, in Guatemala, 106, 117, 121–22,
131
Xinka people, in Guatemala, 131, 135
See also ILO 169
Indio Maíz Biological Reserve, 97
indirect expropriation (regulatory taking),
223–24
Industrias Infinito S.A. (Infinito Gold)
Arias and, 50–51, 157–58
EIA from, 155, 233
extraction permit, application for, 151–52
international investment dispute claim
by, 176, 227–28, 233–36
legal injunctions against, 166–67
PR campaign in Costa Rica, 50
Sala IV, use of, 166
See also Crucitas mining project
influential allies, description of, 49
informal restrictions, as provisional bans,
23
INGOs (international nongovernmental
organizations), 189, 193–94
INMINE (Instituto Nicaragüense de la
Minería), 68–69
institutional actors, access to. See docking
and docking points
institutions
docking points in, importance of, 62–63
institutional activism, 56
institutional development in
Guatemala, 105
institutional engagement, docking and,
54–57
public environmental institutions in
Costa Rica, 146–48
See also bureaucracies; business
associations; courts and judicial
systems; decentralization; docking
and docking points

Instituto Nicaragüense de la Minería
(INMINE), 68–69
Instituto Universitario de Opinión Pública
(IUDOP), 204
Inter-American Commission on Human
Rights (IACHR), 55, 97, 133–34, 236
Inter-American Court for Human Rights
(IACtHR), 55
intermittent approval framework, 104,
105–6, 139
See also Guatemala
International Allies (El Salvador), 194
international arbitration. See International
Centre for the Settlement of
Investment Disputes (ICSID)
International Centre for the Settlement of
Investment Disputes (ICSID)
Daniel W. Kappes and Kappes,
Cassiday & Associates v. Republic of
Guatemala, 236–39
discussion of, 225–26
Infinito Gold Ltd. v. the Republic of Costa
Rica, 156, 233–36
mining companies' use of, 240
NAFTA ratification and, 10–11
Pac Rim Cayman LLC v. Republic of El
Salvador, 180–81, 208, 214, 228–32
See also investor-state dispute
settlement cases
International Commission Against
Impunity in Guatemala (CICIG),
54–55, 132–33, 134–35
International Council on Mining and
Metals (ICMM), 42–43
International Finance Corporation (IFC,
World Bank), 11–12, 42–43, 91, 109
international investment regimes, 223–27
International Monetary Fund (IMF), 145,
148
international nongovernmental
organizations (INGOs), 189, 193–94
international trade agreements, dispute
settlement clauses, 223–24
Invest in Guatemala, 115
Investment and Trade Research Center
(CEICOM, El Salvador), 193
investment decisions, factors affecting,
9–10

298 INDEX

Investment Law (1999, El Salvador), 185, 229, 230
investment rules regime, 224
investor-state dispute settlement cases (ISDS)
in Central American mining conflicts, 227–39
Daniel W. Kappes and Kappes, Cassiday & Associates v. Republic of Guatemala, 236–39
discussion of, 224–27
impacts of, 240–42
Infinito Gold Ltd. v. the Republic of Costa Rica, 233–36
Pac Rim Cayman LLC v. Republic of El Salvador, 180–81, 208, 214, 228–32
See also International Centre for the Settlement of Investment Disputes
Isla, Ana, 151
IUDOP (Instituto Universitario de Opinión Pública), 204

Jalapa, Guatemala, plebiscite in, 125
joint effects process, 3–4
judicial systems. See courts and judicial systems
junior mining companies, 5–6, 11–12, 71, 91
Justice and Corporate Accountability Project (Canada), 126, 132
justice-oriented activists, judicial institutions and, 54
Justicia, Paz e Integridad de la Creación de los Franciscanos (JPIC, Franciscan Justice, Peace and Creation Integrity), 195–96

Kapiszewski, Diana, 127
Kappes, Cassiday & Associates (KCA), 227–28, 236–39
Kappes, Daniel, 227–28
Keith, Minor Cooper, 143n.1
Kirsch, Stuart, 218
Kolb, Felix, 170

labor, flexibilization of, 10
See also unions
LAC (Latin America and Caribbean) countries, ISDS and, 226

La Cruz de la India, Nicaragua, scale conflicts in, 88–93
La India. See La Cruz de la India
La Libertad mine (Nicaragua), 1, 64–65, 71, 80
La Línea tax evasion scheme, 134–35
land reclamation, funding for, 18–19
Lanzas, Lorena, 87
La Puya (activist group, Guatemala), 124–25, 236, 237, 239
large-scale mining (LSM), traditional focus on, 42–43
Las Crucitas mining project (Costa Rica). See Crucitas mining project
Lasky's law, 6–7
lateral transnationalism, 183
Latin America, 218–43
business organizations, 47
commodities consensus, 5
differing attitudes toward mining in, 1–2, 10
environmentalism in, 15
environmental reforms, rollbacks of, 215
factors impacting mining in, 6
family capitalism in, 46
final reflections and conclusions, 239–43
foreign direct investment (FDI) in mining in, 5–6
international investment regimes, 223–27
introduction to, 218–19
investor-state dispute settlement cases, 227–39
mining policy in, 4
mining properties, number of conflicts over, 15
model, restatement of, 219–23
natural resource rents, 8, 9f
overview of, 32–33
presidents' support for extractive sector expansion, 50–51
Latin America and Caribbean (LAC) countries, ISDS and, 226
law
cause lawyers, 167
friend of the court (amicus curiae) briefs, 230–32, 234–35, 239
Guatemala, strategic litigation in, 127
legal challenges to mining bans, 23

legal claims (*denuncias*), 166
legal opportunity structures, 54–55
legal rights infrastructure, 130–33
litigation as anti-mining tool, 166
rule of law, 54–55, 129–30, 130*t*
soft law adaptations, 11–13
See also courts and judicial systems
Law on Monetary Integration (2001, El Salvador), 185
Le Billon, Philippe, 59
Levitsky, Steven, 127
Lewis, Tammy L., 15
Ley de los Consejos de Desarrollo Urbano y Rural (2002, Guatemala), 121
Ley General de Decentralización (2002, Guatemala), 121
linkages, formed by social resistance movements, 39–40
Lizano, Eduardo, 145–46
Llamado Urgente (Urgent Call, Costa Rica), 160
Lobo Segura, Jorge, 160–61, 168
local governments, in Rancho Grande conflict, 87
local populations, recognition and voice of, 20–22
See also community consultation
Los Encuentros, Guatemala, roadblocks in, 118
LSM (large-scale mining), traditional focus on, 42–43
Lula da Silva, Luiz Inácio, 56
Lyon Lake Mines, 151–52

Macri, Mauricio, 46–47
Madre de Díos, Peru, ASM mining in, 43–44
MadreSelva (environmental activist association, Guatemala), 123, 125, 130–31, 193
Maegli Novella, Rodrigo Carlos, 114n.10
Maldonado, Pedro Rafael, 134
Malouf Morales, Roberto Antonio, 113
Mannix, Ronald, 169
marches (*caminatas*), 162
MARENA (Ministerio del Ambiente y los Recursos Naturales, Nicaragua), 72–73
Maritimes-Breaking the Silence (BTS, Canada), 132

Marlin Mine (Guatemala), 109, 119–20, 122–24, 133n.32, 135–36
MARN (Ministerio de Medio Ambiente y Recursos Naturales, Ministry of the Environment and Natural Resources, El Salvador), 187–88, 199–200, 229
MARN (Ministerio de Medio Ambiente y Recursos Naturales, Ministry of the Environment and Natural Resources, Guatemala), 115–16, 236–37
Martínez-Alier, Joan, 15
MAS (Movement toward Socialism, Bolivia), 53
Mata, Guillermo, 198
Maya Programme (Guatemala), 131n.29
Mayer, Joshua L., 59
megaprojects in Guatemala, conflicts over, 116
MEM (Ministry of Energy and Mining, Nicaragua), 76, 96–97
MEM, Guatemala. *See* Ministry of Energy and Mining (MEM, Guatemala)
mercury use in gold mining, 43, 43n.4, 72, 88, 89, 89*f*
Mesa Nacional Frente a la Minería Metálica (National Roundtable on Metallic Mining, El Salvador)
  Catholic Church and, 209, 213
  creation of, 182–83
  discussion of, 190–97
  Funes and, 198–99
  ICSID case and, 230–31
  mining ban, support for, 207–8
  public opinion polling and, 204
Metallic Mining Prohibition Law (2017, El Salvador), 187–88
method of agreement and method of difference, 27–28
Mexican Council of Businessmen, 47
Mexico
  ASMs in, 42–43
  business associations, 47–48
  indigeous consultation, 59n.12
  ISDS cases against, 226
  mining conflicts, 7
  neoliberal reforms, 10–11
  resistance activism, 38–39
  3X3 anti-corruption law, 57
  top-down community consultations, 59

Middeldorp, Nicholas, 59
Mill, John Stuart, 27–28
Minamata Convention (2013), 43, 78n.15, 176
MINEC (Ministry of Economy, El Salvador), 187–88, 201
mine closings, funding for, 18–19
mine-promoting policies, 61*t*
Minera San Rafael S.A. (MSR), 109–10
mine-restricting policies, 61*t*
Mineros S.A., 64
mining (in general)
    acronyms list, xiii–xvii
    in Costa Rica, 142–77
    in El Salvador, 180–215
    final reflections and conclusions, 239–43
    in Guatemala, intermittent mining in, 104–39
    in Latin America, 218–43
    mining conflict and policy alternatives, 1–30
    movements, elites, and state permeability, 34–63
    in Nicaragua, 64–101
    outputs, relationship to profitability, 218–19
    policy reforms, conditions conducive to, 242–43
    question of full costs of, 218
    See also Costa Rica; El Salvador; Guatemala; Latin America; mining conflict and policy alternatives; mining risks; Nicaragua
Mining Code (1982, Costa Rica), 151, 167n.23
mining conflict and policy alternatives, 1–30
    compensation contests, 18–19
    environmental controls, 19–20
    full bans, 25–26
    introduction to, 1–5
    mining and neoliberal reform, 10–11
    mining conflicts, sources of increases in, 84–85
    mining moratorium, 23–24, 105, 116, 187–88, 201–2
    mining prohibition, 22–26

natural resource dependence and mining promotion frameworks, 8–15
    new Latin American extractive complex and its discontents, 5–8
    partial bans, 24–25
    provisional bans, 23–24
    recognition and voice, 20–22
    reform alternatives and proposals for change, 15–26
    resource nationalism, 13–15
    restrictive regulation, 16–22, 17*t*
    soft law adaptations, 11–13
    See also definitional conflicts; distributive conflicts; scale conflicts
mining policy
    sources of divergence on, 4
    types of, 32–33
Mining Reserve (Nicaragua), 77–78
mining resistance movements. See social resistance movements
mining risks
    acid mine drainage, 19, 22, 43
    cyanide, 22, 200
    health impacts, 43
    land reclamation costs, 18–19
    landslides, 19
    mercury use, 43, 43n.4, 72, 88, 89, 89*f*
    natural resource dependence, 8–15
    tailings spills, 6–7, 22
    See also water access and quality
mining sector development, sources of policies shaping, 219–23, 220*t*
MiningWatch Canada, 132, 193–94
Ministerio del Ambiente y los Recursos Naturales (MARENA, Nicaragua), 72–73
Ministerio de Medio Ambiente y Recursos Naturales (MARN, Ministry of the Environment and Natural Resources, Guatemala), 115–16, 236–37
Ministry of Culture (Peru), 59n.12
Ministry of Economy (MINEC, El Salvador), 187–88, 201
Ministry of Energy and Mining (MEM, Guatemala)
    actions of, 107*t*, 109, 118, 136–37, 139, 236–37

legal actions against, 131, 133–34, 135, 136–37, 236–38

Ministry of Energy and Mining (MEM, Nicaragua), 76, 96–97

Ministry of Industry, Energy, and Mines (Costa Rica), 145–46

Ministry of Natural Resources, Energy and Mines (MIRENEM, later Ministry of Environment and Energy, MINAE, Costa Rica), 146–48, 151

Ministry of the Environment and Natural Resources (Ministerio de Medio Ambiente y Recursos Naturales, MARN, El Salvador), 187–88, 199–200, 228–29

Ministry of the Environment and Natural Resources (Ministerio de Medio Ambiente y Recursos Naturales, MARN, Guatemala), 115–16, 236–37

Miramar Front in Opposition to Mining (Costa Rica), 155

MIRENEM (Ministry of Natural Resources, Energy and Mines, later Ministry of Environment and Energy, MINAE, Costa Rica), 146–48, 151

Mische, Ann, 53

Monge Pereira, Claudio, 173

Montana Exploradora de Guatemala, 109, 126n.24

Moore, Jen, 226

Morales, Evo, 14

Morales, Jimmy, 136, 137

Moran, Robert, 119–20, 199–200

Mora Solano, Sindy, 157n.13

Morgan, John, 234

movements, elites, and state permeability, 34–63

docking and community consultation, 57–60

docking and institutional engagement, 54–57

docking points and policy deliberation, 51–60

elites, cohesion of, 45–51

elites and mining, 49–51

introduction to, 34–38

overview of, 30–31

resistance movements, 40–45

social movement organization, 38–45

summary and conclusions, 60–63

See also elites and elite cohesion; social resistance movements; state bureaucracy permeability

Movement toward Socialism (MAS, Bolivia), 53

multisectoralism in social movements, 40

municipal codes

Municipal Code (El Salvador), 183–84, 203

Municipal Code (Guatemala), 121, 125

Murillo, Heidy, 161–62

Murillo, Rosario, 87–88, 97

National Association of Private Enterprise (ANEP, El Salvador), 182, 201, 206

national cleavage structure, 3n.1

National Conciliation Party (PCN, El Salvador), 205–6, 211

National Development Plan (2003, Nicaragua), 73–74

National Environmental Technical Secretariat (Secretaría Técnica Nacional Ambiental, SETENA, Costa Rica), 155–56, 168–69, 233

National Front for the Opposition to Open Pit Mining (Costa Rica), 152

"national interest" declaration (Arias), 50–51, 153, 158, 160, 173n.34, 221–22, 233–34

Nationalist Republican Alliance (ARENA, El Salvador)

attitudes toward mining, summary of, 222

elites and, 46–47, 181–82

mining, support for, 204–5

mining conflict and, 180, 209, 211

mining politics and, 201–2

political control by, 184–85

under Saca administration, 187–88

Salvadoran economic model and, 185–86

National Liberation Party (PLN, Costa Rica), 153–54, 163

National Park Service (Costa Rica), 148n.4

National Roundtable on Metallic Mining (El Salvador). *See* Mesa Nacional Frente a la Minería Metálica

302 INDEX

National System of Conservation Areas
(Sistema Nacional de Áreas de
Conservación, SINAC, Costa Rica),
168
natural resource dependence and mining
promotion frameworks, 8–15
mining and neoliberal reform, 10–11
resource nationalism, 13–15
soft law adaptations, 11–13
natural resource extraction, 218
natural resource rents, 8, 9f
neo-extractivism, 6n.5
neoliberal reform, 10–11, 38
Neptune Gold Mining, 64
Network in Solidarity with the People of
Guatemala (NISGUA), 132
networks, in social resistance movements,
39–40
new constitutionalism, 224
Nicaragua (in general), 64–101
acronym list, xvi
boom period, gold mining during, 75–78
cited interviews, list of, 102t
contra war, 99
democratic deterioration and
deepening conflict, 97–98
El Limón mine, competition over
economic resources in, 81–83
introduction to, 64–68
La India, scale conflict in, 88–93
mining conflict, interpretation of,
98–101
mining opposition, 66, 78–93
mining policy timeline, 73t
mining sector development, summary
of factors shaping, 219–20, 220t
overview of, 31
post-revolutionary mining growth and
development, 70–75
Rancho Grande (El Pavón), struggle
over community identity and
agroecology in, 84–88
revolutionary period, mining
transitions in, 68–70
See also, Bonanza mine; HEMCO
mining company; La Libertad mine;
Daniel Ortega; Sandinista National
Liberation Front

Nicaragua (details)
artisanal and small-scale miners, 42–43,
88, 89
business sector organization, 74
civil society activism, lack of impact by,
95–96
community consultations, 59
docking points, 66–67, 93–98, 100, 101
electoral authoritarianism, 100–1
electoral authorities under FSLN, 95
elite consensus, 65–66, 68–78
El Salvador, comparison with, 27–28
forest cover, 149t
gold exports, 69f, 77–78
gold output, 90, 110f
mine ownership, 1
mining promotion in, 62
mining towns, comparison with nonmining towns, 81–82
natural resource rents, 8, 9f
NGOs in, loss of legal status, 97–98
public opinion on mining, 35t, 36
reforestation projects, 13
rule of law, 55, 130t
sustained promotion policy package on
mining, 220
top-level support for mining, 50–51
Nicaragua Human Rights and
Anticorruption Act (2018, US),
98n.35
Nicaraguan Mining Chamber (Cámara
Minera de Nicaragua, CAMINIC),
49–50, 75, 96–97, 98
Nim Ajpu Association of Maya Lawyers
and Notaries (Guatemala), 131
North American Free Trade Agreement
(NAFTA), later USMCA, 10–11,
225n.6
Northern Union for Life (UNOVIDA,
Costa Rica), 160, 168
Novella family (Guatemala), 114–15

OAS, investigation into Nicaraguan
protest responses, 97
Obando y Bravo, Miguel, 80
Observatorio de Conflictos Mineros de
América Latina (OCMAL), 7
obsolescing bargain, 18

Odio, Elizabeth, 152
Olivos Pact (Nicaragua), 94
Ondetti, Gabriel, 47–48
Open Pit Mining National Opposition Front (Costa Rica), 160
opposition networks. *See* social resistance movements
Organisation for Economic Co-operation and Development (OECD), 62
organization, in business sector, 74
Ortega, Daniel
  docking points under, 94–95
  electoral authoritarianism under, 100–1
  foreign mining investors, support for, 1
  as FSLN leader, 67, 95
  at La Libertad mine reopening ceremony, 1, 50
  mining industry, support for, 65, 75–76
  Obando and, 80
  Olivos Pact and, 94
  populist capitalism, embrace of, 76
  protests against, 97
Otto, James, 8–9
outcomes, factors leading to divergent, 61*t*
Oxfam America, 193–94

PAC (Citizen Action Party, Costa Rica), 163, 171–72
Pacheco, Abel, 153, 154–55, 233
Pacheco, Fabián, 154n.9
Pacific Rim (Pacific Rim Cayman, Canadian mining junior)
  El Dorado mine project, 186–88
  El Dorado mine project, countering of resistance to, 205–6
  El Dorado mine project, EIA for, 200
  El Dorado mine project, limitations on community comments on, 12
  international investment dispute claim, 180–81, 183–84, 208, 227–28
  Pac Rim Cayman LLC v. Republic of El Salvador, 180–81, 208, 214, 228–32
Panama
  ISDS cases against, 226
  natural resource rents, 8, 9*f*
  public opinion on mining, 35*t*, 36
Pan American Silver, 133n.32

Parada, Luis, 229–30, 232
Parque del Agua Juan Castro Blanco (Costa Rica), 150–51
partial bans, 24–25
participatory budgeting, 57
Pastoral Commission for Peace and Ecology (COPAE), 123
Pastoral Social de Pavón (Costa Rica), 160
PCN (National Conciliation Party, El Salvador), 205–6, 211
PDC (Christian Democrat, El Salvador), 210–11
People's Council of the Western Highlands (Consejo de Pueblos de Occidente, CPO, Guatemala), 121–22, 131
Pérez Molina, Otto, 111n.5, 126, 134–35, 136, 236
Pérez-Rocha, Manuel, 226, 236
Peru
  ASMs in, 42–43
  Defensoría del Pueblo, 7n.10
  ISDS cases against, 226
  mining conflicts, 7
  mining sector development, factors shaping, 220
  natural resource rents, 8, 9*f*
  as *país minero*, 77
  public opinion on mining, 35–36, 35*t*
  top-down community consultations, 59
Philippines
  Executive Order 79, 22
  mining bans, 22, 242
Piedras, Colombia, community referenda in, 25
Pineda, Francisco, 194n.11
Piñera, Sebastián, 46–47
Placer Dome, 151–52
Plan de Ordenamiento y Desarrollo Urbano (PODU, HEMCO), 83
PLN (National Liberation Party, Costa Rica), 153–54, 163
Pohl, Lina, 207n.25
policy changes and social movements, research on, 2–4
policymaking cycle, bureaucracies in, 55–56
Policy Perception Index (Fraser Institute), 9–10

304 INDEX

political elites
  business elites and, 48
  discussion of, 46–47
  in El Salvador, 204–5, 206, 214, 222
  mining lobby, rejection of, 51
  in Nicaragua, 219–20
political parties
  in Costa Rica, 153–54, 171–72
  docking and, 53–54
  in El Salvador, connections with social
    movements, 198–99
  in Guatemala, 116–17, 220–21
  impact of activists on, 175–76
  political settlement, 27, 48, 65–66
politics
  Costa Rican political system, 170–72
  in Guatemala, 127–28
  political access mechanism, 170
  political leaders, impact of ISDS on, 227
  political leaders, in Costa Rica, 221–22
  political mediation model, 4, 144
  political participation, in Nicaragua, 94
  political process theory, author's use
    of, 144
  private politics, description of, 13
  Salvadoran political systems, docking
    and, 183
Poma, Ricardo and Poma Group, 206
popular cultures of resistance, 188
power imbalances, in extractive sector, 21–22
privatizations, in post-revolutionary
    period (Nicaragua), 71
Procuraduría General de la República
    (Costa Rica), 168
Programa Estado de la Nación (State of the
    Nation Project, Costa Rica), 163n.19,
    170
Progreso VII Derivada open pit mine
    (Guatemala), 109–10, 119–20, 124–
    25, 134, 135, 136
PRONicaragua, 73–74, 75, 76, 91, 96–97
proposals for change, reform alternatives
    and, 15–26, 17t
protesters and protests
  criminalization of, 20, 50–51, 117–18
  data on, 7
  roadblocks by, 118–19, 126, 136
  See also social resistance movements

PT (Workers' Party, Brazil), 53, 57
public environmental institutions in Costa
    Rica, 146–48
"public interest" declaration. See "national
    interest" declaration
public opinion
  corporate public relations campaigns'
    influence on, 50
  in Costa Rica, 212, 222
  in El Salvador, 204, 212
  impact of variations in, 35–37, 35t
  on mining, 136, 163, 204, 212
  in Nicaragua, 219–20
  possible shifts in, 51
public policy, social movements and, 40,
    213
Public Prosecutor's office (Ministerio
    Público, Guatemala), 132–33
Pulgar-Vidal, Manuel, 201
Puno, Peru, 2011 mobilizations in, 16
PUSC (Social Christian Unity Party, Costa
    Rica), 153–54

Radius Gold, Exploraciones Mineras de
    Guatemala (EXMINGUA), 109–10
Ramazzini, Álvaro, 123, 195
Rancho Grande (El Pavón mine,
    Nicaragua), 50, 84–88, 96–97
rastras (artisanal gold processing centers), 89
Reagan, Ronald, 70n.5
recognition and voice of local populations,
    20–22
referenda
  in Costa Rica, 156–57
  in El Salvador, 183–84
  prevalence of, 57
reform alternatives and proposals for
    change, 15–26, 17t
Refugee and Repopulated Communities
    Coordinator (CCR, El Salvador), 191
regulatory taking (indirect expropriation),
    223–24
Remmer, Karen, 226, 227
rentier populism, 24
Research and Social Studies Association
    (Asociación de Investigación
    y Estudios Sociales, ASIES,
    Guatemala), 116

INDEX   305

research on extractive sector conflict, traditional focus of, 34
resignification, 188
resistance conflicts (*conflictos de resistencia*), 41
resistance movements. *See* social resistance movements
resource nationalism, 10, 13–15, 50, 77–78
restrictive regulation, 15–22, 17*t*
revenue transfers, 13–14
Revista Mejoremos Guate (FUNDESA and CACIF), 115
revolving door, bureaucracies and, 55–56
Rice, Roberta, 4, 52
right to knock and be received (derecho de picaporte), 113
Rio Earth Summit (1992), 146–48
Río Lempa, El Salvador, 194–95
Ríos, Sergio, 90
Rivera, Marcelo, 180
roadblocks, as protest activity, 118–19, 126, 136
Rodríguez, Miguel Ángel, 152, 154, 167
Rojas, Fabio, 159
Roman Catholics. *See* Catholic Church, views and actions on mining
Rosa Chávez, Gregorio, 206n.22
Rosa Chávez, Herman, 202
Rossi, Federico M., 45, 188
royalties, accumulation at central government level, 18–19
rule of law, 54–55, 129–30, 130*t*
Rural Communities Association for Salvadoran Development (CRIPDES), 191, 193, 203–4

Sabana Redonda, Guatemala, plebiscite in, 125
Saca, Antonio "Tony"
    ARENA, expulsion from, 210–11
    ARENA's hold on power under, 187–88
    as business leader, 46–47
    elites and, 181–82
    mining, opposition to, 229
    mining controversy under, 180, 201–2, 204–5
    Pacific Rim and, 208
sacrifice zones, 10

Sáenz Lacalle, Fernando, 196–97
Sagastume, Bernabé, 123n.21, 125
Sagot, Álvaro, 168
Sala Constitucional de la Corte Suprema de Justicia (CSJ, Nicaragua), 95
Sala I (Administrative Chamber of the Supreme Court, Costa Rica), 167–68, 169, 233–34
Sala IV (Constitutional Chamber of the Supreme Court, Costa Rica), 154n.10, 165–66, 169
Salvadoran Ecological Unit (UNES), 193
Salvadoran Social and Economic Development Foundation (FUSADES), 46–47, 184–85
San Casimiro, Ángel, 151–52
Sánchez Cerén, Salvador, 181–82, 198–99
Sánchez-Sibony, Omar, 128
Sandinista National Liberation Front (Frente Sandinista de Liberación Nacional, FSLN, Nicaragua), 67, 68–69, 70, 87, 99
San José del Golfo, Guatemala, 124–25
San Marcos, Guatemala. Mayan indigenous communities in, 134
San Martín mine (Honduras), 24
San Miguel Ixtahuacán, Guatemala, mining concessions in, 109
San Rafael Las Flores, Guatemala, 125
Santa Marta, El Salvador, civil war refugee resettlement in, 191
Santa Rosa, Guatemala
    community consultations in, 122
    resistance network in, 125–26
Santa Rosa de Pocosol, Costa Rica, anti-mining organizing in, 150–51
scale conflicts, 42–43, 44, 66, 81, 88–93, 100, 188–89
Schedler, Andreas, 100–1
Schneider, Ben Ross, 46
Schneiderman, David, 224
scientific activism, 119–20, 199, 213–14
Secretaría Técnica Nacional Ambiental (SETENA, National Environmental Technical Secretariat, Costa Rica), 155–56, 168–69, 233
sectoral breadth (in resistance movement analysis), 37, 189–90, 195–97

306 INDEX

Segovia, Alexander, 111, 113
self-convened (*autoconvocados*), 97
Seltzer, Catherine McLeod, 186–87
Serrano, Jorge Antonio, 111n.5
service conflicts, 82
SETENA (Secretaría Técnica Nacional
  Ambiental, National Environmental
  Technical Secretariat, Costa Rica),
  155–56, 168–69, 233
Shrake, Thomas, 229
Silva, Marina, 56
Simmons, Erica S., 38–39
SINAC (Sistema Nacional de Áreas
  de Conservación, National System
  of Conservation Areas,
  Costa Rica), 168
Sipacapa (Sipakapa), Guatemala
  indigenous consultations process in,
    122–23, 133–34
  mining concessions in, 109
Sipakapa No Se Vende (documentary),
  122–23
Sistema Nacional de Areas de
  Conservación (SINAC, National
  System of Conservation Areas,
  Costa Rica), 168
SLO (social license to operate), 11–13,
  156, 204, 230
slow movement studies, 3
small-scale miners. *See* artisanal and
  small-scale mining
Social and Economic Development
  Association (ADES, El Salvador),
  191, 199
social cascade effects, 211–12
Social Christian Unity Party (PUSC, Costa
  Rica), 153–54
social ecology, 149, 151
social license to operate (SLO), 11–13,
  156, 204, 230
social media, anti-mining activists' use of,
  160–61
social mobilization. *See* social resistance
  movements
social movements
  ability to influence public policy,
    189–90
  challenges to, 159

discussion of, 38–45
framing, frame transformation, 151,
  159
ISDS and, 227
judicialization of, 128–29
legal instruments, use of, 165
networks, 39–40
overview of, 37
political party linkages, processes
  affecting, 171
public policy outcomes, relationship
  to, 213
role in policymaking process, 164
scale shifting, 37, 127, 230–31
social movement networking, 160
social movement partyism, 198
social movement theory, 159
social resistance movements
  alliance variations and organizational
    challenges, 40–45
  collective learning in, 45
  community-level resistance, limited
    impact of, 192
  in Costa Rica, 150–51, 175, 222
  docking and political parties and,
    53–54
  in El Salvador, 182–83, 212–15, 222–23
  factors for success in, 143
  in Guatemala, 104–5, 116–27, 135–36,
    138, 220–21
  importance of, 26
  importance of state organization
    penetration by, 26–27
  ISDS processes' impact on, 240,
    241–42
  in Nicaragua, 100, 219–20
  overview of, 37
  policy impact, means to achieving,
    61–62
  policy results and, research on, 2–4
  service-oriented versus rights-oriented,
    41–42
  summary and conclusions on, 60–63
  tactics and strategies, 118–22, 160–62,
    190, 192–97
  See also docking and docking points;
    elites and elite cohesion
soft law adaptations, 11–13

solidarity state model, in Costa Rica, 146

Solís, Ottón, 172n.33

Spalding, Rose J., argument and methods, 26–30

spatial reach (in resistance movement analysis), 37, 189–90, 192–95

speak without saying (*hablar sin hablar*), 192

Special Mining Exploration and Extraction Law #387 (2001, Nicaragua), 72–73

state bureaucracy permeability, 20, 26–27, 37–38, 51–60

See also docking and docking points

State of the Nation Project (Programa Estado de la Nación, Costa Rica), 163n.19, 170

states

ASM, responses to, 43–44

bureaucracies in, 55–56

Stein, Ernesto, 112

stock of legacies, 188, 192

strategic capital, 183, 188, 213

strategic environmental assessments (SEAs), 187–88, 201, 202

Strategic Group Against Mining (Grupo Estratégico contra la Minería, Matagalpa, Nicaragua), 86

structural adjustment, 43–44, 74–75, 145, 152

Subterranean Struggles (Bebbington and Bury), 5–6

Superior Council of Private Enterprise (COSEP, Nicaragua), 49–50

Supreme Court (Costa Rica). *See* Sala I; Sala IV

Supreme Court (Honduras), 24

Supreme Court of Justice (Guatemala), 132n.31, 134, 135, 221, 237

surface property rights, 205–6, 208

Svampa, Maristella, 14

Tahoe Resources, 109–10, 125

tailings, 7n.6

Tarrow, Sidney, 49

Tatagiba, Luciana, 56

TAU Consultora Ambiental, 202

tax exonerations, 18

TCA (Tribunal Contencioso Administrativo, Administrative Litigation Tribunal, Costa Rica), 167–69, 234–35

technology improvements, impact on mining, 6

temporary and de facto prohibitions (provisional bans), 23–24

territorial prohibitions (partial bans), 24–25

think tanks, in Guatemala, 112–13

third-party financing, 234

tómbolas (artisanal gold processing centers), 89

top-down consultation processes, 58–59

Torres Wong, Marcela, 59

transnationalism, 188–90, 193

Tribunal Contencioso Administrativo (TCA, Administrative Litigation Tribunal, Costa Rica), 167–69, 234–35

Triton Mining Corporation, 71

UCA (Universidad Centroamericana, El Salvador), 210

UCCAEP (Union of Private Sector Chambers and Associations, Costa Rica), 152–53

UCR (University of Costa Rica), University Council (Consejo Universitario), 160

UN Conference on Trade and Development (UNCTAD), 115–16

UNES (Salvadoran Ecological Unity), 193

Unidad Revolucionaria Nacional Guatemalteca (URNG), 236–37

UN Industrial Development Organization (UNIDO), 43

Union of Extractive Industries (Gremial de Industrias Extractivas, GREMIEXT, Guatemala), 49–50, 113

Union of Private Sector Chambers and Associations (UCCAEP, Costa Rica), 152–53

unions, in Nicaragua, 70–71, 83

United States

bureaucracies in, 55n.9

on CACIF, 111

mining bans in, 22, 242

308 INDEX

Universidad Centroamericana (UCA, El Salvador), 210
Universidad Francisco Marroquín (Guatemala), 112–13
universities, in Costa Rica, 51, 160
University of Costa Rica (UCR), University Council (Consejo Universitario), 160
UNOVIDA (Northern Union for Life, Costa Rica), 160, 168
Urgent Call (Llamado Urgente, Costa Rica), 160
Urkidi, Leire, 58
URNG (Unidad Revolucionaria Nacional Guatemalteca), 236–37
Uruguay, business associations in, 47–48
US Agency for International Development (USAID), 72, 145
US–El Salvador Sister Cities network, 193–94

Valle de El General, Costa Rica, proposed bauxite mine, 150–51
Van Harten, Gus, 224
Vannessa Ventures, 151–52, 233
Vargas Leiva, Gerardo, 172
Vásquez, Dominga, 118
Veilman, Carlos, 118–19
Velásquez, Iván, 132–33, 137
Venezuela
    ICSID, withdrawal from, 225
    natural resource rents, 8, 9f
Vernon, Raymond, 18
Villalta, José María, 173
violence
    against anti-mining protests, 50–51, 83, 92, 118–19, 124–26
    against student protests, 97
vulnerability theory, 38–39

Walter, Mariana, 58
water access and quality
    in Costa Rica, 152, 155, 173

in El Salvador, 182–83, 194–95, 206, 207
El Tambor gold mining project and, 236
in Guatemala, 108, 123, 124, 133–34
mining impact on, 19
in Nicaragua, 64, 78–79, 82, 83, 85–86, 89
West, Karleen Jones, 59–60
Western Highlands, Guatemala, community consultations in indigenous territories, 120–23
    See also Marlin Mine (Guatemala)
Wheaton River Minerals Limited, 155
World Bank
    Compliance Advisor Ombudsman, 12
    decentralization initiatives, support for, 57
    International Finance Corporation, 11–12, 42–43, 91, 109
    mining laws, recommendations on, 10
    mining policy reforms, promotion of, 11
    See also International Centre for the Settlement of Investment Disputes
World DataBank, Worldwide Governance Indicators, 129–30
World Development Indicators, on economic impact of natural resource rents, 8
World Trade Organization (WTO), on trade subsidies in Costa Rica, 148
Wright Sol, John, 211

Xinka people (Guatemala), 125, 131, 135, 139

Yagenova, Simona, 116
Yashar, Deborah J., 127

Zaremberg, Gisela, 59
Zarruk, Carlos, 76, 77
Zelaya, Manuel "Mel," 24
zonas de amortiguamiento (buffer zones), 78–79